ENGLISH CHURCH DEDICATIONS

Also available from University of Exeter Press:

Unity and Variety
A History of the Church in Devon and Cornwall
edited by Nicholas Orme (1991)

'An important contribution to general ecclesiastical history'
Journal of Ecclesiastical History

'Coherence, consistency and depth of scholarship'
English Historical Review

'Get it, read it, dip into it; it should be on every Christian bookshelf'
Cornish Churchman

ENGLISH CHURCH DEDICATIONS

WITH A SURVEY OF CORNWALL AND DEVON

Nicholas Orme

UNIVERSITY
of
EXETER
PRESS

First published in 1996 by
University of Exeter Press
Reed Hall, Streatham Drive
Exeter, Devon EX4 4QR
UK

British Library Cataloguing in Publication Data
A catalogue record for this book is
available from the British Library

ISBN 0 85989 516 5

Typeset in 10/12pt Plantin by
Greenshires Icon, Exeter

Printed and bound in Great Britain by
BPC Wheatons Ltd, Exeter

CONTENTS

FIGURES

TABLES

ACKNOWLEDGEMENTS

The publication of this book has been made possible through the generous help of the Marc Fitch Fund, the Lord Bishop of Exeter, and the Council of the Devon and Cornwall Record Society. The Council of the Devonshire Association made a grant towards research costs. The illustration on the cover of the book is reproduced with the kind permission of the Bodleian Library, Oxford, from MS Laud misc. 302, folio 162r. The author and publisher are grateful for the assistance of all those concerned.

ABBREVIATIONS

(References to other works can be traced in the bibliography)

1 Dates

1161 x 1184   The x indicates a precise but unknown date somewhere between the outer limits indicated.

1170 (15th)   This indicates a document of 1170 recorded in a text of the 15th century, raising the possibility that spellings (especially those of names) have been modified.

2 Archives, Libraries and Texts

BL   London, British Library

Bodleian   Oxford, Bodleian Library

CChR   *Calendar of Charter Rolls*

Chanter   Exeter, Devon Record Office, Chanter MSS (Registers of the Bishops of Exeter)

CFR   *Calendar of Fine Rolls*

CIPM   *Calendar of Inquisitions Post Mortem*

CPL   *Calendar of Papal Letters*

CPR   *Calendar of Patent Rolls*

CRO	Truro, Cornwall Record Office
Crockford	*Crockford's Clerical Dictionary*
CuRR	*Curia Regis Rolls*
DB	*Domesday Book*, vol. x: *Cornwall*, ed. Thorn, Caroline and Frank (Chichester, 1979) *Domesday Book*, vol. ix: *Devon*, ed. Thorn, Caroline and Frank, 2 vols (Chichester, 1985)
DCRSL	Exeter, Devon and Cornwall Record Society Library (in West Country Studies Library)
DRO	Exeter, Devon Record Office
ECA	Exeter, Cathedral Archives
EDD	*Exeter Diocesan Directory*
Exon	The Exeter Domesday Book, in *Domesday-Book: Additamenta* (London, Record Commission, 1816)
IPM	Exeter, Devon and Cornwall Record Society Library (in West Country Studies Library), Transcripts of Inquisitions Post Mortem
Kelly	*Kelly's Directory of Cornwall* (London, 1856–1939) and *of Devonshire* (London, 1873–1939)
LPFD	*Letters and Papers, Foreign and Domestic, Henry VIII*
LPL	London, Lambeth Palace Library
MCR	Exeter, Devon Record Office, Exeter City Archives, Mayor's Court Rolls
Moger	Moger, Olive. 'Copies of Transcripts from Wills and other Records' (collected c. 1921–41), 21 vols, two copies: Exeter, Devon Record Office and West Country Studies Library

MS Milles   Oxford, Bodleian Library, MS Top. Devon b.1–2

MS Willis   Oxford, Bodleian Library, MS Willis

Murray   Murray, Sir Oswyn. 'Transcripts of Wills', 41 vols, Exeter, West Country Studies Library

NDRO   Barnstaple, North Devon Record Office

PND   Gover, J.E.B., Mawer, A., and Stenton, F.M. *The Place-Names of Devon*, 2 vols, Cambridge, English Place-Name Society, vols viii-ix (1931-2)

Pole   See bibliography section, Exeter, Devon and Cornwall Record Society Library

PRO   London, Public Record Office

PROB   London, Public Record Office, Prerogative Court of Canterbury, individual wills and registers of wills

RIC   Truro, Royal Institution of Cornwall, Courtney Library

Tax   Taxation of Pope Nicholas IV, 1291, in Hingeston-Randolph, F.C. (ed.) *The Registers of Walter Bronescombe . . . and Peter Quivil . . . Bishops of Exeter* (London and Exeter, 1889), pp. 450-81

TDD   Truro Diocesan Directory

PREFACE

It is a rash historian who says that the topic to be addressed has never been adequately studied. In the case of English parish church dedications this statement is, if not entirely true, very largely so. Of course, information about them is widely available. It appears on church notice-boards, in diocesan handbooks, in Crockford's and Kelly's directories, and in Pevsner's *Buildings of England*. But this material lacks any framework of time. These are the dedications as they are understood to be now, and there is little awareness that, like everything else, they have histories. One has only to read a parish church guide-book to find that while other aspects of the building—fabric, furnishings, incumbents and famous events—are treated historically, the dedication is not. 'The Church *is* dedicated to so and so', irrespective of chronology or change, as if to say like Jesus, 'Before Abraham was, I am'.

The absence of historical commentary is a long-standing one. It stems from the first modern collectors of church dedications: Browne Willis and his successors in the eighteenth century.[1] Their motives were indeed those of historians. They tried to recover the dedications of England after two hundred years of neglect and to publicise them in directories. Unfortunately, they drew on documentary evidence without naming dates or sources and made conjectures (rationally but often wrongly) when they could not find evidence. They mingled facts and speculations, innocent of discussions or references, in simple lists which seemed to say 'this is the dedication and always has been'. Other eighteenth- and nineteenth-century antiquaries, with better access to medieval sources, discovered that some of their predecessors' conjectures were wrong. They corrected them, but did so silently and reissued the lists with the same impression of timeless certainty. By the end of the nineteenth century, it was possible for Frances Arnold-Forster to publish three large volumes, the so-called *Studies in the*

---

1. On Browne Willis, see below, p. 45.

History of English Church Dedications (1899), with scarcely any reference to history. Her third volume printed the church dedications of
England and Wales then current as if they were the medieval originals.
In fact, they were a late-Victorian mixture of ancient truth with modern inventions, guesses, and errors. A subsequent writer, Francis
Bond, in his *Dedications of English Churches* (1914), was a little more
careful. He understood the possibility of dedications changing from the
middle ages to modern times and called for more local research to be
done. But in the meanwhile, he took the modern dedications and wove
conjectures from them, like Arnold-Forster.[2]

Bond's call has elicited little response in the eighty years since it was
made. An honourable exception is that of T.H.B. Graham and W.G.
Collingwood, who published a list of church dedications in the diocese
of Carlisle (1925), showing the earliest dates of record.[3] The dedications of early Anglo-Saxon churches in England were collected by
Wilhelm Levison in 1945–46, and those of religious houses between
1066 and 1216 have been listed and studied by Alison Binns in 1989.[4]
For parish churches since 800, however, Arnold-Forster and Bond
alone are normally cited as authorities in twentieth-century bibliogra-
phies. Historians still consult them for individual dedications and for
statistics concerning patron saints, apparently failing to realize that
much of the evidence they contain is Hanoverian or Victorian, and
medieval only in part.

In Devon, at least 73 of the current dedications of ancient churches
are absolutely different from the pre-Reformation ones, and at least 27
others (where the churches have had a pair of patron saints) are partly different.[5] Since these figures relate only to the 70% of Devon
parishes where pre-Reformation evidence is known, it follows that
about 140 of the county's modern dedications are likely to have been
altered wholly or partly—about 30% of the total. Cornwall presents
contrasting problems. There, a great many patron saints of churches
have been perpetuated in the names of parishes and settlements, so
that they have never been quite forgotten. Instead, changes have taken
place to the forms of the names. Spellings have been modified and mis-
understandings have arisen about the identities and even the genders

---

2. For further discussion of the work of Arnold-Forster and Bond, see below, pp. 55–57.
3. T.H.B. Graham and W.G. Collingwood, 'Patron Saints of the Diocese of Carlisle', *Transactions of the Cumberland and Westmorland Antiquarian and Archaeological Society*, new series, xxv (1925), pp. 1–27.
4. These authors are considered below, pp. 17, 25, 57–58.
5. The 23 churches of Exeter are excluded from this calculation, because most are a special case, have always been known by their dedications, and a few have long disappeared and are known only from historical records.

of the saints concerned. Much has been done to sort out these difficulties by scholars such as G.H. Doble, Charles Henderson, Lynette
Olson and O.J. Padel.[6] Nonetheless, some 30 Cornish parish churches
now celebrate patron saints different in name, gender or identity from
those of the middle ages.

A few people have long expressed dissatisfaction with the lack of
trustworthy reference books in this field. In Devon, the local historian
R. Burnett-Morris wrote in 1924 that 'a complete list (with dates) of
the changes in Devon church dedications seems to be very much wanted'.[7] H.P.R. Finberg expressed a similar wish a quarter of a century
later: 'how badly we need a revised and critically documented list of
church dedications.'[8] Forty-five years after Finberg, the need is still
unsatisfied. Yet no-one would study the history of place-names, for
example, largely from the forms in use today. With dedications, as with
place-names, we require historical evidence to show exactly when each
one is first recorded and how it has changed down the centuries.
Collecting this information is a formidable task. Parish church dedications were not systematically recorded in the middle ages, and there
was no directory of them until John Ecton's *Thesaurus Rerum
Ecclesiasticarum* of 1742. Identifying them before the Reformation
requires the reading of a wide range of sources including records of the
crown, charters, bishops' registers and wills. To attempt this task for
the ten thousand or so medieval parishes of England would require
years of research and produce a row of volumes.

The present study aims merely to start the enterprise. It provides a
general history of church dedications in England and a guide to their
sources and historiography. It then presents a gazetteer of one English
region to show what can be done to collect dedication evidence and
how the evidence may be set out and interpreted. The area chosen
consists of the two counties of Cornwall and Devon, which until 1877
constituted the diocese of Exeter and which contain about 700 ancient
parish churches (about 218 and 482 respectively). This region has the
merit of presenting a contrast in the patron saints of its churches.
Cornwall is a county of many Celtic dedications, while Devon contains
the kinds found commonly in the areas settled by the Anglo-Saxons.
Studying both counties introduces the difficulties and reveals the features likely to be encountered elsewhere in England. The gazetteer also

---

6. The work of these scholars is discussed below, p. 55.
7. R. Burnett-Morris, 'St Michael's, Coleton', *Devon and Cornwall Notes and Queries*, xiii
   (1924–25), p. 99.
8. H.P.R. Finberg, 'Church Dedications in Devon', *Devon and Cornwall Notes and Queries*, xxiv
   (1950–51), pp. 225–26.

collects the dedications of about 100 religious houses and hospitals in the region up to the Reformation. It is not concerned, however, with churches founded since 1600: whether Anglican, Catholic or those of other denominations. Modern church dedications have been less affected by change or uncertainty and can be found more easily in nineteenth- and twentieth-century directories.

In method, the gazetteer adopts a similar approach to that of English place-name studies. The evidence about each church is presented with dates and sources, followed by a commentary based on the data. Details of church dedication dates are provided when known, and parish feast days as observed in the eighteenth and nineteenth centuries. The investigation of church dedications necessarily involves pointing out errors by previous writers. The present author will not have avoided mistakes and apologizes for those which come to light. Ideally, readers should always check the original sources in cases of doubt, and if there is any respect in which this work is better than its predecessors, it is chiefly in listing the sources which enable checks to be made. The author will be glad to receive additions and corrections, and to publish them with acknowledgement. It is hoped that the best features of the present study will provide a stimulus and a model to be followed (with improvements where necessary) in the rest of England. We are at an early stage on a long road. One day, perhaps, we shall have a series of lists not only of the dedications of churches but of all the cult centres and cult objects of the past: religious houses, guilds, chapels, altars, images, writings, holy wells and other hallowed places. Only when that evidence is assembled shall we be able adequately to study the history and geography of devotion to God, the angels and the saints.

My research for this, as for previous projects, has been eased by much kindness from the staff of the Bodleian Library (Oxford), the British Library (London), Canterbury Cathedral Archives, Cornwall Record Office (Truro), the Devon and Exeter Institution (Exeter), the Devon Record Office (Exeter), Exeter Cathedral Archives and Library, Exeter University Library, the Guildhall Library (London), Lambeth Palace Library, the Public Record Office (London), the Royal Institution of Cornwall (Truro), and the West Country Studies Library (Exeter). I owe further debts to the Rt Revd Michael Ball, Lord Bishop of Truro, the Rt Revd Hewlett Thompson, Lord Bishop of Exeter, Dr Caroline Barron, Dr John Blair, Dr Julia Crick, the Revd J. Cruse, the Revd J. Dykes, Mrs Anne P. Fuller, Mr S. Hobbs, Mrs Jeanne James, the Revd W.M.M. Picken, Mr P.A.S. Pool, the Ven. R.L. Ravenscroft, the Revd Prebendary J. Trevelyan, and Mr R.K. Wheeler (Exeter Diocesan

Registrar) for kindly suggesting sources and answering queries. Two
generous scholars, Professor Frank Barlow and Dr Michael Haren,
have supplied me with material from forthcoming publications by
them: the *Acta* of the bishops of Exeter and the *Calendar of Papal
Registers* volume xix respectively. Mr Séan Goddard has once more
provided admirable maps. Dr O.J. Padel has for many years given me
the benefit of his knowledge of Cornish language and history. I am
again obliged to his files of Cornish place-names, to Dr Philip Payton
(Director of the University of Exeter's Institute of Cornish Studies) for
easing my access to them, and to Dr Padel for further wise advice both
general and detailed about this book, though he (and my other helpers)
are in no way responsible for any defects it possesses. Finally, the
project could not have been realised without the support and encouragement of Dr Eamon Duffy, Professor Ronald Hutton and Dr R.N.
Swanson, or the help of Professor Michael Swanton, Mr Simon Baker,
Dr Richard Willis and the staff of the University of Exeter Press. I am
very grateful to them all.

Nicholas Orme,
University of Exeter,
15 May 1996.

PART ONE

CHURCH DEDICATIONS

1

ENGLISH CHURCH DEDICATIONS

Since early times, Christians have inaugurated new churches with special prayers and ceremonies.[9] The historian Eusebius tells us that after the Emperor Constantine granted toleration of Christian worship in 313, churches were widely built and consecrated. He refers to a case at Tyre in the following year, and records an oration spoken on the occasion.[10] The act of inaugurating a church has traditionally centred on dedicating and consecrating the building, and both these verbs occur in the medieval services of inauguration.[11] Dedication involves declaring that the church is devoted to holy purposes; consecration is the action, making the building into a holy place. The process as a whole has generally been called the dedication. In the middle ages, it was a permanent measure. Religious houses and parish churches, once dedicated, remained so.[12] The modern Church of England, however, distinguishes two levels of religious status.[13] Parish churches with a permanent basis are said to be consecrated. Other, 'district' churches are designated on more provisional terms, and are termed dedicated.[14] This distinction needs to be mentioned, since it is current, but it is not

---

9. On what follows, see H. Leclerq, 'Patron', in *Dictionnaire d'Archéologie Chrétienne et de Liturgie*, ed. F. Cabrol and H. Leclerq, 15 vols (Paris, 1924–53), xiii part ii, cols 2513–24; R.W. Muncey, *A History of the Consecration of Churches and Churchyards* (Cambridge, 1939), pp. 10–24; and Antonia Gransden, 'The Question of the Consecration of St Edmund's Church', in *Church and Chronicle in the Middle Ages: Essays Presented to John Taylor*, ed. Ian Wood and G.A. Loud (London, 1991), pp. 59–86.
10. Eusebius, *The Ecclesiastical History and the Martyrs of Palestine*, ed. H.J. Lawlor and J.E.L. Oulton, 2 vols (London, 1954), i, 300–15 (book x, chapters 3–4).
11. See the references below, note 19.
12. There were, however, also temporary places of worship by the later middle ages, such as private chapels and oratories. They were not necessarily dedicated and consecrated, and were licensed for worship by the pope or bishop only during his pleasure.
13. *The Oxford Dictionary of the Christian Church*, ed. F.L. Cross and E.A. Livingstone, 2nd ed. (Oxford, 1983), p. 386; *The Oxford English Dictionary*, ed. J.A. Simpson and E.S.C. Weiner, 2nd ed., 20 vols (Oxford, 1989), s.v. 'dedicate' (1), a usage dated to 1885.
14. In modern Church law, dedication is merely a declaration of intent to use land and its buildings for sacred purposes. Consecration is the setting aside of land and its buildings in perpetuity, solely for sacred purposes. The religious ceremony of consecration is accompanied by a legal instrument called a 'Sentence of Consecration', which causes the land to come within the jurisdiction of the Ordinary, i.e. the bishop and his chancellor in the Consistory Court. A consecrated church is the only sort of church recognised as such in law.

relevant to the present study. The churches with which we are concerned—ancient religious houses and parish churches—were permanent buildings. All were originally sanctioned for use by services which spoke alike of dedication and consecration. Either word may be used to describe their status.

To dedicate a church means dedicating it to God. But by the end of the fourth century it was becoming usual to place the church under an additional patron or patrons—saints, angels, Christ or the Trinity—after whom the church might be named and identified. In 386, St Ambrose, when about to dedicate the cathedral of Milan, found the bodies of Gervase and Protase close by, whom he believed to be Christian martyrs. He translated them to the building and made them its patron saints. In 395, the scholar Paulinus of Nola refers to St Felix as the patron of the church of Nola, while the Roman minister Flavius Rufinus, who died in that year, had already built a church in honour of Peter and Paul near Chalcedon in Asia Minor. The patron saints of the first two examples were buried at or near the churches concerned. In the third case, the dedication followed a pattern which became more common: the choice of any saint or spiritual being, especially a well-known one, as patron of the church. At many churches, the choice must have originated locally. The nobility or clergy who established the building would select a patron for whom they cherished a devotion, as Flavius Rufinus did for Peter and Paul. Alternatively, the church—like that of Nola—might take its name from a saint buried there, or one whose relics it had acquired. A third influence might be that of a mother church elsewhere. Thus, the monastery of Peter and Paul founded at Canterbury in about 600 recalled the fact that its founder had come from Rome, the city of those saints.[15]

Once Christianity was firmly founded, the choice of patron came also to involve the local diocesan bishop. He, as the senior cleric of the district, was the person entrusted with authorising buildings for ecclesiastical use. As early as the fifth century, it was held to be essential for every church or altar to be consecrated by him, and wrong for this to be done by a bishop from elsewhere.[16] In England, the Council of Chelsea (816) ordered that when churches were built they should be consecrated by the bishop of the diocese. The liturgy of the service was to include the blessing and sprinkling of holy water, the celebration of the eucharist, and the enclosure of consecrated bread and wine inside

---

15. Below, p. 16.
16. Muncey, *History of the Consecration of Churches*, pp. 21–22.

the altar, with relics if available.[17] Aelfric, writing in the 990s, added that no mass should be held in a building that had not been consecrated —a statement repeated by the Council of Winchester in 1070.[18] Forms of dedication services survive in England from the Anglo-Saxon period up to the Reformation.[19] They are to be found in the pontifical, the liturgical book containing the services proper to be carried out by bishops, and they have broadly similar features without being uniform. The pontificals contained material for three associated ceremonies: the dedication of a church, the consecration of its altar or altars, and the enclosure of relics within them. Each of these actions included the dedication of the structure to God, while naming it in honour of a saint. Many of the references are to 'the holy martyr N. [i.e. the name of the saint]', implying that the typical patron would be a martyr, as had often been so among the Romans. In practice, however, there were also many dedications to 'confessors', 'matrons' and 'virgins': saints who had died in their beds.

Despite the Anglo-Saxon laws and pontificals, many churches remained undedicated (or were suspected of being so) in the twelfth and thirteenth centuries. Some of these were new foundations. There was a space of seventeen years between the foundation and dedication of Butley Priory (Suffolk) and an even longer one at Cirencester Abbey (Gloucestershire.).[20] Others, it was said, were ancient buildings. In 1237 the papal legate Otto, presiding over the Council of London, complained that numerous churches, even cathedrals, had not been consecrated with holy oil although they were old foundations. He ordered that all those whose walls were complete should have the lack made good by the local bishop within the next two years. If the order were disregarded, the celebration of mass was to be forbidden, and clergy in charge of ancient churches were not to prevaricate on the

17. *Councils and Ecclesiastical Documents relating to Great Britain and Ireland*, ed. A.W. Haddan and W. Stubbs, 3 vols (Oxford, 1869–73), iii, 580.
18. *Councils and Synods I: A.D.871–1204*, ed. D. Whitelock, M. Brett and C.N.L. Brooke, 2 vols (Oxford 1981), i, 205, 210; ii, 575.
19. These include, in chronological order, *The Pontifical of Egbert, Archbishop of York*, [ed. W. Greenwell,] Surtees Society, xxvii (1853), pp. 26–53; *Pontificale Lanaletense*, ed. G.H. Doble, Henry Bradshaw Society, lxxiv (1936), pp. 2–38; *The Leofric Missal*, ed. F.E. Warren (Oxford, 1883), pp. 218–21; *The Pontifical of Magdalen College*, ed. H.A. Wilson, Henry Bradshaw Society, xxxix (1910), pp. 98–124; *Liber Pontificalis of Edmund Lacy, Bishop of Exeter*, ed. R. Barnes, G. Oliver and P. Jones (Exeter, 1846), pp. 18–38; *Liber Pontificalis Chr. Bainbridge Archiepiscopi Eboracensis*, [ed. W.G. Henderson,] Surtees Society, lxi (1875), pp. 53–80. A comparative edition of four texts and an outline of the service is provided by W.H. Frere, *Pontifical Services Illustrated from Miniatures of the XVth and XVIth Centuries*, 2 vols, Alcuin Club Collections, iii–iv (1901), i, 2-54; for further discussion, see Alison Binns, *Dedications of Monastic Houses in England and Wales 1066-1216* (Woodbridge, 1989), pp. 11–14.
20. Binns, *Dedications of Monastic Houses*, p. 10. In Devon, Monkleigh parish church is mentioned as requiring dedication in 1421 (below, p. 184).

grounds that they planned to rebuild.[21] The pronouncements of the
Council of London were repeated by several diocesan bishops in subsequent years; indeed, one or two of them anticipated the Council in
this respect.[22] But these initiatives may not have been wholly effective,
either. From the late twelfth to the mid fourteenth centuries, the monks
of Bury St Edmunds believed that their abbey church had not been
dedicated yet they failed to have this rectified.[23] Such a situation does
not mean, of course, that such churches were without patron saints.
Clearly, St Edmund fulfilled such a role at Bury, dedicated or not.
Indeed, it is difficult to find any positive evidence of churches without
spiritual patrons. The records of Church councils and of the bishops
fail to mention such a circumstance, because they concentrated on the
rite of dedication and the status it conferred, not on the detail of the
patron saints.

The absence of such saints remains a possibility in some medieval
churches, but it seems to have been infrequent. Church legislation,
when it refers to them, assumes that they normally existed. In 1229,
Bishop William of Blois of Worcester required each church in his diocese to display the date of dedication beside the high altar, along with
the names of the officiating bishop and the patron saint—a require-
ment copied in two other dioceses.[24] Patronal images were common in
churches. By the early fourteenth century, English canon law required
that the parishioners of each church should provide the furnishings
and vessels necessary for worship, including 'the principal image in the
chancel'.[25] The fifteenth-century English canon lawyer, William
Lyndwood, explained this as referring to the image 'of that saint in
whose honour the church is consecrated', or as we would say today,
'the patron saint'.[26] The saint's image seems to have been usually
placed to the north of the 'high' or chief altar of the church at the east
end of the chancel, the south end being occupied by an image of
Mary.[27] Lyndwood observed that if there were two patron saints like
Peter and Paul, images of both should be provided. At Exeter
Cathedral—dedicated to Peter and Mary, as well as to Paul by the fourteenth century—the image of Peter stood on the north side of the high

21. *Councils and Synods II: A.D.1205–1313*, ed. F.M. Powicke and C.R. Cheney, 2 vols (Oxford, 1964), i, 245–46.
22. The legislation is well summarised by Antonia Gransden, 'The Question of the Consecration of St Edmund's Church', pp. 69–70.
23. Ibid., pp. 65–77.
24. *Councils and Synods II: A.D.1205–1313*, ed. Powicke and Cheney, i, 172; cf. pp. 296–97, 367, 600.
25. Ibid., ii, 1387.
26. William Lyndwood, *Provinciale* (Oxford, 1679), p. 252.
27. J.C. Cox, *Churchwardens' Accounts from the Fourteenth Century to the Close of the Seventeenth Century* (London, 1913), pp. 142–43.

altar, Paul's on the south side, and Mary's in the neighbourhood of Paul's.[28] Patronal images were often elaborate and might be dressed in clothes. St Ewen, in the Bristol church of that name, wore a coat of tissue, while St Andrew at Ashburton (Devon) owned a tunic of black velvet, buckram and silk.[29] At Morebath (Devon) in 1530-1, the church contracted with an image maker to manufacture 'a new George and a new horse to our dragon'—evidently a large ensemble depicting the saint in action.[30] When a church was named after All Saints, Lyndwood thought that there should be several images or none, because no image was required where the subject was not reproducible.[31] In a parallel case, the church of Holy Trinity Hull solved the problem by displaying an image with three heads.[32]

The emphasis on patron saints in Church law is supported by statistical evidence. In the South West of England, 95% of the parish churches in Cornwall and virtually every religious house in Cornwall and Devon can be shown to have had a patron by the end of the middle ages. The percentage of Devon parish churches in this respect is lower at 70%, but as the missing places are those for which no records survive, the absence in their cases (and in 5% in Cornwall) is provisional not certain. The importance of patron saints before the Reformation cannot therefore be questioned on the grounds of their non-existence. It may, however, have been modified by the competition they faced in their buildings from other heavenly beings. By at least the later middle ages, the dominant image in most churches was that of Jesus on the Cross atop the chancel screen, accompanied by the Virgin Mary and St John. Many places came to acquire a separate Lady chapel in the Virgin's honour, as well as side altars honouring other saints. Images of holy men and women were sculpted in wood, painted on walls and screens, or glazed in windows. Frequently, such images (especially of the Virgin) might acquire a reputation for intercessory powers or working miracles and become the chief object of local veneration, eclipsing the cult of the ancient patron saint. A Somerset vicar who left money for local pilgrimages in 1534 was interested in Our

28. *Ordinale Exon*, ed. J.N. Dalton and G.H. Doble, 4 vols, Henry Bradshaw Society, xxxvii–viii, lxiii, lxxix (1909–40), i, 24, 64, 297.
29. *The Church Book of St Ewen's, Bristol 1454–1584*, ed. Betty R. Masters and Elizabeth Ralph, Bristol and Gloucestershire Archaeological Society, Records Section, vi (1967), p. 9; *Churchwardens' Accounts of Ashburton, 1479–1580*, ed. Alison Hanham, Devon and Cornwall Record Society, new series, xv (1970), p. 81.
30. *The Accounts of the Wardens of the Parish of Morebath, Devon 1520–1573*, ed. J. Erskine Binney (Exeter, 1904), p. 32.
31. Lyndwood, *Provinciale*, p. 253.
32. Eamon Duffy, *The Stripping of the Altars: Traditional Religion in England c.1400–c.1580* (New Haven and London, 1992), p. 458.

Lady of Pity at Sidbury (Devon) and the tomb of Bishop Lacy in Exeter Cathedral, not in the saints after whom these churches were named.[33]

Still, patron saints had honour: inside and outside church. Their feast day or days might be honoured with special attention—an occasion which in modern times has come to be called the 'patronal festival'.[34] Local people might mark the day as a holiday,[35] or name children after the saint.[36] The date on which the bishop dedicated the church and high altar, the 'feast of dedication', was also commonly celebrated as a special day in the church's year. Church leaders encouraged observances of this second kind. The twelfth-century 'Pontifical of Magdalen College' reminded bishops when dedicating churches to tell the people to keep the anniversary as a festival, and the reminder survives in the pontifical used by Archbishop Bainbridge of York between 1508 and 1514.[37] To help parishioners remember the date, bishops often granted indulgences remitting penance to those who came to the church on that day of the year. William Brewer, bishop of Exeter, awarded 24 days of remission in 1231-32 on the anniversary of the dedication of St Mary Arches (Exeter) and 30 days in 1238 on that of St Buryan (Cornwall).[38] Ecclesiastical calendars sometimes mention such dedication feasts, those of Tawstock (Devon) on 8 January and South Molton (Devon) on 10 October being recorded in fifteenth- and early sixteenth-century prayer books used in the district.[39] Because we usually talk of 'church dedications', confusion has arisen in modern times between the spiritual patron and his or her festival on the one hand and the feast of dedication on the other. The dedication feast may have included some memory of, or reference to, the spiritual patron, but the date on which it was held was simply the anniversary of the original dedication of the church. Only very rarely can that have coincided with the patronal festival. Failure to appreciate this fact has led historians in Devon to imagine St Nicholas to

---

33. *Wells Wills*, ed. F.W. Weaver (London, 1890), pp. 97–98.
34. The term 'patronal festival' (or 'fête') is not recorded in English until 1834 (*Oxford English Dictionary*, s.v. 'patronal').
35. See below, note 44.
36. This was not, apparently, common in Devon, but in a few Cornish parishes children (especially girls) were named after the patron saint of the church, e.g. at St Columb, Landulph and St Minver (*Nicholas Roscarrock's Lives of the Saints: Cornwall and Devon*, ed. Nicholas Orme, Devon and Cornwall Record Society, new series, xxxv (1992), pp. 126, 141, 154). Equally, this was not the case in other places with unique local saints, e.g. Newlyn East and St Teath (ibid., pp. 133, 163).
37. *The Pontifical of Magdalen College*, ed. Wilson, p. 122; *Liber Pontificalis Chr. Bainbridge*, ed. Henderson, p. 75.
38. Nicholas Orme, 'Indulgences in Medieval Cornwall', *Journal of the Royal Institution of Cornwall*, new series ii, vol. i (1992), pp. 164, 170.
39. Nicholas Orme, 'Two Early Prayer-Books from North Devon', *Devon and Cornwall Notes and Queries*, xxxvi (1991), p. 347.

be the patron saint of Dunkeswell church because the church was dedicated on the eve of St Nicholas' day, and St Andrew to be the patron saint of Cullompton because the event took place on St Andrew's eve.[40] In truth, no such connection can be made; patronal festivals and dedication festivals were different events both in the liturgy and in the calendar.

We have seen how the authority to dedicate churches and altars came to belong to the diocesan bishops. It followed that, up to the Reformation, any questions relating to such dedications lay within the bishop's jurisdiction because he or his predecessors had named the patron at the consecration of the high altar. There is indeed little evidence that bishops interfered with or changed the spiritual patronage of churches, that clergy or lay people asked for alterations, or that litigation arose over the matter. Occasionally, a bishop may have modified a local choice. When Bishop Brewer dedicated the church of St Buryan in 1238, he named the high altar in honour of SS Andrew the Apostle, Thomas the Martyr and Nicholas the Confessor before mentioning the local patron, the Blessed Virgin Buryan.[41] If this was a new initiative, it may imply that such an obscure saint was felt to need the support of better attested and more powerful colleagues. Equally, given that a bishop had little contact with most of his parishes, local people may have altered church dedications without consulting him. There are several other instances in Cornwall where English or international saints were added to Celtic ones, without any surviving information about when or by whom this was done.[42] More certainly, bishops seem to have demanded and received acknowledgement of their power over church dedication feasts. The registers of the late-medieval bishops of Exeter furnish several examples in which the diocesan bishop allowed a change of date after a formal approach from the clergy and parishioners. Thus Bishop Lacy transferred the dedication feast of Topsham (Devon) from Easter Friday to 3 July in 1436, and that of St Dominick (Cornwall) from 30 August to 9 May in 1445. In the latter case, the parish evidently asked for the change to remove the festival from the harvest season.[43]

The Reformation led to further interventions in these matters. In 1536 Henry VIII, who had become head of the Church of England two years earlier, caused the convocation (or clerical assembly) of the province of Canterbury to command all churches to keep 'the feast of

---

40. Below, pp. 152, 155.
41. *The Register of John de Grandisson, bishop of Exeter*, ed. F.C. Hingeston-Randolph, 3 vols (London and Exeter, 1894–49), i, 84.
42. Below, p. 39.
43. Below, pp. 78, 210. Other examples include St Enodoc in Cornwall and Cullompton, Upton Hellions and Venn Ottery in Devon (below, under these entries).

dedication' on the first Sunday in October. Again the motive was the avoidance of harvest. In addition, 'the feast of the patron' of each church, 'called commonly the church holy day', was no longer to be observed as a holiday unless it was a generally recognized feast, i.e. a major religious festival.[44] In 1538, a proclamation ordered the suppression of the cult of Thomas Becket, and although it did not mention the church dedications in his honour, it implicitly ruled them out.[45] But the interest of the crown in these matters did not last long. As the Reformation developed and took a Protestant direction, the cults of saints and the observance of their feasts lost people's attention rather than attracting it. The Book of Common Prayer of 1549 and its successors provided no material for the celebration of dedication festivals, though equally it did not forbid them. The remembrance of patron saints in parish churches grew weak, and in many places they became forgotten. Bishops remained involved with church dedications only when new churches had to be inaugurated.[46] Such cases were relatively few until the early nineteenth century when new churches proliferated as populations increased. A modern Anglican or Catholic bishop will be concerned with choosing, or at least approving, the spiritual patron of a new church as part of the process of establishing the church and consecrating it. But in the Anglican Church, the bishop's authority has been weakened by the oblivion into which church dedications fell after the Reformation. When, in the 1730s, antiquaries like Browne Willis began to produce church directories and to list church patron saints, they did so independently of the bishops. The antiquaries published the dedications which they believed to be the traditional ones that former bishops had authorized. In fact, many of their dedications were conjectures which differed from those of the middle ages. Later antiquaries and ecclesiologists further modified these conjectures, introduced mistakes and invented spiritual patrons anew without recourse to the bishop. Every modern diocese is likely to contain churches whose dedications come from scholarly or local initiatives which have never been officially sanctioned. By the strict letter of canon law, such innovations ought to be approved and established by a fresh dedication of the high altar. In practice, they have become established over time, buttressed by notice boards, statues and stained-glass effigies, and are assumed to be ancient and official. It would be a bold bishop who set out to regularize them now.

44. D. Wilkins, *Concilia Magnae Britanniae et Hiberniae*, 4 vols (London, 1737), iii, 823–24.
45. *Tudor Royal Proclamations*, ed. P.L. Hughes and J.F. Larkin, 3 vols (New Haven and London, 1964–49), i, 276.
46. On this subject, see below, pp. 43–44.

2

THE PERIOD BEFORE 1066

The earliest churches in Britain were founded in late Roman times, particularly after Christianity received imperial toleration in 313. Their dedications have been lost, except for one or two traditions recorded by the historian Bede (d. 735). He tells us that Alban, martyred probably in the third century, was commemorated by a church at St Albans built after his death as 'a worthy memorial of his martyrdom'.[47] He adds that Augustine of Canterbury found in that city, on his arrival in 597, 'a church built in ancient times, in honour of St Martin, while the Romans were still in Britain'.[48] Some have questioned whether Bede meant that the dedication of St Martin's was Roman, or merely the building. Martin's cult, however, developed quickly after his death in 397, and there is no reason why it should not have reached Canterbury before the Anglo-Saxon conquest in the fifth century.[49] If so, it appears that late Roman Britain possessed church dedications to both of the categories of saints already mentioned. Alban typified the local martyr buried in the church, and Martin bishop of Tours the widely celebrated figure whose cult had spread from elsewhere.

The occupation of much of Britain by the Anglo-Saxons in the fifth century disrupted Christianity, which remained well organised chiefly in the western and northern parts of the island under Celtic rule. The occupation also left those parts more isolated from continental Europe. The Roman custom of dedicating churches to spiritual patrons was followed in the Celtic lands, but the dedications in these regions differ somewhat (at least, as they have been recorded) from those of the Roman world. The topic of Celtic dedications needs to be studied in two stages: first, by dating the evidence about them, and secondly, by

---

47. *Bede's Ecclesiastical History of the English People*, ed. B. Colgrave and R.A.B. Mynors (Oxford, 1991), pp. 34–35.
48. Ibid., pp. 76–77.
49. J.N.L. Myres, 'Reviews of Books', *English Historical Review*, lxx (1955), p. 93; J.M. Wallace-Hadrill, *Bede's Ecclesiastical History of the English People: A Historical Commentary* (Oxford, 1988), pp. 36–37.

interpreting it. In Cornwall, the earliest recorded church dedication is that of Docco, patron of Lanow in St Kew parish, a monastery which is said to have been visited by St Sampson in the early sixth century and is mentioned in his first surviving Life written in the seventh.[50] The name Docco is that of a Celtic saint, further recorded in south Wales where the church of Llandochau Fawr in Glamorgan came to be called after him. Nothing else is known about Cornwall until the tenth century, when a list of 48 saints in a Breton source of that period includes some 25, perhaps more, who are later attested as patrons of Cornish churches. Several were undoubtedly patrons in Cornwall by the date of the list because their names occur in the order of the topography of their churches, showing that the compiler was aware of the links between saints and particular places.[51] All are people with Celtic names. Other Cornish documentary records survive from the tenth century onwards: a few charters of pre-Conquest date, Domesday Book in 1086, and an increasing volume of charters, chronicles, saints' lives and other material after 1100. In these post-900 sources, many other patron saints of Cornish churches are mentioned: some with Celtic names and others who are well-known apostolic or Roman saints. Thus Michael and Stephen are both to be found in Domesday Book, the one as patron of St Michael's Mount, the other of St Stephen by Launceston, at either end of the county. A good many Cornish church saints, however, both Celts and non-Celts, are not recorded until the thirteenth century, or even later.

The fact that virtually no dedication evidence about Cornwall survives until after 900 means that our knowledge is scanty indeed about the matter in earlier centuries. Little can be safely said about the dates when Cornish churches acquired their patron saints or which saints they originally acquired. The Life of St Sampson implies that Cornwall was officially Christian by the early sixth century and had at least one church by then, but whether Cornish churches began in that century, or the fifth, or even the fourth (before the end of Roman Britain) is impossible to say, pending the discovery of archaeological evidence. The adoption of saints by churches is another difficult matter. In later records, Celtic men and women predominate as patrons both in Cornwall and the other Celtic lands, and it has generally been thought that they reflect the original choice of dedication. According to this view, people in Cornwall and Wales preferred Celtic patrons, either

50. *La Vie de Saint Samson*, ed. R. Fawtier (Paris, 1912), p. 142.
51. B. Lynette Olson and O.J. Padel, 'A Tenth-Century List of Cornish Parochial Saints', *Cambridge Medieval Celtic Studies*, xii (1986), pp. 33–71.

because such men and women had strong local cults or because of the relative isolation of the Celtic lands from the Roman world during the fifth and sixth centuries. It is equally possible, however, that the Cornish (and the other Celtic peoples) dedicated churches from the earliest times to non-Celtic figures like Martin or Michael, and that the later records of these dedications are just as indicative of ancient practices. Church dedications may have changed in these early centuries, too—we have no means of knowing. An original non-Celtic patron saint may have been eclipsed by a holy Celtic figure who was subsequently buried in the church, or the reverse may have occurred. Certainly, Celts form a large majority when we reach the era of written records in the tenth century. It also seems that their number was largely complete by that date. Cornwall came under firm English rule, politically and ecclesiastically, during the ninth and tenth centuries, and only about half a dozen Celtic saints seem to have become church patrons after the year 900. These few, moreover—Kenwyn, Ludwan, Morveth, Tallan, and possibly Manacca—appear to be late-medieval inventions from place-names meaning other things.[52] No Cornishman or woman who lived after the English conquest is known to have become a patron saint.

Who were these Celtic patron saints in Cornwall and Wales, and were they saints in the usual sense? Certainly, some were. Sampson, who died in the mid sixth century and of whom we possess a credible early Life, was a monk and bishop with a distinguished career in Wales, Cornwall and Brittany. The monastery of Docco mentioned in Sampson's Life bore the name of a saint of south Wales, and may have been a daughter house of that saint's church in Glamorgan. There are ninth- and tenth-century Lives of Winwaloe and Paul of Leon, attested Church leaders with dedications in the Celtic lands, but the Lives and legends of the other patron saints of Cornwall (and many saints lack anything of the kind) were mostly written in and after the twelfth century. The writers of most of these Lives possessed virtually no knowledge of their subjects as historical figures. Instead, they portrayed them in the manner that saints were traditionally represented: coming from countries overseas and often being killed by local tyrants for whom there is no ancient evidence. In truth, some of these early 'saints' may have been notable local people rather than saintly foreigners. Cuby, patron of Cuby and Duloe, is said to have been born in Cornwall, though characteristically this statement occurs in a Welsh source which likewise presents the saint as an incomer.[53] Three other Cornish churches—Constantine, Gerrans

---

52. Below, pp. 40, 101.
53. A.W. Wade-Evans, *Vitae Sanctorum Britanniae et Genealogicae* (Cardiff, 1944, pp. 234–35).

and Gwithian—are dedicated to men with names similar to those of
kings or lords in Cornwall and Devon during the Celtic period.[54] It is
not improbable that the some such saints were royalty or nobility who
founded the buildings or were buried at the sites. Llansadwrn in
Anglesey still possesses an early inscribed stone to Saturninus, a mar-
ried man after whom the church is apparently named.[55] Other saints,
perhaps, were early parish clergy. The parish of Garway, originally
Lann Guorboe, now in Herefordshire, preserves the name of a priest
called Guoruoe who is mentioned in an early charter relating to the
church and was apparently the first incumbent.[56]

Some of the Cornish patron saints were also unique to one church
and were thought to be buried in the building. The antiquary William
Worcester, who visited Cornwall in 1478, was told about seventeen
such cases including Breac at Breage, Euny at Lelant and Morwenna
at Morwenstow.[57] In other places, the patrons of Cornish churches
were not unique or local, but popular Celtic figures buried elsewhere.
Thus St Petroc, whose body was first enshrined at Padstow and then
removed to Bodmin, came to be the dedicatee of three further Cornish
churches: Egloshayle, Little Petherick and Trevalga. In the nineteenth
and early twentieth centuries, students of early Celtic Church history
liked to think that church dedications to Celtic saints began in the
saint's lifetime, through an act of foundation by the saint or one of veneration by his or her devotees. There is no positive evidence for this,
and it looks unlikely. Sainthood is largely a posthumous award, and the
theory of personal foundations rules out the possibility that a saint's
cult grew after the saint's death, a growth for which there are often historical grounds. We do not assume that non-Celtic saints like Cuthbert
or Martin founded the churches dedicated to them.[58] If a church was
built on a burial ground associated with a famous person, that person's
name may have been attached to the church from the start; so too if it

---

54. On Constantine, see G.H. Doble, *St. Constantine, King and Monk, and St Merryn*,
"Cornish Saints" Series, no. 26 (Truro, 1930); on Gerent, idem, *Saint Gerent*, "Cornish
Saints" Series, no. 41 (Long Compton, 1938); and on Gwithian, *La Vie de Saint Samson*, ed.
Fawtier, p. 144.

55. *An Inventory of the Ancient Monuments in Anglesey* (London, Royal Commission on Ancient &
Historical Monuments in Wales & Monmouthshire, 1937), pp. cv, cix, 110.

56. Wendy Davies, *An Early Welsh Microcosm: Studies in the Llandaff Charters* (London, 1978), pp.
42, 143. O.J. Padel, *Cornish Place-Name Elements*, English Place-Name Society, lvi–lvii (1985),
p. 144, notices a similar case: Iunabui at Llandinabo (Herefordshire).

57. William Worcester, *Itineraries*, ed. J.H. Harvey (Oxford, 1969), pp. 26–29, 86–89, 96–99,
106–7, 114–15.

58. The topic is discussed and rejected by Owen Chadwick, 'The Evidence of Dedications in the
Early History of the Welsh Church', in H.M. and Nora K. Chadwick, *Studies in Early British
History* (Cambridge, 1954), pp. 173–88, especially pp 175–76, 187–88.

was built and dedicated to a figure like Petroc who was already dead and famous. In other cases, it is possible that the person after whom the church is now named is a later noble or cleric who has eclipsed an earlier patron, even a patron from the Roman world. Guoruoe presumably ministered in a church dedicated to somebody else.

Perhaps the most definite judgment to be made about the Celtic saints culted in Cornwall is that they were many rather than few. The 133 ancient churches with Celtic patrons, omitting saints who are apparently late inventions, venerated at least 107 different people. Saint Petroc's monastery at Bodmin was the wealthiest religious house in Cornwall at the time of the Domesday Survey, and he became the patron of at least fourteen churches in Devon. In Cornwall, by contrast, his tally was limited to the five places mentioned above. Winwaloe had the patronage of another five or six,[59] while Euny, Piran and Rumon owned three each. Fourteen, including Cuby, Just, Melor and Wenna, presided over two each, but it is always possible that patrons with the same personal name were different people. Although a wide range of names was used in Celtic Cornwall, names recurred and may have done so among saints.[60] The remaining 88 saints were honoured in single churches, some additionally at chapels or wells. Even David, Paul of Leon and Sampson—saints widely culted in Wales and Brittany—had only one or two parish dedications in Cornwall, showing that the choice of saints in the county was highly localised and little affected by fashionable cults. This pattern differed from most of England. There, where Christianity was largely reintroduced from the continent, dedications to saints like Andrew, Mary, Michael and Peter became very common, while saints of a single church were relatively unusual. Another way of analysing patrons is by gender, but this is difficult in Cornwall because the sources (often written at some distance from the church) sometimes disagree about the sex. Working on the basis that the gender most often found in records is the correct one, Cornwall seems to come closer to England east of the Tamar in preferring male patron saints to female ones. Of the county's 133 churches with early Celtic patrons, 91 honoured men, 37 women, and four a pair of each gender.[61] A similar surplus of males is found in Devon. There too female patron saints were few and their churches a minority, even though Mary was the most popular patron of all (including the men).[62]

---

59. The total for Winwaloe increases to six if St Winnow is included.
60. For wide choice in names, see also Elisabeth Okasha, *Corpus of Early Christian Inscribed Stones of South-west Britain* (London and New York, 1993), pp. 343–45.
61. In addition, there is the patron of St Veep, whose gender is uncertain.
62. Below, pp. 31, 34–35.

In England, the story of church dedications resumes in 597 with the mission of Augustine of Canterbury. Bede tells us that Augustine found another old church in Canterbury besides St Martin's, which he restored in honour of Christ and made his cathedral (the present-day Christ Church).[63] He also built a new church for a monastic community and named it after the apostles Peter and Paul.[64] As the conversion of England proceeded during the seventh and eighth centuries, more large churches were built in the English kingdoms, staffed by communities of monks or priests and eventually known as minsters.[65] Some were founded by kings and others by clerics, sometimes in association with royal estates. Minsters came to acquire definite parishes over which they had rights and responsibilities, and these territories were often much larger than the typical English parishes of later times. In Devon, which was conquered by the kings of Wessex in the seventh century, the minsters included Crediton, Exeter, Hartland, Plympton and Tiverton, all of which are known to have had bodies of clergy and extensive parishes.[66] Smaller local churches appeared alongside the minsters perhaps as early as the seventh century and in significant numbers by the tenth. These were usually built by local lords to serve their households or estates and were served by single clergy. At first, such lesser churches were subordinate to the minsters. The Laws of King Edgar (960–2) distinguished three grades of buildings: 'old minsters', lords' churches with graveyards, and similar churches without them. Those who supported lords' churches were required to pay some or all of their tithes to the local minster.[67] As time passed, however, the churches of the lords acquired their independence and became parish churches—a process in train during the tenth and eleventh centuries and largely completed by the twelfth. The result was the division of England into a patchwork of smaller parishes than before. Sometimes the minsters survived within this system with a community of clergy and a larger than average territory, but sometimes they were reduced to the status of ordinary churches with a single cleric and a parish of average size.

---

63. Bede, *Ecclesiastical History*, ed. Colgrave and Mynors, pp. 114–15.
64. Ibid.
65. On what follows, see *Minsters and Parish Churches: the local Church in Transition, 950–1200*, ed. John Blair (Oxford, 1988), especially pp. 1–8, and *Pastoral Care before the Parish*, ed. John Blair and Richard Sharpe (Leicester, 1992). Contrary views are expressed by Eric Cambridge and David Rollason, 'The Pastoral Organization of the Anglo-Saxon Church: a Review of the "Minster Hypothesis" ', *Early Medieval Europe*, iv (1995), pp. 87–104.
66. On minsters in Devon, see *Unity and Variety: a History of the Church in Devon and Cornwall*, ed. Nicholas Orme (Exeter, 1991), pp. 12–15.
67. *Councils and Synods I: A.D.871–1204*, ed. Whitelock, Brett and Brooke, i, 97–98.

Table 1

English Church Dedications, 597–800

(Source: W. Levison, *England and the Continent in the Eighth Century*, pp. 259–65)

Peter	20
Mary	19
Peter and Paul	6
Andrew	6
Martin	4
Michael	3
Paul	3
John the Baptist	2
Laurence	2
Alban	1
Bartholomew	1
Christ	1
Cuthbert and Oswald	1
Matthias	1
The Four Crowned Martyrs	1

Augustine's foundations helped to influence the dedications of churches in England as well as their constitutions. Later church founders in England followed his preference for Biblical saints, including Peter and Paul. The scholar Wilhelm Levison, who compiled a list of all the dedications recorded in England between 597 and 800 (excluding chapels and subsidiary altars), found that they venerated a relatively narrow group of patrons (Table 1). The two most popular were Peter, appropriately in a country converted from Rome, and the Virgin Mary. These came well ahead of the rest of the field including apostolic figures like Andrew, Bartholomew and Paul, a few Roman figures like Laurence and the Four Crowned Martyrs, and Martin a popular saint of the Christian Roman Empire. Only two dedications are recorded before 800 to British or English figures: one to Alban and one jointly to Cuthbert and Oswald, the latter of which falls just before the concluding date. This native category, however, grew considerably after 800 and is more prominent when records increase in the tenth and eleventh centuries. Kings and Church leaders in the late Anglo-Saxon period encouraged the cults of English saints as a means of extending political power, religious influence, and even national integration. The rulers of Wessex from Alfred onwards are said to have fostered the cult of Cuthbert, while Cnut supported Edmund of Bury and Edward the Martyr, and the monks of Winchester promoted

Table 2

Devon Church Dedications before 1086

(Source: present book)

Church	Dedication	Evidence
Braunton	Brannoc	Place-name
Bridestowe	Bridget	Place-name (Domesday)
Christow	Christina	Place-name (Domesday)
Crediton	Mary (?)	Later document
East Teignmouth	Michael	Document
Exeter Cathedral	Mary and Peter	Documents
Exeter: St Martin	Christ, Holy Cross, Mary and Martin	Later document
Exeter: St Olave	Mary, Thomas the Apostle and Olave	Document
Exeter: St Sidwell	Sidwell	Document
Hartland	Nectan	Place-name (Domesday)
Instow	John	Place-name (Domesday)
Petrockstowe	Petroc	Place-name (Domesday)
Plympton	Peter (and Paul?)	Domesday Book
St Budeaux	Budoc	Place-name (Domesday)
St James (near Exeter)	James	Place-name (Domesday)
St Marychurch	Mary	Place-name (Domesday)
Tavistock Abbey	Mary (and Rumon?)	Document
Totnes	Mary	Domesday Book

Swithin. By the Norman Conquest, native saints like these had probably been chosen as the patrons of numerous churches in England, as
had several holy women such as Aethelthryth (Etheldreda) of Ely,
Mildburg of Much Wenlock and Werburg of Chester.[68]

There was no sharp distinction, it seems, between the choice of
patron saints for the minsters and for their counterparts on lords'
estates. Both grades of churches came to honour the major Biblical and
Roman figures—perhaps because the small foundations copied the
larger in this matter. The minsters were chiefly distinctive because they
were more likely to acquire the bodies of holy kings, bishops or nuns
who became cult figures alongside the original patron saints and might
then be added, officially or unofficially, to the church dedication. Even
so, saints like Cuthbert and Swithin who were buried in minsters

---

68. On the cults of Anglo-Saxon saints, see David Rollason, *Saints and Relics in Anglo-Saxon England*
(Oxford, 1989), especially chapters 6–7, and on royal saints in particular, Susan J. Ridyard, *The
Royal Saints of Anglo-Saxon England: a Study of West Saxon and East Anglian Cults* (Cambridge,
1988).

became popular as patrons of lesser churches. In Devon, the evidence for church dedications in the Anglo-Saxon period is scanty because relatively few early records survive from the county. Only about 18 dedications are known by 1086—including religious houses and parish churches—from records in Domesday Book or other early documents (Table 2). A longer list can be postulated, however, if we are willing to read back church dedications recorded in the twelfth and later centuries. This proposal can be defended on two grounds. First, as mentioned above, evidence suggests that a great many churches existed in England by the tenth century—both minsters and lesser foundations—identical with those of later parishes. In Devon, the 18 churches recorded with dedications by 1086 can be doubled to over 30 if we add those whose mere existence is known by that date: a total representing both major and minor churches of later times.[69] Secondly, medieval dedications (as we shall see) appear to be marked by constancy rather than change, suggesting that they were not generally altered after adoption.[70] It is plausible therefore that many of the dedications recorded in later medieval Devon originated in Anglo-Saxon times. The commonest names involved—Mary, Peter and Paul, Michael, and Andrew—resemble those of Levison's list and imply that Devon was broadly similar to the rest of Anglo-Saxon England in its preferences.[71] Holy Cross, George, John the Baptist, James, Martin, and Thomas the Apostle may also be added by the Conquest with complete or virtual certainty,[72] as may four Anglo-Saxon figures: Cuthbert and Edmund each with two later churches, and Swithin and Edward (doubtless the Martyr) each with three. Finally, the post-

---

69. Archaeological evidence suggests St George Exeter and St Michael Sidbury (Bridget Cherry and Nikolaus Pevsner, *Devon*, The Buildings of England, 2nd ed. (London, 1989), pp. 390, 732). Domesday Book mentions several churches other than those with dedications. They include (with known pre-Reformation dedications in brackets) Axminster (Mary and John the Baptist), Buckfast (Mary and Stephen), Cullompton (Mary), Colyton (Andrew and Mary), Exeter (two unnamed churches, one probably St Stephen), Kingskerswell (Mary), South Molton (Syth) and Yealmpton (Bartholomew). Domesday place-names suggest further churches at Cheriton Bishop (Michael), Cheriton Fitzpaine (All Saints), Churston Ferrers (unknown), Exminster (Martin), Honeychurch (Mary), and Whitchurch (Andrew), while Charford in South Brent (Petroc and Mary), the Cheritons in Brendon (unknown) and Payhembury (Mary), and the Churchill in East Down (unknown) may indicate others (DB, passim).

70. On this subject, see below, pp. 36–37.

71. The cults of the saints concerned had also reached the South West by the Norman Conquest in the form of relics preserved at Exeter Cathedral. The best study of the Exeter relic lists is now Patrick W. Conner, *Anglo-Saxon Exeter: a Tenth-century Cultural History* (Woodbridge, 1993), pp. 171–209. Of the 23 saints with three or more churches later dedicated to them in Devon (below, Table 4), 17 are represented by relics in the Exeter lists (ibid., pp. 206–9).

72. Certain are Holy Cross (co-patron of St Martin's Exeter), James at St James near Exeter, Martin in Exeter, and Thomas the Apostle (co-patron of St Olave's Exeter). Virtually certain are George in Exeter and at Modbury, John the Baptist at Axminster and Martin at Exminster.

Table 3

Devon Minsters and their Dedications

(Source: present book)

(Probable minsters are in roman text; possible minsters in italics)

Church	Dedication(s), with first recorded date(s)
Axminster	Mary (c. 1200) and John the Baptist (1315)
Barnstaple	Peter (c. 1190) and Paul (1370)
Braunton	Brannoc (854)
Buckfast	Mary and Stephen (c. 1143)
Chittlehampton	Urith (15th century)
Colyton	Mary (c. 1200) and Andrew (1301)
Crediton	Mary (c. 950) (?) and Holy Cross (1237)
Cullompton	Mary (13th century)
Exeter	Mary and Peter (925 x 939)
Exminster	Martin (1400)
Hartland	Nectan (1086)
Kingskerswell	Mary (1477)
Lydford	Petroc (1237)
Modbury	Mary (1505) and George (c. 1190)
Pilton	Mary (1261)
Plympton	Peter (1086) and Paul (c. 1186)
South Molton	'Syth' (1517)
Stokenham	Humbert (1343)
Tavistock	Mary (981) and Rumon (c. 1154)
Tiverton	Peter and Paul (1447)
Totnes	Mary (1086)
West Alvington	Unknown
Yealmpton	Bartholomew (1421 x 1432)

Conquest records suggest that Devon followed the pattern of minster dedications proposed above. Many of the county's ministers are later found with apostolic and Roman patrons, while a few acquired resident saints like Brannoc at Braunton, Nectan at Hartland and Rumon at Tavistock (Table 3).[73]

In some western and northern parts of England—Devon, the Welsh Marches and Cumbria, for example—the Saxons conquered areas where Christianity was already strong. In such places, they sometimes took over churches with Celtic patron saints as well as founding

---

73. The only lesser churches in Devon with distinctive, apparently resident saints, are Stoke Fleming (Ermund) and St Sidwell in Exeter, and even these may be candidates as minsters.

new ones with apostolic, Roman or English dedications. The name of Devon perpetuates that of the Celtic Dumnonii who previously ruled the territory, and at least a few of the county's holy sites seem to have existed before the Saxons' arrival. Exeter had a late Roman cemetery near the present cathedral. It contained burials that are likely to be Christian and may have lain close to a church.[74] Four or five rural churches, including East Ogwell, Lustleigh and Stowford, are associated with inscribed stones from the period when Devon was wholly or partly Celtic.[75] These sites appear to have stayed in use from Celtic to Saxon times, but if they ever had churches with Celtic dedications (which is not certain) the dedications had more difficulty in surviving. None of the churches with stones is recorded with such a dedication in historic times. A stronger claim can be advanced on behalf of four other churches: Braunton, Chittlehampton, Hartland and Landkey. The first three of these came to be dedicated to Celtic saints who, in the later middle ages, were believed to be buried in them (Brannoc, Urith and Nectan respectively), implying continuity of shrines and possibly buildings since the pre-Saxon era. Landkey has a typical Celtic church name, meaning 'church site of Cei (or Kea)' an attested Celtic saint, and a fifth church, Instow, gave rise to folklore in the twelfth and thirteenth centuries that a distinctive, apparently Celtic, St John was martyred and buried there, though this cannot be proved. Neither Landkey nor Instow, however, possessed a Celtic dedication strong enough to endure until the end of the middle ages. By 1346, Landkey was under the patronage of St Paul, while Instow by 1476 venerated St John the Baptist.[76]

Four plausibly ancient Celtic dedications in a county of 482 medieval churches is not many, considering that Devon passed to the Saxons at a relatively late date when they were Christians. It is possible that some pre-Saxon churches in Devon had non-Celtic patrons: the one postulated in late-Roman Exeter may have commemorated Mary or an apostle. A great many other Devon churches must be of later, Saxon origin even if, in some cases, they were founded at Celtic burial sites. Equally, names like Landkey, the lost *Lantokay* (another church

---

74. P.T. Bidwell, *The Legionary Bath-House and Basilica and Forum at Exeter* (Exeter, 1979), pp. 112–13; C.G. Henderson and P.T. Bidwell, 'The Saxon Minster at Exeter', *The Early Church in Western Britain and Ireland*, ed. Susan M. Pearce (Oxford, 1982), pp. 145–75.

75. Susan M. Pearce, *The Kingdom of Dumnonia* (Padstow, 1978), p. 71; idem, 'The Early Church in the Landscape: The Evidence from North Devon', *The Archaeological Journal*, cxlii (1985), pp. 255–75; Okasha, *Corpus of Early Christian Inscribed Stones of South-West Britain*, passim.

76. Below, pp. 173, 177.

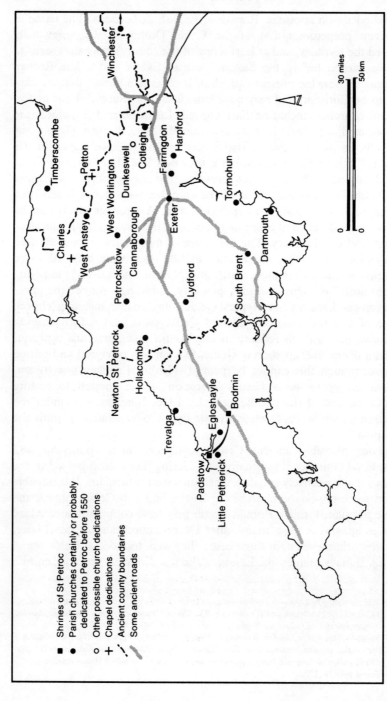

Figure 1. The Cult of St Petroc in Cornwall and Devon

Shrines of St Petroc ■

Parish churches certainly or probably
dedicated to Petroc before 1550 ●

Other possible church dedications ○

Chapel dedications +

Ancient county boundaries ⌐·⌐

Some ancient roads

Winchester

Timberscombe

Petton

Harpford

Charles

West Anstey

West Worlington

Dunkeswell

Cotleigh

Farringdon

Tormohun

Exeter

Petrockstow

Clannaborough

Lydford

Dartmouth

South Brent

Newton St Petrock

Hollacombe

Trevalga

Egloshayle

Bodmin

Padstow

Little Petherick

30 miles

50 km

of Cai) at Leigh-in-Street near Glastonbury (Somerset), and the former *Lanprobi* (church of Probus) at Sherborne (Dorset) suggest
that once there were more churches in the South West with Celtic
patrons.[77] Such churches must have lost their dedications after the
Saxon conquest—not necessarily immediately, but eventually. As time
went on and the Celtic population of Devon became anglicised, it is a
fair assumption that Roman Christianity and its favourite saints
became dominant, replacing earlier Celtic cults.[78] Changes in
patterns of settlement may have helped this process, leading to the
building of new churches on fresh sites and the disuse of older ones.
There are indeed another twenty-four churches in Devon with Celtic
patrons.[79] They include one each named after Budoc, Kerrian, and
Winwaloe, two each after Bridget, David, Nectan (in addition to
Hartland), and Rumon, and at least fourteen after Petroc (Figure 1).[80]
But these dedications may all post-date the Saxon conquest
and need not be explained as Celtic survivals.[81] David and Bridget
could have arrived through social and commercial contacts
with the Celtic lands. Budoc and Winwaloe, saints of Brittany, might
have been imported during the reign of Athelstan (who acquired relics
from that country) or in the time of the Normans (some of whom
came from there). Rumon, Petroc and possibly Kerrian can be
explained as spoils of the Saxon conquest of Cornwall in the
ninth and tenth centuries. It is well-known that, in about the tenth
century, the body of Niot or Neot was taken from St Neot
(Cornwall) to Huntingdonshire and that of Rumon from Ruan
Lanihorne to Tavistock.[82] Saxon control of Bodmin, where Petroc's
body lay, would have enabled his cult and relics to spread to
churches in Devon in a similar fashion during that century or shortly
afterwards.[83] As for Kerrian (whose church was in Exeter), his name
looks likeliest to be a variant of Ciarán, an Irish saint identified in

77. Pearce, *Kingdom of Dumnonia*, pp. 73, 82, 135.
78. A similar paucity of Celtic dedications is also to be found in Cumbria, a similarly Celtic kingdom
    conquered by the English (below, p. 41).
79. This figure excludes saints without a proven Celtic identity like Constantine of Milton Abbot and
    Helen of Abbotsham and Lundy, who could equally be the Roman emperor and his mother.
80. As we do not know the medieval dedications of about a third of the Devon parish churches, we
    can probably postulate a total of about twenty to Petroc throughout the county.
81. This view has already been suggested by Susan Pearce, 'The Dating of some Celtic Dedications
    and Hagiographical Traditions in South Western Britain', *Devonshire Association Transactions*, cv
    (1973), pp. 95–120.
82. *Nicholas Roscarrock's Lives of the Saints*, ed. Orme, pp. 160–61, 167–68.
83. Exeter had relics of several Celtic saints including Bridget, Petroc, Winwaloe and *Morenna* (per-
    haps the saint of Lamorran rather than Morwenna of Morwenstow) by the eleventh century
    (Conner, *Anglo-Saxon Exeter*, p. 208).

medieval times with the different patron saint of St Keverne in west Cornwall.[84] Relics from there may have been transported to Exeter.

Saxons elsewhere in England, as has been observed, generated their own saints from kings, clerics and nuns. Devon's achievement in this respect is small, either because of its distance from the main centres of royalty and religion or through its interest in Celtic saints. St Sidwell's church in Exeter, which appears to have existed by the eleventh century, honoured a female saint of whom little is known. Her late, fourteenth-century legends seem to give her a Saxon rather than a Celtic context, but this may be due to invention.[85] Otherwise, the only signs of distinctive Saxon saints appear in the South Hams. At Stokenham, a St Humbert is mentioned as patron in 1343, and a St Ermund held a similar status nearby at Stoke Fleming in 1364 and 1419. Both these names are recorded in Anglo-Saxon England, making it possible that Humbert (Hunbeorht) and Ermund (Earmund) were Englishmen who lived in or before the eleventh century, perhaps at the places dedicated to them.[86] No further home-grown saints appeared in Devon, and stricter rules about canonisation in the twelfth century made sainthood even harder to achieve. Two late-medieval bishops of Exeter, James Berkeley (d. 1327) and Edmund Lacy (d. 1455), were venerated locally after they died, but neither was formally canonised and neither inspired the dedication of a church or even an altar.[87]

---

84. On Rumon, see *Nicholas Roscarrock's Lives of the Saints*, ed. Orme, pp. 167–68; compare also the removal of St Neot's relics to Huntingdonshire (ibid., pp. 160–61). At Exeter Cathedral in the 14th century, the cathedral observed the feast day of *Keranus*, also called *Kieranus* and *Piranus*, on 5 March (*Ordinale Exon*, ed. Dalton and Doble, i, pp. xxxii–iii, 216, 344). It is reasonable to suppose that *Keranus* is Kerrian, because all the patron saints of the Exeter churches had their festivals observed by the cathedral. The patron saint of St Keverne was also referred to as *Kieranus*, and 5 March was the feast day of that of Ciarán of Saighir, so all these saints appear to have been thought the same—with the addition of Piran for good measure.

85. *Nicholas Roscarrock's Lives of the Saints*, ed. Orme, pp. 170–72. It has been suspected that Sidwell may be identical with Sitofolla, mentioned as the sister of the Celtic St Paul of Leon in his ninth-century Life (ibid.).

86. Nicholas Orme, 'Two Unusual Devon saints', *The Devon Historian*, li (October 1995), pp. 12–13; below, pp. 203–04.

87. Nicholas Orme, 'Two Saint-Bishops of Exeter: James Berkeley and Edmund Lacy', *Analecta Bollandiana*, civ (1986), pp. 403–18.

3

FROM 1066 TO THE REFORMATION

From about the twelfth century onwards, written records shed more light on church dedications than before. It becomes easier to find information about them and to make confident judgments of their range and popularity. The best surviving data relate to religious houses—abbeys and priories—of which large numbers were founded or refounded in the Norman and Angevin periods. Many of these houses were established by written charters which often mention the patron saints. Monastic founders thought of the saints as the recipients of their donations and wished to record that they had granted property 'to God and St Peter', or whoever the saint might be. In turn, foundation charters have tended to endure through their value to those who bought monastic lands at the Reformation. Recently, the topic of monastic dedications has found a thorough historian in Alison Binns, whose *Dedications of Monastic Houses in England and Wales, 1066–1216*, appeared in 1989. This collects the evidence about the main religious orders for men (but not women) from original sources, and provides a directory of individual houses as well as an analysis of the cults after which they were named.

The monastic revival of the twelfth century blended general principles with local traditions. Many monasteries belonged to new international orders: the Cistercians, Premonstratensians and Carthusians. The friars, who appeared in the thirteenth century, were also well-organised bodies common to western Europe. Some of these orders adopted a common patron. The Cistercian houses were usually dedicated to Mary and, so later on, were those of the Carmelite friars.[88] Dominican and Franciscan friaries often remembered their founder saints, Dominic and Francis, while two small orders—the canons of the Holy Sepulchre and the Trinitarian friars—sometimes applied these dedications to their houses. In other cases, particularly those of the

---

88. A few Cistercian abbeys dedicated to saints other than Mary are listed by Binns, *Dedications of Monastic Houses*, p. 159.

Table 4

Monastic Dedications in England, 1086–1216

(Source: Alison Binns, *Dedications of Monastic Houses*, pp. 18–19.)

Mary	235
Peter and Paul	49
Peter and Paul 18	
Peter alone 29	
Paul alone 2	
Trinity	22
John the Baptist	21
John the Evangelist	18
James	18
Mary Magdalene	18
Nicholas	16
Andrew	15
Michael	15
Leonard	13
All Saints	11
Thomas Becket	10
Margaret	8
Cuthbert	7
Bartholomew	6
Saviour	6
George	6
Giles	5
Laurence	5
Holy Cross	5
Holy Sepulchre	5

Benedictine monks and Augustinian canons, monasteries grew out of earlier churches and perpetuated the names of local saints. Thus Bury Abbey was dedicated to Edmund, Chester to Werburg, and Evesham to Mary and Egwin. This happened in the South West too, where the Benedictine and Augustinian monasteries at Bodmin (Petroc), St Germans, Minster (Matherian) and Tavistock (Mary and Rumon) preserved the memory of older regional cults. By the end of the twelfth century, monastic foundations were numerous and prominent enough to stimulate the making of an inventory of them and their patron saints. This first known attempt in England to collect church dedications was the 'Mappa Mundi', produced in about 1200 and attributed to the monk Gervase of Canterbury. The work, which is a gazetteer not a map, lists the counties and regions of Britain, their religious houses and hospitals (with dedications), castles, islands and rivers. It did not achieve completeness, but it provided the names of some 142 monastic and hospital dedications in England: the earliest body of information on the subject, as opposed to individual pieces of evidence.[89]

Binns' researches show that in the period from 1066 to 1216, the male monasteries (excluding the Cistercians) adopted about 101 different spiritual patrons, sometimes singly sometimes jointly. Twenty-four of these patrons owned five or more religious houses (Table 4), 21 owned between two and four, while 56 had one. Comparing Levison's list of AD 600–800 (Table 1), three trends are noticeable. First, Mary has achieved greater popularity both as sole and co-patroness. Even so, her total does not include the Cistercian houses dedicated to her which would further increase the number. Secondly, international saints of the post-apostolic period have grown in prominence, especially George, Leonard and Nicholas. Thirdly, saints local to England have made more impact, notably Cuthbert and Thomas Becket. Because the foundations of many monasteries can be dated within fairly narrow limits, it follows that the same can be done with their dedications, enabling us to measure the relative popularity of cults at particular times. In the immediate post-Conquest period between 1066 and 1100, monastic founders still kept an interest in Peter and Andrew, to which they added the Trinity and Nicholas. Between 1100 and 1150, Peter was overtaken in popularity by James, while the Trinity, John the Evangelist and Mary Magdalene also attracted support. Finally, between 1150 and 1216, John the Baptist and Thomas Becket rose to more prominence. There was still some regard for John the Evangelist and Mary Magdalene, but scarcely any now for Peter and Andrew. Mary remained the favourite patron throughout, ahead of any other figure.[90]

Parish churches were slower to generate records than religious houses. Most probably originated in the Saxon era of few extant documents, so that the dates of their foundations (and therefore of their dedication origins) are rarely known. In the twelfth century, however, the sources increase in volume. These include charters by which lay patrons of churches granted them to monasteries or to other people, and records of the crown which mention churches when (as pieces of property) they became matters of inheritance or litigation. In the thirteenth century, bishops' registers start to record the acts of 'institution'

89. *The Historical Works of Gervase of Canterbury*, ed. W. Stubbs, 2 vols (London, Rolls Series, 1879–80), ii, 414–49.

90. Binns, *Dedications of Monastic Houses*, pp. 22–34.

or 'admission' by which bishops approved the appointment of clergy to parish churches, and papal registers begin to list dispensations to clergy such as the right to hold benefices in plurality. Fiscal records commence in this century too, notably the 'Taxation of Pope Nicholas IV' (1291) which set out to list all religious houses and parish churches with their values and the 'Nonarum Inquisitiones' (1340).[91] The fourteenth and fifteenth centuries furnish three further kinds of evidence. Wills, which exist in large numbers after the 1380s, refer to parish churches extensively as places to be buried or as recipients of bequests. Church court records deal with neglect in maintaining church buildings and with disputes or disturbances which arose inside them. Finally, churchwardens' accounts record, year by year, the income received by churches and the expenditure of money on liturgical activities, furnishings and the repair of the general fabric.

The wealth of references to churches in these sources is great, but it does not extend, unfortunately, to their patron saints. In towns of course, where there were often several churches, it was essential and normal to distinguish them by their dedications. Urban church saints, like St Clement Danes or St Mary Bow in London, have always been widely mentioned and well remembered. In the countryside on the other hand, where most churches were located, there was usually but one in any place. It was more natural to refer to it by its location, which immediately identified it, than by its dedication which might be repeated elsewhere. There was even a legal desirability that a church be described topographically. The right to nominate the clergyman (the advowson) was often associated with the lordship of an adjoining manor, and it was important to keep this connection in mind. So documents commonly record the dedications of rural churches only in Celtic areas, where they continued to be known primarily by their spiritual patrons. In most of England, this was true only in that minority of cases where the dedication was contained in the place-name like Felixstowe (Suffolk), Peterchurch (Herefordshire) or St Neots (Huntingdonshire), or where two churches lay close together as they often did in Lincolnshire and East Anglia. Otherwise, to refer to a church by its dedication as well as by its location was an optional practice in legal documents, infrequently followed. It is rare in charters and uncommon in most records of the crown. In the latter category, the

---

91. *Taxatio Ecclesiastica Angliae et Walliae auctoritate P. Nicholai IV*, [ed. T. Astle, S. Ayscough and J. Caley,] (London, Record Commission, 1802); *Nonarum Inquisitiones* (London, Record Commission, 1807). There is a better text of the former for Cornwall and Devon in *The Registers of Walter Bronescombe . . . and Peter Quivil . . . Bishops of Exeter*, ed. F.C. Hingeston-Randolph (London and Exeter, 1889), pp. 450–81.

'proofs of age' of feudal heirs, filed with the inquisitions post mortem, have been the most useful source for the present study. Their statements from witnesses about births and baptisms produce a larger than usual (though by no means plentiful) supply of references to churches with their saints.[92]

Bishops' registers are not much better in this respect. They mention church saints occasionally, but not as a matter of routine. In Devon, dedications were not used even to distinguish parishes with similar names like the two Bickleighs or the two Littlehams. One abbey (Tavistock) may have made a practice of mentioning patron saints when it forwarded clergy to the bishop for institution. The Exeter registers contain several references to the Tavistock churches of St Helen Abbotsham, St Constantine Milton Abbot, and St Eustace Tavistock.[93] But this was unusual. Either those who owned advowsons rarely bothered to mention patron saints in the documents required for institution, or the bishops' registrars seldom cared to record them. Papal registers are more helpful here, and by the early sixteenth century they frequently mention (and therefore demanded evidence of) patron saints when granting dispensations to hold benefices. More fruitful still are wills. Not only do they often refer to churches, but saints were more prominent in the minds of those who dictated them or drew them up. When a church is specified for burial or a bequest, the patron saint is more liable to be named, though this is not always so or even in the majority of cases. Most testators too seem to have thought of churches in terms of place and a dozen wills mention a church by location alone for every will that refers to its dedication. So many wills have survived from the later middle ages, however, that they constitute an exceptionally valuable source for patron saints, and they are always worth exploring with this in mind.

In other aspects of parish church history, archaeology is an important source. Can it help establish dedications? It may in principle, but in practice the problems of arguing from material remains are formidable. Medieval churches contained cults other than those of their patron saints. The existence of a wall painting, a stone figure or a stained-glass portrait does not prove that the saint it depicts was patron of the whole church. An image must occupy a place of honour on the chancel screen, in the chief east window, in the porch or on the tower before the possibility may be taken seriously. Even such an image,

---

92. *Calendar of Inquisitions Post Mortem*, in progress (London, Public Record Office, 1904–);
   Calendar of Inquisitions Post Mortem, Henry VII, 3 vols (London, Public Record Office, 1898–1956).
93. Below, pp. 126, 183, 207.

especially in a window, may not occupy its original site. Where painted chancel screens survive, the patron saint is not always given a
position of importance. In Devon, Denis, Peter, Andrew and
Winwaloe did not apparently receive it in their churches of Bradninch,
Buckland-in-the-Moor, Kenn or East Portlemouth respectively.[94] It is
also necessary, where archaeology is concerned, to guard against theo-
ries based on anachronistic evidence. Thus Cadeleigh (Devon)
displays a medieval image on its tower which is said to be that of its
patron saint Bartholomew. Yet the saint is not attested as the patron
until 1742 and the designation may be a guess of the eighteenth century. The deduction about the tower image is likely to be based on this
post-medieval information.[95]

So far, some 339 medieval parish church dedications in Devon (70%
of the whole) have been traced between the Norman Conquest and the
end of the sixteenth century. The corresponding figure for Cornwall is
211 (95%), reflecting the fact that most Cornish saint dedications (as
in other Celtic regions) are preserved in place-names and easier to
determine. The churches concerned are those of the ancient parishes
—parishes recognised as such up to the early nineteenth century—
together with a few medieval chapels of ease like Exmouth, Newton
Abbot and Newton Poppleford which have acquired a similar function
and status to parish churches. We shall examine first the evidence for
Devon, which is summarised in Tables 5–7. Table 5 analyses the numbers of churches dedicated to each patron: God, angel or saint. Each
reference to a patron is counted once, whether the saint was the sole
known patron of the church or a joint patron, so that the number of
dedications is consequently larger than that of the churches. Table 6
lists all the cases where two or more saints are mentioned as church
patrons on the same occasion, indicating that they held the function
jointly. Here, the order of the saints follows that which occurs in the
documents. Finally, Table 7 collects the cases where churches are given
different patrons on different occasions. This may have arisen because
the church possessed joint patrons or because the dedication underwent change—a question for discussion later on.

The information in the tables has limitations. First, with only 70% of
the Devon church dedications having been recovered, we must make
allowances for the losses. The numbers of churches owned by the most
popular cult figures may have been nearly half as high again as the

---

94. Frederick Bligh Bond and Bede Camm, *Roodscreens and Roodlofts*, 2 vols (London, 1909), ii, 290,
297, 301, 324, 344.
95. Cherry and Pevsner, *Devon*, p. 241.

Table 5

Spiritual Patrons of Devon Parish Churches, 1066–1600

(Source: present book)

Mary	79
Mary alone 55	
Mary, Assumption, alone 1	
Mary, Nativity, alone 1	
Mary, joint 22	
Peter and Paul	40
Peter and Paul 15	
Peter, other joint 1	
Peter alone 23	
Paul alone 1	
All Saints	32
Michael	32
Andrew	28
George	16
John the Baptist	14
Petroc	14
James	7
Trinity	7
Trinity also known as Saviour 2	
Martin	6
Giles	5
Laurence	5
Pancras	5
Thomas Becket	5
Nicholas	4
Clement	3
Edward	3
Gregory	3
Leonard	3
Margaret	3
Mary Magdalene	3
Nectan	3
Swithin	3
Bartholomew	2
Bridget	2
Holy Cross	2
Cuthbert	2
Cyricus	2
David	2
Edmund	2
Helen	2
Stephen	2
Thomas the Apostle	2

Single dedications: Augustine, Blaise, Brannoc, Cei/Kea, Budoc, Calixtus, Cecilia, Christina, Constantine, Denis, Ermund, Eustace, Gabriel, German, Humbert, John of Instow, Kerrian, Luke, Marina, Mark, Olave, Rumon/Romanus, Seven Maccabees, Sidwell, Syth, Urith, Winwaloe.

Table 6

Joint Patrons of Devon Churches, 1066–1600
(Source: present book)

Peter and Paul: 15 churches (and possibly others
  where only Peter or Paul has been recorded)
Christ, Holy Cross, Mary and Martin (Exeter, St Martin)
Constantine and Giles (Milton Abbot)
George and Mary (Cockington)
Holy Cross and Mary (Crediton)
John the Baptist and the Seven Maccabees (Cookbury)
Mary and All Saints (Clovelly)
Mary and Michael (Awliscombe)
Mary, Thomas the Apostle and Olave (Exeter, St Olave)
Peter and Andrew (Berrynarbor)
Petroc and Mary (South Brent)

Table 7

Anomalous Patrons of Devon Churches, 1066–1600
(Source: present book)

(a) Examples involving Mary (earliest reference first):

Andrew, Mary	Colyton
David, Mary	Dotton
Edward, Mary	St Mary Steps (Exeter)
Mary, Andrew	Colebrooke
Mary, Andrew	Thorncombe
Mary, George	Modbury
Mary, Helen	Lundy
Mary, John the Baptist	Axminster
Mary, John the Baptist	Hatherleigh
Mary, Mary Magdalene	Chulmleigh
Mary, Michael	Bampton
Petroc, Mary	Cotleigh
Trinity, Mary	Burrington

(b) Other examples (earliest reference first):

Cei, Paul	Landkey
Cyricus, Cecily	South Pool
Gregory, possibly George	Goodleigh
John of Instow, John the Baptist	Instow
Mary, Marina	Mariansleigh

totals we have at present. Secondly, the chronological framework of the evidence is weak. As has been pointed out, most parish church dedications originated in an age of few surviving documents. Many achieved record at a relatively late stage of their history, sometimes not until the eve of the Reformation. At only a handful of places such as Cowick, Dartmouth and Kingsbridge, usually chapels of ease of late foundation, is there some indication of when the dedication was given. The cult of the patron saint in itself allows some speculation about the date of its origin, but this can rarely be precise. Many, perhaps most, patron saints were adopted in the pre-Conquest period. It has been argued that the large number of attributions in Devon to Peter, Paul, Andrew and Michael are compatible with Saxon origins, as are the smaller complements to George, Petroc and Martin.[96] Saints like Denis, Giles and Leonard—popular with twelfth-century monastic founders—may often have been chosen as patrons of parish churches in the same period, but it is hard to be sure. Two or three dedications can be dated to the twelfth century or later. Thomas Becket (d. 1170) is the most obvious case, while Gabriel at Stoke Gabriel (as we shall see) appears to be a choice of the thirteenth century.[97]

Nor can much be done to explain why this or that church has a particular patron. Why were so many churches in Devon dedicated to Mary, Peter, Andrew and Michael? The cult-devotions of parish church founders were crucial, but they have not been recorded. Choice may have followed fashion, the encouragement of kings or bishops, or the availability of relics for hallowing the chief church altar. Sometimes, adjoining churches have the same dedication, raising the question whether they once had a mother and daughter relationship. More often, the saint of the church distinguishes it from its immediate neighbours. In Devon, where only half a dozen saints were widely chosen as patrons, churches usually replicate the dedication not of the next parishes but the next but one. Local lords or people, it appears, wanted to give their church and community a special identity. Topography may have played a part in the choice of Michael, who was associated with rocks and mountains (Monte Gargano in Italy, Mont St Michel in France) and whose English churches are often (though not always) in high places. Place-names, on the other hand, seem to have had rather little influence. In Cornwall, St Dennis may have been suggested by the nearby hill-fort (*dinas* in Cornish), but in Devon ancient place-names which indu-

---

96. Above, pp. 18–19.
97. Below, pp. 37, 205.

bitably match the local church-saint, like Braunton or Bridestowe, result from the dedication not the other way round. Some other present-day parallels—Bridgerule (Bridget), Ide (Ida), Martinhoe (Martin) and Wembury (Werburg)—have not yet been traced back beyond the eighteenth-century. The first certainly is, and the others may be, the result of ingenious speculation in that period: a time when dedications had often been forgotten and needed to be supplied.[98]

Relics were another factor in making choices. This can be seen at churches which had a resident saint in the manner of Braunton, Chittlehampton and Hartland, each of which came to adopt the saint as patron. Evidence of this kind is otherwise rare, but Devon had a large number of churches dedicated to All Saints especially in smaller or less-populous parishes. That option, perhaps, reflects the use of modest unidentifiable relics for putting into altars. Mother houses may have had influence too, though this is also difficult to prove. The chief church of Devon after 1050 was Exeter Cathedral. The cathedral had a significant impact on the county in terms of architecture, church organization and liturgy, but its patron saints (Mary and Peter) were so common that their transmission is hard to establish even to those churches which the cathedral owned. The great expansion of monasteries in the twelfth century postdated the establishment of most parish churches, and cannot be expected to have left much mark on their dedications. We are left, in Devon, with a handful of examples where the saint of a mother church appears to have been copied at a satellite building. Petroc of Bodmin is found at Bodmin's churches of Hollacombe and Newton St Petrock, and Nectan of Hartland at Hartland's chapel of ease (later parish church) of Welcombe. Other possible influences are the Knights of St John on Clayhanger, Mont St Michel on Otterton, Mary of Rouen on Ottery St Mary, and Rumon of Tavistock on Romansleigh.

Mary was the favourite parish church patron in Devon, as in the English monasteries. Next in popularity, but well behind, came Peter and Paul together and individually, closely followed by Michael, All Saints and Andrew. Only three other dedications were fairly widespread: George, John the Baptist and Petroc. The remaining 54 patrons were all relatively uncommon and none appears to have had more than about ten parish churches throughout the county, even making allowances for the unknown cases. Twenty-five patrons owned between two and seven recorded churches, while 28 had a single known church. Nearly all were men. Only eleven were women, of whom Mary alone

---

98. On this period, see below, pp. 45–51.

has weight in statistical terms. The next most frequent, Margaret and Mary Magdalene, each owned but a handful of churches, and if Mary's are discounted the women's total at present is only 16. Dedications to aspects of the Godhead were unusual. A few founders fixed on the Trinity, but it is interesting to note that when this happened popular usage preferred to call the church after Christ or the Saviour, a practice also found in England generally. Apparently people empathised more with Christ—the Godhead in human form—than with a cult as theological as the Trinity. Quite how Devon varied in its dedications from other counties awaits more careful research elsewhere, but most of its patron saints seem to have been common to England as a whole, albeit with differences in popularity. The county was most distinctive in its Celtic cults, as we have seen, but these should not be overemphasized. They do not quite reach 10% of the documented churches.

The greatest variety of patron saints in relation to area was usually to be found in towns. In Devon, Exeter best shows this characteristic. The city and its suburbs contained a cathedral dedicated to Mary, Peter and eventually Paul, and three monasteries honouring Andrew, James and Nicholas. Its parish churches, numbering about 25, celebrated three kinds of patrons. The largest group of 17 bore the names of apostolic and western European saints. These included All Saints, George, James, John the Baptist, Laurence, Leonard, Martin, Mary, Mary Magdalene, Pancras, Paul, Stephen and the Trinity (sometimes called Christ Church).[99] The hospitals of St Alexius, founded in the twelfth century, and St Roche, inaugurated in the early sixteenth, added two more exotic names to this category. Three parish churches were called after Saxon saints—Cuthbert, Edmund of East Anglia and Edward (doubtless the Martyr)—and with them may be grouped two which commemorated the Viking saint Olave (Olaf of Norway) and Sidwell (allegedly Saxon at least).[100] Finally, there was a triplet of church dedications to definite Celtic saints—David, Kerrian and Petroc—who (we have argued) are more likely to have originated in the late Saxon period than in the pre-Saxon one.[101] Exeter resembled the rest of Devon in the predominance

99. Two very popular Devon saints, however, are missing. There was no parish church of St Michael although a chapel was founded to him (now in the cathedral deanery) which did not become parochial. Andrew too had none within the city, but the priory at Cowick close by was dedicated to him and seems to have been parochial in the twelfth century, possibly having been founded at an earlier parish church.
100. Above, p. 24.
101. There is no good evidence, as Exeter antiquaries have liked to think, that the Exeter church dedications reflected a division of the city into Celtic and Saxon halves. The theory was propounded by T. Kerslake, 'The Celt and the Teuton in Exeter', *The Archaeological Journal*, xxx (1873), pp. 211–225, and repeated in Beatrix F. Cresswell, *Exeter Churches* (Exeter, 1908), pp. 1–2.

of mainstream saints of the Church, but it was wider in the range of figures it commemorated. Several of its saints were rare in the South West, and Alexius and Roche were unique as patrons of whole buildings. The region has only one other known pre-Reformation church dedication each to Edmund, Olave, Sidwell and possibly Kerrian, and two each to Cuthbert, David and Edward.

Dedications were not necessarily to a single saint, however. Most of the evidence about them consists of late, casual allusions in which naming one saint may have been enough for convenience. In the few cases where we have documents associated with the act of dedication, we find three patrons at St Olave Exeter (1063), four at St Martin Exeter (1065), and four at St Buryan in Cornwall (1238). In each of these instances, the saint listed last is attributed with the sole patronage in other documents. At a number of other churches, records mention two saints as joint patrons (Table 6). The most common linkages are Mary with another saint and Peter with Paul. Other saint pairings are uncommon, though Milton Abbot is once said to have been dedicated to Constantine and Giles, while Cookbury certainly commemorated John the Baptist and the Seven Maccabees. It is also possible that the churches of Cyricus were jointly dedicated to his mother Julitta, though this is not recorded. More frequently still, we come across references to different saints at different times, explicable either as cases of joint patronage or changes of dedication (Table 7). These examples can be put into two groups. First, there are fourteen churches which are once said to be dedicated to Mary and once to another saint. It is possible that Mary replaced another patron as her cult grew in importance, but we are not obliged to believe that she did. She could have joined the other saint, or they could always have been co-patrons. We know of at least six instances (listed in Table 6) where Mary and another saint were definitely linked together, making it look as though the arrangement was recurrent. There is another, smaller group of churches where the two saints have similar names: South Pool (Cyricus and Cecilia), Goodleigh (Gregory and George), Instow (John of Instow and John the Baptist) and Mariansleigh (Mary and Marian). Here we can permissibly allow for confusion; the people making the records have misremembered or misunderstood the saints.

None of these 'anomalous' references to saints, therefore, proves that the dedications underwent change. Indeed, we have no positive evidence of any such alteration in Devon. No church patron is known to have been formally repudiated in the county until we reach the Reformation and the unique and national example of Thomas Becket. There are a very few churches, however, where alterations seem to have occurred at least in the addition of a co-patron to an existing saint. Landkey, as we have seen, originated as 'the church of St Cei' but its patron by 1346 was Paul, so that Cei was either given a colleague or was forgotten altogether.[102] At Stoke Gabriel, the archangel appears to have been introduced by Bishop Bronescombe (whose special patron he was) in the second half of the thirteenth century. If the church was older, Gabriel must have joined or replaced an earlier patron.[103] Similarly, at South Molton which was said to be dedicated to Syth in 1517, Syth (if Zita) must have been a newcomer since the latter was a late medieval saint.[104] But, on the whole, the evidence for change is not compelling. None of the cases mentioned proves the replacement of a patron rather than the adoption of a companion. When evidence survives about church dedications over a long period, it shows that saints were honoured consistently. Thus, Helen is mentioned at Abbotsham from 1193 to 1521, Michael at Alphington from about 1150 to 1546, Peter at Brampford Speke from about 1150 to 1366, and there are numerous other examples. It looks as though most parish churches acquired their patron saints well before the end of the twelfth century and kept to them. When new saints became popular, as some did after 1150 like Anne, Gabriel, Raphael, Roche and Thomas Becket, they were rarely adopted as the patrons of whole parish churches. Even Becket managed to acquire only a few in Devon, most of them plausibly founded after his martyrdom. Rather, such cults were commemorated in churches by additional images, altars or chapels, or in free-standing chapels elsewhere.[105]

Cornwall was different; here change is more evident. After the county became part of the English Church and more of the population was touched by English speech and culture, it was inevitable that people's spiritual interests should range more widely than the Celtic saints popular in the previous era. Cornwall already had churches with non-Celtic patrons—St Michael's Mount and St Stephen Launceston—by the time of Domesday Book (1086). In later centuries, both the Church authorities and the Cornish people came to feel that Celtic saints were not enough. Churches acquired altars and

102. Below, p. 177.
103. Below, p. 205.
104. Below, p. 202. On the cult of St Syth, see Sebastian Sutcliffe, 'The Cult of St Sitha in England: an Introduction', *Nottingham Medieval Studies*, xxxvii (1993), pp. 83–89.
105. On the proliferation of chapels in late medieval England, see Nicholas Orme, 'Church and Chapel in Medieval England', *Transactions of the Royal Historical Society*, 6th series, vi (1996), pp. 75–102. The cult of St Raphael in Devon is discussed by Orme in *Analecta Bollandiana*, civ (1986), pp. 403–18.

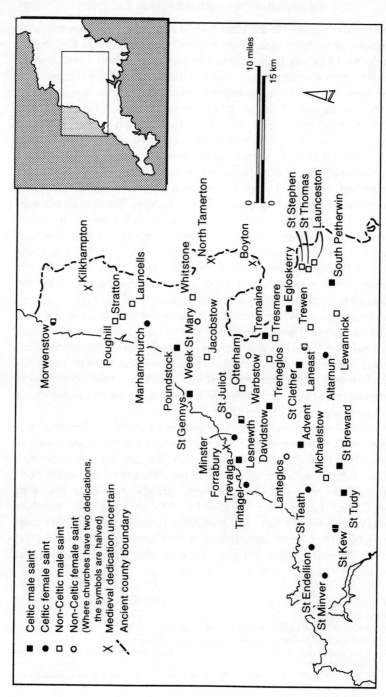

Figure 2. Parish Church Dedications in North Cornwall

Legend:
- Celtic male saint
- Celtic female saint
- Non-Celtic male saint
- Non-Celtic female saint
  (Where churches have two dedications, the symbols are halved)
- X Medieval dedication uncertain
- Ancient county boundary

Morwenstow
Kilkhampton
Poughill
Stratton
Launcells
Marhamchurch
Poundstock
Week St Mary
Whitstone
North Tamerton
Jacobstow
Boyton
St Stephen
St Thomas
Launceston
South Petherwin
Otterham
Warbstow
Tremaine
Tresmere
Egloskerry
Trewen
St Juliot
Trevalga
Lesnewth
Davidstow
Treneglos
St Clether
Laneast
Minster
Forrabury
Tintagel
Lanteglos
Advent
Michaelstow
Altarnun
Lewannick
St Teath
St Breward
St Endellion
St Kew
St Tudy
St Minver
St Gennys

chapels of Mary, Peter, James and other great international figures, and in some places one or more of these saints became co-patron of the whole building. A dated example of this is the dedication of St Buryan church, already mentioned, which Bishop Brewer named in 1238 in honour of Andrew, Thomas Becket, Nicholas and Buryan.[106] During the later middle ages, some other Celtic patron saints appear with more familiar companions. Grade was joined by the Holy Cross at Grade by 1261, Morwenna by John the Baptist at Morwenstow by about 1285, Meriasek by Martin at Camborne by 1448, Delech by Leonard at Landulph by 1451, and Manakneu by Dunstan at Lanreath by 1472. There are at least 12 such cases before the Reformation.

In these churches the Celtic saints at least maintained a foothold; in some others they lost it completely. This may have happened by the late Saxon period in the parts of Cornwall north-east of Bodmin Moor (Figure 2). Here, the countryside became largely Anglicized in its place-names and therefore in the speech of its people, presumably through settlement from Devon. Some of its churches took patron saints similar to those east of the Tamar. Andrew was patron of Launcells and Stratton, George or Gregory of Treneglos, James of Jacobstow, Mary of Week, Nicholas of Tresmere and Whitstone, Olaf of Poughill and Werburg of Warbstow. Elsewhere in Cornwall two trends are apparent. In one of these the Celtic saint was given a Latin name similar to that of a better-known international figure, raising the possibility that the Celt was reinterpreted as this person. Entennin became Antonius in the two parishes of St Anthony, Felec of Phillack became Felicity and Carroc of St Carrock became Cyricus. Less commonly, the Celt was eclipsed by a different international saint. An early name for the church of St Stephen in Brannel was *Eglosselans* or *Egloshellans*, 'church of Elenn', a person mentioned in the tenth-century Breton list of saints with Cornish connections.[107] From the mid twelfth century onwards, however, the church was chiefly linked with Stephen and came to be called after him. At St Veep, contemporaries were evidently puzzled as to whether the saint was male or female, latinising it sometimes in one gender, sometimes in the other. In 1336 Bishop Grandisson dedicated the high altar of the church to SS Cyricus and Julitta, patrons of the nearby priory of St Carrock, which suggests that the memory of Veep had dwindled to that of a place-name.[108] Luxulyan may be a similar example. The place-name means

106. Below, p. 72.
107. Below, p. 117.
108. Below, p. 122.

'the chapel of Sulien' but this church too was dedicated to Cyricus and Julitta by 1412.[109]

Yet the history of Celtic dedications was not altogether one of decline. The latinization of names may be misleading. The patron saints of St Erme and St Ervan were given the Latin form Hermes, but the church of St Michael's Mount celebrated a 'St Hermes confessor of the Cornish people' in 1478, so Hermes (to the Cornish) may have remained a local saint.[110] In the same year, 'St *Sirus* the priest' was believed to be buried at St Carrock, implying that the saint there went on being viewed as a distinct person despite officially possessing the name and identity of the Roman child saint Cyricus.[111] Popular belief about such saints may have differed from that of the bishop or of learned opinion. A sense that Cornish churches usually had Celtic patrons remained strong enough in the later middle ages to cause the invention of new Celtic saints based on church place-names. Thus we hear that Kenwyn, which probably means 'white ridge', was dedicated to a male St Keynwyn in 1342; Ludgvan, 'place of ashes', to a male St Ludwan in 1319; Morvah, 'sea grave', to a female St Morveth in 1390; and Talland, 'hill-brow church site', to a male St Tallan in 1452.[112] If these churches followed the precepts of canon law, they would have erected statues to these saints and venerated them. There is even an example of a church adding a new Celtic co-patron to an earlier non-Celtic one. St Martin by Looe is first attested in about 1220 and normally bore that name alone until the early sixteenth century. In 1547 and 1563, however, the church was said to be dedicated to St Keyne, and the parish became known as 'Keyne the great' to distinguish it from the smaller one of St Keyne nearby.[113]

In 1925, Graham and Collingwood published their survey of dedications in the modern diocese of Carlisle—a careful historical study of parish churches. This diocese covers the ancient counties of Cumberland and Westmorland with the Furness region of Lancashire—an area roughly the size of Devon which it resembles as a peripheral part of England where Celtic political control survived until comparatively late. The authors took pains to identify medieval dedications from historical records, but their sources enabled them to establish the fact for only about 78 of the 174 ancient churches in the

---

109. Below, p. 99. For another possible case, see St Pinnock (below, p. 111).
110. Worcester, *Itineraries*, ed. Harvey, pp. 102–3.
111. Ibid., pp. 106–7.
112. Below, pp. 89–90, 99, 106, 118.
113. Below, p. 101.

Table 8

Medieval Dedications of Parish Churches in Carlisle Diocese

(Source: T.H.B Graham and W.G. Collingwood, 'Patron Saints of the Diocese of Carlisle', *Transactions of the Cumberland and Westmorland Antiquarian and Archaeological Society*, new series, xxv (1925), pp. 1–27)

Michael	11
Cuthbert	11
Mary 8 (+1 shared)	9
Andrew	7
Bridget	3
Kentigern	3
Laurence	3
Peter	3
Trinity	3
All Saints	2
James	2
John the Baptist	2
John the Evangelist	2
Margaret	2
Oswald	2
Patrick	2
16 other saints	1 each

diocese (Table 8).[114] The results show that most were dedicated to international or English saints, resembling Devon not Cornwall in that respect. The relative popularity of these saints, however, differed from what we have found in Devon. Churches of Mary do not predominate; rather, they come below Michael and Cuthbert to lie only third in numerical order. Cults of Peter and Paul are also rare by Devon standards. Carlisle and Devon share more in common in the respect paid to Andrew and in the presence of one strong local saint cult in each case: Cuthbert's and Petroc's. Another resemblance lies in a relative lack of Celtic saint dedications. Those of Carlisle—Bridget, Kentigern and Patrick (plus Columba with a single dedication)—are usually outsiders rather than purely local figures, a feature also visible in Devon. It is a paradox that, although each region bordered on the Celtic world and had Celtic rulers well into the Anglo-Saxon period, they both demonstrate the victory of the saint cults of Europe and England.

114. Graham and Collingwood, 'Patron Saints of the Diocese of Carlisle', pp. 1–27.

4

FROM THE REFORMATION TO 1800

The Reformation, beginning in the 1530s, greatly modified the status of both patron saints and dedication feasts. As we have seen, Henry VIII's regime initiated change when it consolidated dedication feasts on the first Sunday in October in 1536 and forbade the veneration of Thomas Becket two years later. At Plympton (Devon), the Becket dedication was quickly altered to Maurice,[115] and at Cowick, the saint's church became known simply as 'St Thomas', as if its patron was the doubting apostle.[116] During the 1530s and 40s, Reformist Church leaders and writers grew more hostile towards all aspects of saint cults, and public opinion adjusted itself accordingly. The mention of church dedications in wills, hitherto common, declined between 1535 and 1550 and became rare. When Henry died in 1547 and the Reformation continued under the government of Edward VI (1547–53), church dedications, though not forbidden, were further marginalized. A campaign against images in churches, going back to 1538, was completed in 1548 with an order that they should all be removed, thus taking away the saints' chief local memorials.[117] The Books of Common Prayer of 1549 and 1553 abolished most saints from the calendar, except for Mary and the apostles.[118] The old liturgies relating to patronal festivals and dedication feasts became obsolete along with the rest of the medieval Latin services, and no new ones were provided.

The concept of dedicating churches, however, did not die out completely. Henry VIII caused a number of cathedrals and university colleges to be refounded between 1541 and 1546, and followed precedent in giv-

---

115. One wonders why Maurice; though not a cleric, he had suffered for the faith under an earlier ruler. Was this covert defiance?
116. Below, pp. 151, 193.
117. Thomas Cranmer, *Miscellaneous Writings and Letters*, ed. J.E. Cox, Parker Society (1846), p. 510.
118. F. Procter and W.H. Frere, *A New History of the Book of Common Prayer* (London, 1902), pp. 337–40. In 1553 four saints' days, and in 1561 57 more, were restored to the Prayer-Book calendar, but no liturgical material was provided for them and they henceforth meant more for private remembrance or calendar purposes than for public veneration (ibid., p. 340).

ing them spiritual patrons, although he preferred the names of Christ or the Trinity to those of saints.[119] His example was generally followed in the relatively small number of other mid- and late-Tudor church foundations. Sir Thomas White dedicated his new Oxford college to St John the Baptist in 1557 (when Mary Tudor was queen), but the other Oxford and Cambridge founders of the mid sixteenth century chose divine names: Emmanuel, Jesus and Trinity. The second half of the century, however, did not see many even of these dedications. A strong Puritan current ran through the Church of England during Elizabeth's reign, including the bench of bishops. Many Puritans disliked the commemoration of saints as encroaching on the worship due to God, and bishops were chary of involving themselves in dedication ceremonies on those (relatively few) occasions when new churches came into use. In 1564, Bishop Grindal of London entrusted the dedication of the church of Woodham Walter (Essex) to his archdeacon—a departure from traditional practice. In 1597, his successor Bishop Bancroft gave the task at St Anne's Blackfriars (London) to his vicar general, a mere official.[120] When Richard Hooker published the fifth book of his *Laws of Ecclesiastical Polity* in 1597, he felt it necessary to write a chapter in defence of church dedication and another in that of remembering patron saints.[121] Reproving those who 'cast up their poison' at such practices, he justified dedication as a custom used in early Christian times, helpful in establishing the status of churches as places for public worship. It was hardly frequent nowadays, he observed ironically. He quoted Augustine of Hippo to point out that churches were dedicated to God alone. Naming them in honour of saints and martyrs was intended to remember such men and women for their virtues, not to set up gods alongside God.

Hooker accorded with, and helped to shape, a revival of respect for Church traditions which produced more sympathy for the practice of church dedication after 1603. It became more common for bishops to carry out the rite when churches were rebuilt or newly built, and some bishops devised special liturgies to supply the lack in the Book of Common Prayer.[122] Sometimes these liturgies involved naming the

---

119. *Letters and Papers, Foreign and Domestic, Henry VIII*, ed. J.S. Brewer and others (London, 1862–1932), xvi, 420, 424–25, 572, 575; xvii, 255; xxi part ii, 333 (but note Christ and Mary: xvii, 490).

120. *English Orders for Consecrating Churches in the Seventeenth Century*, ed. J. Wickham Legg, Henry Bradshaw Society, xli (1911), p. xviii.

121. Richard Hooker, *The Laws of Ecclesiastical Polity*, 2 vols (London, 1907, reprinted 1963), ii, 39–46 (book v, chapters 12–13).

122. On what follows, see *English Orders for Consecrating Churches*, ed. Legg, passim. A further form of consecration, dated 1714, is printed in Wilkins, *Concilia Magnae Britanniae et Hiberniae*, iv, 668–69.

church in honour of a spiritual patron and sometimes they did not, but as there was no longer a belief in hallowed objects, the naming invariably ceased to be directed to the altar, or holy table as it was now called. Instead, the name was given to the building in general and it was not always conferred liturgically. The spiritual patron might simply be mentioned in the legal instrument read out in church, recording the terms in which the bishop had established and dedicated the building. Some seventeenth-century bishops, though venturing to name churches to patrons, followed Henry VIII in avoiding saints. Bishop Andrewes of Winchester dedicated a chapel at Peartree (Hampshire) in 1620 in the name of Jesus, and the bishop of St David's made the former abbey of Dore (Hereford) into a parish church in 1635 in honour of the Trinity.[123] The previous monastery had borne the name of Mary. Other bishops allowed saints, especially if they were already associated with the building. Fulmer church (Buckinghamshire) was dedicated to St James (its former patron) in 1610, Blackfriars to St Anne in 1617 (again, an earlier church) and Meltham (Yorkshire) to St Bartholomew in 1651.[124]

The tradition of dedicating churches survived, then, but it was rarely carried out and should not be overemphasized. In most parishes, the removal of images and the disuse of festivals weakened the memory of the ancient patron saints. Hostility to their cults and to ceremonies like dedications remained strong in some quarters. One of the charges levied against Archbishop Laud at his trial in 1645 was that he had dedicated his private chapel to St John the Baptist while he was bishop of St David's.[125] In towns indeed, where there were several churches, their names remained in speech. There, though Puritans might carefully drop the 'St', even they could not avoid referring to churches as 'Peter's' or 'Mary's'. In Cornish churches named after their saints, and in English ones such as Jacobstow or St Marychurch, it was also easy to remember the ancient patron. In the majority of parishes, however, his or her identity lacked imagery, documentation or use in speech and was often forgotten. It is true that the late sixteenth and early seventeenth centuries saw the growth of antiquarian studies in England which aimed to preserve and recover the medieval past through documentary research. These studies, however, were slow to include church dedications. The earliest antiquaries tended to focus on family, manorial and urban history. A great historical survey of England's churches

---

123. *English Orders for Consecrating Churches*, ed. Legg, pp. 50, 67–68, 173, 178; compare p. 45.
124. Ibid., pp. 15, 207, 290.
125. Ibid., p. 108.

did not appear until Roger Dodsworth and William Dugdale published their *Monasticon Anglicanum* (1655–73). This work, moreover, centred on monastic houses and although it began to bring their dedications to light, the patron saints of the parish churches had to wait longer. Not until the 1720s did they become the object of large-scale historical research.

That they did so was primarily due to the initiative of Browne Willis (1682–1760), scion of a wealthy family in Buckinghamshire.[126] Willis inherited Whaddon Hall and the nearby manor of Bletchley, and further improved his means by marrying Katherine, the only daughter and heiress of Daniel Eliot of Port Eliot in Cornwall. She brought him a fortune of £8,000 and duly bore him ten children. After a brief political career as MP for Buckingham between 1705 and 1708, Willis gave most of his time to antiquarian research and charitable projects. Very much the heir of Dodsworth and Dugdale, he began in their tradition by publishing a *History of the Mitred Parliamentary Abbies and Conventual Cathedral Churches*, i.e. the most important monasteries, in 1710–19. Next, with more originality, he extended historical study to other kinds of Church institutions. Between 1717 and 1721, he published accounts of the four cathedrals of Wales, followed by a three-volume *Survey of the Cathedrals* of England (1727–30), describing fourteen of them. He seems to have planned to cover the remaining eight English cathedrals and started collecting data, but never finished the task. Perhaps this was because, in the 1720s, his attention was diverted to the larger, richer field of English parish history. This topic was still unexplored except in those few counties such as Warwickshire where a good local historian (like Dugdale) had listed the parish churches and their incumbents. Little had yet been done towards providing general information about such churches in England. In 1535, Henry VIII's government had drawn up the *Valor Ecclesiasticus*, which enumerated most parish benefices and their values as part of the survey of Church property carried out at the Reformation. By the end of the seventeenth century, the parish information from the *Valor* was in print in order to provide the clergy with details about what benefices were worth.[127] The best edition of the material came to be John Ecton's *Liber Valorum et Decimarum*, published in 1711, which listed the names of the parish benefices under dioceses and rural deaneries, together with their 1535 values and the ecclesiastical taxes payable on them. His

---

126. On Willis, see the *Dictionary of National Biography* article by William Prideaux Courtney.
127. E.g. *Valor Beneficiorum: or, a Valuation of all Ecclesiastical Preferments in England and Wales* (London, 1695).

volume was well received since it went into two further editions in the 1720s, but it was primarily financial in purpose; it was, however, the nearest thing to a Church directory until the year 1730.

Willis set out to broaden Ecton's work by collecting other relevant information. This was to include the owners of advowsons responsible for nominating clergy, the names of the monasteries which (in some cases) had formerly appropriated tithes, and the church dedications. He also gathered evidence about parish feast days or 'revels' as they were often called, though he never printed this material. The motive for his work was partly utilitarian. Identifying those who owned advowsons enabled the clergy to know the people who might further their careers. Monastic appropriations and church dedications, on the other hand, were largely matters of historical interest, and here Willis was influenced by his antiquarian leanings. The first fruits of his research were published in 1727–30 as part of his *Survey of Cathedrals*. This listed the parishes of the fourteen English dioceses whose cathedrals Willis had studied, together with their patrons and some of their dedications. He continued the task with a volume called *Parochiale Anglicanum* (1733), containing similar lists for the remaining English and Welsh dioceses, including Exeter. Finally, in 1742, he allowed this material (with copious additions of his own) to be integrated with Ecton's *Liber Valorum* to form a consolidated work called *Thesaurus Rerum Ecclesiasticarum*. The title page bore only Ecton's name, but the publishers' preface acknowledged their debt for the dedication evidence to Willis, 'that Learned and Communicative Antiquary'.[128] The result was the first comprehensive directory of the Church of England. Each diocese was divided alphabetically into rural deaneries, and within the deaneries the parish benefices were listed in two groups: those liable to tax and those discharged through poverty. The entry for each benefice gave its status as a rectory or vicarage, the church dedication where known, the patron of the living, the medieval and modern impropriators of the tithes, the valuation of 1535 and the dues and taxes payable.

Willis shares the credit for this achievement. He supplied church dedications for most of the parishes, bringing them to notice after years of neglect. Indeed, he created a new historical topic: their study, listing and elucidation. Whence did he gain his information about them? In the Celtic areas, he was able to identify patron saints from placenames, though the latter sometimes led him astray. Thus he, or his informants, invented a Saint Lanty as patron of the two Cornish

---

128. J. Ecton, *Thesaurus Rerum Ecclesiasticarum* (London, 1742), p. iii.

churches of Lanteglos, a name which truly means 'a valley with a church'.[129] In Cornwall, where he had a close family connection, he either pursued enquiries personally or did so through correspondents. Copies of letters from Cornish clergy and gentlemen survive among his papers, conveying information about particular places, and the antiquary Thomas Tonkin gave him special assistance.[130] His list of Cornish dedications was fairly complete by the time that *Parochiale Anglicanum* was published in 1733, although corrections and additions were subsequently made in the *Thesaurus*. Elsewhere in England, including Devon, the recovery of church dedications was a more difficult matter as it is still today. Although Devon was included in *Parochiale Anglicanum*, Willis had found hardly any of its church dedications at that point and was able to list the majority of them only in 1742. He collected documentary references when he could, personally or through friends, from the records of the crown, from stray charters, and from wills which he soon realized to be the richest source. He made or commissioned inspections of the wills in the archbishop of Canterbury's prerogative court in London and gained valuable material from them, although his searches were not exhaustive.[131] Thomas Baker of St John's College Cambridge sent him notes from wills about the churches of Cambridgeshire.[132] Willis' documentary enquiries, however, proved to have limited results in the case of Devon, and he devised an ingenious way of solving the problem.

The Treasury, centred at Westminster, had at its disposal a network of professional local agents covering the whole of England: collectors of customs duties, excise duties and duties on salt.[133] Willis evidently obtained the favour of one of the senior treasury officers, probably William Pinney of the Excise Office, and through him sent out letters to the tax collectors of Devon asking for the desired information. The correspondence which initiated this process has not been found, but several of the returns sent back by the Devon collectors survive among Willis' papers. They show that he asked for four pieces of information: the name of the parish, the patron saint of the church, the calendar date of the dedication and that of the annual feast or revel. Dates of feasts were easy to find because they were still being held, and Willis

129. Below, p. 95.
130. E.g. Oxford, Bodleian Library, MS Willis 41, ff. 244, 260–61.
131. The wills are now in the Public Record Office, London, classified as Prerogative Court of Canterbury, Prob 11.
132. MS Willis 25, f. 1a verso.
133. The organization is described by Edward Hughes, *Studies in Administration and Finance 1558–1825* (Manchester, 1934).

gained a good response though he did not print the results. Patron saints and dedication dates, on the other hand, were often quite forgotten. More than one of Willis' correspondents testified to the lack of knowledge and even of interest about them. Nicholas Webber, writing from Devon in 1733, confessed that 'the dedications of churches I know not how to find out at present'.[134] William Peirie, in a letter of 1740 from Plymouth, stated that, in his experience, 'when the churches were dedicated, or to what saint, the country people are so ignorant that they have not the least tradition relating thereto'.[135] A correspondent from Holcombe Burnell (Devon) said that he 'never heard anything in the least of a dedicatory title fixed to the church'.[136] Faced with such poor information, the tax collectors seem to have made up their lists by conjecturing saints from the dates of parish feasts. If, say, the feast was held on Midsummer Day (originally the festival of St John the Baptist), it was assumed that he had been the patron saint of the local church. This assumption was one that Willis shared, and he may well have proposed it to his informants in the first place.

Eighteenth-century parish feast dates, unfortunately, do not support this conjecture. True, Henry VIII's law of 1536 about parish church feasts stated that 'the feast of the patron of every church' was 'called commonly the church holy day',[137] but by the 1740s, these two events were no longer always the same. In the pre-Reformation calendar, the patronal festival had been just one of several important days involving holidays and public revelry. Others included Christmas, Easter, Rogation week, Whitsuntide, and the major saints' festivals. After the Reformation, Protestant hostility to holy days cut down the number of holidays considerably. Most parishes kept but a single major celebration each year which might be observed on any of the former important feast days. Some held it at Eastertide, some at Rogationtide, some at Whitsuntide. Others did so on or near the major saints' days of the summer and early autumn: St John the Baptist or Midsummer Day (24 June), SS Peter and Paul (29 June), St Thomas Becket (7 July), St James the Great (25 July), St Peter in Chains or Lammas Day (1 August), St Bartholomew (24 August) and St Michael (29 September). These days were not necessarily the days on which the medieval parishes had celebrated their patronal festivals. In 178 parishes in Devon where we know both the name of the medieval saint and the

---

134. MS Willis 41, f. 200.
135. Ibid., f. 229.
136. Ibid., f. 242.
137. Above, note 44.

date of the parish feast day observed in the eighteenth century, the saint's day and the feast day coincide in 54 examples at best: about 31%. Most parish feast days were not held on the ancient patronal festival which, through disuse of saint cults, was frequently forgotten by the 1740s. Willis' theory might be rational but it was not correct.

Its consequences, however, have been long-lasting. Directories carry more weight than monographs, and the *Thesaurus* became an influential work as time went on. Later students of Church history came across evidence about medieval church dedications which contradicted the 1742 edition, but they tended to make silent corrections in later editions or other works. The extent of Willis' conjectures did not become clear; instead, sanctified by print, they often became accepted as the truth. By the nineteenth century, some of them were so firmly established that even evidence about their incorrectness was liable to be disregarded. Of the 339 churches in Devon whose medieval dedications we now know, the *Thesaurus* of 1742 reproduced 135 correctly, 20 half correctly (where two patrons were involved) and 88 incorrectly; the rest were returned as unknown or were omitted.[138] This has implications for the remaining 143 Devon churches, about 30%, where we have no medieval evidence. If Ecton is astray in the same proportions, a substantial proportion of their dedications are also likely to be eighteenth-century inventions. Anyone who wishes to measure the strength of oral traditions would do well to consider the extent to which the medieval saints had been forgotten by Willis' time. Not only had common patrons like Mary and All Saints passed out of memory but rare ones such as Calixtus at West Down, Pancras at Widecombe, and Petroc at Cotleigh. The losers in this process were chiefly Mary, who lost 25 sole or joint dedications, All Saints (13), Paul (11), Peter (10), Andrew (9), Michael (8), and George (5). The winners, as the result of Ecton's new conjectures, were Mary, who acquired 13 new dedications to offset her losses, John the Baptist (13), James (10), Trinity (7), Peter (5), and Thomas Becket (5). The greatest overall losses were suffered by Mary (12), Paul (11), All Saints (10), Andrew (7), and Peter (5). The largest net gains were made by the Baptist (11), James (8), the Trinity (5), and Thomas Becket (5), reflecting the fact that their festivals occurred in high summer at favourite times for parish revels. In truth, most English churches already had patron saints when Becket died and his cult was incorporated into parish religion in other ways. Of the eleven churches in Devon with which he is credited in Ecton,

---

138. The figures in this sentence omit the 23 ancient parish churches of Exeter, for the reasons given above, p. xii, note 5.

five can be shown to be wrong and this casts doubt on the six which lack earlier references.[139] Much the same is true of the churches of James.

Willis was not the only person to collect dedications in Devon in the eighteenth century. Within a dozen years or so of the appearance of the *Thesaurus*, Jeremiah Milles, precentor of Exeter Cathedral, set out on a similar quest.[140] Milles planned to acquire general information about the natural resources, history and monuments of the Devon parishes through circulating printed enquiries to the parish clergy. Each document consisted of a double sheet of questions with spaces for answers, of which some 250 completed copies survive, representing about half of the Devon parishes.[141] The exact date of the exercise is not clear, but three of the returns contain references ranging from 1754 to 1756, so that the date '*c*.1755' has been adopted in the present study. Some of the returns were made by local incumbents and others by lay people. The schoolmaster of Barnstaple obliged at several parishes in north Devon. One question on the sheet asked for evidence about dedications, another about parish feast days. Milles put these questions, perhaps, because he aimed at completeness in his enquiries rather than through lack of confidence in the *Thesaurus*. The reactions he got were similar to those evoked by Willis. Feast days were still observed; dedications were largely forgotten. Many parishes returned the latter as unknown or, as before, conjectured them from the feast day. This confirms the lack of popular interest in dedications, found by Willis' correspondents and shows that the *Thesaurus* had yet made little impact. It is rarely referred to by Milles' informants and had evidently stimulated little curiosity.

A modest interest in church patron saints continued, however, at least among scholars. Three further editions of Ecton's *Thesaurus* appeared during the eighteenth century. Each of them contained revisions of dedications and all are worth checking for evidence. The second edition of 1754 altered some 63 attributions in Devon and about 26 in Cornwall. The third edition of 1763 amended a further 18 in Devon and 10 in Cornwall. Most of these changes replaced the feast-day conjectures with evidence from medieval sources: chiefly the bishops' registers but in a few cases (including Monkton, Shute and

---

139. Willis failed to discover the undoubted medieval dedications to Becket at Dodbrook, Exeter, Plympton and perhaps Loddiswell—probably because they had been changed in Henry VIII's reign.

140. For Milles' career, see the *Dictionary of National Biography* article by William Prideaux Courtney and also Joan Evans, *A History of the Society of Antiquaries* (Oxford, 1956).

141. Bodleian Library, MS Top. Devon b.1–2.

West Anstey) the cathedral archives. The second and third editions bore Willis' name on the title-page below that of Ecton, and it is likely that he collected or received the new material up to his death in 1760. The dean of Exeter at this time, Charles Lyttelton (1747–62), was a leading antiquary, and both he and Milles who succeeded him may have contributed data.[142] The last edition of the *Thesaurus*, published in 1786, discarded the names of Ecton and Willis in favour of a new author, John Bacon, and a fresh title, *Liber Regis vel Thesaurus Rerum Ecclesiasticarum*. The format was much the same, however, and further changes were made to eleven dedications in Devon and one or two in Cornwall. Meanwhile, in 1782, a local church directory called *Thesaurus Ecclesiasticus Provincialis* was published anonymously at Exeter—a work now attributed to William Jones. His book, which covers only the diocese of Exeter, resembles Ecton in format but adds the names of incumbents, thus coming another stage closer to modern practice. Its dedications are largely based on Ecton, and an eight-page *Supplement* issued in 1787 seems to have been prompted by the revised material in Bacon. Jones' work thus has little independent value, but it gave further publicity to dedications in the region. Unobtrusively, they were becoming a natural element of church description. When Richard Polwhele published his *History of Devonshire* in three volumes between 1793 and 1806, he included them under the parishes, taking them largely from the directories. He was the first historian of Devon to make this a standard procedure.

---

142. Lyttelton is also discussed in Evans, *History of the Society of Antiquaries*, passim.

5

CHURCH DEDICATIONS SINCE 1800

The study of church dedications owes much to the eighteenth-century antiquaries. Not only did they revive it; they made the subject an essential part of Church history. Ever since, those who have treated of churches in detail have felt obliged to list their patron saints: Samuel Lewis' *Topographical Dictionary of England* (published from 1831 until 1849), the county directories like Kelly's (1845 until 1941) and White's (1850 until 1896), the ecclesiastical ones of *The Clergy List* (1841 until 1917) and *Crockford's Clerical Dictionary* (since 1860), and architectural guides such as Pevsner's *Buildings of England* (since 1951).[143] The Georgian concern with dedications was largely a scholarly one, but by Victoria's reign it was taking root in the parishes. The Romantic Movement stimulated an increasing curiosity about the middle ages. Interest grew in the medieval features of churches: architecture, sculpture and furnishings. Dedications and patron saints shared the appeal of aumbries, piscinas and squints. From the 1830s, the Tractarian Movement in the Church extended this interest to worship. The veneration of saints revived to a modest extent. They were celebrated more often in the calendar, in patronal festivities, in stained-glass windows and in sculptures. By the end of the nineteenth century many more Anglican clergy and congregations were aware of their church dedications and saw them as adding to the dignity and distinction of their buildings.

The period since 1800 has also been marked by greater research into medieval records. This has had positive effects in recovering more of the original dedications, but the coexistence of directories, scholarly works and popular devotion has led to further confusion. Conjectures like those of Willis have been repeated and believed alongside more authentic evidence unearthed by historians. Sometimes, research has caused churches to change their dedications back to those of the middle ages, and the change has eventually been reported to the directories.

---

143. The standard guide to directories is Gareth Shaw and Allison Tipper, *British Directories: A Bibliography and Guide* (London and New York, 1988).

In other places, clergy and congregations have stayed loyal to the conjectures and research has made no impact. A feeling that all churches should have dedications has caused patron saints to be invented when they could not be discovered, and this too has conflicted with research. The absence of much episcopal control over dedications has allowed the intrusion of imaginative and even idiosyncratic changes. In early twentieth-century Devon, love of Celtic romance led a rector of Bradninch, Charles Croslegh, to replace the historical Denis by a pseudo-Irish Disen, and a vicar of Staverton, E.D. Drake-Brockman, to discard the attested Paul the Apostle in favour of the more exotic Paul of Leon in Brittany.[144] In Cornwall, on the other hand, where one would expect Celtic saints to be especially cherished, a few have been obscured or supplanted by non-Celtic figures in late- and post-Victorian times. The Trinity is now often regarded as the patron of St Austell, All Saints of St Ewe, St James of St Kew and St Thomas Becket of St Merryn.

Several regions of nineteenth-century England produced antiquarians who worked to recover medieval church dedications.[145] In the South West, the major name is that of George Oliver (1781–1861), pioneer priest of the Catholic Church in Exeter and a careful, scholarly historian of the middle ages.[146] Oliver ministered to a small and still unpopular sect, but he worked to develop good relationships with Anglicans and expounded Church history as the common heritage of Christians. At first he concentrated on visiting churches and describing their architecture; later this led him to documentary research. Advancing notably on his precursors in Devon, he gained access to the archives of the bishop, the cathedral and city of Exeter, the Courtenays of Powderham, the British Museum and the Public Records in London. His most ambitious work, *Monasticon Dioecesis Exoniensis* (1846), was inspired by Dodsworth and Dugdale. It contained outline histories of all the medieval religious houses in Cornwall and Devon, supported by copious transcripts of documents. In a *Supplement* to this work, he added a list of all the parish churches in the two counties with their dedications, noting correctly that 'every printed list of the saints, to whom the churches within the diocese of Exeter were dedicated, is defective and erroneous'. Accordingly, 'we have endeavoured to supply the deficiency to the best of our power'.[147] Some revisions to the list appeared in a second *Supplement*, published in 1854.

---

144. Below, pp. 135, 203.
145. For a list, see Francis Bond, *Dedications and Patron Saints of English Churches* (London, 1914), pp. xii–xiii.
146. For Oliver's life, see the *Dictionary of National Biography*, article by Thompson Cooper.
147. G. Oliver, *Monasticon Dioecesis Exoniensis* (Exeter and London, 1846), p. 436.

In gathering sources and editing documents, Oliver reached high standards. For dedications he used the Ecton volumes, making further corrections from his own researches. He himself claimed to have 'thoroughly sifted the episcopal registers and examined many ancient wills and documents'.[148] His work on the registers was certainly more thorough than before, although (as the volumes had not yet been printed) he overlooked some details. He also found most of the relevant material in the cathedral archives—a source hitherto little used. He saw some of the pre-Reformation wills of Exeter diocese but not all which were then extant, because two later scholars who used them—Olive Moger and Sir Oswyn Murray—found references that he had missed. Outside Exeter, he was not able to make much effective use of the Public Record Office (whose archives had scarcely begun to be printed), and none of the wills of the prerogative court of Canterbury in London, a place notoriously difficult of access until about 1860. The presentation of his dedication evidence is disappointing by our standards because, in the Willis tradition, it normally excludes references to sources. Usually, we can follow his tracks, but his notes are now lost and we are often left wondering why he made emendations or new proposals.[149] Sometimes he appears to have found a medieval source; at other times his reason is unclear. He was capable of making mistakes as well, so that we cannot safely assume that his statements were based on reliable evidence. He ascribed Modbury to Peter from a reference to the 'aisle of St Peter' in the church; East Buckland to Guy from one which related to its Anglo-Norman owner not its saint; and Westleigh to Petroc because its church was mentioned in the same document as West Anstey of which the saint was patron. He attributed Petroc to Harford instead of to Harpford, and Andrew to Christow instead of to Yarnscombe, citing pre-Reformation wills made by the incumbents. Recourse to the bishops' registers would have shown him that neither cleric belonged to the parish he thought! Perhaps his most surprising error was to identify a reference to the chapel of St Giles in Great Torrington parish with Little Torrington. The latter was a distinct parish; the chapel was St Giles in the Wood.

The subject of dedications in Devon has not been taken much further since Oliver's time, though there have been useful short papers

---

148. Oliver, *Monasticon*, Supplement, passim.

149. A volume entitled 'Extracts made by Dr Oliver, collected together and bound by Wm. Harding' was in Exeter City Library until at least 1939, with the reference 009.03/57745. It contained transcripts from deeds, wills and other documents, of which the deeds alone were further copied into G. Oliver, *Précis of Leases etc. 1253–1803 from Powderham Castle*, 3 vols, now in the Devon Record Office, Exeter. I have not located the original volume; it may have been lost when the library was bombed in 1942.

and published notes about particular churches. The chief progress in the South West has been made in Cornwall, where it has taken a somewhat different form. The patron saints of most of the ancient Cornish churches are enshrined in place-names but, as has already been stated, these names were often modified over the centuries, obscuring the saints' identities. Important progress in unravelling this problem has been made in the twentieth century. Between the 1920s and his death in 1945, Canon G.H. Doble published a large number of studies of individual saints, chiefly in a succession of 48 pamphlets entitled the 'Cornish Saints' series. Doble's interests were primarily literary and hagiographical, and although the studies are chiefly associated with his name, those issued up to the 1930s included valuable contributions by Charles Henderson, the foremost documentary historian of Cornwall in the early twentieth century. It is a pity that, when most of Doble's work on saints was reissued in five volumes called *The Saints of Cornwall* between 1960 and 1970, Henderson's material was largely omitted. Modern researchers should therefore consult the original pamphlets in preference to the reprinted edition.[150] More recently, Dr O. J. Padel and Dr Lynette Olson have taken further the study of Cornish saints through his two studies of the county's place-names, her history of early monasteries, and their joint edition of the important tenth-century list of saints many of whom were patrons of Cornish churches.[151] Their work, building on that of Doble and Henderson, has greatly improved our knowledge on several fronts: names, identities, sites and churches.

Most branches of history since the mid nineteenth century have been brought to higher standards through academic study. Dedications have been slow to share in this process. The first attempt to compile a book about them that was more than a gazetteer was Frances Arnold-Forster's *Studies in Church Dedications, or England's Patron Saints*, published in three volumes in 1899. It centred on the patron saints commemorated in English churches (estimated by her at about 600) and ranged in time from the middle ages to her own day. Volumes 1 and 2 of the work consisted of studies of the saints, largely hagiographical in nature, with some references to the places associated with them. Volume 3 contained lists. Two of these named the saints, the places where they were culted and the numbers of churches dedicated to them. The third

150. For bibliography about Doble, see below, p. 232.
151. O.J. Padel, *Cornish Place-Name Elements*; idem, *A Popular Dictionary of Cornish Place-Names* (Penzance, 1988); [B.] Lynette Olson, *Early Monasteries in Cornwall* (1989); and Olson and Padel, 'A Tenth-Century List of Cornish Parochial Saints', pp. 33–71.

catalogued the parishes of England (some 14,000) with their dedications. Arnold-Forster divided dedications into four historical periods, depending on the origins of the churches to which they were attached. The periods were 'ancient' (i.e. pre-Reformation), the eighteenth century, between 1800 and 1850, and between 1850 and 1900. She was thus not unaware that her subject had a history. She knew that many churches had been founded since 1700, and that their dedications should be analysed separately.[152] She understood that some ancient churches had lost their original patron saints and had been credited with different, modern ones.[153] She appreciated that forgotten dedications could be discovered in medieval wills and other documents.[154] She conceded that parish feast days were but 'a slender clue' to church patrons and should be used judiciously in this quest.[155] She modestly anticipated that 'numerous imperfections and mistakes' would be found in her work.[156] Unfortunately, her work still persuades the unwary reader that it provides reliable statistics about medieval church dedications. It does no such thing. It is a list and analysis of church dedications as they were reckoned to be in 1900, with all the alterations that had been made since the 1730s. She herself did no systematic work to separate the medieval evidence from the conjectures and inventions of later times. Much of the secondary literature of the twentieth century which draws on her work misunderstands this fact. In truth, we cannot use her book as a source for pre-Reformation church dedications, either for general statistics or to verify individual cases.

The misleading notions to which Arnold-Forster's work gave rise are illustrated in Francis Bond's *Dedications & Patron Saints of English Churches* (1914). Bond, who acknowledged that his book was inspired by hers, also possessed some historical understanding. He too accepted that new dedications had 'not infrequently' been substituted for old ones.[157] He recognised that many had been lost.[158] He urged that investigations should be carried out into the dedications of each county, starting with those observed today but verifying them from medieval wills and other documents.[159] But these insights occur remarkably late in his work—in its fourteenth chapter! The substance of the book pre-

---

152. Frances Arnold-Forster, *Studies in Church Dedications or England's Patron Saints*, 3 vols, (London, 1899), i, p. x.
153. Ibid., p. xi.
154. Ibid., p. xii.
155. Ibid.
156. Ibid., p. xiv.
157. Bond, *Dedications & Patron Saints of English Churches*, p. 191.
158. Ibid., pp. 191–92.
159. Ibid., pp. 201–2.

cedes that point. It consists of discussions of saints with more attention to their iconography than Arnold-Forster had given and with a more definite focus on the middle ages. Its use of statistics is similar to hers, however, and as likely to mislead. Bond claimed that he had 'stripped off' all the dedications of the eighteenth and nineteenth century, 'leaving only those of more ancient date'.[160] What this means is that he removed the evidence relating to new churches dedicated after 1700, not the new dedications attributed to medieval churches by antiquarians since that date. His statistics and his individual examples are vitiated, no less than Arnold-Forster's, by the fact that they represent the situation of 1900, not that of 1550.

The study of church dedications has developed rather slowly since these pioneers. In England, the best work of the early and mid twentieth century was done by Graham and Collingwood in 1925 and by the great German historian Wilhelm Levison in 1945–6. The first two scholars, as we have seen, researched and dated the medieval dedications of Carlisle diocese,[161] while Levison published a characteristically careful paper on dedications in general and collected the early Anglo-Saxon examples in his book on *England and the Continent in the Eighth Century* (1946).[162] Unfortunately, two of these three works appeared only in local journals, and Levison's lectures (though generally influential) have been little known outside the field of Anglo-Saxon studies. The lack of progress in the subject is well illustrated by Bishop Kirk's *Church Dedications of the Oxford Diocese* (1946) and the Revd C.S.L. Linnell's *Norfolk Church Dedications* (1962). Kirk eschewed (and may not have known) the historical approach of the Carlisle scholars. Rather, he conducted an analysis of the churches in his diocese solely on the evidence of his own day, like Arnold-Forster and Bond.[163] Linnell, who acknowledged Kirk as a model, claimed to have done better by comparing modern dedications with those given in medieval wills, but his lists of pre-Reformation dedications lack precise references and the historical context is weak. Neither author's work would receive consideration in a better studied and more rigorous field. In the field of monastic history, the standard list of *Medieval Religious Houses: England and Wales* by David Knowles and R.N. Hadcock (1953; 2nd ed., 1971) gathered large numbers of dedications, though these were

---

160. Ibid., p. v.
161. Above, pp. 40–1.
162. Levison, *England and the Continent in the Eighth Century* (Oxford, 1946), pp. 259–65; idem, 'Medieval Church-Dedications in England: Some problems', *Transactions of the Archaeological and Antiquarian Society of Durham and Newcastle upon Tyne*, x (1946), pp. 57–79.
163. K.E. Kirk, *Church Dedications of the Oxford Diocese* (Oxford, 1946), pp. 18–19.

sometimes drawn from early, less reliable sources like Dodsworth and Dugdale. But the best large-scale work of the century has been Binns' careful and scholarly collection and discussion of *Dedications of Monastic Houses* (1989). This follows the good practice of Levison and the Carlisle scholars in basing its work on original sources of the middle ages, not on post-medieval and secondary ones. It observes academic standards and provides both a sound analysis of the material and a helpful account of its context.

Meanwhile, irrespective of scholars, the dedications of the ancient English parish churches continue in use. Like the Church of England itself, they have grown up organically during several centuries. Some churches possess patron saints who have been venerated or at least remembered since medieval times, probably since the churches were founded. Others are believed to have ancient dedications which are, in truth, the conjectures of Willis and others in the eighteenth century. In further cases, the Victorian period has been influential. Some dedications were invented then, and others were given distinctive casts—Anglican, Anglo-Catholic or antiquarian—like 'St Michael and All Angels', 'Our Lady', 'the Blessed Virgin Mary' or 'All Hallows'. A few churches cherish dedications which are based on egregious mistakes. In some parishes, the spiritual patrons are taken seriously, with annual commemorations both liturgical and social; in others, the saint is little more than a name like that of a house. Yet there has never been an absolute breach between the study and use of church dedications. Most of the books about them can be shown to have had some influence on Church practice. It will be interesting to see if modern research continues to have such an impact, or if the established dedications are now set in tablets of stone.

6

THE GAZETTEER AND HOW TO USE IT

The gazetteer that follows includes all the medieval religious houses and hospitals in Cornwall and Devon, and all the ancient parish churches, i.e. those in existence up to about 1800. A few other churches are listed which are (or were until recently) chapels of ease but which, being old foundations or similar in appearance to parish churches, are often taken for them. Churches founded since about 1700, whether Anglican or non-Anglican, are not mentioned because their dedications have been less subject to change and can usually be traced with accuracy in printed directories. The inclusion of some chapels of ease means that the book needs to be used with care in matching statistics of dedications with those of parish churches. It is a complex matter to decide which churches had parochial status at any one time in the past. National surveys of Church property, like the 'Taxation of Pope Nicholas IV' in 1291 and the *Valor Ecclesiasticus* in 1535, are broadly helpful in this matter, but they are not altogether reliable as inventories. The compilation of an historical directory of the English parish system is another project calling out to be done.

The information about dedications in this book is based on both archival and secondary sources. In the first category, a thorough search has been made of the surviving *acta* of the bishops of Exeter up to 1257, the bishops' registers from that year up to the Reformation, and the printed calendars of British and Irish entries in the papal registers up to 1513.[164] The records of relevant religious houses have been searched: notably the archives of Exeter Cathedral and the cartularies of monasteries with west-country property.[165] An attempt has been made to examine all the wills relating to Devon and Cornwall before the Reformation. Nationally, these include the wills of the prerogative

---

164. The *acta* have now been edited as *English Episcopal Acta*, vols xi–xii, *Exeter 1046–1184* and *1186–1257*, ed. Frank Barlow (London, British Academy, 1996).
165. For a list of cartularies, see G.R.C. Davis, *Medieval Cartularies of Great Britain: A Short Catalogue* (London, 1958).

court of Canterbury in the Public Record Office, those registered at
Canterbury Cathedral during vacancies of the archbishopric, and
those of the various courts in London preserved in the Guildhall
Library. Locally, the testamentary records of Exeter diocese and its
peculiar jurisdictions seem to have suffered losses during the nineteenth century and the remainder were destroyed in the Exeter air raids
of 1942. Fortunately, some transcripts of these wills were made before
that event by Charles Henderson, Olive Moger and Sir Oswyn Murray,
and these have been consulted along with the several dozen other wills
that survive in the Devon Record Office. Turning to the Public
Records in London, a full investigation has been made of the inquisitions post mortem (and proofs of age) for Devon and Cornwall, using
the modern printed calendars and the complete transcript of entries
relating to the two counties in the West Country Studies Library,
Exeter. It has not been feasible to make an exhaustive scrutiny of the
other classes of documents in the Public Record Office, even of their
printed calendars, but many references and leads have been pursued.
In the Devon and Cornwall Record Offices, a wide search has been
made through all the main pre-Reformation documents, though here
too the scale of the archives makes full investigation difficult. Various
other primary sources have been consulted and are listed in the bibliography, notably Oliver's *Monasticon* and the one or two surviving
cartularies of west-country families.

The main secondary sources used are the four major previous
gazetteers of dedications—Willis (1733), Ecton (1742), Jones (1782)
and Oliver (1846)—along with the present-day directories of the dioceses of Exeter and Truro. A reference to each of these sources is given
for each church,[166] and citations of the three later editions of Ecton are
given when they provide new material. Modern directories, chiefly
Kelly's and occasionally Crockford's, have been used to chart the history of dedications since Oliver's list of 1846. Other secondary sources,
including church guide books, have not been much employed because
they rarely treat church dedications in an historical way or include references to sources. Compared with Oliver's work—the last general list
to be based on original research—the present study has been able to
add material from several important sources. These include the published papal registers, the inquisitions post mortem and other Public
Record Office calendars, the evidence of the wills in London, a wider
range of those formerly in Exeter, and the archival collections of the

---

166. Willis's *Parochiale Anglicanum* (London, 1733), however, contains very few dedications in
Devon.

two county record offices. Even so, the possible sources for dedications have not yet been exhausted. In particular, more remain to be found in those pre-Reformation papal registers which have not yet been published and among the English Public Records, especially (one envisages) legal records.

The gazetteer of churches in Cornwall and Devon which follows is arranged alphabetically, compound place-names being listed under the first element. East Down, for example, appears under E, not D. In Cornwall, however, the book observes the traditional practice of ignoring the word 'Saint' which occurs before many parish names, because it is (or often has been) omitted in practice. Thus St Endellion is listed under E, not S, while North Hill is still under N as in Devon. All churches in Devon should be regarded as belonging to the diocese of Exeter, unless otherwise stated, and all those in Cornwall as lying in the same diocese until 1877 and in Truro since that date. The small number of anomalous parishes and those which have been transferred into or out of the dioceses and counties since the 1840s are noted in the entries concerned.

Each church entry contains two or three paragraphs. The first lists the evidence for the spiritual patron or patrons in chronological order, with names, dates, and abbreviated sources which can be identified in the List of Abbreviations and in the Bibliography (Sections 1 and 2a). The name of each saint or other spiritual patron is given before the earliest date and reference to it. When further dates and references follow after a comma without a fresh name, this indicates that the same form of the name applies in those cases. Variant forms of the name are separated by a semi-colon, and absolutely different evidence is placed in a separate sentence. Where printed directories fail to list a patron saint of a parish, or declare that the saint is unknown, this book puts the word 'Unknown'.[167] Such evidence is often positively useful in showing how patron saints became forgotten, and helps to explain why new ones were proposed. The names of familiar saints like Andrew, Mary, Michael and Peter have usually been standardized in their common form. Mary includes 'Our Lady' and 'the Blessed Virgin Mary', which have not been separately noted.

Other saints, chiefly in Cornwall, have names and identities which are less easy to establish. In their case, it is often important to give the original spelling and this is indicated by putting the name (or phrase in which the name occurs) into italics which means that it appears in that

---

167. This procedure is not followed in the case of the Devon entries in Willis's *Parochiale Anglicanum* of 1733, because there are too few of these to be meaningful.

form in the original source. When unusual saints are recorded in less than half a dozen medieval sources, all the sources are reproduced in the entry for the church. When such saints are recorded more frequently, a selection of medieval references has been made so as to suggest the most common form of the name and the main variants found. The sources for church dedications are frequently in Latin and give the saint's name in a Latinized form, usually in the genitive case. A modern scholar needs to identify and detach the Latin endings from these names in order to recover the vernacular form which was used in everyday speech. Modern Cornish practice is inconsistent in rendering some Celtic saints in the vernacular (Petroc rather than Petrocus), while in other cases it follows the Latin form (Endelienta rather than Endelient). In this book, references to the saints in Part I, the parish commentaries in Part II, and the index, give the vernacular Celtic or Saxon forms, not the Latin ones. In a few cases like Kewa, Morwenna and Wenna, the final -a is indeed the Latin form but it also approximates to the original vernacular usage. The Cornish vernacular forms presented in this book are compromises between medieval and modern spellings, and the reader must go to more specialized works (like those of Dr Padel) in order to understand the history of these names and how they were spelt.

Because direct references to patron saints of churches are often lacking, the historian of dedications is obliged to consider indirect evidence too. One such source consists of medieval references to the 'store' or 'image' of a saint. Stores were funds, of which most west-country churches had several before the Reformation. One was usually that of the chief saint of the church, while others belonged to other saints and images in the building. A mention of the 'store of St Peter', for example, does not therefore establish that the church was dedicated to him. However, if the store of St Peter is mentioned first in a list of stores, or is the same as the church dedication recorded in an earlier or later period, there is some likelihood that it is the store of the chief saint. It is therefore relevant to include such information, but it must be interpreted cautiously. References to the 'chancel' or 'cemetery' of a saint more plausibly indicate the patron saint of the church and have been so interpreted.

Another kind of indirect evidence requiring cautious treatment is that of place-names. In Cornwall in particular, place-names sometimes seem to contain the name of a saint, especially names beginning *Eglos*, 'church of', and *Lan*, 'church site of', followed by a second element. Popular belief and scholarly conjecture alike have often led to this element being interpreted as the name of the patron saint. The assumption is a dangerous one, given that Egloshayle means 'church on an estuary' and Lanivet 'church site at a place called *Neved*', not the churches of saints called Helie or Nyvett as has sometimes been thought.[168] When such place-names do contain a personal name as their second element, the latter need not be that of the patron saint but might refer to an early founder or owner of the church. Dr Padel has noted that, in about fifty cases of Cornish parish churches with names beginning in *Lan*, only twenty contain the name of the patron saint while in another twenty the name is different, the patron saint being known from other sources.[169] Even a case like Landulph, which occurs in Domesday Book as *Landelech*, meaning 'church site of a person called Dylyk or Delek', may not be quite straightforward. A Cornish saint with a similar name is known, and the patron saint of Landulph itself was called (in Latin) *Dilecta* by the early sixteenth century. The evidence may encourage us to interpret the Domesday name as including that of the patron saint, but it is still possible that the saint was a later invention from the place-name as seems to have happened in places like Ludgvan and Talland.[170] In another Cornish parish, Lansallos meaning 'church site of Salwys', local opinion after the Reformation came to believe that the church was dedicated to that person, reinterpreted as Alwys, instead of the earlier patron Ildiern. It is necessary to use place-name evidence in church dedication study, if only to explain some of the conjectures that have arisen about patron saints, but the evidence must be regarded with great respect for the problems which it presents.

Most parish entries include a middle paragraph. This collects all the known evidence about the dates when church buildings were dedicated and when parish feasts were held. References to fairs are added when they may be relevant to local dedications, but the book does not list them otherwise and it is not a complete record of them. Feasts and fairs offer further indirect evidence about the patron saints of a church, although like other such evidence it is fraught with difficulty. When a church saint is first recorded in the eighteenth century, it may look as though a parish feast, held on that saint's day, establishes the likelihood of the saint's patronage stretching back into the past. On the contrary; the eighteenth-century statement about the patron saint may be a con-

---

168. This question is thoroughly discussed by Padel: in 'Cornish Names of Parish Churches', *Cornish Studies*, iv/v (1976–77), pp. 15–27; *Cornish Place-Name Elements*, e.g. pp. 91, 142–45; and under the appropriate place-names in *A Popular Dictionary of Cornish Place-Names*, passim.
169. Padel, 'Cornish Names of Parish Churches', pp. 15–27, and *Cornish Place-Name Elements*, p. 142.
170. Discussed above, p. 40.

jecture based on the parish feast day, and most parish feasts were held on different days from that of the local patron saint. Church dedication dates and feast dates often help to explain why eighteenth- and nineteenth-century antiquaries made conjectures about patron saints, but they rarely lend independent support in identifying the patron saint of the church before the Reformation.

The final paragraph of each entry is in italics and contains the author's commentary on the evidence. Further assistance can be found at the back of the book, where an index of saints enables the reader to analyse the dedications name by name and to see how widely they were (or have been believed to be) honoured.

PART TWO

GAZETTEER OF CHURCH DEDICATIONS

CHURCH DEDICATIONS IN CORNWALL

In Cornwall, as in Devon, the form of place-names follows that of modern secular usage; ecclesiastical usage may differ.

Advent

Adwen (saint's name) 12th century (14th) (Grosjean, 1953, pp. 397–8); *capella Sancti Adweny* 1302 (PRO, JUST 1/117); *parochia Sancti Adweni* 1334 (Glasscock, 1975, p. 33); *capella Sancte Athewenne* 1340 (*Nonarum*, p. 346); *capelle Sancti Audewini* 1447 (Chanter XI, f. 292v); *Adwhen* (place) 1447 (ibid., f. 292); *Adven* (place) 1535 (*Valor*, ii, 402), 1553 (Snell, c.1955, p. 50); *Athawin* 1733 (Willis, p. 172); *St. Adven* 1742 (Ecton, p. 181); *St. Advent* 1782 (Jones, p. 111). 'Commonly called St Ann' 1814 (Lysons, p. 8). *Adwen* 1846 (Oliver, p. 437), 1883 (Kelly); *Athwenna* 1925 (Henderson, p. 19); *Adwena* or *Athwenna* 1939 (Kelly); *Adwena* 1996 (*TDD*).

Adwen since at least 1302, but probably since at least the 12th century when his name occurs in a list of saints connected with north Cornwall (Orme, 1992c, p. 115). He was then believed to be one of the 24 children of the Welsh king Brychan. With one exception in 1334, the medieval records regarded him as male; the modern female attributions come from that exception.

St Agnes

Agnes 1327 (Padel, 1988, p. 49), 1331 (ECA, D&C 2851), 1340 (*Nonarum*, p. 348), 1425 (Jacob, ii, 345), 1482 (DRO, Chanter 1063–4), 1733 (Willis, p. 169), 1742 (Ecton, p. 179), 1782 (Jones, p. 105), 1846 (Oliver, p. 437); *Agnes the Virgin* 1925 (Henderson, p. 19); *Agnes* 1939 (Kelly), 1996 (*TDD*).

In the early 18th century the parish feast was held on the Sunday after St Agnes' Day (Polsue, 1867–72, i, 4), and on St Agnes' Day (21 January) in 1878 (Boase, 1890, col. 1587).

Agnes since at least 1327.

St Allen

Church of *Sanctus Allunus* 1261 (Padel, 1988, p. 50); *ecclesiarum... Sancti Aluni* 1269 (Chanter I, f. 35 (i)); *ecclesie Sancti Alluni* 1261 (ibid. f. 24); *ecclesia de Sancto Aluno* 1291 (Tax.); *ecclesie . . . Sancti Aluni* 1421 (Chanter X, f. 47); *ecclesie . . . Sancti Alani* 1474 (Chanter XII (ii), f. 29v); *Aleyn* or *Allen* 1733 (Willis, p. 169); *Alleyn* 1742 (Ecton, p. 176), 1782 (Jones, p. 98); *Alunus* or *Elwinus* 1846 (Oliver, p. 437); *Allen* 1883 (Kelly); *Alunus* 1925 (Henderson, p. 10); *Allen* 1939 (Kelly); *Alleyne* 1996 (*TDD*).

In 1878 the parish feast was held on Rogation Sunday (Boase, 1890, col. 1587).

Alun, a male saint otherwise unknown, since at least 1261.

Altarnun

Altrenune (place) *c.*1100 (14th) (Holmes and Weaver, 1894, p. 119); *Alternon* (place) 1224 x 1244 (Chanter I, at end of register); *ecclesiam Sancte Nonne* 1236 (Chanter I, f. 25v); *Alternun* (place) 1282 (15th) (Hull, 1987, p. 2); *vicaria Sancte Nonite* 1349 (Chanter X, f. 83; *Nunn* 1733 (Willis, p. 171), 1742 (Ecton, p. 179); *Nonita* 1754 (Ecton, p. 628); *Nun* 1782 (Jones, p. 106); *Nonnet* or *Nun* 1814 (Lysons, p. 14); *Nonna* 1846 (Oliver, p. 437); *Nun* 1883 (Kelly); *Nonna* 1925 (Henderson, p. 20); *Nun* or *Nonna* 1939 (Kelly); *Nonna* 1996 (*TDD*),

Nonn, the mother of St David, since at least about 1100.

St Anthony in Meneage

Ecclesiam Sancti Antonini 1162 x 1170 (Oliver, 1846, p. 41); *vicariam Sancti Antonini* 1266 (Chanter I, f. 34v); *ecclesias Sancti Antonii* 1281 (Oliver, 1846, p. 43); *Sancti Antonii de Lanyntenyn* 1344 (Chanter V, f. 51v); *vicaria Sancti Antonii* 1370 (Chanter VII, f. 8v); *ecclesie . . . Sancti Antonini* 1435 (Chanter X, f. 135v); *ecclesie . . . Sancti Antonini* 1467 (Chanter XII (ii), f. 7v), 1498 (ibid., Redmayn, f. 6v), 1514 (Chanter XIII, ff. 55v–56); *Antonies c.*1540 (Leland, 1907–10, i, 195); Anthony 1733 (Willis, p. 166), 1742 (Ecton, p. 174), 1782 (Jones, p. 93), 1846 (Oliver, p. 437), 1883 (Kelly); *Anthoninus* or *Antonius* 1925 (Henderson, p. 21); Anthony 1939 (Kelly), 1996 (*TDD*).

In 1867 the parish feast was held on the Sunday nearest to St Stephen's Day (26 December) (Polsue, i, 36) and in 1878 on St Stephen's Day (Boase, 1890, col. 1587).

The place-name Lanyntenyn suggests that the saint was originally Entenin, who was also venerated at St Anthony in Roseland (below). He was latinized as Antoninus by the late 12th century and as Antonius by the late 13th.

St Anthony in Roseland: Augustinian priory and parish church

Entenin (saint's name) 10th century (Olson and Padel, 1986, p. 45); *ecclesiam Sancti Antonini regis et martyris* 1154 x 1189 (PRO, C 53/115, m. 13; Oliver, 1846, p. 135); *ecclesiam Sancti Antonini martyris* 1186 x 1188 (Barlow, 1996, no. 168); *Sancti Antonii c.*1200 (Gervase, 1867, ii, 424); *ecclesiam Sancti Antonii* 1259 (Chanter I, f. 7v); *Sancti Antonii in Rosland* 1291 (Tax.); *capella Sancti Antonii* 1340 (*Nonarum*, p. 347); *Antonie c.*1540 (Leland, 1907–10, i, 200). Anthony 1733 (Willis, p. 170). Not in Ecton (1742). Anthony 1782 (Jones, p. 102), 1846 (Oliver, p. 437), 1883 (Kelly); *Antoninus* king and martyr 1925 (Henderson, p. 21); Anthony 1939 (Kelly), 1996 (*TDD*).

Bishop Bronescombe dedicated the church on 3 October 1259 (Chanter I, f. 7v). In 1878 the parish feast was held on 3 October (Boase, 1890, col. 1587).

Originally dedicated to Entenin, a male saint believed in the 12th century to be a king and martyr. He was latinized as Antoninus by the late 12th century and eventually as Antonius.

Antony

James 1405 (Chanter IX, f. 87), 1479 (Chanter XII (ii), f. 87v); store of James the bishop (RIC, Henderson, HC 66, p. 165); James the Great 1538–9 (CRO, DDP 7/5/1 (A&B)). Anthony 1733 (Willis, p. 165), 1742 (Ecton, p. 173). John 1754 (Ecton, p. 627). Anthony and John the Baptist 1763 (Ecton, p. 127), 1782 (Jones, p. 90). James 1786 (Bacon, p. 301), 1846 (Oliver, p. 437), 1883 (Kelly), 1925 (Henderson, p. 22), 1939 (Kelly); James the Great 1996 (*TDD*).

Bishop Bronescombe dedicated the church on 14 October 1259 (Chanter I, f. 8). In 1878 no parish feast was held (Boase, 1890, col. 1587).

The place-name means 'Anta's farm' and has nothing to do with any Saint Anthony (Padel, 1988, p. 51). James since at least 1405 until the Reformation, then forgotten. Anthony in the 18th century, on the basis of the place-name, and John the Baptist perhaps because of the neighbouring church of St John. James was recovered in 1786.

St Austell

Austoll (saint's name) 10th century (Olson and Padel, 1986, p. 59); *ecclesiam de Austol* 1155 x ?1160 (Barlow, 1996, no. 74); *sanctuarium de Sancto Austolo* 1169 (PRO, C 53/28, m. 10); *ecclesie Sancti Austol* 1259 (Chanter I. f. 6v); *ecclesias . . . Sancti Austoli* 1281 (Oliver, 1846, p. 43); *de Sancto Austolo* 1291 (Tax.); *ecclesie . . . Sancti Austoli* 1446 (Chanter X, f. 200); *S. Austelles c.*1540 (Leland, 1907–10, i, 201–2); *Austel* 1733 (Willis, p. 169); *Austell* 1742 (Ecton, p. 176); *Austle* 1782 (Jones, p. 98); *Austolus* 1846 (Oliver, p. 437). Trinity 1856 (Kelly). *Austolus* 1925 (Henderson, p. 23). Trinity 1939 (Kelly), 1996 (*TDD*).

Bishop Bronescombe dedicated the church on 9 October 1259 (Chanter I, f. 8). In 1878 the parish feast was held on Trinity Sunday and the three following days (Boase, 1890, col. 1587).

Austol, a male saint, since at least the 10th century, believed to be a companion of St Mewan. Since 1856, however, some directories have given the dedication as Trinity, through conjecture from (or preference for) the parish feast day.

St Blazey

Capellas...Sancti Blasii 1440 (Chanter XI, f. 213v); *Blasio* 1450 (ibid., f. 334); *Seynt Blasy* 1535 (*Valor*, ii, 396); *paroch church of S. Blase c.*1540 (Leland, 1907–10, i, 202); *Blase* 1733 (Willis, p. 169); *Blasye* 1742 (Ecton, p. 176), 1782 (Jones, p. 98); *Blaze* 1814 (Lysons, p. 24), 1846 (Oliver, p. 437); *Blasye* or *Blaize* 1883 (Kelly); Blaise 1925 (Henderson, p. 24); *Blasye* or *Blaize* 1939 (Kelly); Blaise 1996 (*TDD*).

In 1878 the parish feast was held on 24 June (Boase, 1890, col. 1587).

Blaise since at least 1440.

Blisland

Prothus and *Jacinctus* 1436 (*CPR 1429–36*, p. 513). *Pratt* 1733 (Willis, p. 172), 1742 (Ecton, p. 181), 1782 (Jones, p. 110); *Proto* or *Prat* 1814 (Lysons, p. 26); *Protasius* 1846 (Oliver, p. 437); *Protho* or *Pratt* 1883 (Kelly); *Prothus* or *Pratt* 1889 (Kelly); *Pratt* 1925 (Henderson, p. 24); Protus (or *Pratt*) and Hyacinth 1926 (Kelly), 1939 (ibid.), 1996 (*TDD*).

In 1867 the parish feast was held on 11 September (Polsue, i, 69), and in 1878 on 22 September or the Sunday following (Boase, 1890, col. 1587).

Protus and Hyacinth, two brothers and early Roman martyrs, before the Reformation. By the 18th century, Protus alone was remembered and then only in the mysterious form of Pratt. The original dedication was at first conjectured from this, but can now be confirmed from the record of 1436.

Boconnoc

Unknown 1733 (Willis, p. 173), 1742 (Ecton, p. 183), 1782 (Jones, p. 116), 1846 (Oliver, p. 437), 1925 (Henderson, p. 24), 1939 (Kelly), 1996 (*TDD*).

Bishop Stapledon dedicated the church on 18 October 1321 (Chanter II, f. 162). In 1878 there was no settled feast day (Boase, 1890, col. 1587).

The medieval dedication has not been discovered, and it was forgotten after the Reformation.

Bodmin: Augustinian priory

Petroc 946 x 955 (Finberg, 1963, p. 12), 939 x 946 (ibid., p. 18), 1086 (DB 4/3), ?1107 (15th) (Hull, 1987, p. 2; *Regesta*, ii, 72), 1146 (Blake, 1981, p. 309), *c.*1200 (Gervase, 1867, ii, 424). Mary and Petroc 1485 (*CPL*, xv, 22), 1492 (*CPL*, xvi, 42; PROB 11/9, f. 168v).

The priory church was dedicated on 24 August (Worcester, 1969, p. 88).

Petroc since the 10th century, to whom Mary was added by at least 1485.

Bodmin: Franciscan friary

The medieval dedication has not been discovered.

Bodmin: St Anthony's hospital

Anthony 1492, 1553 (Orme and Webster, 1995, pp. 186–7).

Anthony, probably of Egypt.

Bodmin: St George's hospital

George 1492, 1531 (ibid., p. 187).

Bodmin: St Laurence's hospital

Laurence 1368, 1531 (ibid., pp. 188–9).

Bodmin: parish church

Petroc 1299 (ECA, D&C 2125), 1417 (Chanter IX, f. 183), 1448 (*CPL*, x, 28), 1476 (*CPL*, xiii (ii), 494); *Patryk* 1543 (RIC, Henderson, HC 66, p. 157); Petroc 1733 (Willis, p. 172), 1742 (Ecton, p. 181), 1782 (Jones, p. 112), 1846 (Oliver, p. 437), 1925 (Henderson, p. 26), 1939 (Kelly), 1996 (*TDD*).

A feast was kept on the Sunday and Monday after St Thomas Becket's Day (7 July) in 1867 (Polsue, i, 104).

Petroc, like the adjoining priory, since at least 1299.

Boscastle—see Forrabury

Botus Fleming

Mary 1504 (Chanter XII (ii), Reg. Arundell, f. 11v). Unknown 1733 (Willis, p. 165), 1742 (Ecton, p. 172), 1782 (Jones, p. 87), 1846 (Oliver, p. 437). Mary 1883 (Kelly), 1925 (Henderson, p. 29), 1939 (Kelly), 1996 (*TDD*).

Bishop Bronescombe dedicated the church on 18 October 1259 (Chanter I, f. 8v). In 1878 there was no feast day (Boase, 1890, col. 1587).

Mary before the Reformation; it was then forgotten and was recovered in the late 19th century.

Boyton

Unknown 1733 (Willis, p. 171), 1742 (Ecton, p. 180), 1782 (Jones, p. 109), 1846 (Oliver, p. 437), 1883 (Kelly). The Holy Name 1889 (Kelly), 1925 (Henderson, p. 30), 1939 (Kelly); Holy Name 1996 (*TDD*).

Until about 1863 there was a fair and parish feast on the third Monday in August (Boase, 1890, col. 1587).

The medieval dedication has not been discovered, and it was forgotten after the Reformation. The Holy Name looks like a late-Victorian conjecture that the feast day, adjusted back to the pre-1752 calendar, related to the commemoration of the Name of Jesus on 7 August. This commemoration, however, was a late-medieval invention, and Boyton church, being much older, would have had a different patron.

Braddock (Broadoak)

Mary 1343 (Chanter V, f. 49), 1733 (Willis, p. 173), 1742 (Ecton, p. 183), 1782 (Jones, p. 116), 1846 (Oliver, p. 437), 1925 (Henderson, p. 30), 1939 (Kelly), 1996 (*TDD*).

In 1878 there was no settled feast day (Boase, 1890, col. 1587).

Mary since at least 1343.

Breage

Ecclesia de Egglosbrec (place) *c.*1170 (13th) (BL, Cotton MS Cleopatra A.vii, f. 74); *ecclesiam de Sancta Breaca* 1246 (ECA, D&C 1381; Barlow, 1996, no. 321); *vicariam Sancte Breace* 1264 (Chanter I, f. 31); *ecclesia Sancte Breace* 1291 (Tax.); *vicariam . . . Sancte Briace/Breace* 1439 (Chanter X, f. 180v); *ecclesie . . . Sancti Briaci* 1467 (Chanter XII (ii), f. 7); *Sancta Briaca virgo* 1478 (Worcester, 1969, p. 29); *ecclesie . . . Sancte Breace* 1510 (Chanter XIII, f. 41v); *Breaca* 1733 (Willis, p. 166); *Breoke alias St. Breage* 1742 (Ecton, p. 173), 1782 (Jones, p. 91); *Breaca* 1814 (Lysons, p. 43), 1846 (Oliver, p. 437); *Breage* 1883 (Kelly); *Breaca* 1925 (Henderson, p. 30); *Breage* 1939 (Kelly); *Breaca* 1996 (*TDD*).

In 1878 the parish feast was held on St Stephen's Day (26 December), and a fair on the third Monday in June (Boase, 1890, col. 1588).

Breac, a female saint, since at least the late 12th century. In the 15th and 18th centuries, she was confused with Brioc, the male saint of St Breock.

St Breock

Ecclesiam Sancti Brioci 1259 (Chanter I, f. 7v), 1328 (Chanter IV, f. 46v); *ecclesiam . . . Sancti Breaci*, corrected to *Breoci* 1362 (Chanter V, f. 141v); *ecclesiam . . . Sancti Brioci* 1500 (Chanter XII (ii), Redmayn f. 14v); *Breock* 1733 (Willis, p. 168), 1742 (Ecton, p. 178), 1782 (Jones, p. 103); *Briocus* 1846 (Oliver, p. 437); *Breoke* 1883 (Kelly); *Briocus* 1925 (Henderson, p. 31); *Breoke* 1939 (Kelly), 1996 (*TDD*).

Bishop Bronescombe dedicated the church on 24 September 1259 (Chanter I, f. 7v) and Bishop Stapledon the high altar on 11 July 1318 (Chanter II, f. 128).

Brioc or Breoc, a male saint, since at least 1259; he was believed to have come from Wales and to have worked chiefly in Brittany.

St Breward

'In Cornwall, *Sancti Branwalarethi martyris*' early 12th century (Dalton and Doble, 1909–41, ii, 381; iv, 14, 39–40). *Ecclesiam Sancti Brewveredi c.*1190 (Oliver, 1846, p. 42); *ecclesiam de Sancto Bruereto* 1272 (Chanter I, f. 49v); *ecclesiam Sancti Brueredi* 1276 (ibid., f. 69v); *Bruard* 1733 (Willis, p. 172), 1742 (Ecton, p. 181), 1782 (Jones, p. 112); *Bruerdus* 1846 (Oliver, p. 437); *Breward* 1883 (Kelly); *Brueredus* 1925 (Henderson, p. 32); *Breward* 1939 (Kelly), 1996 (*TDD*).

In 1878 the parish feast was held on the first or second Sunday after Candlemas (2 February) and a fair on the Thursday after Midsummer Day (24 June) (Boase, 1890, col. 1588).

Bruered, a male saint, probably identical with the Breton St Branwalader, since at least the late 12th century.

Budock

Richard *de Sancto Budoco* (name) 1208 (*Book of Fees*, i, 43); *ecclesia Sancti Budoci* 1265 (Chanter I, f. 32v), 1291 (Tax.), 1331 (Chanter IV, f. 33), 1340 (*Nonarum*, p. 348); *Budocus c.*1540 (Leland, 1907–10, i, 196); *Budiocke* 1569 (RIC, Henderson, HC 66, p. 152); store of St *Bedocke* 1571 (ibid.); *Budock* 1733 (Willis, p. 166); *Budoke* 1742 (Ecton, p. 174), 1782 (Jones, p. 91); *Budocus* 1846 (Oliver, p. 437), 1925 (Henderson, p. 33), 1939 (Kelly); *Budock* 1996 (*TDD*).

Budoc, a Breton saint said to have been archbishop of Dol, since at least 1208.

St Buryan: parish and collegiate church

Berion (saint's name) 10th century (Olson and Padel, 1986, p. 48); *ecclesia Sancte Beriane* allegedly 925 x 939 (14th) (Chanter IV, f. 25v); *canonici S' Berrione* 1086 (DB 4/27). Andrew the Apostle, Thomas the Martyr, Nicholas the Confessor and *beate Beriane virginis* 1238 (Chanter II, f. 25v; Barlow, 1996, no. 287). *Ecclesie Berriane* 1259 (Chanter I, f. 6); *ecclesia Sancte Beriane* 1291 (Tax.); 1340 (*Nonarum*, p. 348); *S. Burien, S. Buriana c.*1540 (Leland, 1907–10, i, 189); *Buriena* 1733 (Willis, p. 167); *Borian* alias *Burien* 1742 (Ecton, p. 175), 1782 (Jones, p. 94); *Buriana* 1846 (Oliver, p. 437); *Beriana* virgin 1925 (Henderson, p. 34); *Berriana* 1939 (Kelly); *Buriana* 1996 (*TDD*).

Bishop Brewer dedicated the church in honour of Andrew the Apostle, Thomas the Martyr, Nicholas the Confessor and beate Beriane virginis on 26 August 1238 (Chanter II, f. 25v; Barlow, 1996, no. 287). In 1867 the parish feast was held on 29 May (Polsue, i, 165) and in 1878 on the nearest Sunday to Old May Day, with a fair on the first Tuesday in March (Boase, 1890, col. 1588).

Berian, a female saint, since at least the 10th century.

Callington

Mary 1233 (15th) (Hull, 1987, p. 195), 1438 (Chanter XI, f. 162), 1467 (PROB 11/5, f. 106v), 1733 (Willis, p. 166). Not in Ecton (1742). Mary 1763 (Ecton, p. 127). Unknown 1782 (Jones, p. 90). Mary 1846 (Oliver, p. 437), 1925 (Henderson, p. 37), 1939 (Kelly), 1996 (*TDD*).

Fair on the Nativity of the Virgin Mary (8 September) 1267 (*CChR 1257–1300*, p. 84). In 1438 the feast of dedication was ordered to be held on 4 October (Chanter XI, f. 163v).

Mary since at least 1233.

Calstock

Store of Andrew 1368 (DRO, 158M/T3; Webster, 1989, p. 182). Unknown 1733 (Willis, p. 165). Andrew 1742 (Ecton, p. 172), 1782 (Jones, p. 87), 1846 (Oliver, p. 437), 1925 (Henderson, p. 38), 1939 (Kelly), 1996 (*TDD*).

In 1878 no parish feast was held (Boase, 1890, col. 1588).

Andrew, probably since at least 1368 and certainly since 1742.

Camborne

Ecclesiam . . . Sancti Mereadoci 1426 (Chanter X, f. 74). Martin 1448 (Chanter X, f. 239v; Chanter XI, f. 303v), 1449 (Chanter X, f. 246; Chanter XI, f. 324). *Ecclesiam . . . Sancti Mereadoci* 1500 (Chanter XII (ii), Redmayn f. 15); . . . *Meriadoci* 1501 (ibid., f. 21), 1522 (Chanter XIV, f. 13v). Parish of *Mereadok* and Martin 1535 (CRO, DDP 322/1–8, f. 49v); parish of *Merasak* (also *Marasake, Marasak*) 1556–7 (ibid., ff. 41–8).

Peter, with a query 1733 (Willis, p. 167). Mary 1740 (MS Willis 41, f. 237). Peter 1742 (Ecton, p. 175); Peter with a query 1754 (Ecton, p. 128), corrected to Martin (ibid., p. 627); Peter 1782 (Jones, p. 95). *Mariadoci* 1814 (Lysons, p. 55); *Meriadocus* or Martin 1846 (Oliver, p. 437), 1925 (Henderson, p. 38). Martin 1939 (Kelly). Martin and *Meriadoc* 1996 (*TDD*).

In 1878 the parish feast was held on St Martin's Day (11 November) if a Monday, or else the Monday afterwards (Boase, 1890, col. 1588).

The Breton male saint Meriadoc (Meriasek in Cornish) since at least 1426, with Martin as a co-patron from the 15th century until the Reformation. Both saints became forgotten in the 18th century and were permanently restored only by scholars in the 19th.

Cardinham

Ecclesiam . . . Sancti Mebbredi martiris 1473 (Chanter XII (ii), f. 22v); *Sanctus Mybbard heremita, Sancti Midbard* 1478 (Worcester, 1969, pp. 96, 98). Unknown 1733 (Willis, p. 173), 1742 (Ecton, p. 182). John the Baptist 1754 (Ecton, p. 134). *Mewbred* 1763 (Ecton, p. 134), 1782 (Jones, p. 114); *Meubredus* 1846 (Oliver, p. 437); *Mewbred* 1883 (Kelly); *Meubredus* martyr 1925 (Henderson, p. 39); *Meubred* 1939 (Kelly), 1996 (*TDD*).

In 1740 and in 1878 the parish feast was said to be held at Whitsuntide (MS Willis 41, f. 237; Boase, 1890, col. 1588).

Meubred, an otherwise unknown male saint believed to be a martyr, since at least 1473, but not always remembered in the 18th century.

St Carrock: Cluniac priory

St *Carroc* 1189 x 1199 (14th) (Holmes and Weaver, 1894, p. 128). *Prioratus Sancti Ciriaci c.*1200 (Gervase, 1867, ii, 424); *cellulam Sancti Cyrici* 1236 (Chanter I, f. 25v). *Prior de Sancto Caroco,* also *Karoco* 1291 (Tax.); *priore de Sancto Carroco* 1338 (Chanter IV, f. 213; cf. f. 230); *celle Sancti Karoci* 1385, with mention of the feast of *Sanctorum Cirici et Julitte* in the priory (Chanter VI, f. 141). *Sanctus Sirus presbyter . . . in ecclesia . . . Sancti Keryk* 1478 (Worcester, 1969, p. 106). *Cella Sancti Karoci* 1535 (*Valor Ecclesiasticus,* i, 196). *Cyret and Julette, S. Carak c.*1540 (Leland, 1907–10, i, 206). *Cannock* 1733 (Willis, p. 174).

Carroc, a male saint, by at least about 1200. One tradition, going back to about the same date, gave him the Latin name Cyricus and seems to have identified him with the Roman saint of that name, Julitta the mother of the Roman Cyricus being added by the late 14th century. However, another tradition recorded by William Worcester in 1478 regarded him as a priest who was buried in the church.

St Cleer

Ecclesiam de Sancto Claro 1212 (*CuRR 1210–12,* p. 202); *Seintcler* (place) (*Close Rolls 1227–31,* p. 354); *ecclesia Sancti Clari* 1280 (Chanter I, f. 95); *Clari* 1291 (Tax.); *Clary* 1340 (*Nonarum,* p. 342); *ecclesie . . . Sancti Clari* 1448 (Chanter X, f. 236v); *vicariam . . . Sancti Cleri* 1541 (Chanter XIV, f. 104v); *ecclesie Sancti Clari* 1547 (ibid., f. 123v); *St Clare* 1548 (Snell, *c.*1953, p. 18). *Clair* 1733 (Willis, p. 173); *Clere* 1742 (Ecton, p. 182), 1782 (Jones, p. 114); *Clarus* 1846 (Oliver, p. 437); *Cleer* 1883 (Kelly); *Clarus* 1925 (Henderson, p. 41); *Cleer* 1939 (Kelly); *Clarus* 1996 (*TDD*).

In 1878 no parish feast was held (Boase, 1890, col. 1588).

Apparently one of the European male saints called Clair since at least 1212.

St Clement

*Fontem Sancti Clementis c.*1175 (late 14th) (Hull, 1962, p. 58); Clement 1329 (Chanter V, f. 12), 1419 (Jacob, ii, 173), 1480 (Chanter XII (ii), f. 141-v), 1733 (Willis, p. 169); *St. Clemens* 1742 (Ecton, p. 176); Clement 1782 (Jones, p. 98), 1846 (Oliver, p. 437), 1925 (Henderson, p. 41), 1939 (Kelly), 1996 (*TDD*).

In 1878 the parish feast was held on the nearest Sunday to St Clement's Day (23 November) (Boase, 1890, col. 1588).

Clement, probably since at least the late 12th century, certainly since at least 1329.

St Clether

Cleder (saint's name) 12th century (14th) (Grosjean, 1953, pp. 397–8); *Seyncleder* 1249 (Rowe, 1914–50, i, 65–6); *ecclesiam Sancti Clederi* 1259 (Chanter I, f. 8v), 1261 (ibid., p. 168), 1291 (Tax.), 1457 (Chanter XII (i), f 4v); *Clether* or *Gladred* 1733 (Willis, p. 171); *Clether* 1742 (Ecton, p. 180), 1782 (Jones, p. 108); *Clederus* 1846 (Oliver, p. 437); *Clether* 1883–1939 (Kelly); *Clederus* 1925 (Henderson, p. 42), 1996 (*TDD*).

Bishop Bronescombe dedicated the church on 23 October 1259 (Chanter I, f. 8v).

Cleder since at least 1249, but probably since at least the 12th century when his name occurs in a list of saints connected with north Cornwall (Orme, 1992c, p. 125). He was then believed to be one of the twenty-four children of the Welsh king Brychan.

Colan

Hamelin *de Sancto Culano* (name) 1201 (Stenton, 1952, p. 369); *Sancto Culano* 1262 (Rowe, 1914–50, i, 109); *ecclesia de Sancto Choulano* 1272 (Chanter I, f. 49v); *ecclesiam Sancti Culani* 1276 (ibid., f. 72); *ecclesiam Sancti Coelani* 1276 (ibid. f. 73v); *ecclesia Sancti Colani* 1291 (Tax.); *ecclesie . . . Sancti Colani* 1509 (Chanter XIII, f. 36); *Colan* 1733 (Willis, p. 168), 1742 (Ecton, p. 179), 1782 (Jones, p. 105); *Colanus* 1846 (Oliver, p. 437); *Colan* 1883 (Kelly); *Colanus* 1925 (Henderson, p. 42); *Colan* 1939 (Kelly); 1996 (*TDD*).

Bishop Grandisson dedicated the high altar on 14 July 1336 (Chanter II, f. 201). In 1878 the parish feast was held on the first Sunday after the first Thursday in May (Boase, 1890, col. 1588).

Colan or Culan, a male saint, since at least 1201.

St Columb Major

Ecclesiarum Sancte Columbe . . . 1232 x 1244 (CRO, AR 140/232; Barlow, 1996, no. 314); *ecclesie Sancte Columbe majoris* 1264 (Chanter I, f. 30), 1291 (Tax); *S. Columbes c.*1540 (Leland, 1907–10, i, 181); *Columba* 1733 (Willis, p. 168), 1742 (Ecton, p. 178); *Columb* 1782 (Jones, p. 103); *Columba* 1846 (Oliver, p. 437); *Columba* virgin 1925 (Henderson, p. 42); *Columb* 1939 (Kelly); *Columba* 1996 (*TDD*).

A fair was granted on St Columb's Day in 1333 (*CChR 1327–41*, p. 301). In the early 18th century the dedication feast was in November, near the day of St Columb (Polsue, i, 225), and in 1867 on the nearest Sunday to 17 November (ibid., p. 225). In 1878 the parish feast was held on St Columb's Day, on the Sunday after the second Thursday before 13 November (Boase, 1890, col. 1588). St Columb's Day seems to have been a fixed or moveable day round about 15–17 November (see also St Columb Minor, below).

Columb since at least the mid 13th century. The saint was usually perceived as a female and there was a legend of her martyrdom in the neighbourhood, but the name was also sometimes interpreted as male—perhaps through identification with Columba of Iona (Orme, 1992c, pp. 125–6).

St Columb Minor

Capelle Sancte Columbe 1284 (Chanter I, f. 124), 1340 (*Nonarum*, p. 348). Not in Willis (1733). *Columb* 1742 (Ecton, p. 179), 1782 (Jones, p. 106); *Columba* 1846 (Oliver, p. 437); *Columba* virgin 1925 (Henderson, p. 45); *Columba* 1939 (Kelly), 1996 (*TDD*).

In 1878 the parish feast was held on about 15 November (depending on the full moon) (Boase, 1890, col. 1588).

Columb, as at St Columb Major, since at least 1284.

Constantine

Sanctus Constantinus 1086 (DB 4/29); *ecclesiam de Sancto Costantino* 1258 (Chanter I, f. 4v); *parochiis Sanctorum Constantini . . .* 1387 (Chanter VI, f. 175v); *ecclesiam . . . Sancti Constantini* 1415 (Chanter VIII, f. 212), 1534 (Chanter XIV, f. 70v); Constantine 1733 (Willis, p. 166), 1742 (Ecton, p. 174), 1782 (Jones, p. 93); *Constantinus* 1846 (Oliver, p. 437); *Constantine* 1883 (Kelly); *Constantinus* 1925 (Henderson, p. 47); *Constantine* 1939 (Kelly), 1996 (*TDD*).

In 1867 the parish feast was held on the nearest Sunday to 9 March (Polsue, i, 248), and in 1878 similarly to 10 March with a fair on the nearest Wednesday to Midsummer Day (24 June) (Boase, 1890, col. 1588).

Constantine, a male saint, since at least the late 11th century.

Cornelly

Instauro Sancti Cornelii 1502 (PROB 11/13, f. 162); *Cornely* 1549 (Snell, *c.*1955, p. 11); *Cornelius* 1733 (Willis, p. 170); *Cornelly* 1742 (Ecton, p. 175); *Cornelius* 1754 (Ecton, p. 128), 1782 (Jones, p. 94), 1846 (Oliver, p. 437), 1883 (Kelly); *Cornelly* 1925 (Henderson, p. 46); *Cornelius* 1939 (Kelly), 1996 (*TDD*).

In 1878 the parish feast was held on the Sunday nearest to 29 September (Michaelmas Day) (Boase, 1890, col. 1588).

A male saint since at least 1502, apparently the Roman pope Cornelius unless the name is a latinization of some different person.

Crantock: collegiate and parish church

Canonici S' Carentoch 1086 (DB 4/25); *canonichi Sancti Carentochi* 1086 (Exon, p. 187); church of St *Carentoc c.*1100 (14th) (Holmes and Weaver, 1894, p. 119); *ecclesiam Sancti Karantaci* 1146 (Blake, 1981, p. 309); *ecclesia Sancti Karentoci* 1236 (Chanter I, at end); *ecclesia Sancti Karantoci* 1258 (ibid., f. 3v); *ecclesia Sancti Karentoci* 1291 (Tax.); *prebenda Carantoci* 1311 (Chanter II, f. 61v); *decano Sancti Carentoci* 1390 (Chanter VI, f. 214v); *S. Carantokes c.*1540 (Leland, 1907–10, p. 193); *Carantock* 1733 (Willis, p. 168); *Cranstock* 1742 (Ecton, p. 179). *Cadock* 1754 (Ecton, p. 131). *Cranstock* 1782 (Jones, p. 106); *Carantoc* 1814 (Lysons, p. 69); *Carantocus* 1846 (Oliver, p. 438), 1883 (Kelly), 1925 (Henderson, p. 47), 1939 (Kelly); *Carantoc* 1996 (*TDD*).

In 1867 the parish feast was held on the nearest Sunday to 16 May (Polsue, i, 256).

The Welsh male saint Carantoc since at least the 11th century, briefly confused with Cadoc in 1754.

Creed

Crite (saint's name) 10th century (Olson and Padel, 1986, p. 60); Thomas de *Sancta Crida* (name) *c.*1260 (Moulton, 1929, p. 128); vill of *Sancta Crida* mid 13th century (14th) (CRO, AR 1/248); *ecclesia Sancte Cride* 1291 (Tax.), 1310 (Chanter II, f. 48); *ecclesia Sancte Cryde* 1340 (Nonarum, p. 343); *ecclesie . . . Sancte Crede virginis* 1394 (Chanter VII, f. 152); *Crada* 1733 (Willis, p. 169); *Crade* alias *Creede* 1742 (Ecton, p. 176), 1782 (Jones, p. 99); *Crida* 1846 (Oliver, p. 438); *Crida* virgin 1925 (Henderson, p. 49); *Crida* 1939 (Kelly), 1996 (*TDD*).

In 1878 the parish feast was held on the Sunday after St Andrew's Day (30 November) (Boase, 1890, col. 1588).

Cride, a female saint otherwise unknown, since at least the mid 13th century and probably since at least the 10th century when her name appears in the early list of Cornish saints.

Crowan

Eggloscrauuen (place) *c.*1147 x 1179 (13th) (BL, Cotton MS Cleopatra A.vii, f. 74); *ecclesia de Sancte Orewano* (*sic*) 1201 (Stenton, 1952, p. 130); *patronorum . . . sancte Crowenne* 1238 (Barlow, 1996, no. 296); *ecclesie Sancte Crewenne; taxacio Sancte Crouwenne* 1269 (Chanter I, f. 41); *ecclesia Sancte Crowenne* 1291 (Tax.); *ecclesie . . . Sancte Crewenne* 1362 (Chanter V, f. 146v); *parochiam Sancte Crowenne* 1387 (Chanter VI, f. 171v); *ecclesie . . . Sancte Crewenne* 1403 (Chanter IX, f. 69v); *parochia Sancte Cruenne* 1415 (Chanter VIII, f. 209); *Crowan* 1711 (Ecton, p. 122). *Crowan* alias *Uni-Crowan* 1723 (Ecton, p. 79), 1728 (Ecton, p. 84). *Crowena* 1733 (Willis, p; 167). *Unine* 1742 (Ecton, p. 175); *Unnine* 1754 (Ecton, p. 129), corrected to *Crewenne* (ibid., p. 627); *Unine* 1782 (Jones, p. 95). *Crewena* 1846 (Oliver, p. 438), 1883 (Kelly); *Cruenna* 1925 (Henderson, p. 50); *Crewenna* 1939 (Kelly), 1996 (*TDD*).

In 1867 the parish feast was held on the Sunday nearest to 1 February (Polsue, i, 269) and in 1878 similarly to 2 February, with a fair on 15 July unless a Sunday (Boase, 1890, col. 1588).

Crowan or Crewan, a female saint, since at least the 12th century; she was later thought to be a companion of Breac of Breage. By 1723, the name of the church was believed to be Uny-Crowan, implying that Crowan had been joined or supplanted as patron by the male saint Euny. The two names first appear together in the 2nd edition of Ecton's Liber Valorum, *where they do not seem to be an editorial mistake because Uny is spelt differently from the patron saints of Lelant and Redruth where the spelling is Ewny. Rather, Uny looks like a name reported or researched locally and, with the other 18th-century references, suggests a genuine tradition of Euny's connection with Crowan church. Crowan alone, however, has been dominant since 1846.*

Cubert

Vicariam Sancti Cuberti 1269 (Chanter I, f. 41); *ecclesia Sancti Cuberti* 1291 (Tax.); *vicaria Sancti Cuthberti* 1328 (Chanter V, f. 88v); *ecclesie Sancti Cutberti* 1383 (Chanter VII, f. 82); *ecclesie . . . Sancti Cuthberti* 1430 (Chanter X, f. 97); Cuthbert 1733 (Willis, p. 168); *Kilbord* 1742 (Ecton, p. 179); Cuthbert 1754 (Ecton, p. 628), 1782 (Jones, p. 105), 1846 (Oliver, p. 438), 1883 (Kelly); *Cubertus* 1925 (Henderson, p. 51); *Cubert* 1939 (Kelly), 1996 (*TDD*).

In 1867 and 1878 the parish feast was held on the Sunday after 4 October (Polsue, i, 276; Boase, 1890, col. 1588).

The English saint Cuthbert since at least 1269. His name occurs in a parallel form at Gwbert-on-Sea (Cardiganshire), so there is no need to postulate a Celtic saint with a similar name.

Cuby

Ecclesiam Sancti Kybi 1267 (BL, Cotton MS Cleopatra C.vii, f. 129v); *ecclesias . . . Sancti Kybi* 1282 (Chanter I, f. 124v); *ecclesiam S' Kibii* 1286 (ibid., f. 131v); *Sancti Cuvy* 1502 (*CPL*, xvii part i, 457); *Keby* and *Januarius* 1733 (Willis, p. 170); *Keby* 1742 (Ecton, p. 177), 1782 (Jones, p. 100), 1846 (Oliver, p. 438), 1883 (Kelly); *Cuby* 1925 (Henderson, p. 51); *Cubey* 1939 (Kelly); *Cuby* 1996 (*TDD*).

For the parish feast day, see Tregony.

Cuby (Cybi in Welsh), since at least 1267. He was said to have been born in east Cornwall (compare Duloe), and to have died in Wales.

Cury

Egloscuri (place) 1219 (Padel, 1988, p. 77); *ecclesia de Sancto Corentino* 1284 (PRO, JUST 1/111); *capellanum Sancti Corentini* 1310 (Chanter II, f. 48); *capella Sanctorum Corenti . . .* 1340 (Nonarum, p. 344); *Sayntt Corenttyn* 1549 (Snell, *c*.1955, p. 15). Ninian 1733 (Willis, p. 166), 1742 (Ecton, p. 173), 1782 (Jones, p. 91). *Corentinus* 1846 (Oliver, p. 438); *Corantyn* 1883 (Kelly); *Corentin* 1925 (Henderson, p. 52); *Corentyn* 1939 (Kelly); *Corentine* 1996 (*TDD*)

In 1867 and 1878 the parish feast was held on the nearest Sunday to 2 November, and fairs were formerly held on the first Tuesday in February and 3 August (Polsue, i, 289; Boase, 1890, col. 1588).

The Breton male saint Corentin, also known in the hypocoristic or 'pet' form Cury, since at least 1219.

Davidstow

Ecclesiarum . . . S. Davyd' de Treglast 1224 x 1244 (14th) (Chanter IV, f. 4; Barlow, 1996, nos. *234–5); *ecclesie Sancti David* 1269 (Chanter I, f. 42); David 1291 (Tax.), 1410 (Chanter VIII, f. 314v), 1429 (*CPL*, viii, 117), 1733 (Willis, p. 171), 1742 (Ecton, p. 179), 1782 (Jones, p. 106), 1846 (Oliver, p. 438), 1925 (Henderson, p. 52), 1939 (Kelly), 1996 (*TDD*).

In 1878 the parish feast was held on the Sunday before Midsummer Day (24 June), with fairs on 12 July and 5 October (Boase, 1890, col. 1588).

David since at least the early 13th century.

St Dennis

Parochia Sancti Dyonisii 1334 (Glasscock, 1975, p. 31); *capella Sancti Dyonisii* 1340 (*Nonarum*, p. 343); *Dennis* 1733 (Willis, p. 169); *Denys* 1742 (Ecton, p. 176); *Dennys* 1782 (Jones, p. 102); *Dennis* 1846 (Oliver, p. 438), 1883 (Kelly); *Dionisius* 1925 (Henderson, p. 55); *Dennis* or *Denys* 1939 (Kelly); *Denys* 1996 (*TDD*).

In 1878 the parish feast was held on the Sunday of or after St Denis's Day (9 October), with fairs on Rogation Tuesday and the third Tuesday in October (Boase, 1890, col. 1588).

Denis since at least 1334, perhaps suggested by the nearby hill-fort, 'dinas' in Cornish (Padel, 1988, p. 78).

St Dominick

Ecclesiam Sancte Dominice 1259 (Chanter I, f. 8v); 1291 (Tax.); *Sancta Dominica* 1340 (*Nonarum*, p. 341); *ecclesie Sancti Dominici* 1362 (Chanter V, f. 142v); *ecclesiam . . .*

Sancte Dominice 1437 (Chanter X, f. 149); *ecclesie Sancti Dominici* 1445 (Chanter XI, f. 266); *Dominica* (Willis, p. 165); *Dominick* 1742 (Ecton, p. 172), 1782 (Jones, p. 88); *Dominica* 1846 (Oliver, p. 438); *Dominic* 1883 (Kelly); *Dominica* 1925 (Henderson, p. 55); *Dominic* 1939 (Kelly); *Dominica* 1996 (*TDD*).

Bishop Bronescombe dedicated the church on 20 October 1259 (Chanter I, f. 8v). In 1445 Bishop Lacy changed the dedication festival from the morrow of the decollation of St John the Baptist (30 August) to 9 May (Chanter XI, f. 266). In 1867 the parish feast was held on 4 August (Polsue, i, 300), and in 1887 a fair had been recently introduced on the Thursday after 12 May (Boase, 1890, col. 1589).

Dominic, an otherwise unknown female saint, since at least 1259, but twice recorded as a male—perhaps through being identified with the well-known Saint Dominic of Bologna.

Duloe

Lankyp (place) *c.*1286 (Padel, 1976–7, p. 17); *ecclesia Sancti Kybii de Dulo* 1299 (CRO, ME 595–6); *ecclesie Sancti Kibii* 1397 (Rowe, 1914–50, ii, 49); *ecclesia . . . Sancti Kyby* 1411 (Chanter VIII, f. 323). SS Leonard the Abbot and *Koby* the Confessor 1486 (*CPL*, xv, 57); *Cuby* and Leonard 1509 (PROB 11/16, f. 148). *Cuby* 1733 (Willis, p. 173), 1742 (Ecton, p. 182), 1782 (Jones, p. 114); *Keby* 1846 (Oliver, p. 438); *Cuby* 1883 (Kelly); *Cuby* and Leonard 1925 (Henderson, p. 56); *Cuby* 1939 (Kelly), 1996 (*TDD*).

Bishop Stapledon dedicated the church on 15 October 1321 (Chanter II, f. 161v). In 1867 the parish feast was held on 9 November (Polsue, i, 309), and in 1887 there had formerly been a fair on the second Monday in April (Boase, 1890, col. 1589).

The male saint Cuby (Welsh Cybi) since at least the late 13th century (compare Cuby). Leonard was added as co-patron by 1486—a fact forgotten from the Reformation till the 20th century.

East Looe

Mary 1259 (Chanter I, f. 8), 1519 (PROB 11/19, f. 201). Not in the 18th-century directories. Mary 1814 (Lysons, p. 217). Anne 1846 (Oliver, p. 441). Mary 1883 (Kelly), 1925 (Henderson, p. 125), 1939 (Kelly).

Bishop Bronescombe dedicated the chapel on 11 October 1259 (Chanter I, f. 8). In 1887, no parish feast was held but there was a fair on 13 February (Boase, 1890, col. 1591).

Mary since at least 1259, Oliver alone dissenting.

Egloshayle

Patricke 1563 (RIC, Henderson, East Cornwall Book, p. 115, quoting a now lost will). Unknown 1733 (Willis, p. 172), 1742 (Ecton, p. 181), 1782 (Jones, p. 110), 1846 (Oliver, p. 438). *Helie* 1883–1928 (Kelly). *Petrocus* 1925 (Henderson, p. 57); *Petroc* 1935 (Kelly), 1939 (ibid.), 1996 (*TDD*).

In 1887, no parish feast was held but there was a fair on Whit Monday (Boase, 1890, col. 1589).

Probably Petroc before the Reformation, since there are no clearly attested church dedications in the South West to Patrick, whereas Petroc was often spelt in this way by the 16th century. The dedication was forgotten after the Reformation. By the late 19th century, Egloshayle (actually meaning 'church on an estuary') was interpreted as 'church of a saint called Helie', because such a person occurs in the Cornish legend of Brychan (Orme, 1992c, p. 137). This is a mistake, but is sometimes repeated by 20th-century scholars. The 1563 evidence was recovered by Henderson in 1925, and has since become established.

Egloskerry

Keri (saint's name) 12th century (14th) (Grosjean, 1953, pp. 397–8); *capellam de Eglescheria* (place) 1159 x 1181 (15th) (Hull, 1987, p. 6); *Egloskery* (place) 1194 x 1202 (15th) (Barlow, 1996, no. 201c); *capellam . . . Sancte Kerie* 1506 (Chanter XIII, f. 148). Petroc 1733 (Willis, p. 171), 1742 (Ecton, p. 180), 1782 (Jones, p. 109). *Kyryasius* or *Kyriacus* 1814 (Lysons, p. 84). *Ide* and *Lydy* (a mistake for St Issey) 1846 (Oliver, p. 438). *Cyriacus* or Petroc 1883–1926 (Kelly). *Keria* 1925 (Henderson, p. 58); *Kyriacus* or Petroc 1939 (Kelly). Petroc and *Keri* 1996 (*TDD*).

In 1887 the parish feast was held on Whit Monday (Boase, 1890, col. 1589).

The patron saint is first recorded in the latinized female form Keria in 1506. But Keri appears in the 12th century in a list of saints with associations with north Cornwall, probably as patron of this church (Orme, 1992c, p. 145). He was then believed to be male and was regarded as one of the 24 children of the Welsh king Brychan. Eglescheria means 'church of Keri', and it may have been the latinization of the place-name with a female ending that caused Keri later to be regarded as a female. The saint was forgotten after the Reformation, being replaced by Petroc in the 18th century and by other suggestions in the 19th.

St Endellion: parish and prebendal church

Endilient (saint's name) 12th century (14th) (Grosjean, 1953, pp. 397–8); *ecclesia Sancte Endeliente* 1268 (Chanter I, f. 38); *Endelienta* 1291 (Tax.); *ecclesia . . . Sancte Endeliente* 1376 (Chanter VII, f. 46); *Endelian* 1733 (Willis, p. 172), 1742 (Ecton, pp. 1, 81); *Endelion* 1782 (Jones, p. 110); *Endelienta* 1846 (Oliver, p. 438), 1925 (Henderson, p. 59), 1939 (Kelly), 1996 (*TDD*).

In 1887 the parish feast was held on Ascension Day and a fair on the second Tuesday in September (Boase, 1890, col. 1589).

Endilient or -elient, a female saint, since at least 1268 and probably since at least the 12th century when she occurs in a list of saints connected with north Cornwall (Orme, 1992c, p. 130).

St Enoder

Heglosenvder (place) 1086 (DB 4/12); *ecclesias . . . de Sancto Enodoro* 1270 (Chanter I, f. 44v); *ecclesie Sancti Enodri* 1263 (ibid., f. 48); *ecclesie Sancti Ennederi* 1272 (ibid., f. 49v); *ecclesia Enodry* 1291 (Tax.); *St Tenoder* 1522 (PROB 11/20, f. 229v); *Ennoder* 1733 (Willis, p. 169); *Enoder* alias *Eneder* 1742 (Ecton, p. 178); *Enoder* alias *Enedor* 1782 (Jones, p. 103); *Athenodorus* 1814 (Lysons, p. 88); *Ennodorus* 1846 (Oliver, p. 438), 1883 (Kelly); *Enodrus* 1925 (Henderson, p. 62); *Enoder* 1939 (Kelly), 1996 (*TDD*).

In 1887 the parish feast was held on the Sunday nearest to the last Thursday in April, with fairs on Ascension Day and Michaelmas Day (Boase, 1890, col. 1589).

Enoder, an otherwise unknown male saint, since at least the 11th century.

St Enodoc

Capellis . . . de Sancto Wenedoco 1299 (ECA, D&C 2125); *capelle . . . Sancti Guinedoci* 1434 (Chanter XI, f. 107v). *Ennoder* (*sic*) 1733 (Willis, p. 173). Not in Ecton (1742) or Jones (1782). *Enodor* 1846 (Oliver, p. 441). *Enodock* 1883 (Kelly); *Guinedocus* 1925 (Henderson, p. 144); *Enodoc* 1939 (Kelly), 1996 (*TDD*).

In 1434 the dedication feast was moved from 24 to 13 July (Chanter XI, f. 107v).

Enodoc (perhaps from Guenodoc), an otherwise unknown male saint, since at least 1299, sometimes confused with Enoder.

St Erme

Ecclesie Sancti Hermetis 1250 (late 14th) (Hull, 1962, p. 18); *ecclesiam Sancti Ermetis* 1283 (Chanter I, f. 120v); *ecclesia Sancti Hermetis* 1283 (ibid., f. 122); *ecclesia de Sancto Ermete* 1291 (Tax.); *ecclesie Sancti Ermetis* 1391 (Chanter VI, f. 220), 1432 (Chanter X, f. 108); *Seynt Irme*, also *Erme* (place) 1503 (Chanter XII (ii), Arundell f. 8v); *Ermets* 1733 (Willis, p. 170); *Ermett* 1742 (Ecton, p. 176); *Ermet* 1782 (Jones, p. 99); *Hermes* 1846 (Oliver, p. 438), 1925 (Henderson, p. 62), 1939 (Kelly), 1996 (*TDD*).

Bishop Stapledon dedicated the high altar of the church of *Sancti Ermetis*, i.e. this church or St Ervan, on 16 July 1318 (Chanter II, f. 128). In 1878 the parish feast was said to have been held on the last Sunday in August until 1788, when it was moved to the last Sunday in October (Boase, 1890, col. 1589).

The saint may originally have been a distinct Celtic Erme, like the place-name (compare St Ervan). His name first occurs in 1250, however, in the latinized form of Hermes and he may therefore have been identified with the Roman saint of that name. On the other hand, William Worcester noted in 1478 a 'St Hermes confessor of the people of Cornwall' (Worcester, 1969, p. 102), so the saint may have continued to be regarded as Cornish, albeit with a latinized name.

St Erney

Capella Sancti Ter . . . 1269 (Chanter I, f. 42); *capelle Sancti Ternini* 1430 (Chanter X, f. 36v); *capella Sancti Ternini* 1434 (ibid., f. 118); *capelle . . . Sancti Terninii* 1449 (Chanter XI, f. 324v); *Erney* (Willis, p. 165). Not in Ecton (1742). Unknown 1754 (Ecton, p. 627). Not in Jones (1782). *Erney* 1787 (Jones supplement, p. 4), 1846 (Oliver, p. 438); *Terninus* 1925 (Henderson, p. 63); *Erney* 1939 (Kelly), 1996 (*TDD*).

In 1878 no parish feast was held (Boase, 1890, col. 1589).

Terney, an otherwise unknown male saint (compare North Hill), since at least 1269. Later, the initial T was lost through the use of the title 'St'.

St Erth

Ecclesie de Erchi, ecclesiam Sancti Erchi 13th century (15th) (ECA, D&C 3672, p. 55); *vicarie Sancti Ercii* 13th century (ECA, D&C 3625, f. 92v), 1349 (Chanter V, f. 84v), 1391 (Chanter VI, f. 220); *ecclesiam . . . Sancti Erci*, also *Ercy* 1440 (Chanter X, f. 183); *ecclesie . . . Sancti Erci* 1460 (Chanter XII (i), f. 14); *S. Erth(e) c.*1540 (Leland, 1907–10, i, 191–2). *Hiertha* 1733 (Willis, p. 167). *Earth* 1742 (Ecton, p. 175), 1782 (Jones, p. 95); *Ercus* 1846 (Oliver, p. 438), 1925 (Henderson, p. 63), 1939 (Kelly); *Erth* 1996 (*TDD*).

In 1878 the parish feast was held on the nearest Sunday to All Souls' Day (2 November) (Boase, 1890, col. 1589).

Erch, a male saint, since at least the 13th century. He is sometimes regarded as identical with the Irishman Erc of Slane, but as there is little evidence of Irish saint cults in medieval Cornwall he may have been distinct and Cornish.

St Ervan

Ecclesiam Sancti Hermetis 1258 (Chanter I, f. 4); *ecclesia Sancti Hermetis* 1291 (Tax.); *Ervan* 1733 (Willis, p. 168); *Erven* 1742 (Ecton, p. 178); *Ervan* 1782 (Jones, p. 103); *Hermes* 1846 (Oliver, p. 438); *Ervan* 1883 (Kelly); *Hermes* 1925 (Henderson, p. 64); *Ervan* 1939 (Kelly), 1996 (*TDD*).

Bishop Stapledon dedicated the high altar of the church of *Sancti Ermetis*, i.e. this church or St Erme, on 16 July 1318 (Chanter II, f. 128). In 1878 the parish feast was held on the first Sunday after 10 October, with fairs on 25 May and the first Tuesday in October (Boase, 1890, col. 1589).

This saint may originally have been a distinct Celtic Ervan or Erven, but the medieval references to him are latinized as Hermes. For possible identifications, see above under St Erme.

St Eval

Ecclesie Sancti Vuelis 1260 (Chanter I, f. 14; *ecclesia de Sancto Uvelo* 1291 (Tax.); *ecclesiam Sancti Uvely* 1297 (ECA, D&C 1471; Oliver, 1861, p. 429); *ecclesie ... Sancti Vueli* 1424 (Chanter X, f. 68); *Eval* 1733 (Willis, p. 168); *Evall* 1742 (Ecton, p. 178), 1782 (Jones, p. 104); *Uvelus* 1846 (Oliver, p. 438); *Eval* or *Uval* 1883 (Kelly); *Uvelus* 1925 (Henderson, p. 64); *Eval* or *Uval* 1939 (Kelly); *Uvelas* 1996 (*TDD*).

In 1878 the parish feast was held on the Sunday nearest to 20 November (Boase, 1890, col. 1589).

Eval or Uvel, a male saint also honoured in Brittany, since at least 1260.

St Ewe

Euai (saint's name) 10th century (Olson and Padel, 1986, p. 61); *ecclesia Sancte Ewe* 1282 (Chanter I, f. 116), 1291 (Tax;), 1396 (Chanter VIII, f. 8); *ecclesiam ... de Sancta Ewa* 1427 (Chanter X, f; 78); *ecclesiam ... Sancte Ebbe alias Sancte Ewe* 1479 (Chanter XII (ii), f. 86v); *ecclesiam ... de Sancta Ewa alias Sancto Eustachio* 1524 (Chanter XIV, f. 19); *Eva alias Ewe* 1733 (Willis, p. 170); *Eva alias Tue* 1742 (Ecton, p. 176); *Eva alias Ewe* 1782 (Jones, p. 99); *Ewa* or *Eustachius* 1846 (Oliver, p. 438). All Saints or *Ewe* 1883 (Kelly). *Ewa* 1925 (Henderson, p. 65). All Saints or *Ewe* 1939 (Kelly); All Saints 1996 (*TDD*).

In 1878 the parish feast was held on 1 November, with fairs on the second Tuesday in April and October (Boase, 1890, col. 1589).

Ewa since at least 1282 and probably since at least the 10th century, since she occurs in the early list of Cornish saints. She is otherwise unknown, but at times she was interpreted as being the Saxon female saint Ebbe (1479) and the male St Eustace (1524). Since 1883, directories have given All Saints as an alternative or sole dedication, presumably through a conjecture from (or preference for) the parish feast day.

Falmouth

Charles king and martyr 1665 (Oliver, 1846, p. 438); *King Charles the Martyr* 1733 (Willis, p. 166); *Charles I* 1814 (Lysons, p. 103); *Charles the Martyr* 1742 (Ecton, p. 182); *St, also King, Charles the Martyr* 1754 (Ecton, pp. 128, 134), 1782 (Jones, p. 91); *King Charles the Martyr* 1883 (Kelly), 1925 (Henderson, p. 65), 1939 (Kelly), 1996 (*TDD*).

In 1878 no parish feast day was held (Boase, 1890, col. 1589).

King Charles I since the foundation (compare Plymouth).

Feock

Lanfioc (place) *c.*1160, 1167 (17th) (Bodleian, MS James 23, pp. 156, 168); *ecclesiam Sancte Feoce* 1264 (Chanter I, f. 171); *ecclesia de Sancto Feoco* 1291 (Tax.); *ecclesie Sancte Feoce* 1315 (Chanter II, f. 108v), 1393 (Chanter VII, f. 145); *vicaria de Sancto Feoco* 1463 (Chanter XII (i), f. 46); *ecclesiam ... Sancte Feoce* 1501 (ibid., (ii), Redmayn f. 20v); *Feoke* 1733 (Willis, p. 170); *Feoke* 1742 (Ecton, p. 178), 1782 (Jones, p. 102); *Feoca* 1846 (Oliver, p. 438), 1883 (Kelly), 1925 (Henderson, p. 66); *Feock* 1939 (Kelly), 1996 (*TDD*).

In 1878 the parish feast was held on 2 February (Boase, 1890, col. 1589).

Fioc since at least 1264 and probably (in view of the place-name) since at least the mid 12th century. The saint, otherwise unknown, was usually regarded as female but twice as male.

Forrabury

John Leland, visiting Boscastle in about 1540, noted that 'there is a chirch in it, as I remembre, of S. Simphorian' (Leland, 1907–10, i, 176); *Simphorian* 1733 (Willis, p. 172); *Symphorian* 1742 (Ecton, p. 182); *Simphorian* 1754 (Ecton, p. 133), 1782 (Jones, p. 113); *Symphorianus* 1846 (Oliver, p. 439); *Symphorian* 1883 (Kelly). Unknown 1925 (Henderson, p. 66). *Symphorian* 1939 (Kelly), 1996 (*TDD*).

In 1878 fairs were held on 5 August and 22 November (Boase, 1890, col. 1589).

Leland's reference may be either to Forrabury or to Minster nearby, church of St Matherian. Minster church is called the parish church of Minster and Boscastle in 1468 (Chanter XII (ii), f. 12v). If his reference was to Forrabury, then this church was indeed dedicated to the male Roman martyr Symphorian before the Reformation, perhaps suggested by the place-name. If he meant Minster, then Symphorian is a misunderstood or rationalized form of Matherian. It has, however, been associated with Forrabury since the 18th century.

Fowey

Ecclesiam Sancti Barriani 1100 x 1135 (Oliver, 1846, pp. 37–8); *ecclesiam Sancti Barriani* 1162 x 1170 (Oliver, 1846, p. 41). *Ecclesias . . . Sancti Fymbriani* 1281 (Oliver, 1846, p. 43); *ecclesie Sancti Fimbarri* 1412 (Chanter IX, f. 143); *ecclesie . . . Sancti Fymbarri* 1461 (Chanter XII (i), f. 16); *ecclesie . . . Sancte Fymbarry* 1465 (ibid., f. 26v). *Sanctus Barnic Episcopus callid anglice Seynt Barre* 1478 (Worcester, 1969, p. 106). *Ecclesiam Sancti Finbarri*, also church of St *Barry* 1500 (PROB 11/12, f. 154). *Saynt Barre* 1504 (PROB 11/14, f. 164v). *S. Fimbarrus c.*1540 (Leland, 1907–10, i, 203); *Fimbarrus* 1733 (Willis, p. 170), 1742 (Ecton, p. 178), 1782 (Jones, p. 102). *Barre*, later Nicholas 1814 (Lysons, p. 111). Nicholas or *Fimbarr* 1846 (Oliver, p. 439). *Fimbarrus* 1883 (Kelly); *Fimbarrus* or *Barry*, later Nicholas 1925 (Henderson, p. 67); *Fimbarrus* 1939 (Kelly), 1996 (*TDD*).

A fair was granted on St Barri's Day in 1316 (*CChR 1300–26*, p. 306). Bishop Grandisson dedicated the church (also the high altar and two others) in honour of St Nicholas, bishop and confessor, on 3 July 1336 (Chanter IV, f. 201). In 1878 the parish feast was held on 31 July and a fair on 1 May (Boase, 1890, col. 1589).

Barri, a male saint (perhaps the Welsh saint Barruc), since at least the 12th century, often identified with the Irish Finbar by the late 13th. Nicholas was a co-patron of the church by 1336 (and was perhaps introduced then).

St Gennys

Sanguinas, also *Sanwinas* 1086 (DB 1/4, 5/7/9); *ecclesiam Sancti Genesii* 1177 x 1184 (15th) (Barlow, 1996, no. 111); Saint *Ginnes* 1244 (Rowe, 1914–50, i, 39); *Sancto Ginasio* 1246 (Rowe, 1914–50, i, 55); *ecclesiam Sancti Genesii* 1238 (15th) (Barlow, 1996, no. 274); *ecclesie Sancti Genisi* 1263 (Chanter I, f. 26v); *ecclesia Sancti Genesii* 1291 (Tax.); *ecclesie . . . Sancti Genisii* 1427 (Chanter X, f. 79); *ecclesie . . . Sancti Genesii* 1548 (Chanter XIV, f. 130); *Ginnis* 1733 (Willis, p. 171); *Genys* alias *Gennes* 1742 (Ecton, p. 179), 1782 (Jones, p. 107); *Genesius* 1846 (Oliver, p. 439), 1883 (Kelly), 1925 (Henderson, p. 68); *Gennys* 1939 (Kelly), 1996 (*TDD*).

In 1878 the parish feast was held on Whit Sunday (Boase, 1890, col. 1589).

Guinas (modern Gennys), a male saint latinized as Genesius, since at least the

11th century. There were Roman and Irish saints with similar names, but he may well have been unique to Cornwall.

St Germans: Augustinian priory and parish church

Missa . . . Germani episcopi 10th century (Bodleian, MS Bodley 572, f. 1); *episcopatus . . . Beati Germani* 936 (17th) (Bodleian, MS James 23, p. 170); *Sancto Germano* 1018 (11th) (ECA, D&C 2524; Kemble, 1839–48, iv, 2–3); *aecclesia S' Germani* 1086 (DB 1/6); *manerium Sancti Germani* 1146 (Blake, 1981, p. 309); *prior Sancti Germani* 1291 (Tax.); *monasterii Sancti Germani Autisiodoren'* 1361 (Chanter III, f. 211v); *S. Germanes* (place) *c.*1540 (Leland, 1907–10, i, 210); *German* 1733 (Willis, p. 165), 1742 (Ecton, p. 173), 1782 (Jones, p. 91); *Germanus* 1846 (Oliver, p. 439), 1883 (Kelly), 1925 (Henderson, p. 70); *Germans* 1939 (Kelly); *Germanus* of Auxerre 1996 (*TDD*).

Bishop Bronescombe dedicated the priory church on 28 August 1261 (Chanter I, f. 21). In 1878 no parish feast was held but there was a fair on 28 May (Boase, 1890, col. 1589).

German since at least the 10th century, identified by at least 1361 with German of Auxerre.

Germoe

Sancto Tyrno (sic) 1270 (PRO, JUST 1/179, m. 3); *Germogh* (place) 1334 (Glasscock, 1975, p. 30); *capelle Sancti Girmow* 1410 (Chanter VIII, f. 314v); *capella . . . Sancti Girmoci* 1418 (Chanter IX, f. 264v); *instauro Sancte Gyrmoce* 1445 (Chanter XI, f. 512); *Sanctus Gyermocus episcopus* 1478 (Worcester, 1969, p. 28); *S. Germocus, S. Germoke c.*1540 (Leland, 1907–10, i. 188); *Germock* 1733 (Willis, p. 166); *Germowe* 1742 (Ecton, p. 173); *Germoe* 1782 (Jones, p. 91); *Germocus* 1846 (Oliver, p. 439); *Germoe* 1883 (Kelly); *Germochus* 1925 (Henderson, p. 72). Not stated 1939 (Kelly). *Germoe* 1996 (*TDD*).

In 1878 the parish feast was held on the Sunday after the first Saturday in May (Boase, 1890, col. 1589).

Germoc or Girmoc, a male saint, since at least 1270. By the 16th century he was regarded as a companion of Breac of Breage.

Gerrans

Gerent (saint's name) 10th century (Olson and Padel, 1986, p. 45); *ecclesiam Sancti Gerent'* 1202 (ECA, D&C 1397; Barlow, 1996, no. 208); *ecclesiam Sancti Gerendi* 1260 (Chanter I, f. 15v), 1291 (Tax.); *ecclesie Sancte Gerende* 1333 (Chanter IV, f. 169); *capella Sancte Gerende* 1335 (ibid., f. 12); *ecclesie . . . Sancti Gerendi* 1362 (Chanter V, f. 139v); *Sancti Gerendi . . . ecclesiarum* 1422 (Chanter X, f. 56); *S. Geron's c.*1540 (Leland, 1907–10, i, 201); *Gerens* 1733 (Willis, p. 170). *Gurons* 1742 (Ecton, p. 177); *Guron* 1782 (Jones, p. 99). *Gerendus* 1846 (Oliver, p. 439), 1883 (Kelly), 1925 (Henderson, p. 72), 1939 (Kelly); *Gerrans* 1996 (*TDD*).

In 1868 the parish feast was held on the second Sunday in August (Polsue, ii, 77), and in 1878 on the first Sunday after 10 August with a fair on the Tuesday two weeks before Whit Tuesday (Boase, 1890, col. 1589).

Gerent, usually a male saint, since at least 1201 and probably since at least the 10th century when he appears in the early list of Cornish saints.

Glasney: collegiate church

Mary and Thomas 1267 (Chanter I, preliminary folios). Thomas the Martyr 1334 (Oliver, 1846, p. 51), 1498 (*CPL*, xvii part i, 53); Thomas 1535 (*Valor*, ii, 392).

Mary and Thomas Becket before the Reformation, Becket being a canonised saint when the church was founded.

St Gluvias

Ecclesia Sancti Glyviaci 1291 (Tax.); *ecclesiarum Sanctorum . . . Gluviaci* 1331 (Chanter IV, f. 33); *ecclesia Sancti Gliwyaci* 1340 (*Nonarum,* p. 348); *Gluvias* 1733 (Willis, p. 166), 1742 (Ecton, p. 174), 1782 (Jones, p. 91); *Gluviacus* 1846 (Oliver, p. 439); *Gluvias* 1883 (Kelly); *Gluviacus* martyr 1925 (Henderson, p. 74); *Gluvias* 1939 (Kelly), 1996 (*TDD*).

Bishop Stapledon dedicated the church on 25 July and the high altar on 18 August 1318 (Chanter II, f. 128-v). In 1878 the parish feast was held on the first Sunday in May (Boase, 1890, col. 1589).

Gluviac, a male saint, since at least 1291.

Golant—see St Sampson

St Goran (Gorran)

Guron (saint's name) 10th century (Olson and Padel, 1986, pp. 60–1); *Sanctus Goranus* 1086 (Exon, p. 66); *Langoron* (place) 1201 (Stenton, 1952, pp. 464, 505); *ecclesias . . . de Sancto Gorono* 1270 (Chanter I, f. 44v); *ecclesie de Sancto Gorrono* 1270 (ibid., f. 45v); *ecclesia Sancti Goroni* 1291 (Tax.), 1340 (*Nonarum,* p. 343), 1372 (Chanter VII, f. 19v), 1422 (Chanter X, f. 55); *Goran* 1733 (Willis, p. 170), 1742 (Ecton, p. 177), 1782 (Jones, p. 99); *Goronus* 1846 (Oliver, p. 439); *Goran* 1883 (Kelly); *Goronus* 1925 (Henderson, p. 74); *Goran* 1939 (Kelly); *Goranus* 1996 (*TDD*).

In 1878 the parish feast was held on the Sunday after Easter Day (Boase, 1890, col. 1589).

Guron or Goron, a male saint said to have moved here from Bodmin, since at least 1086 and probably since at least the 10th century as he appears in the early list of Cornish saints.

Grade

Ecclesie Sancte Crucis 1261 (Chanter I, f. 18). *Ecclesia Sancte Grade* 1291 (Tax.); *ecclesie Sancte Grande* (*sic*) 1310 (Chanter II, f. 192v). *Ecclesia Sancte Crucis* 1317 (ibid., f. 119v), 1409 (Chanter IX, f. 107v). *Grade* 1733 (Willis, p. 166); *Grada* 1742 (Ecton, p. 174). Holy Cross 1754 (Ecton, p. 627). *Grada* 1782 (Jones, extra p. 4). Holy Cross and *Gradus* 1846 (Oliver, p. 439); *Grade* and Holy Cross 1883 (Kelly); Holy Cross or *Grada* 1925 (Henderson, p. 75); *Grade* and Holy Cross 1939 (Kelly); *Grada* and Holy Cross 1996 (*TDD*).

In 1868 the parish feast was held on the nearest Sunday to St Luke's Day (18 October) (Polsue, ii, 111).

Grade, an otherwise unknown female saint, since at least 1291: probably the original patron. The church was also dedicated to Holy Cross by 1261.

Gulval

Sancte Weluede (*sic*) 1302 (PRO, JUST 1/117, m. 69); *vicaria Sancte Welvele* 1328 (Chanter V, f. 3v); *ecclesie . . . Sancte Golvele* 1410 (Chanter VIII, f. 314v); *ecclesie . . . Sancte Weluele* 1435 (Chanter X, f. 128); *ecclesie . . . Sancte Welvele* 1508 (Chanter XIII, f. 27v). *Eval* 1733 (Willis, p. 168). *Gulwall* 1742 (Ecton, p. 175), 1782 (Jones, p. 96); *Gudwal* 1846 (Oliver, p. 439); *Gulwal* 1883 (Kelly); *Wolvela* 1925 (Henderson, p. 76); *Gulval* 1939 (Kelly), 1996 (*TDD*).

Bishop Grandisson dedicated the high altar on 10 July 1336 (Chanter IV, f. 201). In 1878 the parish feast was held on the Sunday nearest to 12 November (Boase, 1890, col. 1590).

Gwelvel (modern Gulval) since at least 1302. The saint, a female, is otherwise unknown, since the form of her name and her gender differ from those of the better-known Breton saint Gudwal.

Gunwalloe

Capelle Sancte Wynwole (sic) 1433 (Chanter XI, f. 503); *Wynwallow* 1549 (Snell, c.1955, p. 14); *Wynnwallow* 1733 (Willis, p. 166); *Wynwallow* 1742 (Ecton, p. 173), 1782 (Jones, p. 91); *Winwaloe* 1814 (Lysons, pp. 126–7); *Wynwolaus* 1846 (Oliver, p. 439); *Wynwallow* 1883 (Kelly); *Winwolaus* 1925 (Henderson, p. 77); *Winwalloe* 1939 (Kelly), 1996 (*TDD*).

In 1878 the parish feast was held on the last Sunday in April (Boase, 1890, col. 1590).

The Breton saint Winwaloe since at least 1433.

Gwennap

Lanwenap (place) 1199 (Henderson, 1932–3, p. 350); *ecclesie Sancte Weneppe* 1269 (Chanter I, f. 41); *ecclesia Sancte Veneppe* 1291 (Tax.); *Sancte Wenneppe . . . ecclesiarum* 1391 (Chanter VI, f. 220), 1411 (Chanter VIII, f. 143v); *Wenapa* 1733 (Willis, p. 166); *Wenap* 1742 (Ecton, p. 174), 1782 (Jones, p. 93); *Wenepe* or *Wenap* 1814 (Lysons, p. 127); *Weneppa* 1846 (Oliver, p. 439); *Wennap* 1883 (Kelly); *Weneppa* 1925 (Henderson, p. 77), 1939 (Kelly), 1996 (*TDD*).

In 1878 the parish feast was held on Whit Monday and the following days (Boase, 1890, col. 1590).

Gwenep or Gwenap, a female saint, since at least 1269 and probably since at least 1199 in view of the place-name.

Gwinear

Ecclesie Sancti Wyneri 1258 (Chanter I, f. 5); *ecclesia de Sancto Wyniero* 1286 (ibid., f. 130v); *ecclesia Sancti Wynieri* 1291 (Tax.); *ecclesie . . . Sancti Winneri* 1438 (Chanter X, f. 164v); *ecclesie . . . Sancti Wynneri* 1442 (Chanter XI, f. 509); *fraternitati sancti Whynnery* 1445 (Chanter XI, f. 512); *ecclesie . . . Sancti Winnieri* 1523 (Chanter XIV, f. 15); *Wymer* 1733 (Willis, p. 168); *Wynar* 1742 (Ecton, p. 176), 1782 (Jones, p. 97); *Winnierus* 1846 (Oliver, p. 439); *Gwinear* or *Wynar* 1883 (Kelly); *Winierus* or *Fingar* 1925 (Henderson, p. 78); *Gwinear* 1939 (Kelly); *Winnear* 1996 (*TDD*).

In 1878 the parish feast was held on the Sunday after the first Thursday in May (Boase, 1890, col. 1590).

Gwinear or Gwinier since at least 1258, a male saint later believed to have been martyred in the vicinity.

Gwithian

Guidian (saint's name) 10th century (Olson and Padel, 1986, p. 49); *parochia Sancti Goythiani* 1334 (Glasscock, 1975, p. 30); *Gwithian* 1733 (Willis, p. 168); *Gothian* 1742 (Ecton, p. 175), 1782 (Jones, p. 96); *Gothianus* 1846 (Oliver, p. 439). *Felix* and *Gothian* 1883–1906 (Kelly). *Gothian* 1910–1939 (Kelly); *Gocianus* 1925 (Henderson, p. 80); *Gwithian* 1996 (*TDD*).

In 1868 and 1887 the parish feast was held on the nearest Sunday to All Saints' Day (1 November) (Polsue, ii, 162; Boase, 1890, col. 1590).

Gwithian, a male saint also honoured in Brittany, since at least 1334 and pos-

sibly since at least the 10th century since he appears in the early list of Cornish saints. Felix was imported by mistake from Phillack nearby.

Helland

Church of *Sancti Senniani* (or *Seninani*) 1443 (DRO, Catalogue of Exeter City Library Deeds, 31,931 (the original deed is lost); Picken, 1947–9, pp. 342–3); *Sancti Siniani* (or *Simani*, or *Sunani*) 1502 (*CPL*, xvii part i, 423). Unknown, corrected to Helena 1733 (Willis, pp. 172, 231). Helena 1742 (Ecton, p. 181), 1782 (Jones, p. 111), 1846 (Oliver, p. 439), 1883 (Kelly). Unknown 1925 (Henderson, p. 81). Helena 1939 (Kelly), 1996 (*TDD*).

In 1878 the parish feast was held on Easter Monday with a fair formerly on 2 October (Boase, 1890, col. 1590).

The two medieval references can each be deciphered in different ways, but together they seem to point to a male saint called Sennian or Sinian. The form of his name is different from that of Sithney; it comes closer to that of Sennan, but that saint was regarded as a woman, so the saint of Helland may be unique. The dedication was forgotten after the Reformation, and from 1733 to 1939 Helena was usually postulated from the place-name which actually means 'ancient church site' (Padel, 1988, p. 96).

Helston: St John hospital

John the Baptist 1240, 1548 (Orme and Webster, 1995, pp. 193–6).
John the Baptist, a common hospital dedication.

Helston: St Mary Magdalene hospital

Mary Magdalene 1398, 1411; Margaret 1419 (Orme and Webster, 1995, pp. 197–8).
Mary Magdalene, a common hospital dedication; Margaret in 1419 must be a mistake.

Helston: parish church

Michael 1420 (PROB 11/2B, f. 400), 1549 (Snell, *c.*1955, p. 18), 1733 (Willis, p. 167), 1742 (Ecton, p. 174), 1782 (Jones, p. 92), 1814 (Lysons, p. 134), 1846 (Oliver, p. 439), 1883 (Kelly), 1925 (Henderson, p. 81), 1939 (Kelly), 1996 (*TDD*).

In 1868 the parish feast was held on 8 May (one of the feasts of St Michael) (Polsue, ii, 182), and in 1878 on 8 May and 29 September with various other fair days (Boase, 1890, col. 1590).
Michael since at least 1420.

St Hilary

Hilary 1179 (*Cartulaire des Iles Normandes*, Société Jersiaise, 1920, i, 16–19), 1205 (Oliver, 1846, p. 253), 1261 (Chanter I, f. 20v), 1291 (Tax.); *Hillary* 1733 (Willis, p. 168); *Illarii* 1742 (Ecton, p. 175); *Illarii* alias *Hillary* 1782 (Jones, p. 96); Hilary 1846 (Oliver, p. 439), 1883 (Kelly), 1925 (Henderson, p. 82), 1939 (Kelly), 1996 (*TDD*).

In 1878 the parish feast was held on 13 January (St Hilary's Day) (Boase, 1890, col. 1590).
Hilary bishop of Poitiers since at least 1179.

Illogan

Ecclesia Sancti Illogani 1291 (Tax.); *ecclesiam Sancti Elugani*, also *Eulugani* 1308 (Chanter II, f. 31); *ecclesie Sancti Yllugani* 1310 (ibid., f. 47); *ecclesiam Sancti Yllogani*

1310 (ibid., f. 50v); *ecclesiam Sancti Illogani* 1382 (Chanter VII, f. 77), 1436 (Chanter X, f. 146v), 1479 (Chanter XII (ii), f. 86v), 1493 (ibid., f. 164), 1533 (Chanter XIV, f. 66). *Illogan* and Edmund 1543, 1548 (Henderson, 1953–60, p. 224). *Illogan* 1733 (Willis, p. 168), 1742 (Ecton, p. 175), 1782 (Jones, p. 96); *Ylloganus* or *Euluganus* 1846 (Oliver, p. 439); *Illogan* 1883 (Kelly). *Illoganus* and Edmund 1925 (Henderson, p. 83). *Illogan* 1939 (Kelly), 1996 (*TDD*).

In 1860 the parish feast was held on the Sunday nearest to St Luke's Day (18 October) (Polsue, ii, 225), and in 1878 on the Sunday nearest to 20 October (Boase, 1890, col. 1590).

Illogan, a male saint believed to be buried in the church, since at least 1291. Edmund was apparently added as a co-patron by the mid 16th century, but has rarely been remembered in modern times.

St Issey

Feudum Sancti Iti ?1161 x ?1162 (Barlow, 1996, no. 122); *in Sancto Ydi* 1195 (Stenton, 1929, p. 134); *villa de Seint Idde* 1198–9 (*Feet of Fines*, 1900, p. 237); *villa de Sancto Idi* 1198–9 (ibid., p. 224); *ecclesia Sancte Ide* 1257 x 1280 (ECA, D&C 3625, f. 91). *Parochia Sanctorum Id' et Lid'* 1287 (CRO, ME 595–6). *De Sancta Ida* 1302 (PRO, JUST 1/117, m. 58d); *ecclesie . . . Sancte Ide* 1334 (Chanter V, f. 28), 1334 (Glasscock, 1975, p. 32), 1340 (*Nonarum*, p. 349). *Ecclesie Sanctorum Ide et Lydi* 1382 (Chanter VI, f. 71); *parochia Sanct' Ide et Lide* 1383 (ibid., f. 109); *ecclesie . . . Sanctorum Ide et Lydy* 1384 (ibid., f. 112); *ecclesia Sanctorum Idi et Lidi* 1399 (Chanter VIII, f. 31). *Parochia Sancte Cisie* 1424 (Chanter XI, f. 35); *ecclesie . . . Sancte Ide* 1440 (Chanter X, f. 190); *ecclesie Sancti Ide* 1444 (Chanter X, f. 213); *ecclesie . . . Sancte Ide* 1462 (Chanter XII (i), f. 16v); *ecclesie . . . Sancte Ide* 1522 (Chanter XIII, f. 13); *ecclesie . . . de Sancta Ida*, also *Sancte Ide* 1543 (Chanter XIV, ff. 110v–111); *Essy* 1733 (Willis, p. 168); *Esye* alias *Issye* alias *Ithy* 1742 (Ecton, p. 178), 1782 (Jones, p. 104). *Filius* 1846 (Oliver, p. 439). *Issey* 1883 (Kelly); *Ida* or *Idi* 1925 (Henderson, p. 83); *Issey* 1939 (Kelly), 1996 (*TDD*).

In 1878 the parish feast was held on the Sunday nearest to 20 November (Boase, 1890, col. 1590).

The earliest saint mentioned was latinized as Ida or Idus and recorded at first as male but later usually as female. He or she was probably the same as Idi, the joint patron saint of Mevagissey, where the saint was usually female and was coupled with another female saint. At St Issey he or she shared the patronage between at least 1287 and 1399 with a saint latinized as Lydus and usually regarded as male. He was possibly identical with Elid or Lyde of the Isles of Scilly.

St Ive

Ecclesie Sancti Hyvon' 1258 (Chanter I, f. 5); *ecclesia Sancti Ivonis* 1291 (Tax.); *Ivo* 1733 (Willis, p. 165); *Ives* 1742 (Ecton, p. 172), 1782 (Jones, p. 88); *Ivo* 1846 (Oliver, p. 439), 1883 (Kelly), 1925 (Henderson, p. 84); *Ive* 1939 (Kelly), 1996 (*TDD*).

The bishop of Waterford dedicated the church in 1338–9 (Chanter IV, f. 220v). In 1878 no parish feast was held but a fair formerly took place on the last Thursday in April (Boase, 1890, col. 1590).

Ivo or Ives, a male saint, since at least 1258. He was apparently the so-called Persian bishop, patron of St Ives near Huntingdon.

St Ives

Roda Sancte Ye 1284 (PRO, JUST 1/112, m. 3); *Porthye* (place) 1284 (ibid., m. 24); *Porthia* (place) 1291 (Tax); *capella Sancte Hye* 1340 (*Nonarum*, p. 348); *capellarum*

Sanctorum . . . Ye virginis 1409 (Chanter IX, f. 232v); *Sent Ives* (place) 1478 (Worcester, 1969, p. 34); *Sancta Hya* 1478 (ibid., p. 114); store of *Sancte Iye virginis* 1503 (PROB 11/14; 36 Holgrave); *Ja c.*1540 (Leland, 1907–10, i, 192); *Iia* 1733 (Willis, p. 167); *Jesse* alias *Ives* 1742 (Ecton, p. 175); *Jia* 1754 (Ecton, p. 129); *Ives* 1782 (Jones, p. 95); *Hya* or *Ia* 1814 (Lysons, p. 147); *Hya, Ia* or *Ya* 1846 (Oliver, p. 439); *Hya* or *Ia* 1883 (Kelly); *Ia* virgin 1925 (Henderson, p. 85); *Ia* 1939 (Kelly); *Ia* the virgin 1996 (*TDD*).

In 1868 and 1887 the parish feast was held on the Sunday nearest to St Blaise's Day (3 February), with a fair on the Sunday nearest to St Andrew's Day (30 November) (Polsue, ii, 271; Boase, 1890, col. 1590).

Ia or Ya, a female saint since at least 1284, believed in the late legends about her to have come from Ireland. The place was confused with St Ives (Huntingdonshire) as early as 1478.

Jacobstow

Jacobestowe (place) 1270 (Chanter I, f. 44); James 1272 (ibid., f. 50); *Jacobstowe* (place) 1291 (Tax.); *Stawe Sancti Jacobi* (place) 1452 (Chanter X, f. 283). James 1733 (Willis, p. 171), 1742 (Ecton, p. 179), 1782 (Jones, p. 107), 1846 (Oliver, p. 440), 1883 (Kelly), 1925 (Henderson, p. 86), 1939 (Kelly), 1996 (*TDD*).

In 1878 the parish feast was held on the Sunday after 5 August (Boase, 1890, col. 1590).

James since at least 1270.

St John

Ecclesiam Sancti Johannis 1155 x 1160 (13th) (Finberg, 1947, pp. 358, 364, 368; Barlow, 1996, no. 71); John 1272 (Chanter I, f. 49); John the Baptist 1402 (Chanter IX, f. 56v), 1517 (Chanter XIII, f. 70v), 1524 (Chanter XIV, f. 19), 1531 (ibid., f. 53v), 1733 (Willis, p. 165); John 1742 (Ecton, p. 172), 1782 (Jones, p. 88); John the Baptist 1846 (Oliver, p. 440). John the Evangelist 1883 (Kelly). John the Evangelist, later John the Baptist 1925 (Henderson, p. 86). John the Evangelist 1939 (Kelly). John the Baptist 1996 (*TDD*).

In 1878 no parish feast was held (Boase, 1890, col. 1590).

John since at least the mid 12th century. The Baptist would be more likely than the Evangelist, and this was understood to be the case by 1402. However, the Evangelist has sometimes been preferred since the 1880s.

St Juliot

Sangviland (place) 1086 (DB 5/4/6); *Sanguilant* (place) 1086 (Exon, p. 218). *Capellis . . . Sancte Iulitte* 1177 x 1184 (15th) (Barlow, 1996, no. 111); *capelle beate Iulite* 1238 (15th) (Barlow, 1996, no. 274); *capella Sancte Julitte* 1291 (Tax.), 1340 (*Nonarum*, p. 346); *Seynt Julett* 1549 (Snell, *c.*1955, p. 7); *Juliatte* (ibid., p. 50); *Julit* 1733 (Willis, p. 171); *Julet* 1742 (Ecton, p. 180); *Juliet* 1782 (Jones, p. 109); *Julitta* 1846 (Oliver, p. 440); *Julietta* 1883 (Kelly); *Julitta* 1925 (Henderson, p. 86); *Julietta* 1939 (Kelly); *Julitta* 1996 (*TDD*).

In 1878 the parish feast was held on the last Sunday in June or the first Sunday in July (Boase, 1890, col. 1590).

The forms of 1086 point to a place named after a saint called Guiland or Guilant. The saint's name may have been latinized as Julitta while the saint kept a distinct identity (compare Cyricus at St Veep); alternatively, Julitta may indicate that the saint became identified with or replaced by the Roman female saint Julitta.

St Just in Penwith

Ecclesia Sancti Justi 1291 (Tax.); *ecclesie . . . Sancti Justi* 1425 (Chanter X, f. 71); *Sanctus Justus martir* 1478 (Worcester, 1969, p. 96); *Sancti Justi martiris* 1495 (*CPL*, xvi, 280). *S. Just alias Justinian c.*1540 (Leland, 1907–10, i, 317); *Justus* 1733 (Willis, p. 168); *Juste* 1742 (Ecton, p. 175), 1782 (Jones, p. 96); *Justus* 1846 (Oliver, p. 440); *Just* 1883 (Kelly); *Justus* 1925 (Henderson, p. 87); *Just* 1939 (Kelly), 1996 (*TDD*).

Bishop Grandisson dedicated the high altar on 13 July 1336 (Chanter IV, f. 201). In 1878 the parish feast was held on All Saints' Day (1 November), with a fair on St John's Day (Boase, 1890, col. 1590).

Just, a male saint, since at least 1291 (compare the next entry). In the 15th century he was believed to be a martyr buried in the church.

St Just in Roseland

Iust (saint's name) 10th century (Olson and Padel, 1986, pp. 44–5); *ecclesiae Sancti Justi* 1046 x 1072 (17th) (Bodleian, MS James 23, p. 168); *ecclesiam Sancti Justi martyris* 1154 x 1189 (Oliver, 1846, p. 135; cf. p. 138); *ecclesiam Sancti Justi* 1261 (Chanter I, f. 20v); *ecclesia de Sancto Justo* 1291 (Tax.); *S. Just(e) c.*1540 (Leland, 1907–10, i, 200); *Justus* 1733 (Willis, p. 170); *Juste* 1742 (Ecton, p. 177), 1782 (Jones, p. 100); *Justus* 1846 (Oliver, p. 440); *Just* 1883 (Kelly); *Justus* martyr 1925 (Henderson, p. 88); *Just* 1939 (Kelly), 1996 (*TDD*).

Bishop Bronescombe dedicated the church on 14 August 1261 (Chanter I, f. 20v). In 1878 the parish feast was held on 14 August (Boase, 1890, col. 1590).

Just, a male saint, since at least the eleventh century, and probably since at least the tenth as he occurs in the early list of Cornish saints. He is presumably the same as the patron of St Just in Penwith, being regarded as a martyr at both places.

Kea

Sanctus Che 1086 (Exon, p. 66); *Landighe* (place) 1086 (DB 5/24/12). *Parochia Sancte Kycladoce* 1390 (Chanter VI, f. 208); *ecclesiarum . . . Kekaladoci* 1437 (Chanter X, f. 153). *Ecclesie . . . Sancte Kee* 1451 (Chanter X, f. 266v); *S. Cay c.*1540 (Leland, 1907–10, i, 198); *Caius* 1733 (Willis, p. 170). *Cuby* 1742 (Ecton, p. 177), 1782 (Jones, p. 100). Unknown 1846 (Oliver, p. 440). *Kea* 1883 (Kelly); *Keus* or *Ke* 1925 (Henderson, p. 89).

Kea or Cai since at least the 11th century. Usually regarded elsewhere as a male (though twice here as female), he was venerated in Brittany and early churches were named after him at Landkey (Devon) and Leigh-on-Street (Somerset). The form 'Kycladoca' is perhaps a latinization of a Cornish epithet Ke Colethek, 'Kea the cherished' (Dr O.J. Padel, personal communication). In 1896, however, the church was superseded by the present church of All Hallows.

Kenwyn

Capella Sancti Keynwyny 1340 (*Nonarum*, p. 347); *ecclesie Sancti Benewyny* (sic) 1419 (Jacob, ii, 173); *parochie . . . Sancti Kelnewyni* 1419 (PROB 11/2B, f. 365). *Kenwen* 1733 (Willis, p. 170); *Kenwyn* 1742 (Ecton, p. 177), 1782 (Jones, p. 100). Unknown 1846 (Oliver, p. 440). *Kenwyn* 1883 (Kelly). *Cuby* with a query, or *Kenwyn* probably *Keyne* 1925 (Henderson, p. 90). Not stated 1939 (Kelly). *Keyne* 1996 (*TDD*).

Bishop Bronescombe dedicated the church on 27 September 1259 (Chanter I, f. 7v). In 1878 the parish feast was held on the Sunday nearest to 9 October (Boase, 1890, col. 1590).

The place-name Kenwyn probably means 'white ridge' (Padel, 1988, p. 102). By 1340, however, it was regarded as the name of a male saint, who was apparently venerated as its patron during the 14th and 15th centuries. In modern times, other conjectures have been made.

St Keverne

Achobran (saint's name) 10th century (Olson and Padel, 1986, pp. 47–8); *canonici Sancti Achebranni,* also *Sanctus Achabranus* 1086 (DB 4/23); *Sancto Akeverano* 1201 (Rowe, 1914–50, i, 7); *ecclesia Sancti Caveran'* 1235 x 1236 (Barlow, 1996, no. 233); *vicaria Sancti Kerani* 1266 (Chanter I, f. 34v); *vicariam Sancti Keverani* 1269 (ibid., f. 41); *ecclesie Sancti Kaverani* 1269 (ibid., f. 82); *ecclesia Sancti Kerani* 1291 (Tax.); *ecclesia de Kierani* 1340 (*Nonarum,* p. 348); *ecclesiam Sancti Keverani* 1330 (Chanter IV, f. 4v); *ecclesie Sancti Kyerani* 1342 (Chanter IV, f. 46); *ecclesie Sancti Kierani* 1362 (ibid., f. 146v); *ecclesie . . . Sancti Keuerani siue Kyerani* 1464 (Chanter XII (i), f. 17); *Sancti Pierani alias Sancti Kierani* 1497 (CPL, xvi,, 538); *ecclesie . . . de Sancto Kierano* 1524 (Chanter XIV, f. 18); *ecclesie . . . de Sancto Kewrano* 1528 (ibid., f. 37); *Saynt Keuerayne* 1532 (ibid., f. 59v); *Keyran* 1535 (*Valor,* ii, 393); *S. Piranes alias Keuerine c.*1540 (Leland, 1907–10, p. 195); *ecclesie . . . Sancti Keverani alias dicte Sancti Kerani* 1547 (Chanter XIV, f. 126); *Keverne* 1733 (Willis, p. 166); *Keyran* alias *Keverne* 1742 (Ecton, p. 174); *Keverne* 1782 (Jones, p. 92); *Kyeran* 1814 (Lysons, p. 159); *Keveran* or *Kieran* 1846 (Oliver, p. 440); *Kevern* or *Akebronwas* 1883 (Kelly); *Akeveranus* 1925 (Henderson, p. 90); *Kevern* or *Achebron* 1939 (Kelly); *Keverne* 1996 (*TDD*).

In 1868 the parish feast was held five weeks before Christmas (Polsue, ii, 351), and in 1878 on the Sunday nearest 18 November with fairs on the Tuesday after Old Christmas Day and on the Tuesday before Midsummer Day (24 June) (Boase, 1890, col. 1590).

Achevran or Achovran (modern Keverne), a male saint, since at least 1086 and probably since at least the 10th century as he occurs in the early list of Cornish saints. He was probably in origin an independent figure, but by 1266 he was equated with the Irish saint Ciarán of Saighir, and by the 15th both were identified also with Piran. Keverne has been gradually re-established in modern times. See also Exeter: St Kerrian.

St Kew

Docco 7th century (Fawtier, 1912, p. 142). *Monasterium Sancti Dochou et Sancte Cypa* (error for *Cywa*) *c.*962 (14th) (PRO, C47/52/1/1 m. 3; Picken, 1960, p. 38). *Honore S. Chei* 1086 (Exon, f. 245b). *Lannohoo* (place) 1086 (Exon, f. 101a); *Dohou* ?1107 (15th) (Hull, 1987, p. 2); *ecclesiam Sancti Doho* 1146 (Blake, 1981, p. 309); *ecclesia de Lannou* 1291 (Tax.); *Lanhou* 1335 (Chanter II, f. 12). Fraternity of St Kew at *Lannow* 1368 (Webster, 1989, p. 181); chapel *de Seint Kewe* in the cemetery of *Lannou* 1373 (Chanter VII (part ii), f. 21). *Parochia Sancti Doquini* 1400 (Chanter VIII, f. 48). *Ecclesie . . . Sancte Kewe* 1443 (Chanter X, f. 204); *S. Cua c.*1540 (Leland, 1907–10, i, 191); *Kew* 1733 (Willis, p. 172); *Knee* alias *Kew* 1742 (Ecton, p. 181); *Kew* 1782 (Jones, p. 111), 1846 (Oliver, p. 440). James 1883 (Kelly). *Kewa* 1889 (ibid.). *Daw* or *Doquinus* and *Kewa* virgin 1925 (Henderson, p. 93). *Kew* 1939 (Kelly). James the Great 1996 (*TDD*).

In 1868 the parish feast was held on the Sunday nearest to St James's Day (25 July) (Polsue, ii, 362), and in 1878 on St James's Day with a fair on the first Tuesday in April (Boase, 1890, col. 1590).

The first recorded saint cult here is that of Docco or Dochau, whose monastery at Lanow in the modern parish of St Kew is mentioned in the 7th-century Life of St

Sampson. Names like Lanehoc *and* Lanhou *mean 'the church of Docco'; the saint, a man, was also commemorated at Landochau Fawr in Glamorgan.* Docco's *patronage later extended to the parish church along with that of a co-patron, the female saint Cywa (later Kewa or Kew), who is first mentioned in about 962. The parish church was more commonly named after him until the later middle ages, when Kewa gained chief place instead. James has also been current in modern times, influenced by (or through preference for) the parish feast day.*

St Keyne

Ecclesia Sancti (sic) (also *Sancte*) *Kayne* 1291 (Tax.); *Cayne* 1340 (*Nonarum*, p. 342); *ecclesiam . . . Sancte Kayne* 1422 (Chanter X, f. 33v); *ecclesiam . . . Sancte Keyne* 1462 (Chanter XII (i), f. 23v); *Kayne* 1733 (Willis, p. 173); *Kean* 1742 (Ecton, p. 183); *Keane* 1782 (Jones, p. 116); *Keyna* 1846 (Oliver, p. 440); *Keyne* or *Keyna* 1883 (Kelly); *Kayna* virgin 1925 (Henderson, p. 95); *Keyna* 1939 (Kelly), 1996 (*TDD*).

In 1868 the parish feast was held on 30 September (Polsue, ii, 315).

The Welsh female saint Keyne since at least 1291 (compare St Martin by Looe).

Kilkhampton

Mary, with a query 1733 (Willis, p. 171). Philip and James the Less 1740 (MS Willis 41, f. 226a). James 1742 (Ecton, p. 180), 1782 (Jones, p. 108), 1846 (Oliver, p. 440), 1883 (Kelly), 1925 (Henderson, p. 95), 1939 (Kelly); James the Great 1996 (*TDD*).

In 1740 the parish feast was said to be held on 1 May (SS Philip's and James' Day) (MS Willis 41, f. 226a), and in 1878 on St James' Day (25 July), with various other fair days (Boase, 1890, col. 1590).

The medieval dedication has not been discovered, and it was probably forgotten after the Reformation. Philip and James the Less was evidently a conjecture from the parish feast day, carried forward as James alone (implying James the Great) in Ecton's directory and subsequently (compare Huish and Iddesleigh in Devon). It would be unwise to assume from this that James the Great was the medieval dedication, although the church belonged to the priory of St James (Bristol) in the 12th century.

Ladock

Latoc (saint's name) 10th century (Olson and Padel, 1986, p. 52); *ecclesie Sancte Ladoce* 1268 (Chanter I, f. 39); *ecclesia de Sancta Ladoca* 1291 (Tax.); *ecclesiam . . . Sancti Ladoci* 1463 (Chanter XII (i), ff. 25, 81); *ecclesiam Sancte Ladoce* 1472 (ibid., (ii), f. 19v); *Ladoca* 1733 (Willis, p. 170), 1742 (Ecton, p. 177), 1782 (Jones, p. 100), 1846 (Oliver, p. 440), 1883 (Kelly), 1925 (Henderson, p. 98); *Ladock* 1939 (Kelly); *Ladoca* 1996 (*TDD*).

In 1878 the parish feast was held on the first Sunday after 1 January (Boase, 1890, col. 1590).

Ladoc, an otherwise unknown female saint, since at least the 10th century.

Lamanna in Talland: Benedictine priory

Michael x 1114 (Dugdale, 1817–30, iv, 690), 1289 x ? (15th) (Hull, 1987, pp. 168–9); *capelle de Sancta Lamana* 1291 (Tax.).

Michael since at least the early 12th century; the place-name was misunderstood as a saint's name in 1291.

Lamford (now Maudlin) in Lanlivery: hospital

Mary Magdalene 1258 (CRO, AR 50/1; Orme and Padel, 1995, p. 106).

Mary Magdalene, a common hospital dedication.

Lamorran

Lannmoren (place) 969 (Birch, 1885–93, no. 1231); Adam *de Lammoren* (name) 1194 (Stenton, 1928, p. 172); *ecclesiam . . . Sancte Morenne* 1464 (Chanter XII (i), f. 26v); *ecclesiam . . . Sancte Morenne virginis* 1480 (ibid., (ii), f. 89); *ecclesiam . . . Sancte Moreane virginis* 1500 (ibid., Redmayn f. 13v); *chirch of S. Moran* c.1540 (Leland, 1907–10, i, 199); *Moran* 1733 (Willis, p. 170); *Moun* 1742 (Ecton, p. 177); *Moren* 1754 (Ecton, p. 130); *Moran* 1782 (Jones, p. 100). Unknown 1846 (Oliver, p. 440). *Moran* 1883 (Kelly); *Morenna* virgin 1925 (Henderson, p. 99); *Moran* 1939 (Kelly). Not mentioned 1996 (*TDD*).

Bishop Bronescombe dedicated the church on 12 August 1261 (Chanter I, f. 20v). In 1878 no parish feast was held (Boase, 1890, col. 1591).

Lamorran means 'church site of Moren', and by at least the 15th century a saint of this name was regarded as the patron, as a woman and as a virgin; she is otherwise unknown.

Landewednack

Ecclesiam Sancti Wynewali 1279 (Chanter I, f. 91); *ecclesia Sancti Winwolay* 1291 (Tax.); *ecclesiam Sancti Wynwolayi* 1314 (Chanter II, f. 83); *ecclesie Sancti Wynwolay* 1315 (ibid., f. 234v); *ecclesie Sancti Wynvolay* (or *Wynnolay*) 1329 (Chanter IV, f. 28); *ecclesie Sancti Winwolay* 1404 (Chanter IX, f. 78); *Wednack* 1733 (Willis, p. 166). *Lanty* 1742 (Ecton, p. 174); *Lanty* 1754 (Ecton, p. 128), corrected to *Wynwaelog* (ibid., p. 627). *Wynwolas* 1763 (Ecton, p. 128). *Lanty* 1782 (Jones, p. 93), 1786 (Bacon, p. 304). *Winwolaus* 1846 (Oliver, p. 440). *Lanty* or *Winwallow* 1883–1926 (Kelly). *Wynwolaus* 1925 (Henderson, p. 100); *Winwallow* 1935–1939 (Kelly), 1996 (*TDD*).

In 1878 the parish feast was held on the Sunday nearest to 19 June (Boase, 1890, col. 1591).

The Breton saint Winwaloe since at least 1279. This was partly but not altogether forgotten in the 18th century when a St Lanty was invented from the place-name (compare the two churches of Lanteglos). The latter was current as late as 1926.

Landrake

Michael 1434 (Chanter X, f. 118). Peter 1733 (Willis, p. 165), 1742 (Ecton, p. 173), 1782 (Jones, p. 90), 1846 (Oliver, p. 440), 1883–1926 (Kelly). Michael 1925 (Henderson, p. 100), 1935–1939 (Kelly), 1996 (*TDD*).

In 1878 the parish feast was held on 29 June (SS Peter and Paul), with various fair days (Boase, 1890, col. 1591).

Michael before the Reformation; it was then forgotten. Peter from 1733, evidently on the basis of the parish feast day; Michael was recovered in 1925.

Landulph

Landelech (place) 1086 (DB 5/3/26); *Landilp* (place) 1345 (Rowe, 1914–50, i, 342); *Landilpe* (place) 1490 (Chanter XII (ii), f. 113). Leonard 1451 (Oliver, 1854, p. 37). *Dilecta* and Leonard 1515 x 1518 (PRO, C 1/425/25), 1559 (Henderson, 1929). *Dilp* 1733 (Willis, p. 165), 1742 (Ecton, p. 172), 1782 (Jones, p. 88). Unknown 1846 (Oliver, p. 440). *Dilpe* 1856–1889 (Kelly). Leonard 1902–1939 (Kelly). *Dilp* and Leonard 1925 (Henderson, p. 102). Leonard and *Dilpe* 1996 (*TDD*).

In 1878 no parish feast was held (Boase, 1890, col. 1591).

By the early sixteenth century, Landulph had two patron saints: a female one, latinized as Dilecta, and the well-known Leonard. The place-name Landelech recorded in 1086 probably means 'church site of Dylyk or Delyk' (Padel, 1988, p. 106). This may refer to the saint later known as Dilecta, in which case she was originally a Celtic figure; this theory is supported by the existence of a saint with a similar name and gender (Dilic) as patron of a chapel in St Endellion parish (Orme, 1992c, pp. 140–1). Alternatively, Dilecta may be a conjecture based on the place-name. After the Reformation, Leonard was forgotten and Dilp(e) was conjectured from the place-name.

Laneast

Bishop Lacy consecrated the major altar in honour of *Sancte Satiuole virginis* and St Thomas the Martyr 1437 (Chanter XI, f. 143v; another report of the event mentions *capelle . . . Sancte Satiuole virginis et matris (sic)* alone (ibid., f. 424v); *capelle . . . Sancte Satiuole* 1448 (Chanter XI, f. 304). Unknown 1733 (Willis, p. 171), 1742 (Ecton, p. 180). *Gulval* 1754 (Ecton, p. 628); *Gulval* 1782 (Jones, p. 109). *Welvela* and *Sativola* 1846 (Oliver, p. 440), 1883 (Kelly). *Sativola* virgin, or Michael 1925 (Henderson, p. 103). *Sativola* and *Welvella* 1939 (Kelly); Sidwell and *Gulval* 1996 (*TDD*).

The church was dedicated by Bishop Lacy on 21 March 1437 (Chanter XI, f. 427v). In 1878 the parish feast was held on the first Sunday in August (Boase, 1890, col. 1591).

Sidwell (Latin Sativola) and possibly Thomas Becket from at least 1437 until the Reformation; they were then forgotten. Sidwell was a female saint honoured in Exeter (see Exeter: St Sidwell), so this looks like a comparatively late (rather than an early Celtic) dedication. In 1754, the patron saint was believed to be Gulval due to confusion between the names Laneast and Lanestly, the alternative name for the parish of Gulval. Although Sidwell was recovered in 1846, Gulval has continued to be regarded as co-patron saint without any historical justification.

Lanhydrock

Lanhiderek (place) 1302 (Rowe, 1914–50, i, 209–10); *Sanctus Ydrocus* (saint's name) 1478 (Worcester, 1969, p. 88); *Kydrock* 1733 (Willis, p. 172); *Hydrock* 1742 (Ecton, p. 182); *Hydroek* 1782 (Jones, p. 113). Unknown 1846 (Oliver, p. 440). *Hydrock* 1883 (Kelly); *Hydroc* with a query 1925 (Henderson, p. 104); *Hydrock* 1939 (Kelly), 1996 (*TDD*).

In 1878 no parish feast was held (Boase, 1890, col. 1591).

Lanhydroc means 'church site of someone called Hydroc'. Such a person was not necessarily the patron saint, but Worcester's reference to Ydrocus in 1478 (taken from a calendar of saints that he saw at Bodmin Priory, whose canons owned Lanhydroc church) suggests that Hydroc was regarded as the church patron saint by that date. A similar belief has been current since 1742.

Lanivet

Unknown 1733 (Willis, p. 169), 1742 (Ecton, p. 178), 1782 (Jones, p. 104), 1846 (Oliver, p. 440), 1925 (Henderson, p. 104). *Nyvett* with a query 1935–1939 (Kelly). Ia 1996 (*TDD*).

Bishop Stapledon dedicated the high altar and four others on 6 July 1318 (Chanter II, f. 128). The bishop of Waterford dedicated the high altar in 1338–9 (Chanter IV, f. 220v). In 1870 and 1887 the parish feast was held on the Sunday nearest to the last Thursday in April (Polsue, iii, 20; Boase, 1890, col. 1591).

The medieval dedication has not been discovered, and it was forgotten after the Reformation. Nyvett was deduced in 1935 from the place-name, but the latter means 'church site at a place called Neved' (Padel, 1988, p. 106) and therefore tells us nothing about the patron saint. Ia has been adopted in recent times.

Lanlivery

Sancte Breutte, Sancti Breute (sic) 1473 (*CPL*, xiii (i), 337); chancel of *Synt Bryvyth* 1539 (RIC, Henderson, HC 66, p. 134). *Verek* 1733 (Willis, p. 170); *Vorech* 1742 (Ecton, p. 177). *Brevita* 1763 (Ecton, p. 130). *Vorech* 1782 (Jones, p. 100); *Vorck* 1814 (Lysons, p. 179). *Manaccus* and Dunstan (a mistake for Lanreath) 1846 (Oliver, p. 440). *Brevita* 1883 (Kelly); *Bryvyth* 1925 (Henderson, p. 106); *Brevita* 1939 (Kelly), 1996 (*TDD*).

In 1878 and 1887 the parish feast was held on the first Sunday after the first Tuesday in May (Polsue, iii, 20; Boase, 1890, col. 1591).

Bryvyth, apparently regarded as a female saint but otherwise unknown, since at least 1473. The 1763 reference to the Latin form Brevita must be based on a medieval document not yet discovered, as the papal registers were not then known. Vorech and its variants perhaps arose from a mistaken belief that Lavorek, an ancient name for Mevagissey, related to Lanlivery and meant 'church site of Vorech'.

Lanreath

Manakneu 1266 (*CChR 1257–1300*, p. 62); *ecclesiam . . . Sancti Marnarci* 1429 (Chanter X, f. 92v); *ecclesiam . . . sanctorum Manacci* (*Manaci* in margin) *et Dunstani confessorum* 1472 (Chanter XII (ii), f. 21v); *Sanctus Mancus episcopus* 1478 (Worcester, 1969, pp. 96, 106); *Sancti Manacti* (perhaps for *Manacci*) 1497 (*CPL*, xvi, 527). Unknown 1733 (Willis, p. 173), 1742 (Ecton, p. 182). *Marnerch* 1754 (Ecton, p. 628); *Marnarch* 1763 (Ecton, p. 134), 1782 (Jones, p. 114). *Sancredus*; also *Manaccus* and Dunstan 1846 (Oliver, p. 440). *Marnarch* 1883 (Kelly). *Manacus* and Dunstan 1925 (Henderson, p. 106). *Marnarch* 1939 (Kelly); *Marnarck* 1996 (*TDD*).

Bishop Stapledon dedicated the church on 17 October 1321 (Chanter II, f. 162). In 1878 no parish feast was held but there were fairs on Whit Tuesday, 18 November and three weeks after Shrove Tuesday (Boase, 1890, col. 1591).

Manakneu or Manac, a male saint otherwise unknown, since at least 1266. The saint's name is similar to Manacca, said to be the patron saint of Manaccan, but that saint was believed to be female. By 1472 the saint had acquired Dunstan as a co-patron, but the latter was forgotten after the Reformation and revived only as a result of historical research.

Lansallos

St *Heldenus* (saint's name) 925 x 939 (18th) (Bates, 1899, p. 118; Padel, 1978, p. 20); *ecclesiam Sancte Ildierne* 1320 (Chanter II, f. 150); *ecclesiam Sancte Ilderne* 1326 (LPL, Reg. Reynolds, f. 157v; Hingeston-Randolph, 1894–9, i, 21); *ecclesiam de Ildierne* 1326 (LPL, Reg. Reynolds, f. 159v; Hingeston-Randolph, 1894–9, i, 24); *Sanctus Hyldren* 1478 (Worcester, 1969, p. 106). *Alwys* 1733 (Willis, p. 173); *Alwys* 1742 (Ecton, p. 182), 1782 (Jones, p. 114). *Ildierna* 1846 (Oliver, p. 440). *Alwys* or *Ildierna* 1883 (Kelly). *Ildierna* 1925 (Henderson, p. 107). *Alwys* or *Ildierna* 1939 (Kelly). *Ildierna* 1996 (*TDD*).

Bishop Stapledon dedicated the church on 16 October 1321 (Chanter II, f. 162). In 1878 no parish feast was held (Boase, 1890, col. 1591).

The name Lansallos means 'church-site of someone called Salwys', who was not necessarily the patron saint (Padel, 1988, p. 107). By the 10th century, the patron was reckoned to be a saint variously spelt in the sources, Ildiern being a plausible vernacular form. The saint is male in the earliest reference and that of 1478 claims that

*he was a bishop, so perhaps they should carry more weight than the two in the bishops'
registers which are female. In the 18th century, learned opinion considered that the
patron was Salwys, or Alw(e)ys as it was spelt. This was probably a new assumption
drawn from the place-name. Ildiern was recovered in 1846 but in the female form.*

Lanteglos by Camelford

Ecclesia Sancte Julitte 1291 (Tax.), 1340 (*Nonarum,* p. 346). *Lanty* 1733 (Willis, p.
172), 1742 (Ecton, p. 181), 1782 (Jones, p. 111). *Julitta* 1846 (Oliver, p. 440). *Lanty*
1883–1889 (Kelly). *Julitta* 1902–1939 (Kelly), 1925 (Henderson, p. 108), 1996 (*EDD*).
In 1878 no parish feast was held (Boase, 1890, col. 1591).

*The Roman female saint Julitta before the Reformation (compare St Juliot). This
was forgotten by 1733, when the antiquaries interpreted Lanteglos (which actually
means 'valley with a church': Padel, 1985, p. 171) as 'the church of a saint called
Lanty' (compare the next entry). Lanty survived until the late 19th century, when
Julitta was restored.*

Lanteglos by Fowey

Sanctus Wyllow heremita et martir 1478 (Worcester, 1969, pp. 98, 106); *ecclesiam Sancti
Willei* 1502 (PROB 11/13, f. 100v); *stauro Sancti Willei* 1507 (PROB 11/16, f. 40). *Lanty*
1733 (Willis, p. 173), 1742 (Ecton, p. 182), 1782 (Jones, p. 115). Unknown 1846
(Oliver, p. 440). *Lanty* 1883–1889 (Kelly). *Wylley* or *Wyllow* 1902–1939 (Kelly); *Willeus*
or *Willow* 1925 (Henderson, p. 109); *Wyllow* 1996 (*TDD*).
In the 15th century, the church dedication feast was held on 17 September (Aberystwyth,
NLW 22253A, calendar). In 1878 no parish feast was held (Boase, 1890, col. 1591).

*Wyllow, a male saint regarded as a local martyr, since at least 1478. This was for-
gotten after the Reformation and, as at Lanteglos by Camelford, the antiquaries
invented a St Lanty to whom they supposed the church to have been dedicated. Here
too Lanty survived until the late 19th century, before Wyllow was restored.*

Launcells

Andrew 1403 (Chanter IX, ff. 26, 69v), 1508 (*CPL,* xix (forthcoming), no. 19).
Unknown 1733 (Willis, p. 171). Thomas Becket 1742 (Ecton, p. 179; source, MS Willis
41, f. 226a). Andrew 1754 (Ecton, p. 628), 1782 (Jones, p. 107), 1846 (Oliver, p. 440),
1883–1889 (Kelly). Swithin 1902–1939 (Kelly). Andrew 1925 (Henderson, p. 112).
Andrew and Swithin 1996 (*TDD*).
In 1740 the parish feast was said to be held on 13 July (MS Willis 41, f. 226a), and in
1878 on 15 July (St Swithin's Day) (Boase, 1890, col. 1591).

*Andrew from at least 1403 until the Reformation; it was then forgotten. Thomas
Becket was evidently a conjecture from the parish feast day; Andrew was recovered
in 1754. Since 1902 Swithin has appeared, also a conjecture from the parish feast
day and perhaps because of a wish to distinguish the church from Stratton close by,
which also honours Andrew.*

Launceston: Augustinian priory

The priory of St Stephen by Launceston moved to the new town at Launceston in
*c.*1155 (Hull, 1987, p. xi). Stephen *c.*1200 (Gervase, 1867, ii, 424).
Bishop Stapledon dedicated the church and two altars on 18 August 1318 (Chanter II,
f. 128v). Between 1395 and 1419, Bishop Stafford moved the dedication feast from 18
August to 20 October (BL, Harley MS 3300, p. 148).
Stephen from about 1155 until the Reformation.

Launceston: hospital

Leonard 1245 x 1257, 1535 (Orme and Webster, 1995, pp. 200–3).
Leonard before the Reformation.

Launceston: St Mary Magdalene

Mary Magdalene 1291 (15th) (Hull, 1987, p. 20), 1733 (Willis, p. 171), 1742 (Ecton, p. 180), 1782 (Jones, p. 110), 1814 (Lysons, p. 190). Mary 1846 (Oliver, p. 440). Mary Magdalene 1883 (Kelly), 1925 (Henderson, p. 113), 1939 (Kelly), 1996 (*TDD*).

The bishop of Waterford dedicated the high altar of the church of St Mary Magdalene in 1338–9 (Chanter IV, f. 220v). In 1878 no parish feast was held (Boase, 1890, col. 1591).
Mary Magdalene since at least 1291.

Launceston: St Thomas

Capella Sancti Thome 1291 (Tax.); Thomas the Martyr 1438 (Chanter XI, f. 168v); Thomas 1733 (Willis, p. 171), 1742 (Ecton, p. 180), 1782 (Jones, p. 110), 1846 (Oliver, p. 440). Thomas the Apostle 1883–1939 (Kelly), 1925 (Henderson, p. 185), 1996 (*TDD*).

Bishop Grandisson dedicated the cemetery on 6 November 1333 (Chanter IV, f. 172v).
Thomas, i.e. Becket, from at least 1291 until the Reformation. In accordance with Henry VIII's order in 1538, that dedication should have been discontinued. By the late 19th century, the saint was understood to be Thomas the Apostle.

Lawhitton

Michael 1496 (*CPL*, xvi, 346). Unknown 1733 (Willis, p. 165). Michael 1742 (Ecton, p. 173), 1782 (Jones, p. 88). Unknown 1846 (Oliver, p. 440). Michael 1883–1939 (Kelly), 1925 (Henderson, p. 115), 1996 (*TDD*).

A fair was granted on St Michael's Day in 1311 (*CChR 1300–26*, p. 183). In 1878 no parish feast day is mentioned being held (Boase, 1890, col. 1591).
Michael, possibly since at least 1311 and certainly since at least 1496.

Lelant

Ecclesiam Sancti Euni 1162 x 1170 (Oliver, 1846, p. 41); *ecclesiam Sancti Euny* 1235 (Oliver, 1846, pp. 37–8). *Lanante* (place) *c.*1241 (ECA, D&C 3672, p. 54); *ecclesias de Lananta . . .* 1241 (ibid., pp. 56–7); *Lananta* (place) 1261 (Chanter I, f. 16v). *Ecclesie Sancti Eunini* 1393 (Chanter VII, f. 144v); *ecclesia Sancti Eunyny* 1409 (Chanter IX, f. 232v); *Sanctus Vny* 1478 (Worcester, 1969, p. 114); *ecclesie . . . Sancti Eunini* 1491 (Chanter XII (ii), f. 117); *S. Vnine c.*1540 (Leland, 1907–10, i, 192); *vicariam . . . Sancti Ewny* 1548 (Chanter XIV, f. 130v); *Uny* 1733 (Willis, p. 167); *Ewny* 1742 (Ecton, p. 175), 1782 (Jones, p. 95); *Uny* 1814 (Lysons, p. 169); *Ewinus* 1846 (Oliver, p. 440); *Uny* 1883–1939 (Kelly), 1925 (Henderson, p. 116), 1996 (*TDD*).

In 1878 the parish feast was held on the Sunday nearest to 2 February (Purification of Mary) with a fair on 15 August (Assumption of Mary) (Boase, 1890, col. 1591).
The place-name Lelant means 'church-site of Anta', a saint (allegedly female) commemorated by a chapel in the parish (Padel, 1988, p. 108). The parish church itself, since at least the mid 12th century, has been dedicated to the male saint Euny.

Lesnewth

Michael 1421 (Chanter X, f. 32v). *Knett* 1733 (Willis, p. 172); *Knet* 1742 (Ecton, p. 182), 1782 (Jones, p. 113). Michael 1846 (Oliver, p. 440). *Knet* 1883 (Kelly). *Knet* or

Michael 1889 (Kelly). Michael 1902–1939 (Kelly), 1925 (Henderson, p. 118); Michael and All Angels 1996 (*TDD*).

In 1878 the parish feast was held on the Sunday nearest to 20 October (Boase, 1890, col. 1591).

Michael is the earliest patron recorded, but the 18th-century Knet(t) looks like a genuine local saint remembered in popular tradition. The name Knett may be a vernacular form of the Welsh and Cornish saint Conet (Cenewit, Cunetus) whose feast day in Wales fell on the day before Michael's. If a Celtic saint, he is likely to have been the original dedicatee, to whom Michael was added later (Orme, 1992b, pp. 55–8). Knet dominated the directories up to 1889, but has since been superseded by Michael.

St Levan

Salamun (saint's name) 10th century (Olson and Padel, 1986, p. 42). *Parochia Sancti Silvani* 1334 (Glasscock, 1975, p. 30); *capella Sancti Silvani* 1340 (*Nonarum*, p. 348); *capella Sancti Siluani* 1461 (Cambridge, King's College, MS SMM/2); *Selewan* (place) 1524 (Stoate, 1985, p. 11); *Selevan* (place) 1545 (ibid.); *Levan* 1733 (Willis, p. 167). Not in Ecton (1742). *Levan* 1782 (Jones, p. 95); *Livinus* 1846 (Oliver, p. 440); *Levan* 1883–1939 (Kelly); *Selevan* 1925 (Henderson, p. 118); *Levan* 1996 (*TDD*).

In 1878 the parish feast was held on the Sunday nearest to 15 October (Boase, 1890, col. 1591).

The earliest references to the patron saint, from 1334 onwards, occur in the latinized form Silvanus, but the presence of a saint called Salamun in the 10th-century list of Cornish saints, together with the later vernacular form Selevan, point to the male saint originally called Salamun, later Selevan, who also has church dedications in Brittany. Silvanus may simply be a latinization of Selevan, or an attempt to identify him with a Roman saint of the same name.

Lewannick

Martin 1428 (Chanter X, f. 85), 1479 (Chanter XII (ii), f. 86). *Wynnock* 1733 (Willis, p. 165); *Wenner* 1742 (Ecton, p. 172); *Winnoc* 1754 (Ecton, p. 126). Martin 1763 (Ecton, p. 126), 1782 (Jones, p. 88), 1846 (Oliver, p. 440), 1883–1939 (Kelly), 1925 (Henderson, p. 119), 1996 (*TDD*).

In 1878 no parish feast was held (Boase, 1890, col. 1591).

Martin from at least 1428 until the Reformation; it was then forgotten. The place-name, however, means 'church-site of someone called Gwenek' (Padel, 1988, p. 109), and in the 18th century there was a belief that the church saint had a similar Celtic name. This may well be a mistaken conjecture by antiquarians from the place-name by analogy with St Winnow, unless it represents a genuine local tradition (compare Lesnewth). Martin was recovered in 1763.

Lezant

Stores of All Saints, Katherine, Mary and Michael are mentioned 1543–7 (RIC, Henderson, HC 66, pp. 141–4). St Michael's Meadow, Orchard and Well 1680 (Potts, 1974, p. 90). Unknown 1733 (Willis, p. 165), 1742 (Ecton, p. 173). *Breok* (a mistake for St Breock) 1754 (Ecton, p. 627); *Breock* 1782 (Jones, p. 89). Unknown 1786 (Bacon, p. 300). *Briocus* 1846 (Oliver, p. 440); *Breoke* or *Breage* 1883–1936 (Kelly). Michael 1925 (Henderson, p. 119). Not stated 1935–1939 (Kelly). *Briochus* 1996 (*TDD*).

Bishop Grandisson dedicated the high altar on 27 July 1336 (Chanter IV, f. 201v). In 1878 no parish feast was held (Boase, 1890, col. 1591).

Apparently Michael before the Reformation; it was then forgotten. The suggestion of Brioc arose because the original spelling of Lezant was Lansant which was also an alternative place-name for St Breock (Padel, 1988, pp. 59, 109), causing some antiquaries to confuse the two places. Michael was recovered in 1925, but Brioc still lingers.

Linkinhorne

Ecclesie . . . Sancti Melori 1401 (Chanter IX, f. 54v), 1403 (LPL, Reg. Arundel, i, 288v); *Melorius* 1407 (*CPL*, vi, 121); *ecclesie . . . Sancte Meloris* 1468 (Chanter XII (ii), f. 14v). Unknown 1733 (Willis, p. 165). *Mellor* 1742 (Ecton, p. 172), 1782 (Jones, p. 88); *Meliora* 1814 (Lysons, p. 198); *Milorus* 1846 (Oliver, p. 440); *Mellor* 1883 (Kelly); *Melorus* 1925 (Henderson, p. 120); *Melor* 1939 (Kelly); *Mellor* 1996 (*TDD*).

In 1878 no parish feast was held (Boase, 1890, col. 1591).

The place-name means 'church-site of someone called Kenhoarn' (Padel, 1988, p. 110), but the patron saint since at least 1401 has been Melor, a male saint also venerated at Mylor and in Brittany.

Liskeard: hospital

Mary Magdalene 1323 x 1326, 1368 (Orme and Webster, 1995, pp. 206–7).

Mary Magdalene, a common hospital dedication.

Liskeard: parish church

Martin 1399 (*Cal. Inquisitions Miscellaneous, 1392–9*, p. 227), 1410 (Hull, 1987, p. 187), 1415 (Chanter IX, f. 169v), 1423 (Chanter X, f. 63v), 1473 (Chanter XII (ii), f. 23), 1540 (Chanter XIV, f. 100v; Leland, 1907–10, i, 208), 1733 (Willis, p. 167), 1742 (Ecton, p. 183), 1782 (Jones, p. 115), 1846 (Oliver, p. 440), 1883 (Kelly), 1925 (Henderson, p. 122), 1939 (Kelly), 1996 (*TDD*).

Bishop Brantingham transferred the dedication feast from the eve of St Bartholomew's Day (23 August) to the translation of St Martin (4 July) in 1381 (Chanter VI, f. 90v). In 1878 no parish feast was held (Boase, 1890, col. 1592).

Martin since at least 1399.

Little Petherick

Parochia Sancti Petroci Minoris 1334 (Glasscock, 1975, p. 32); Petroc 1371 (Chanter VII, f. 14v), 1500 (Chanter XII (ii), Redmayn f. 15); *Pedrok Minor* 1535 (*Valor*, ii, 399). Petroc 1733 (Willis, p. 169), 1742 (Ecton, p. 178), 1782 (Jones, p. 104); *Petrocus* 1846 (Oliver, p. 442); Petroc 1883–1939 (Kelly), 1925 (Henderson, p. 164), 1996 (*TDD*).

In 1878 the parish feast was held on 6 October—a recent innovation (Boase, 1890, col. 1594).

Petroc since at least 1334; the place was 'minor' in relation to Padstow nearby.

Lostwithiel

Bartholomew 1350 (PRO, C 143/299/25), 1493 (Harper-Bill, 1991, p. 90), 1543 (RIC, Henderson, HC 66, p. 157), 1733 (Willis, p. 170), 1742 (Ecton, p. 178), 1782 (Jones, p. 102), 1846 (Oliver, p. 441), 1883 (Kelly), 1925 (Henderson, p. 126), 1939 (Kelly), 1996 (*TDD*).

In 1878 the parish feast was held on the Sunday after St Bartholomew's Day (24 August) (Boase, 1890, col. 1592).

Bartholomew since at least 1350.

Ludgvan

Ecclesiam Sancti Ludwani 1312 (Chanter II, f. 72); *ecclesiam Sancti Ludewani* 1319 (ibid., f. 140); St *Ludevon* 1319 (*CIPM*, vi, 123); *ecclesiam Sancti Ludowani* 1382 (Chanter VII, f. 75); *parochiis Sanctorum . . . Ludvoni* 1387 (Chanter VI, f. 175v); *ecclesie . . . Sancti Luduoni* 1418 (Chanter IX, f. 194); *Ludgian* 1733 (Willis, p. 168); *Ludgvan* 1742 (Ecton, p. 175). Paul 1754 (Ecton, p. 627). *Ludgvan* 1782 (Jones, p. 96); *Ludowanus* 1846 (Oliver, p. 441). Paul 1883–1939 (Kelly); Paul the Apostle 1925 (Henderson, p. 127). *Ludgvan* and Paul 1996 (*TDD*).

Bishop Grandisson dedicated the high altar on 14 July 1336 (Chanter IV, f. 201). In 1870 the parish feast was held on the Sunday nearest to St Paul's Day (25 January) (Polsue, iii, 184), and in 1878 on the Sunday after 22 January (Boase, 1890, col. 1592).

The place-name probably means 'place of ashes' (Padel, 1988, p. 112), but by at least 1312 it was supposed to enshrine the name of a male saint, Ludwan, who may well therefore have been venerated in the church. This tradition continued after 1742. Paul has also appeared since 1754; it is difficult to know whether this is a conjecture from the parish feast day, or whether the latter arose from him being co-patron of the church.

Luxulyan

Ecclesie . . . Sanctorum Ciricii et Julitte 1412 (Chanter VIII, f. 160v); *ecclesie Sancti Cirici* 1493 (LPL, Reg. Morton, i, f. 131; Harper-Bill, 1991, p. 90); *Seint Sire and Julett* 1522 (PROB 11/20, f. 229v); *Cyr* 1733 (Willis, p. 170), 1742 (Ecton, p. 177); *Cyr* corrected to *Cyricius* and *Juliette* 1754 (Ecton, pp. 130, 627); *Cyricus* and *Julietta* 1782 (Jones, p. 101); *Cyrus* and *Julitta* 1846 (Oliver, p. 441); *Cyriacus* and *Julitta* 1883–1939 (Kelly); *Ciricius* and *Julitta* 1925 (Henderson, p. 127); *Cyrus* and *Julietta* 1996 (*TDD*).

In 1878 the parish feast was held on the Sunday before 24 June and on the following days (Boase, 1890, col. 1592).

The place-name means 'the chapel of someone named Sulyen' (Padel, 1988, p. 112); that person may or may not have been the original patron saint. By 1412, the patrons were the Roman martyrs Cyricus and Julitta (compare St Veep).

Mabe

De Sancto Laudo 1201 (Stenton, 1952, pp. 270, 348, 579, 586, 708); *capelle sancti Laudi* 1309 (Chanter VII (part iii), f. 27); *parochia Sancti Laudi* 1334 (Glasscock, 1975, p. 30); *capella Sancti Laudy* 1340 (*Nonarum*, p. 348); *Loo*, also *Lowe* 1555 (RIC, Henderson, HC 66, pp. 150–1). *Mabe* 1733 (Willis, p. 167), 1742 (Ecton, p. 174), 1782 (Jones, p. 92). Unknown 1846 (Oliver, p. 441). *Mabe* 1883–1919 (Kelly). *Laudus* or *Loe* 1925 (Henderson, p. 128); *Laudus* 1926–1939 (Kelly), 1996 (*TDD*).

In 1878 the parish feast was held on the Sunday nearest to St Matthew's Day (21 September) (Boase, 1890, col. 1592).

The place-name is based on a personal name, Mab (Padel, 1988, p. 113), but the patron saint by 1201 and probably until the Reformation was Laud, a male saint. The dedication was then forgotten and in the 18th century a saint Mabe was deduced from the place-name, Laud being restored in 1925.

St Mabyn

Mabon (saint's name) 12th century (14th) (Grosjean, 1953, pp. 397–8); *ecclesie de Sancto Malbano* 1234 (Rowe, 1914–50, i, 27); *ecclesie Sancte Mabene* 1266 (Chanter I, f. 74), 1291 (Tax.); *ecclesie . . . Sancte Mabene* 1424 (Chanter X, f. 68); *Mabena* 1733

(Willis, p. 172); *Mabyn* 1742 (Ecton, p. 181), 1782 (Jones, p. 111); *Mabena* 1846 (Oliver, p. 441), 1883 (Kelly), 1925 (Henderson, p. 128); *Mabyn* 1939 (Kelly); *Mabena* 1996 (*TDD*).

In 1878 no parish feast was held (Boase, 1890, col. 1592).

Mabon, usually a female saint, since at least 1234 and probably since at least the 12th century when she occurs in a list of saints connected with north Cornwall (Orme, 1992c, p. 148). She was then believed to be one of the 24 children of the Welsh king Brychan.

Madron

Ecclesia Sancti Maderi 1205 (*CuRR 1205–6*, p. 50); *ecclesie Sancti Maderni* 1276 (Chanter I, f. 74), 1291 (Tax.), 1390 (Chanter VI, f. 206). Church of St *Madernus alias* St *Paternus* 1437 (*CPL*, viii, 672–3); *ecclesie . . . Sancti Paterni alias Sancti Maderni* 1498 (Chanter XII (ii), Redmayn, ff. 6v, 28v); *ecclesie Sancti Maderni alias Sancti Paterni* 1534 (Chanter XIV, f. 76). *Maderne* 1733 (Willis, p. 168). Unknown 1742 (Ecton, p. 176). *Madern* 1782 (Jones, p. 96); *Maddern* 1814 (Lysons, p. 238). *Madernus* or *Paternus* 1846 (Oliver, p. 441). *Madron* 1883–1939 (Kelly). *Madernus* or *Paternus* 1925 (Henderson, p. 128). *Maddern* 1996 (*TDD*).

Bishop Grandisson dedicated the high altar on 13 July 1336 (Chanter IV, f. 201). In 1878 the parish feast was held on Advent Sunday and in the following week (Boase, 1890, col. 1592).

Madern, a male saint not certainly found elsewhere, since at least 1276. By 1437, the saint was identified with Padern, the patron of North and South Petherwin. This conjecture was forgotten after the Reformation, until revived by modern scholars.

Maker

Julian *c*.1539 (Oliver, 1846, p. 133). Michael, with a query 1733 (Willis, p. 166). *Macra* 1740 (MS Willis 41, f. 237). Michael 1742 (Ecton, p. 173). *Macra* 1754 (Ecton, p. 627), 1782 (Jones, p. 90). Julian 1846 (Oliver, p. 441). Julian, Mary and *Macra* 1883–1939 (Kelly). Julian 1925 (Henderson, p. 129). Mary and Julian 1996 (*TDD*).

In 1878 no parish feast was held (Boase, 1890, col. 1592).

Julian before the Reformation; it was then forgotten. Macra was a conjecture based on the place-name, and Michael perhaps from a parish feast day. Julian was recovered in 1846, but Macra and Mary (a newcomer) have also been honoured in recent times.

Manaccan

Ecclesia Sancte Manace 1308 (Chanter II, f. 39); *ecclesie . . . Sancte Manacce* 1424 (Chanter X, f. 72); *Managhan* (place) 1395 (Chanter IX, f. 1v); *ecclesia de . . . Manacca* 1453 (Chanter XI, f. 400); *Manacca* 1477 (Chanter XII (ii), f. 45v), 1505 (Chanter XIII, f. 5); *stauro Sancti Manache* (*sic*) 1500 (PROB 11/12, f. 164v); *Manaca* 1535 (*Valor*, ii, 393). Unknown 1733 (Willis, p. 167). *Manacca* 1742 (Ecton, p. 174). *Menacus* and Dunstan (a mistake for Lanreath) 1763 (Ecton, p. 128). *Manaccan* 1782 (Jones, p. 93). *Antoninus* 1846 (Oliver, p. 441). *Mennaccus* and Dunstan 1883–1926 (Kelly). *Manacca* with a query 1925 (Henderson, p. 129); *Monachus* 1935 (Kelly); *Manacca* or *Manaccus* 1939 (Kelly). *Manaccus* and Dunstan 1996 (*TDD*).

In 1870 and 1878 the parish feast was held on the Sunday nearest to 14 October (Polsue, ii, 262; Boase, 1890, col. 1592).

The place-name Managhan recorded in 1395 could mean 'the place of monks' which accords with Minster, an alternative name for Manaccan first recorded in 1259 (Padel, 1988, p. 114). By 1308, however, the church was regarded as dedicated to a female saint Manacca—possibly real, possibly invented from the place-name as at Kenwyn, Ludgvan, Morvah and Talland. The saint's name is similar to that of Manakneu or Manac, patron saint of Lanreath and there considered to be male, and since 1763 the dedication of Manaccan has sometimes been confused with that of Lanreath.

Marhamchurch

Maronecirche (place) 1086 (DB 5/5/5); *Merewenne* (saint's name) 12th century (14th) (Grosjean, 1953, pp. 397–8); *ecclesia de Marwynechirche* 1291 (Tax.); *ecclesie . . . Sancte Merwenne* 1400 (Chanter IX, f. 45v); *ecclesiam . . . Sancte Marenne* 1433 (Chanter X, f. 115v); *Marhamchurche alias Marwynchurche* 1458 (Chanter XII (i), f. 8v); *Marvenne* 1733 (Willis, p. 171), 1742 (Ecton, p. 179), 1782 (Jones, p. 107). *Morwenna* 1846 (Oliver, p. 441). *Marham* or *Maravina* 1883 (Kelly); *Marwen* or *Morwenna* 1925 (Henderson, p. 130); *Marwenne* 1939 (Kelly), 1996 (*TDD*).

In 1740 the parish feast day was said to be held on 1 August (MS Willis 41, f. 226a). In 1878 it was held on the Sunday after 12 August, with a fair on an adjoining day and another on the Thursday before 25 March (Boase, 1890, col. 1592).

Merewenne, a female saint, since at least the 11th century. In the following century, she was said to be one of the children of the Welsh king Brychan but she may have been identical with the 10th-century English saint Merwenn, abbess of Romsey (Padel, 1988, p. 115; Orme, 1992c, p. 155). Oliver and Henderson were inclined to identify her with Morwenn, patroness of nearby Morwenstow, but the names are different.

St Martin by Looe

Martin 1283 (Chanter I, ff. 119, 120), 1291 (Tax.); *ecclesia Sancte Martine (sic)* 1519 (PROB 11/19, f. 201). *'Martin . . . otherwyse called Kayne the moore'* 1547 (PROB 11/32, f. 9v). *Kayen* 1563 (Torr, 1965–7, p. 82). Martin also *Kayne* 1733 (Willis, p. 173); *Kayn* alias *Martin* 1742 (Ecton, p. 182). Martin 1782 (Jones, p. 114). Martin alias *Kayne* 1814 (Lysons, p. 216). Martin 1846 (Oliver, p. 441). *Kayne* 1856 (Kelly). Martin 1883–1939 (Kelly). Keyne and Martin 1925 (Henderson, p. 132). Martin 1996 (*EDD*).

In 1878 no parish feast was held (Boase, 1890, col. 1592).

Martin since at least 1283. However, by the mid 16th century the church was also dedicated to Keyne, patron of the nearby church of St Keyne, a fact remembered until as late as 1925 but now usually forgotten.

St Martin in Meneage

Parochia Dedynini 1334 (Glasscock, 1975, p. 30); *Sancti Dedymin'* 1334 (PRO, E 179/87/10); *Sancti Dedyinni* (or *Dedymin*) 1337 (PRO, E 179/87/5). *Ecclesie Sancti Martini alias Dydemin* 1385 (Chanter VI, f. 142v; Chanter VII (part ii), ff. 36, 39); *Martyn alias Dedimus* 1535 (*Valor*, ii, 393). Martin 1733 (Willis, p. 167). *Martin* alias *Dedimus* 1742 (Ecton, p. 174), 1782 (Jones, p. 92), 1814 (Lysons, p. 215). Martin 1846 (Oliver, p. 441), 1883 (Kelly), 1925 (Henderson, p. 133), 1939 (Kelly), 1996 (*TDD*).

In 1878 the parish feast was held on 14 November (Boase, 1890, col. 1592).

The earliest recorded saint is Dedymin (the forms vary), latinized as Dedimus and regarded as male. The two references to 'Saint' seem to rule out the possibility of a mere place-name. By 1385, he had become subordinate to Martin, who has dominated the dedication ever since.

St Mary de Valle in Cardinham: church or priory

Mary 1162 x 1170 (Oliver, 1846, p. 41), c.1200 (Gervase, 1867, ii, 424).
Mary before the Reformation. The place was described as a church in the earliest reference and as a priory in the next.

St Mawes

Villata de Sancto Maudeto (place) 1284 (PRO, JUST 1/111); *Mauduit* (place) 1302 (PRO, JUST 1/117, m. 39d); *Seyntmaudit* (place) 1431 (Chanter X, f. 101); *S. Maudite* c.1540 (Leland, 1907–10, i, 200); *Mawes* 1782 (Jones, p. 100); *Mawes* or *Mauditus* 1846 (Oliver, p. 440); *Mawes* or *Mauduit (Maudit)* 1883–1939 (Kelly); *Maudutus* 1925 (Henderson, p. 88).
Maudith, a male saint widely venerated in Brittany, since at least 1284.

Mawgan in Meneage

Maucan (saint's name) 10th century (Olson and Padel, 1986, p. 47); *Scanct' Mawan*, also *Scanctus Maiuian, Santmauuant* 1086 (DB 1/1; Exon, pp. 91, 205); *in Sancto Maugan* (place) 1206 (*CuRR 1205–6*, p. 91); *ecclesia Sancti Maugani* 1291 (Tax.), 1385 (Chanter VI, f. 142v); *S. Mogun's* c.1540 (Leland, 1907–10, i, 195). *Mawnan (sic)* 1733 (Willis, p. 167). *Mogun* 1742 (Ecton, p. 174), 1782 (Jones, p. 92); *Mauganus* 1846 (Oliver, p. 441); *Mawgan* 1883–1939 (Kelly); *Mauganus* 1925 (Henderson, p. 133); *Mawgan* 1996 (*TDD*).
In 1870 the parish feast was said to be held on the Sunday nearest to 11 November (Polsue, iii, 284) but in 1878 on 10 June (Boase, 1890, col. 1592).
Maugan, a male saint venerated in Wales and Brittany, since at least the 1086 and probably since at least the 10th century as he occurs in the early list of Cornish saints (see also the next entry).

St Mawgan in Pydar

Ecclesia Sancti Maugani 1291 (Tax.); *ecclesie . . . Sancti Mawgani* 1451 (Chanter XI, f. 374v); *Maugan* 1733 (Willis, p. 169), 1742 (Ecton, p. 178), 1782 (Jones, p. 104); *Mauganus* 1846 (Oliver, p. 441); *Mawgan* 1883–1939 (Kelly). *Mauganus* and Nicholas 1925 (Henderson, p. 133). *Mawgan* 1996 (*TDD*).
In 1870 the parish feast was said to be held on the Sunday nearest to St James' Day (25 July) in 1870 (Polsue, iii, 298), and in 1878 on St James' Day (Boase, 1890, col. 1592).
The same saint as in the previous entry, since at least 1291. The origin of Nicholas is not clear.

Mawnan

Ecclesie Sancti Maunani 1281 (Chanter I, f. 112v), 1348 (Chanter V, f. 63v). *Ecclesiam . . . Sancti Stephani de Mawnan* 1476 (Chanter XII (ii), f. 33v); *ecclesiam . . . Sanctorum Stephani et Mavnani* 1492 (ibid., ff. 117, 142v), 1499 (ibid., Redmayn f. 11v); similarly but with *Mawnagi* for *Mawnani* 1511 (Chanter XIII, f. 42); *ecclesiam de Sancto Stephano in Mawnano (de Mawnano* in margin) 1526 (Chanter XIV, f. 29); *S. Mawnon* c.1540 (Leland, 1907–10, i, 197); *Mawnan* 1733 (Willis, p. 167), 1742 (Ecton, p. 174), 1782 (Jones, p. 92). *Maunanus* and Stephen 1846 (Oliver, p. 441); *Mawnan* and Stephen 1883–1919 (Kelly); *Maunanus* and Stephen 1925 (Henderson, p. 134). *Mawnan* 1926–1939 (Kelly), 1996 (*TDD*).
In 1878 the parish feast was said to be held on St Stephen's Day (26 December) (Boase, 1890, col. 1592).

Maunan, a male saint, since at least 1281; he was later believed to be a companion of Breac of Breage. Stephen was added as a co-patron by 1476, though he has sometimes been overlooked in directories since the 18th century.

St Mellion

Robert *de Sancto Melano* (name) 1198 (Stenton, 1932, p. 176); *ecclesiam Sancti Melani* 1259 (Chanter I, f. 8v), 1291 (Tax.), 1340 (*Nonarum*, p. 341); *Melania* 1733 (Willis, p. 166); *Melyan* alias *Mellyn* 1742 (Ecton, p. 173), 1782 (Jones, p. 89); *Melanus* 1846 (Oliver, p. 441), 1883 (Kelly), 1925 (Henderson, p. 135); *Melanius* 1939 (Kelly); *Melanus* 1996 (*TDD*).

Bishop Bronescombe dedicated the church on 17 October 1259 (Chanter I, f. 8v). In 1878 no parish feast was held but there was a fair on the last Thursday in March (Boase, 1890, col. 1592).

Melaine, bishop of Rennes, since at least 1198 (compare Mullion).

Menheniot

Lallu (saint's name) 10th century (Olson and Padel, 1986, p. 56); *Sancti Laluwy* 1293 (Rowe, 1914–50, i, 195); *Sancti Lallawy* 1318 (PRO, CP 25/32/17, no. 13); *fraternitati Sancti Lalluly* 1426 (PROB 11/3, f. 44 (or 43)); *stauro Sancti Lalluei* 1509 (PROB 11/16, f. 184v); 'image of *Saynt Lalloe*', '*Saynt Lalo is* store' 1532 (CRO, AR 24/21). George, with a query 1733 (Willis, p. 166). Neot 1742 (Ecton, p. 173), 1782 (Jones, p. 89). *Antoninus* 1846 (Oliver, p. 441). Neot 1883–1889 (Kelly). *Antoninus* 1902–1926 (Kelly). *Lalluwy* 1925 (Henderson, p. 135). Not stated 1935–1939 (Kelly). *Lalluwy* 1996 (*TDD*).

In 1878 no parish feast was held but there were fairs on 23 April, 11 June and 28 July (Boase, 1890, col. 1592).

Lallu, an otherwise unknown male saint, since at least 1293 and possibly since at least the 10th century as he occurs in the early list of Cornish saints. Laluwy and Lalluly are the genitive cases of Latin forms like Lalluus; the vernacular form is shown in the references of 1532. The place-name Menheniot probably means 'land of someone called Hunyad' (Padel, 1988, p. 119), not necessarily a saint, but from the 18th to the 20th centuries the name was often believed to mean 'monastery of Neot'—hence Neot. Oliver's Antoninus, popular up to 1926, may arise from a similar conjecture from the place-name.

St Merryn

Vicariam Sancte Marine 1259 (Chanter I, f. 6); *ecclesia Sancte Maryne* 1340 (*Nonarum*, p. 348); *ecclesie . . . Sancte Marine Virginis* 1437 (Chanter XI, f. 144); *Seynt Meryn* 1477 (Chanter XII (ii), f. 41); *Merin* 1733 (Willis, p. 169), 1742 (Ecton, p. 178), 1782 (Jones, p. 104). Unknown 1846 (Oliver, p. 441). *Merryn* 1883–1926 (Kelly). Thomas Becket 1890 (Boase, 1890, col. 1592). *Marina*; later Thomas the martyr 1925 (Henderson, p. 136); *Merin* and Thomas of Canterbury 1935–1939 (Kelly). *Merryn* 1996 (*TDD*).

In 1878 the parish feast was held on the Sunday of or after 7 July (St Thomas Becket's Day), with a fair on the Monday before the second Tuesday in May (Boase, 1890, col. 1592).

A female saint identified as Marina since at least 1259. Thomas Becket, found since 1890, is a conjecture from the parish feast day.

Merther

'*Cohan* the martyr' 1480 (RIC, Henderson MSS, Ecclesiastical Antiquities, x; source not given); *instauro Sancti Coani* 1512 (PROB 11/18, f. 101). *St Murther* 1569 (Padel, 1988, p. 120). *St Coan Well c.*1691 (Lanhydrock House, FS 2/32/1/42); *Cohan* early 18th century (BL, Add. MS 29,762, p. 174; Polsue, 1867–72, iii, 323). *Merther* 1733 (Willis, p. 170). Unknown 1742 (Ecton, p. 177). *Merther* 1754 (Ecton, p. 130). *Coanus* 1846 (Oliver, p. 441); *Cohan* 1883–1939 (Kelly); *Coanus* 1925 (Henderson, p. 137). Not mentioned 1996 (*TDD*).

In 1878 the parish feast was held on the Sunday nearest to 17 September (Boase, 1890, col. 1592).

Coan or Cohan, an otherwise unknown male saint, since at least the later middle ages. This was not always remembered and between the 16th and 18th centuries a St Merther was invented from the place-name, Coan being recovered in 1846.

Mevagissey

Memai and *Iti* (saints' names) 10th century (Olson and Padel, 1986, p. 62); *ecclesie . . . Sanctarum Meve et Ide* 1422 (Chanter X, f. 42v); *ecclesie . . . Sanctarum Mewe et Ide* 1506 (Chanter XIII, f. 7); *ecclesie . . . Sanctarum Meve et Ide* 1512 (ibid., f. 47v); *Mevy* and *Isse* 1733 (Willis, p. 170); *Mevan* and *Issi* 1742 (Ecton, p. 177), 1782 (Jones, p. 101); *Mewa* and *Ida* 1846 (Oliver, p. 441); *Mevan* and *Issey* 1883 (Kelly); *Meva* and *Ida* 1925 (Henderson, p. 138); *Meva* and *Issey* 1939 (Kelly). Peter 1996 (*TDD*).

Bishop Bronescombe dedicated the church on 8 October 1259 (Chanter I, f. 8). In 1878 the parish feast was held on SS Peter's and Paul's Day (29 June) (Boase, 1890, col. 1592).

Meva and Idi (compare St Issey), two saints regarded as women, since at least the 10th century when they occur together in the early list of Cornish saints, evidently because they were joint patrons of this church. The church-name consists of their two names; Peter is a recent innovation based on the parish feast day.

St Mewan

Megunn (saint's name) 10th century (Olson and Padel, 1986, pp. 59–60); *ecclesia Sancti Mawani* 1291 (Tax.); *ecclesiarum . . . de Sancto Mewano* 1297 (*CPR 1292–1301*, p. 272); *ecclesia Sancti Mewani* 1318 (Chanter II, f. 128v); *ecclesiam Sancti Mewany* 1370 (Chanter VII, f. 10v); *Manwan* 1733 (Willis, p. 170); *Mewan* 1742 (Ecton, p. 177), 1782 (Jones, p. 101); *Mewanus* 1846 (Oliver, p. 441); *Mewan* 1883–1939 (Kelly); *Mewanus* 1925 (Henderson, p. 138); *Mewan* 1996 (*TDD*).

In 1878 the parish feast was held on the Sunday of or after 13 November (Boase, 1890, col. 1593).

The Breton male saint Mewan since at least 1291 and probably since at least the 10th century, as he appears in the early list of Cornish saints.

St Michael Caerhays

Michael 1259 (Chanter I, f. 7v), 1733 (Willis, p. 169), 1742 (Ecton, p. 176). Michael and *Denys* 1782 (Jones, p. 98). Michael 1846 (Oliver, p. 441), 1883 (Kelly), 1925 (Henderson, p. 36), 1939 (Kelly), 1996 (*TDD*).

Bishop Bronescombe dedicated the church on 5 October 1259 (Chanter I, f. 7v). In 1878 no parish feast was held (Boase, 1890, col. 1593).

Michael since at least 1259.

St Michael's Mount: Benedictine priory, later chantry

Sanctum Michaelem qui est iuxta mare possibly 1042 x 1066 (later text) (Hull, 1962, p. 61); *montem Sancti Michaelis de Cornubia c.*1070 (14th) (ibid., p. 1); *ecclesia S' Michaelis* 1086 (DB 4/1); Michael *c.*1200 (Gervase, 1867, ii, 424), 1754 (Ecton, p. 128), 1782 (Jones, p. 94), 1883 (Kelly), 1925 (Henderson, p. 138), 1939 (Kelly).

Michael since at least the 11th century.

St Michael Penkevil: parish and collegiate church

Michael 1261 (Chanter I, f. 20v), 1264 (ibid., f. 30), 1516 (Chanter XIII, f. 65), 1733 (Willis, p. 170), 1742 (Ecton, p. 177), 1782 (Jones, p. 101), 1846 (Oliver, p. 441), 1883 (Kelly), 1925 (Henderson, p. 140), 1939 (Kelly), 1996 (*TDD*).

Bishop Bronescombe dedicated the church on 13 August 1261 (Chanter I, f. 20v). In 1878 the parish feast was held on 29 September (St Michael's Day) (Boase, 1890, col. 1593).

Michael since at least 1261.

Michaelstow

Michael 1282 (Chanter I, ff. 115, 116), 1291 (Tax.), 1490 (Chanter XII (ii), f. 111), 1733 (Willis, p. 172), 1742 (Ecton, p. 182), 1782 (Jones, p. 113), 1846 (Oliver, p. 441), 1883 (Kelly), 1925 (Henderson, p. 142), 1939 (Kelly), 1996 (*TDD*).

In 1878 no parish feast was held (Boase, 1890, col. 1593).

Michael since at least 1282.

Minster: Benedictine priory and parish church

*Ecclesiam Sancte Merthiane c.*1200 (15th) (Oliver, 1846, p. 64). Andrew *c.*1200 (Gervase, 1867, ii, 424). *Sancta Matheriana virgo* 1478 (Worcester, 1969, p. 28). *Gennis* 1733 (a mistake for St Gennys) (Willis, p. 172), 1742 (Ecton, p. 182). *Metherian* 1763 (Ecton, p. 133), 1782 (Jones, p. 113); *Mather* or *Maddern* 1814 (Lysons, p. 238); *Merthiana* 1846 (Oliver, p. 441); *Metherian* 1883 (Kelly); *Merteriana* virgin 1925 (Henderson, p. 143); *Merthiana* 1939 (Kelly); *Merteriana* 1996 (*TDD*).

John Leland, visiting Boscastle in about 1540, noted that 'there is a chirch in it, as I remembre, of S. Simphorian' (Leland, 1907–10, i, 176). This may be a reference to Forrabury (see above), or a misunderstanding of Martherian of Minster.

In 1878 fairs were held on 5 August and 22 November (Boase, 1890, col. 1593).

A female saint, also patron of Tintagel, apparently called Matherian or Mertherian, although the recorded forms differ. She may have had Andrew associated with her in about 1200, unless that reference arises from confusion with Tywardreath Priory.

St Minver

Menfre (saint's name) 12th century (14th) (Grosjean, 1953, pp. 397–8); *Sancte Menfrede* 1256 (Rowe, 1914–50, i, 80); *ecclesie Sancte Menwrede* 1269 (Chanter I, f. 42); *ecclesie Sancte Menurede* 1272 (ibid., f. 51v); *ecclesie Sancte Minefrede* 1276 (ibid., f. 76); *ecclesia de Menvirehede* 1291 (Tax.); *ecclesiam de Sancta Menefreda* 1299 (ECA, 2125); *ecclesie Sancte Mynirede* 1348 (Chanter V, f. 67v); *ecclesie . . . Sancte Minerue* (Chanter VIII, f. 107v); *ecclesie . . . Sancte Menefrede* 1434 (Chanter X, f. 127); *vicaria Sancte Minefride* 1463 (Chanter XII (i), f. 46); *Minvereda* 1733 (Willis, p. 172); *Mynfray* alias *Miniver* 1742 (Ecton, p. 181), 1782 (Jones, p. 111); *Menefrida* 1846 (Oliver, p. 441); *Minifreda* 1883 (Kelly); *Minefreda* virgin 1925 (Henderson, p. 144); *Menefrida* 1939 (Kelly); *Menefreda* 1996 (*TDD*).

In 1878 no parish feast was held (Boase, 1890, col. 1593).

Menfre, a female saint, since at least 1256 and probably since at least the 12th century as she occurs in a list of saints connected with north Cornwall. She was then believed to be one of the 24 children of the Welsh king Brychan.

Morvah

Parochia Sancte Moruede 1348 (PRO, E 179/87/22). *Capellis . . . necnon Sanctarum Brigide et Morvethe* 1390 (Chanter VI, f. 206). *Sancte Morph'e* 1435 (PROB 11/3, f. 156v (157v)). *Capella Sancte Brigide* 1447 (Chanter XI, f. 294v). *Sanctus Morianus* (possibly relating to Morvah) 1478 (Worcester, 1969, p. 96). Unknown 1733 (Willis, p. 168), 1742 (Ecton, p. 176), 1782 (Jones, p. 96), 1846 (Oliver, p. 441). *Morvah* 1883–1912 (Kelly). Not stated 1919–1939 (Kelly). *Morwetha* or Bridget, the latter with a query 1925 (Henderson, p. 145). *Morwetha* 1996 (*TDD*).

In 1878 the parish feast was held on the nearest Sunday to 16 October and a fair on the first Sunday in August (Boase, 1890, col. 1593).

The place-name Morvah probably means 'sea-grave' (Padel, 1988, p. 124), but by 1348 it was interpreted as the name of a female saint, to whom Bridget was added as co-patron by 1390. Bridget seems as likely to be Bridget of Kildare as Bridget of Sweden, since the latter died only in 1371 and was canonized in 1391. Worcester's reference, albeit to a male saint, may be to the same church. Both medieval saints were forgotten after the Reformation; Morvah or Morwetha has been restored since the late 19th century.

Morval

Ecclesie . . . Sancte Wenne 1435 (Chanter X, f. 143), 1514 (Chanter XIII, f. 56); *stauro Sancte Wenne* 1519 (PROB 11/19, f. 201). Unknown 1733 (Willis, p. 173). *Wenn* 1742 (Ecton, p. 183), 1782 (Jones, p. 115); *Wenna* 1846 (Oliver, p. 441), 1883 (Kelly), 1925 (Henderson, p. 145); *Wenn* 1939 (Kelly); *Wenna* 1996 (*TDD*).

Bishop Stapledon dedicated the high altar on 18 June 1318 (Chanter II, f. 128). In 1878 no parish feast was held (Boase, 1890, col. 1593).

Wenna, a female saint, since at least 1435 (compare St Wenn). In north Cornwall in the 12th century, she was believed to be one of the 24 children of the Welsh king Brychan.

Morwenstow

Morewenna (saint's name) 12th century (14th) (Grosjean, 1953, pp. 397–8); Lucy *de Morewestewe* (name) 1201 (Stenton, 1952, p. 399). John the Baptist *c.*1285 (MS Willis 41, f. 235; dated by *CPR 1281–92*, p. 176). *Ecclesia de Morwenestowe* (place) 1291 (Tax.). John the Baptist 1476 (*CPL*, xiii (ii), 487). *Sancta Morwinna* 1478 (Worcester, 1969, p. 26). John the Baptist 1509 (DRO, Exeter City Library, DD 39156). *Marvenne* 1733 (Willis, p. 171). John the Baptist 1740 (MS Willis 41, f. 226a). *Morvenna* 1742 (Ecton, p. 179), 1782 (Jones, p. 107); *Morwenna* 1846 (Oliver, p. 441), 1856 (Kelly), 1925 (Henderson, p. 146). John the Baptist 1939 (Kelly), 1996 (*TDD*).

In 1740 and 1878 the parish feast was said to be held on 24 June (St John the Baptist's Day) (MS Willis 41, f. 226a; Boase, 1890, col. 1593).

The church took its name from Morwenna, a female saint, by at least 1201 and probably since at least the 12th century when she occurs in a list of saints connected with north Cornwall. She was then believed to be one of the 24 children of the Welsh king Brychan. She was accompanied and probably superseded as patron by John the Baptist from about 1285. He was perhaps the choice of William de Monkton who gave the church in that year to the hospital of St John the Baptist at Bridgwater (Somerset), rather than being a result of the hospital's ownership. Since the 18th century, each saint has been mentioned in directories, but not together.

Mullion

Ecclesiam Sancti Melani 1262 (Chanter I, f. 25), 1291 (Tax.); *Melania* 1733 (Willis, p. 167); *Melan* 1742 (Ecton, p. 174), 1782 (Jones, p. 93); *Melanus* 1846 (Oliver, p. 441); *Melan* 1883 (Kelly); *Melanus* 1925 (Henderson, p. 147), 1939 (Kelly); *Mellanus* 1996 (*TDD*).

In 1870 the parish feast was said to be held on the Sunday nearest to 4 November (Polsue, iii, 385), and in 1878 similarly to 6 November (Boase, 1890, col. 1593).

Melaine, also patron of St Mellion, since at least 1262.

Mylor

Meler (saint's name) 10th century (Olson and Padel, 1986, pp. 46–7); *ecclesiam Sancti Melori* 1258 (Chanter I, f. 4v); *ecclesia de Sancto Meloro* 1291 (Tax.); *ecclesie Sancti Miloris* 1514 (Chanter XIII, f. 55); *ecclesie. . . . de Sanct' Milor'* 1527 (Chanter XIV, f. 34); *Melor* 1733 (Willis, p. 167), 1742 (Ecton, p. 174), 1782 (Jones, p. 92); *Milorus* or *Melorus* 1846 (Oliver, p. 441); *Mylor* or *Melorus* 1883–1939 (Kelly); *Melorus* 1925 (Henderson, p. 147); *Mylor* 1996 (*TDD*).

In 1878 the parish feast was said (confusingly) to be on 28 August but currently held on the Sunday nearest to 25 October (Boase, 1890, col. 1593).

The Breton saint Melor, also patron of Linkinhorne, since at least 1258 and probably since at least the 10th century as he occurs in the early list of Cornish saints.

St Neot

A church 'in which *Sanctus Gueriir* lies in peace (and now *Sanctus Niot* lies there as well)' 10th century (Asser, 1959, p. 55; Orme, 1992c, p. 125). *Nioth* (saint's name) 10th century (Olson and Padel, 1986, pp. 49–51); *clerici S' Neoti*, also *Neotestov* (place) 1086 (DB 4/28); *presbiteri de Sancto Nieto* 1086 (Exon, p. 121); *Sanctus Anietus* 1086 (ibid., p. 66); *Sennet* (place) *c.*1100 (14th) (Holmes and Weaver, 1894, p. 119); *ecclesie Sancti Neoti* 1265 (Chanter I, f. 33v), 1291 (Tax.); *ecclesiam Sancti Nyoti* (Chanter II, f. 161v); *Nyoty* 1340 (*Nonarum*, p. 342); *ecclesia . . . Sancti Nioti* 1412 (Chanter VIII, f. 161); *vicaria Sancti Nioti* 1453 (Chanter XI, f. 400), 1469 (Chanter XII (ii), f. 15); *Nyott* 1553 (Snell, *c.*1953, p. 48); *Neott* 1733 (Willis, p. 173); *Nyote* alias *St. Neot's* 1742 (Ecton, p. 183), 1782 (Jones, p. 115); *Neot* 1814 (Lysons, p. 246); *Neotus* 1846 Oliver, p. 441). *Neot* or *Gueri(e)r* 1883–1939 (Kelly). *Anietus* 1925 (Henderson, p. 148); *Neot* 1996 (*TDD*).

Bishop Stapledon dedicated the church on 14 October 1321 (Chanter II, f. 161v). In 1878 the parish feast was said to be held on the last Sunday in July for one week (Boase, 1890, col. 1593).

If Asser's information is correct, St Neot church originally housed, and may therefore have had as its patron, the body of an otherwise unknown male saint Gueriir. It has, however, taken the name of Niot or Neot, also a male, since at least the 11th century. Most of Neot's body was taken in the 10th or 11th century to St Neot's (Huntingdonshire), where he was believed to be an Englishman and contemporary of King Alfred, but the 10th-century evidence of a saint in Cornwall called Nioth may make a Celtic origin for him more plausible. Gueriir has sometimes been remembered in modern times.

Newlyn East

Ecclesiam Sancte Niweline 1259 (Chanter I, f. 7v); *ecclesia Sancte Neuline* 1264 (ibid., f. 30); *ecclesiarum Sancte Niwyline . . .* 1269 (ibid. f. 35(a)v); *ecclesiam Sancte Neweline, ecclesia Sancte Newlyne* 1291 (Tax.); *ecclesie . . . Sancte Neuline*, also *Newline* 1429

(Chanter X, f. 37); *Newlina* 1733 (Willis, p. 169); *Newlyn* 1742 (Ecton, p. 178); *Newlin* 1782 (Jones, p. 104); *Newelina* 1846 (Oliver, p. 441); *Newlyn* 1883–1939 (Kelly); *Neulina* virgin 1925 (Henderson, p. 150); *Newlina* 1996 (*TDD*).

Bishop Bronescombe dedicated the church on 26 September 1259 (Chanter I, f. 7v). In 1872 and 1878 the parish feast was held on the last Sunday in April, with a fair on 8 November (Polsue, iv, 5; Boase, 1890, col. 1593).

Newlyn, an otherwise unknown female saint, since at least 1259.

North Hill

Unknown 1733 (Willis, p. 166). *Turney* or *Torney* 1739 (MS Willis 41, f. 244); *Torney* 1742 (Ecton, p. 173), 1782 (Jones, p. 89). Unknown 1846 (Oliver, p. 441). *Torney* 1883 (Kelly), 1925 (Henderson, p. 152), 1939 (Kelly), 1996 (*TDD*).

In 1878 no parish feast was held but there were fairs on 8 September and the first Thursday in November (Boase, 1890, col. 1593).

The medieval dedication has not been discovered, but the 1739 evidence (although late) looks like a plausible local tradition. If so, the saint would be Terney, also patron of St Erney.

North Petherwin (transferred from Exeter to Truro diocese 1877, and from Devon to Cornwall 1966)

Andrea de Pidrewin (name) 1138–55 (13th) (Chanter I, f. 35v); *ecclesiam Sancti Paterni* 1171, 1186 x 1191 (Finberg, 1947, pp. 361, 369; Barlow, 1996, nos. 130, 174), 1193 (Chanter XV, f. 43v; Oliver, 1846, p. 95), 1284 (Chanter I, f. 123; dated by Finberg, 1969, p. 24). *Ecclesia de Northpydrewyn* (place) 1291 (Tax.). *Ecclesie . . . Sancti Paterni* 1501 (Chanter XII (ii), Redmayn f. 19v); *gildii Sancti Paterni* 1509–10 (CRO, DDP 167/5/1); *ecclesie . . . Sancti Paterni* 1529 (Chanter XIV, f. 40); *Paternus* 1733 (Willis, p. 172), 1742 (Ecton, p. 180), 1782 (Jones, p. 107), 1846 (Oliver, p. 452), 1925 (Henderson, p. 152), 1996 (*TDD*).

Bishop Bronescombe dedicated the church on 22 October 1259 (Chanter I, f. 8v). In 1878 the parish feast was formerly held on Trinity Sunday and a fair formerly on 20 September (Boase, 1890, col. 1594).

Padern, a male saint, since at least the 12th century, and patron also of South Petherwin.

North Tamerton

Unknown 1733 (Willis, p. 171), 1742 (Ecton, p. 180). *Dennis* 1754 (Ecton, p. 132). Unknown 1782 (Jones, p. 109), 1846 (Oliver, p. 441). Denis 1883–1939 (Kelly); Denis, with a query 1925 (Henderson, p. 152); Denis 1996 (*TDD*).

In 1740 and 1878 the parish feast was said to be held on Whit Sunday (MS Willis 41, f. 226a; Boase, 1890, col. 1595), with a fair in 1878 on 1 October (ibid.).

The medieval dedication has not been discovered; Denis since 1754. As this does not seem to be a conjecture from a parish feast day, it may be a genuine tradition.

Otterham

Lands called *St Tenye* 1613 (RIC, Henderson, East Cornwall Book, p. 428) and *St Iny* 1616 (ibid.). Unknown 1733 (Willis, p. 175). *Dennis* 1739 (MS Willis 41, f. 244v), 1742 (Ecton, p. 182), 1782 (Jones, p. 109); Denis 1846 (Oliver, p. 441), 1883–1939 (Kelly); Denis, with a query 1925 (Henderson, p. 153); Denis 1996 (*TDD*).

In 1878 the parish feast was held on the last Sunday in October (Boase, 1890, col. 1593).

The medieval dedication has not been unequivocally established, but Denis looks possible from the 1613–16 evidence and from the later tradition, and he has certainly been regarded as the patron saint since 1739.

Padstow

Sancte Petroces stow (place) (referring to Padstow or possibly Bodmin) 981 (Rositzke, 1940, p. 51); *Sanctus Petrocus* early 11th century (Liebermann, 1889, p. 17). *Lanwenehoc* (place) 1086 (DB 4/4); *Lan Wethnocke* (place) 12th century (14th) (Grosjean, 1956, p. 153). Petroc 1352 (Chanter V, f. 98), 1421 (Chanter X, f. 30), 1458 (Chanter XII (i), f. 8v), 1472 (ibid., (ii), f. 21), 1510 (Chanter XIII, f. 40); *Patrickstow alias Padstowe* (place) 1549 (Chanter XIV, f. 133v); Petroc 1733 (Willis, p. 169), 1742 (Ecton, p. 179), 1782 (Jones, p. 105), 1814 (Lysons, p. 251); *Petrocus* 1846 (Oliver, p. 442); Petroc 1883 (Kelly), 1925 (Henderson, p. 153), 1939 (Kelly), 1996 (*TDD*).

In 1872 the parish feast was held on 1 May (Polsue, iv, 20); Whitsuntide is mentioned as a holiday in 1878 (Boase, 1890, col. 1593)..

Petroc from at least the early 11th century, here as elsewhere sometimes confused with Patrick. The place-name Lanwenehoc, found in this and similar forms from the 11th century onwards, means 'church site of Gwethenek', a saint who is said to have lived at Padstow before Petroc and who was honoured locally until at least the 15th century (Olson and Padel, 1986, pp. 53–4; Padel, 1988, p. 131); it is not clear if he was ever a patron saint of the church, however.

Paul

Ecclesie Sancti Paulini 1259 (Chanter I, f. 5v), 1266 (*CChR 1257–1300*, p. 62), 1291 (Tax.); *ecclesie Sancti Pauli* 1317 (Chanter II, f. 119), 1340 (*Nonarum*, p. 348), 1362 (Chanter V, f. 139), 1418 (Chanter IX, f. 264), 1439 (Chanter X, f. 180v); *ecclesie . . . Sancti Pawli* 1475 (Chanter XII (ii), f. 35); *ecclesie . . . Sancti Paulini* 1494 (ibid., ff. 168v, 170v), 1504 (LPL, Reg. Warham, i, f. 205), 1523 (Chanter XIV, f. 17), 1530 (ibid., f. 49v); *Paulinus* 1733 (Willis, p. 168); *Paul* 1742 (Ecton, p. 176), 1782 (Jones, p. 97); *Paulinus* bishop of Rochester 1814 (Lysons, p. 255); *Paulinus* 1846 (Oliver, p; 442). Paul 1883–1939 (Kelly); *Paulinus, Paulus*, really Pol de Leon 1925 (Henderson, p; 155); Pol-de-Lion 1996 (*TDD*).

Bishop Grandisson dedicated the high altar *ecclesie Sancti Pauli* on 11 July 1336 (Chanter IV, f. 201). In 1878 the parish feast was held on the Sunday nearest to 10 October (Boase, 1890, col. 1593).

Paulinus or Paul, usually interpreted nowadays as Paul of Leon in Brittany rather than Paul the Apostle. This is likely in an area of Celtic dedications, but it is also probable that the saint was often identified with the Apostle or with Paulinus of Rochester.

Pelynt

Plvnent (place) 1086 DB (5/15/3); *vicariam . . . Sancti Nunit* 1442 (Chanter X, f. 202v). *Sanctus Juncus* 1478 (Worcester, 1969, p. 106). *Nunn* 1733 (Willis, p. 173), 1742 (Ecton, p. 183), 1782 (Jones, p. 115). Mary 1846 (Oliver, p. 442). Nun or *Nonna* 1883–1939 (Kelly). *Nonna*, or Mary with a query 1925 (Henderson, p. 155). *Nun* 1996 (*TDD*).

A fair was granted on St John the Baptist's Day (24 June) 1356 (*CChR 1341–1427*, p. 153). In 1878 the parish feast was held on 25 and 26 June (Boase, 1890, col. 1593).

Two traditions are recorded about the patron saint of this parish. Plunent in 1086 means 'the parish of Nennyd', and a male saint of this name is known in Wales (Padel, 1988, p. 132). The 1442 reference also makes the saint male (Worcester's Juncus may be a distorted form of the same saint, or of the saint of Lanreath).

However, a chapel of St Nynnyna, a female saint, also existed in the parish by 1291 (Tax.), and by the 18th century the patron saint was considered to be a female who was identified with Nonn, the mother of St David and patron of Altarnun.

Perranarworthal

St *Peran c.*1260 (Moulton, 1930, p. 178); *stauro Sancti Perrani* 1500 (PROB 11/12, f. 164v); *St Peran Arwothal* 1543 (Stoate, 1985); Piran 1742 (Ecton, p. 174), 1782 (Jones, p. 92); *Pieran* 1846 (Oliver, p. 442); Piran 1883–1939 (Kelly); *Pieranus* 1925 (Henderson, p. 158); Piran 1996 (*TDD*).

In 1878 no parish feast was held (Boase, 1890, col. 1594).

The Cornish saint Piran of Perranzabuloe since at least the 13th century.

Perranuthnoe

Ecclesiam Sancti Pierani 1348 (Chanter V, f. 66v), 1372 (Chanter VII, f. 20v); *parochia Sancti Perani* 1400 (Chanter VIII, f. 47v); *ecclesiam . . . de Seynt Perane* 1433 (Chanter X, f. 113); *ecclesiam Sancti Pierani* 1433 (ibid., f. 115), 1499 (Chanter XII (ii), f. 11); Piran 1733 (Willis, p. 168), 1742 (Ecton, p. 176); *Peran* 1782 (Jones, p. 97); *Pieran* 1846 (Oliver, p. 442). Piran and Nicholas 1856–1939 (Kelly). *Pieranus* 1925 (Henderson, p. 159). Michael and Piran 1996 (*TDD*).

In 1872 the parish feast was said to be held on the Sunday nearest to 5 March (Polsue, iv, 47), and in 1872 on 5 March with a fair on 5 August (Boase, 1890, col. 1594).

Piran since at least 1348, to whom first Nicholas and then Michael have been added in modern times on unknown grounds.

Perranzabuloe

Canonici S' Pierani 1086 (DB 4/26); *ecclesiam . . . Pirani* ?1107 (15th) (Hull, 1987, p. 2; *Regesta,* ii, 72); *ecclesiam Sancti Perani* 1146 (Blake, 1981, p. 309); *ecclesie Sancti Pyrani* 1269 (Chanter I, f. 41); *ecclesia Sancti Pirany* 1291 (Tax.); *ecclesie . . . Sancti Pierani* 1376 (Chanter VII, f. 41v), 1421 (Chanter X, f. 27v); *vicarie Sancti Pierani alias Kyerani* 1449 (Chanter XI, f. 311v). *S. Piranes* (place) *c.*1540 (Leland, 1907–10, i, 193); Piran 1733 (Willis, p. 169); *Peran* 1742 (Ecton, p. 179), 1782 (Jones, p. 105); Piran 1814 (Lysons, pp. 260, 264); *Pieran* 1846 (Oliver, p. 442); Piran 1883–1939 (Kelly); *Pieranus* 1925 (Henderson, p. 159); Piran 1996 (*TDD*).

In 1878 the parish feast was held on the last Sunday in October with a fair on the Monday after 16 March (Boase, 1890, col. 1594).

Piran since at least the 11th century. By the 13th, he was identified with the Irish saint Ciarán of Saighir, who was also believed to be the same as Keverne, patron of St Keverne.

Phillack

Felec (saint's name) 10th century (Olson and Padel, 1986, pp. 48–9). *Ecclesie Sancte Felicitatis* 1259 (Chanter I, f. 7), 1291 (Tax.), 1329 (Chanter V, f. 6v), 1476 (Chanter XII (ii), f. 37v). *Parochie Sant Felicis* 1497 (Taylor, 1932, p. 181); *ecclesiam de Felys* 1503 (ibid., Arundell f. 12v); *St Felix, Felyx* 1546, 1548 (Snell, *c.*1953, pp. 24–5); Felix 1733 (Willis, p. 167), 1742 (Ecton, p. 175), 1782 (Jones, p. 96). *Felicitas* 1846 (Oliver, p. 438). Felix 1883 (Kelly). *Felicitas* 1889–1902 (Kelly); *Felicitas* originally *Piala* 1906–1939 (Kelly); *Felicitas* 1925 (Henderson, p. 164), 1996 (*TDD*).

In 1878 the parish feast was held on the nearest Sunday to 23 November (Boase, 1890, col. 1594).

The earliest references to the church patron-saint occur in the Latin form Felicitas, but this appears to be a latinization of an earlier Celtic saint who is mentioned in the 10th-century list of Cornish saints. By 1259, the saint was regarded as a female. In turn, this tradition was replaced by 1546 with a belief that the saint was a male with the Latin name Felix (compare Philleigh). Felix lasted as late as 1883, when Felicity triumphed again; Piala comes from a medieval legend of St Gwinear but has no proven connection with Phillack (Orme, 1992c, p. 165).

Philleigh

Filii (saint's name) 10th century (Olson and Padel, 1986, pp. 45–6); *ecclesia Sancti Filii* 1312 (Chanter II, f. 68v). Felix 1733 (Willis, p. 170), 1742 (Ecton, p. 177), 1782 (Jones, p. 99). *Filius* 1846 (Oliver, p. 439). Felix 1883–1939 (Kelly). *Filius* 1925 (Henderson, p. 165); *Philleigh* 1996 (*TDD*).

In 1878 the parish feast was held on 3 November (Boase, 1890, col. 1594).

As at Phillack, the name Filius first recorded in 1312 appears to be the latinization of an earlier Celtic one, in this case Filii who is also mentioned in the 10th-century list of Cornish saints. By 1312 the saint was understood to be male; eventually, by 1733, he was latinized as Felix, and perhaps identified with one of the saints of that name. Filius was recovered in 1846.

Pillaton

Odulphus the Confessor 1411 (*CPL*, vi, 290); *ecclesie Sancti Odulphi* 1468 (Chanter XII (ii), Reg. Bothe, f. 11v). Unknown 1733 (Willis, p. 166), 1742 (Ecton, p. 173), 1782 (Jones, p. 89), 1846 (Oliver, p. 442). Odulph 1883–1939 (Kelly); *Odulphus* 1925 (Henderson, p. 165); Odulph 1996 (*TDD*).

Bishop Bronescombe dedicated the church on 16 October 1259 (Chanter I, f. 8). In 1878 no parish feast was mentioned but a fair was held on Whit Tuesday (Boase, 1890, col. 1594).

Odulph (d. 855), apostle of Frisia, by at least 1411 until the Reformation. He was then forgotten, but recovered in the late 19th century.

St Pinnock

Ecclesia Sancti Pynnoci 1284 (Chanter I, f. 123v), 1291 (Tax.). Church of St Andrew of *Seint Pynnok* 1385 (Rowe, 1914–50, ii, 26). *Ecclesiam . . . Sancti Pinnoci* 1460 (Chanter XII (i), f. 25); *Pinnock* 1733 (Willis p. 173); *Pynnoke* 1742 (Ecton, p. 183), 1782 (Jones, p. 115); *Pynocus* 1846 (Oliver, p. 442); *Pinnock* 1883–1939 (Kelly); *Pynnocus* 1925 (Henderson, p. 166); *Pinnock* 1996 (*TDD*).

In 1878 there was no parish feast day other than a moveable harvest festival (Boase, 1890, col. 1594).

Pynnoc, an otherwise unknown male saint, since at least 1284. By 1385, however, he had apparently been accompanied or superseded by Andrew, although he continued to be known through the place-name and has had the sole honour since 1733.

Porthilly

Michael 1299 (ECA, 2125). Unknown 1733 (Willis, p. 173). Not in Ecton (1742) or Jones (1782). Unknown 1846 (Oliver, p. 441). Michael 1883 (Kelly), 1925 (Henderson, p. 144), 1939 (Kelly), 1996 (*EDD*).

Michael since at least 1299 until the Reformation; it was then forgotten, and recovered in the late 19th century.

Poughill

Olave 1228 (15th) (Hull, 1987, p. 150), 1417 (Chanter IX, f. 186); Olave the Martyr 1427 (Chanter X, f. 84); Olave 1504 (LPL, Reg. Warham, i, f. 204). Unknown, corrected to *Tooleda* 1733 (Willis, pp. 171, 231). *Tolida* 1742 (Ecton, p. 180). Olave 1754 (Ecton, p. 628), 1782 (Jones, p. 108), 1846 (Oliver, p. 442), 1883 (Kelly); Olave martyr 1925 (Henderson, p. 166); *Olaf* 1939 (Kelly); *Olaf* king and martyr 1996 (*TDD*).

In 1740 the parish feast day was said to be held on 1 August (St Olave's day is 29 July) (MS Willis 41, f. 226a), and in 1878 on 2 August (Boase, 1890, col. 1594).

Olaf of Norway, king and martyr, since at least 1228 (compare St Olave, Exeter). By the 18th-century, he seems to have survived only in the memory of his feast-day, Tooleda being 'St Olave's Day', but his proper name was recovered in 1754.

Poundstock

Ecclesie Sancti Wynwolai 1333 (PRO, SC 6/161/74 m. 8d; Picken, 1947–9, pp. 342–3). Unknown 1733 (Willis, p; 171). Neot, with a query 1742 (Ecton, p. 180); Neot 1782 (Jones, p. 109), 1846 (Oliver, p. 442), 1883–1939 (Kelly); Neot, with a query 1925 (Henderson, p. 167). Winwaloe 1996 (*TDD*).

In 1878 the parish feast was held on Rogation Sunday (Boase, 1890, col. 1594).

The Breton saint Winwaloe from at least 1333 until the Reformation; it was then forgotten. Neot was a guess based on the local river name; Winwaloe has been recovered only through Picken's discovery in the 1940s.

Probus: collegiate and parish church

Propus (saint's name) 10th century (Olson and Padel, 1986, pp. 51–2); *canonici S' Probi* 1086 (DB 4/24); *Probos* ?1107 (15th) (Hull, 1987, p. 2); *ecclesiam Sancti Probi* 1146 (Blake, 1981, p. 309), 1241 x 1242 (15th) (Chanter XII (ii), ff. 44–5; Barlow, 1996, no. 256), 1269 (Chanter I, f. 39v), 1291 (Tax.); *Probus* 1733 (Willis, p. 170), 1742 (Ecton, p. 177), 1782 (Jones, p. 101), 1846 (Oliver, p. 442). Probus and Grace 1856–1939 (Kelly), 1872 (Polsue, iv, 94), 1925 (Henderson, p. 168), 1996 (*TDD*).

In 1872 the parish feast was held early in July (Polsue, iv, 100), the second Sunday in July being specified in 1878 (Boase, 1890, col. 1594).

Probus, a male saint, since at least 1086 and probably since at least the 10th century when he appears in the early list of Cornish saints. He may also have been the patron of the church of Lanprobi, *an early church at or near Sherborne (Dorset). Grace seems to appear only in about the 1850s, perhaps suggested by a bench-end inscription of 1591 asking for 'grace and good' or by the discovery of two skulls in the sanctuary wall in 1850, implying two patron saints. Since that period, a local fair on 23 September has been known as 'St Grace's fair', but it is not clear if the name comes from an earlier date (information kindly contributed by the Ven. R.L. Ravenscroft).*

Quethiock

Hugh 1297 (*CPR 1292–1301*, p. 284); *ecclesiam Sancti Hugonis* 1317 (Chanter II, f. 119v); Hugh (in the Latin form *Hugo*) 1318 (ibid., f. 127v), 1335 (*CPR 1334–8*, pp. 183, 197), 1337 (Chanter IV, f. 13v), 1346 (Chanter V, f. 57). Unknown 1733 (Willis, p. 166), 1742 (Ecton, p. 172). Hugh 1754 (Ecton, p. 126), 1782 (Jones, p. 87), 1846 (Oliver, p. 442), 1883–1939 (Kelly); *Hugo* 1925 (Henderson, p. 170); Hugh 1996 (*TDD*).

In 1878 no parish feast was held but there was a fair on the last Monday in January (Boase, 1890, col. 1594).

Hugh since at least 1297. Though often reproduced in the Latin form Hugo, there is no reason why the saint should not have been Hugh of Cluny (d. 1109) or Hugh of Lincoln (d. 1200).

Rame

German possibly by 1309 (Picken, 1956–8, p. 106); *ecclesia Sancti Germani* 1340 (Chanter IV, f. 231), 1341 (ibid., f. 240). Michael 1733 (Willis, p. 166); Michael, with a query 1742 (Ecton, p. 173). Michael 1754 (Ecton, p. 127), corrected to German (ibid., p. 627). German 1782 (Jones, p. 89); *Germanus* 1846 (Oliver, p. 442), 1925 (Henderson, p. 170), 1939 (Kelly), 1996 (*TDD*).

Bishop Bronescombe dedicated the church on 15 October 1259 (Chanter I, f. 8) and Bishop Stapledon on 10 October 1321 (Chanter II, f. 161v). In 1878 no parish feast was held (Boase, 1890, col. 1594).

German by at least 1309 until the Reformation (compare St Germans); it was then forgotten. Michael in the 18th century, until German was recovered in 1754.

Redruth

Church of *Sancti Eunini* 1297 (*Cal. Chancery Rolls*, p. 55); *ecclesia Sancti Ermini* 1316 (Chanter II, f. 112v); *ecclesiam Sancti Eunyny* 1325 (ibid., f. 184); *ecclesia Sancti Eunini* 1333 (Chanter V, f. 23v; cf. f. 87); *ecclesiam . . . Sancti Ewini* 1362 (ibid., f. 146v); *ecclesiam Sancti Ewniny*, also *Euniny* 1393 (Chanter VII, f. 143v); *ecclesiam . . . Sancti Eunini* 1421, 1423 (Chanter X, ff. 47v, 57v); *Uny* corrected to *Ewin* 1733 (Willis, pp. 167, 231); *Ewny* 1742 (Ecton, p. 175); *Ewney* 1754 (Ecton, p. 129); *Ewny* alias *Uny* 1782 (Jones, p. 95); *Euinus* or *Erminus* 1846 (Oliver, p. 442); *Uny* 173 (Kelly); *Eunius* or *Uny* 1925 (Henderson, p. 172); *Euny* 1939 (Kelly), 1996 (*TDD*).

The Cornish male saint Euny since at least 1297; compare Crowan and Lelant.

Roche

Ecclesia Sancti Goenandi 1242 (CRO, ME 595–6), 1306 (ibid.); church of St *Gunand* 1294 (*Cat. Ancient Deeds*, ii, 507); *ecclesia Sancti Gonandi* 1357 (Chanter V, f. 112); *ecclesiam . . . Sancti Goeniandi* 1474 (Chanter XII (ii), f. 24); *ecclesiarum . . . Sancti Goniandi* 1475 (ibid., f. 34v); *ecclesiam . . . Sancti Gonandi* 1497 (ibid., Redmayn, f. 2). *Conant* corrected to *Roch* 1733 (Willis, pp. 171, 231). *Roche* 1742 (Ecton, p. 177). *Gomonde* 1763 (Ecton, p. 130), 1782 (Jones, p. 101); *Gomonda* 1814 (Lysons, p. 278); *Goemandus* or *Conandus* 1846 (Oliver, p. 442); *Gomonda* 1883–1939 (Kelly); *Gonandus* 1925 (Henderson, p. 172); *Gomonda* 1996 (*TDD*).

The bishop of Waterford dedicated the high altar in 1338–9 (Chanter IV, f. 220v). In 1878 the parish feast was held on the Sunday before the second Tuesday in June, and there were three fair days (Boase, 1890, col. 1594).

Gonand, Goniand or Gunand, an otherwise unknown male saint, since at least 1242. Two 18th-century sources wrongly supposed the saint to be the French St Roche, on the basis of the place-name which simply means 'rock' (Padel, 1988, p. 150). Since the 19th century, the name and even the gender of the saint have been distorted.

Rock—see Porthilly

Ruan Lanihorne

Rumon (saint's name) 10th century (Olson and Padel, 1986, p. 46); 'the relics . . . of St Rumon (*Sancti Rumoni*) . . . were placed in the church of the township which is called *Lanrihorn*' 13th-century source, referring to *c*.980 (Grosjean, 1953, p. 397); *ecclesiam . . . Sancti Rumoni* 1458 (Chanter XII (i), f. 9); *ecclesiam . . . Sancti Rumonis* 1517 (Chanter XIII, f. 73); *Rumon* 1733 (Willis, p. 170), 1742 (Ecton, p. 177), 1782 (Jones, p. 101); *Rumonus* 1846 (Oliver, p. 442); *Rumon* 1883–1939 (Kelly); *Rumonus* 1925 (Henderson, p. 173); *Rumon* 1996 (*TDD*).

In 1878 the parish feast was held on the second Sunday in September (Boase, 1890, col. 1594).

Rumon, probably since at least the 10th century when his name occurs in the early list of Cornish saints. He was originally buried here, but was taken to Tavistock Abbey in the late 10th or the 11th century.

Ruan Major

Ecclesia Sancti Romon' 1208 (*Rotuli Litterarum Patentium*, f. 81a); *ecclesia Sancti Rumoni* 1291 (Tax.), 1325 (Chanter II, f. 184), 1394 (Chanter VII, f. 148), 1398 (Chanter IX, f. 10), 1533 (Chanter XIV, f. 62v); *Rumon* 1733 (Willis, p. 167), 1742 (Ecton, p. 174), 1782 (Jones, p. 92); *Rumonus* 1846 (Oliver, p. 442); *Rumon* 1883–1939 (Kelly); *Rumonus* 1925 (Henderson, p. 174); *Rumon* 1996 (*TDD*).

In 1878 the parish feast was held on the Sunday after Ascension Day (Boase, 1890, col. 1594).

Rumon since at least 1208.

Ruan Minor

Ecclesia de Sancto Rumono 1277 (Chanter I, f. 81); *ecclesiam Sancti Rumoni* 1314 (Chanter II, f. 82v), 1441 (Chanter XI, f. 225), 1533 (Chanter XIV, f. 63); *Rumon* 1733 (Willis, p. 167), 1742 (Ecton, p. 174), 1782 (Jones, p. 93); *Rumonus* 1846 (Oliver, p. 442), 1925 (Henderson, p. 174); *Rumon* 1939 (Kelly).

Rumon since at least 1277.

Saltash

Nicholas 1351 (Chanter III, f. 168v), 1492 (Harper-Bill, 1991, p. 89), 1733 (Willis, p. 166), 1742 (Ecton, p. 173), 1782 (Jones, p. 91). Unknown 1846 (Oliver, p. 442). Nicholas 1856 (Kelly). Nicholas and Faith 1883–1939 (Kelly), 1925 (Henderson, p. 174), 1996 (*TDD*).

In 1878 no parish feast was held but there were three fair days (Boase, 1890, col. 1594).

Nicholas since at least 1351. Faith was added in about 1883, on the supposition that a chapel of St Faith mentioned in a 15th-century reference formed part of the church; in fact it stood in a different location.

St Sampson (Golant)

Mostier Saint Sanson late 12th century (Ewert, 1939–70, i, 89); *capella Sancti Sampsonis* 1281 (Oliver, 1846, p. 43), 1374 (Chanter VII, f. 7); *Sampson* 1733 (Willis, p. 171), 1742 (Ecton, p. 178), 1782 (Jones, p. 102), 1814 (Lysons, p. 281), 1846 (Oliver, p. 442), 1883–1939 (Kelly), 1925 (Henderson, p. 175), 1996 (*TDD*).

The church was dedicated by Thomas Chard, bishop of Selymbria on 7 May 1509 (Chanter XIII, f. 168v). In 1878 the parish feast was held on the first Sunday after 28 July (Boase, 1890, col. 1594).

The Breton saint Sampson, bishop of Dol, since at least the late 12th century.

Sancreed

Ecclesiam Sancti Sancreti 1235 (13th) (Luard, 1864, p. 99); *ecclesias . . . de Sancto Sancredo* 1242 x 1243 (ECA, D&C 1942; Barlow, 1996, no. 257); *ecclesiam Sancti Sancredi* 1289 (ECA, D&C 3672, p. 57), 1291 (Tax.), 1313 (Chanter II, f. 70); *ecclesie . . . Sancti Sancreti* 1378 (Chanter VII, f. 55); *ecclesie . . . Sancte Sancrede* 1494 (Chanter XII (ii), f. 168v); *Sancred* 1733 (Willis, p. 168); *Sancret* 1742 (Ecton, p. 176); *Sancreet* 1782 (Jones, p. 97); *Sancredus* 1846 (Oliver, p. 442); *San Creed* 1883–1939 (Kelly); *Sancredus* 1925 (Henderson, p. 175); *Creden* 1996 (*TDD*).

In 1872 and 1878 the parish feast was held on Whit Sunday (Polsue, iv, 141; Boase, 1890, col. 1594).

Sancred, usually a male saint said to have lived as a swineherd, since at least 1242. The modern references suggest a confusion with the patron saint of Creed or with some other saint.

Scilly Isles: St Agnes

*S. Agnes Isle c.*1540 (Leland, 1907–10, i, 190); Agnes 1883–1939 (Kelly), 1996 (*TDD*).

Agnes since at least about 1540. The dedication was evidently suggested by the older, non-saintly, name of the island, Hagenes (Padel, 1988, p. 49).

Scilly Isles: St Helen

Insula Sancti Elidii 1140 x 1175 (15th) (Finberg, 1947, pp. 359–60); *insulam Sancti Egidii* 1193 (16th) (Chanter XV, f. 43v; Oliver, 1846, p. 95); *Saynct Lides Isle c.*1540 (Leland, 1907–10, i, 190).

Elid or Lyde, a male saint, since at least 1193 (compare St Issey). Egidius (Giles) in the 16th-century text is evidently a mistake, as is Helen which first occurs in 1569 (Padel, 1988, p. 95).

Scilly Isles: St Martin

*S. Martines Isle c.*1540 (Leland, 1907–10, i, 190); Martin 1883–1939 (Kelly), 1996 (*TDD*).

Martin since at least about 1540.

Scilly Isles: St Mary

Ecclesia Sancte Marie de Heumor 1161 x 1184 (13th) (Finberg, 1947, p. 362; Barlow, 1996, no. 131); *S. Mary Isle c.*1540 (Leland, 1907–10), i, 190); Mary 1782 (Jones, p. 94), 1883–1939 (Kelly), 1996 (*TDD*).

In 1878 no parish feast was held (Boase, 1890, col. 1594).

Mary since at least the late 12th century.

Scilly Isles: St Samson

Insula . . . sancti Sampsonis 1140 x 1175 (15th) (Finberg, 1947, pp. 359–60); *insulam Sancti Sampsonis* 1193 (16th) (Chanter XV, f. 43v; Oliver, 1846, p. 95).

Sampson since at least the late 12th century.

Scilly Isles: Tean

Insula . . . sancte Teone 1140 x 1175 (15th) (Finberg, 1947, pp. 359–60); *insulam Sancte Theone virginis* 1193 (16th) (Chanter XV, f. 43v; Oliver, 1846, p. 95).

Tean, an otherwise unknown female saint, since at least the late 12th century.

Scilly Isles: Tresco, St Nicholas, Benedictine priory and parish church

Nicholas x 1177 (15th) (Finberg, 1947, p. 365; Barlow, 1996, no. 132), 1193 (16th) (Chanter XV, f. 43v; Oliver, 1846, p. 95), c.1200 (Gervase, 1867, ii, 424), 1883–1939 (Kelly), 1996 (*TDD*).

Nicholas since at least 1176.

Sennen

Parochia Sancte Senane 1334 (Glasscock, 1975, p. 30); *capellam Sancte Senane* 1448 (Chanter XI, f. 302); *Sennan* 1733 (Willis, p. 167). Not in Ecton (1742). *Sennan* 1782 (Jones, p. 95). *Senara* (a mistake for Zennor) 1846 (Oliver, p. 442). *Sennen* 1883–1939 (Kelly); Senana and John the Baptist 1925 (Henderson, p. 176); *Sennen* 1996 (*TDD*).

An inscription on the church font records the dedication of the church on St John the Baptist's Day 1441; however, the dedication was also in prospect in August 1448 (Chanter XI, f. 302). In 1872 and 1878 the parish feast was held on Advent Sunday (the nearest Sunday to St Andrew's Day) (Polsue, iv, 144), with a fair in 1878 on St Peter's Day (Boase, 1890, col. 1594).

Senan or Sennen, a female saint not certainly found elsewhere, since at least 1334. Henderson's conjecture of John the Baptist apparently rests on the irrelevant date of the church dedication in 1441.

Sheviock

Mary 1193 (Oliver 1846, p. 95), 1278 (Chanter I, f. 85v), 1497 (*CPL*, xvi, 528); store of Mary 1521 (RIC, Henderson, HC 66, p. 165); Mary 1733 (Willis, p. 166); Mary, with a query 1742 (Ecton, p. 173); Mary 1754 (Ecton, p. 627), 1782 (Jones, p. 89). Peter and Paul 1846 (Oliver, p. 442). Mary 1883–1939 (Kelly). Mary, Peter and Paul 1925 (Henderson, p. 177). Mary 1996 (*TDD*).

Bishop Bronescombe dedicated the church on 13 October 1259 (Chanter I, f. 8). In 1878 no parish feast was held (Boase, 1890, col. 1594).

Usually Mary since at least 1193. In 1427, however, the rector of Sheviock wished to be buried 'in the cemetery of SS Peter and Paul' (Chanter XI, f. 500v), so either the dedication was jointly to Mary, Peter and Paul or the rector was referring to a different church. In modern times Mary alone, and Mary with Peter and Paul, have both been favoured.

Shipstors (or Sheepstall) in Veryan: hospital

The hospital adjoined a chapel of, and may have been dedicated to, Margaret in 1301 (Orme and Webster, 1995, p. 212).

Sithney

Ecclesia Sancti Sythynini 1230 (*CuRR 1230–3*, p. 23); *Merthersithun* (place) 1230 (Rowe, 1914–50, i, 23); *ecclesias de Sancto Sydnio* . . . 1270 (Chanter I, f. 44v); *ecclesia Sancti Sydeny* 1291 (Tax.); *ecclesie* . . . *Sancti Sidenini* 1393 (Chanter VII, f. 144v); *ecclesie* . . . *Sancti Sithnini* 1432 (Chanter X, f. 108); *ecclesie* . . . *Sancti Sidnini* 1436 (ibid., f. 144); *Sanctus Senseus* perhaps for *Sesneus* 1478 (Worcester, 1969, p. 88); *parochia Sancti Sydnyny* 1549 (Snell, c.1955, p 18); *Sithney* 1733 (Willis, p. 167); *Sithne* 1742 (Ecton, p. 174), 1782 (Jones, p. 94); *Siduinus* or *Sithuinus* 1846 (Oliver, p. 442); *Sithney* 1883–1939 (Kelly); *Sidinius* 1925 (Henderson, p. 177); *Sithney* 1996 (*TDD*).

In 1872 and 1878 the parish feast was held on the first Sunday in August (Polsue, iv, 155; Boase, 1890, col. 1594).

Sydhni (modern Sithney), a male saint also venerated in Brittany, since at least 1230.

South Hill

Ecclesie parochialis Sancti Sampsonis 1333 (Chanter IV, f. 172v); store of Sampson 1467 (PROB 11/5, f. 106v); Sampson 1477 (Chanter XII (ii), f. 41v). Unknown 1733 (Willis, p. 166), 1742 (Ecton, p. 173). Sampson 1754 (Ecton, p. 127). Unknown 1782 (Jones, p. 90). Sampson 1846 (Oliver, p. 442), 1883 (Kelly), 1925 (Henderson, p. 178), 1939 (Kelly), 1996 (*TDD*).

Bishop Grandisson dedicated the high altar on 4 November 1333 (Chanter IV, f. 172v).

The Breton saint Sampson since at least 1333 until the Reformation; it was then forgotten and recovered in 1754.

South Petherwin

*Paer c.*1200 (Padel, 1988, p. 138); *Pyderwyne* (place) 1291 (Tax.); chaplain of *sancti Paterni de Piderwyne c.*1293 (15th) (Hull, 1987, p. 19); *Patron* 1555 (RIC, Henderson, HC 66, p. 149); *Paternus* 1733 (Willis, p. 171), 1742 (Ecton, p. 180), 1782 (Jones, p. 108), 1846 (Oliver, p. 442), 1883 (Kelly), 1925 (Henderson, p. 178), 1939 (Kelly), 1996 (*TDD*).

In 1878 no parish feast was held (Boase, 1890, col. 1594).

Padern, a male saint, since at least about 1200 (compare North Petherwin).

St Stephen in Brannel

[Ecclesiam] Sancti Stephani 1261 (Chanter I, f. 20v), 1291 (Tax.). *Eglosselans* (place) 1297 (*Cal. Chancery Rolls*, p. 56); *Egloshellans* (place) 1379 (Henderson, 1953–60, p. 445). Stephen the Martyr 1394 (Chanter VII, f. 150); Stephen 1733 (Willis, p. 169), 1742 (Ecton, p. 183), 1782 (Jones, p. 116), 1846 (Oliver, p. 442), 1883 (Kelly), 1925 (Henderson, p. 179), 1939 (Kelly), 1996 (*TDD*).

Bishop Bronescombe dedicated the church on 20 August 1261 (Chanter I, f. 20v). In 1878 the parish feast was held on the first Sunday in August (Boase, 1890, col. 1594).

Stephen from at least 1261. The settlement by the church also had the Cornish name Eglosselans *by 1297, meaning 'church of Helans'. This need not refer to the patron saint, but a saint called* Elenn *occurs at a suitable place in the 10th-century list of Cornish saints so the church may originally have been dedicated to that person (Olson and Padel, 1986, pp. 57–8).*

St Stephen by Launceston: priory and parish church

Ecclesie Sancti Stephani 1076 (15th) (Hull, 1987, pp. 3–4); *canonici S' Stefani* 1086 (DB 4/2); *ecclesiam . . . Sancti Stephani* ?1107 (15th) (Hull, 1987, p. 2; *Regesta*, ii, 72); *ecclesiam Sancti Stephani* 1146 (Blake, 1981, p. 309), 1291 (Tax.); Stephen 1733 (Willis, p. 171), 1742 (Ecton, p. 180), 1782 (Jones, p. 110), 1846 (Oliver, p. 440), 1883 (Kelly), 1925 (Henderson, p. 180), 1939 (Kelly), 1996 (*TDD*).

Bishop Bronescombe dedicated the church on 25 October 1259 (Chanter I, f. 8v).

Stephen since at least the 11th century. The priory, but not the parish church, moved to the new town of Launceston in about 1155 (Hull, 1987, p. xi).

St Stephen by Saltash

Ecclesiam Sancti Stephani 1187 x 1190 (Barlow, 1996, no. 171); *Sancti Stephani de Seint Estevene* 1270 (Rowe, 1914–50, i, 117); Stephen 1276 (Chanter I, f. 72), 1291 (Tax.), 1315 (Chanter II, f. 110v); *S. Stephan's c.*1540 (Leland, 1907–10, i, 210); Stephen 1733 (Willis, p. 166), 1742 (Ecton, p. 173), 1782 (Jones, p. 90), 1846 (Oliver, p. 442), 1883 (Kelly), 1925 (Henderson, p. 182), 1939 (Kelly), 1996 (*TDD*).

In 1878 no parish feast was held (Boase, 1890, col. 1595).

Stephen since at least the late 12th century.

Stithians

Ecclesie Sancte Stethyane 1268 (Chanter I, f. 37v); *ecclesia Sancte Stediane* 1291 (Tax.), 1354 (Chanter III, ff. 176v–177); *ecclesie . . . Sancte Stediane* 1421 (Chanter X, f. 48v); *Stythian* 1733 (Willis, p. 167); *Stedian's* or *Stythians* 1742 (Ecton, p. 174); *Stedians* alias *Stythyans* 1782 (Jones, p. 92); *Stedianus* 1846 (Oliver, p. 443); *Stythians* 1883 (Kelly); *Stedyana* 1925 (Henderson, p. 183); *Stythian* 1939 (Kelly); *Stythians* 1996 (*TDD*).

The bishop of Waterford dedicated the high altar in 1338–9 (Chanter II, f. 220v).

Stithian, an otherwise unknown female saint, since at least 1268.

Stoke Climsland

All Saints 1508 (*CPL*, xix (forthcoming), no. 33). Unknown 1733 (Willis, p. 166), 1742 (Ecton, p. 173), 1782 (Jones, p. 90), 1846 (Oliver, p. 443), 1925 (Henderson, p. 182), 1996 (*TDD*).

Bishop Stapledon dedicated the church on 6 October 1321 (Chanter II, f. 161). In 1878 a fair was held on 29 May (Boase, 1890, col. 1595).

All Saints before the Reformation; it was then forgotten and, unusually, no other dedication has been conjectured or substituted.

Stratton

Andrew *c.*1146 x 1165 (15th) (Hull, 1987, pp. 152–3), 1433 (Chanter X, f. 113v), 1541 (Chanter XIV, f. 106v), 1551 (RIC, Henderson, HC 66, p. 146b; Oliver, 1837, p. 173), 1733 (Willis, p. 171), 1742 (Ecton, p. 180), 1782 (Jones, p. 109), 1846 (Oliver, p. 443), 1883 (Kelly), 1925 (Henderson, p. 182), 1939 (Kelly), 1996 (*TDD*).

In 1740 the parish feast day was said to be held on 30 November (St Andrew's Day) (MS Willis 41, f. 226a). In 1878 no feast day was mentioned but three fairs were held (Boase, 1890, col. 1595).

Andrew since at least the mid 12th century.

Talland

Ecclesie . . . Sancti Tallani 1452 (Chanter X, f. 272v), 1465 (Chanter XII (ii), f. 2v), 1472 (ibid., f. 21), 1479 (ibid., f. 86), 1514 (Chanter XIII, f. 56). Unknown 1733 (Willis, p. 173). *Tallan* 1742 (Ecton, p. 183), 1782 (Jones, p. 116); *Tallanus* 1846 (Oliver, p. 443); *Tallan* 1883 (Kelly); *Talland* 1889–1919 (Kelly). Unknown or *Tallanus* 1925 (Henderson, p. 183). Not stated 1926–1939 (Kelly). *Tallan* 1996 (*TDD*).

In 1878 no significant parish feast was held (Boase, 1890, col. 1595).

The place-name appears to mean 'hill-brow church site' (Padel, 1988, p. 160). By 1452, it was interpreted as the name of a male saint Tallan, who has generally been regarded as the patron ever since.

St Teath

Tedda (saint's name) 12th century (14th) (Grosjean, 1953, pp. 397–8); *de Sancta Tecla (sic)* 1201 (Stenton, 1952, p. 382); *Tethe* 1259 (Chanter I, f. 6); *ecclesie Sancte Thetthe* 1266 (ibid., f. 34v); *porcionis Sancte Tethe* 1270 (ibid., f. 45v); *Thetha* 1291 (Tax.); *ecclesia Sancte Tethe* 1389 (Chanter VI, f. 195v); *ecclesie . . . Sancti (sic) Tethe virginis* 1520 (Chanter XIV, f. 2); *ecclesie . . . Sancte Tethe virginis* 1522 (ibid., f. 12v); *S. Esse c.*1540 (Leland, 1907–10, i, 178); *Seynt Ethe* 1548 (Snell, *c.*1953, p. 48); *Tethe* 1733 (Willis, p. 173), 1742 (Ecton, p. 181), 1782 (Jones, p. 112); *Tetha* 1846 (Oliver, p. 443), 1883 (Kelly); *Tetha* virgin 1925 (Henderson, p. 184); *Tetha* or *Etha* 1939 (Kelly); *Teatha* 1996 (*TDD*).

In 1878 the parish feast was held on Whit Tuesday, with fairs on the last Tuesday in February and the first Tuesday in July (Boase, 1890, col. 1595).

Tetha, a female saint, since at least 1201 and probably since at least the 12th century when she occurs in a list of saints connected with north Cornwall (Orme, 1992c, p. 132). She was then believed to be one of the 24 children of the Welsh king Brychan.

Temple

Unknown 1733 (Willis, p. 173). John 1740 (MS Willis 41, f. 237). Unknown 1742 (Ecton, p. 182), 1782 (Jones, p. 113), 1846 (Oliver, p. 443). Catherine 1883 (Kelly), 1925 (Henderson, p. 185), 1939 (Kelly), 1996 (*TDD*).

The medieval dedication has not been discovered, and it was forgotten after the Reformation. John was probably a conjecture from the place having once belonged to the Knights of St John; the origin of Catherine is not clear.

St Thomas by Launceston—see Launceston

Tintagel

Ecclesie Sancte Marcelliane 1258 (Chanter I, f. 4); *ecclesie Sancte Merteriane* 1259 (ibid. f. 7v); *vicariam Sancte Merth'* 1276 (ibid., f. 74v); *ecclesie . . . Sancte Marthariane* 1422 (Chanter X, f. 42v). *S. Symphorian, ther caullid Simiferian c.*1540 (Leland, 1907–10, i, 177). *Symphorian* 1733 (Willis, p. 173), 1742 (Ecton, p. 181). *Simphorian* corrected to *Marteriane* 1782 (Jones, p. 112; extra page 4). *Marcelliana* or *Materiana* 1846 (Oliver, p. 443). *Symphorian* 1883–1889 (Kelly). *Materiana* 1902–1914 (Kelly); *Merteriana* virgin 1925 (Henderson, p. 186); *Materiana* or *Madryn* 1919–1939 (Kelly), 1996 (*TDD*).

In 1878 no parish feast was held (Boase, 1890, col. 1595).

A female saint, also patron of Minster, apparently called Matherian or Mertherian, although the recorded forms differ. Leland recorded Symphorian, perhaps by mistake, which endured until as late as 1889; modern writers have restored the original saint, but have had difficulties in agreeing on a spelling or identification.

Towednack

Parochia Sancti Tewynnoci 1334 (Glasscock, 1975, p. 30); *parochia Sancti Thewynnoci* 1337 (PRO, E 179/87/15); *capellarum sanctorum Tewennoci confessoris . . .* 1409 (Chanter IX, f. 232v); *Widnock* 1733 (Willis, p. 167). Not in Ecton (1742). *Widnock* 1754 (Ecton, p. 129); *Twinnock* 1763 (Ecton, p. 129). Not in Jones (1782). Unknown 1846 (Oliver, p. 443). *Twinnock* 1883 (Kelly); *Tewennoc* 1889–1902 (Kelly); *Tewinnock* the confessor 1906–1926 (Kelly); *Tewennocus*, i.e. Wynwallo 1925 (Henderson, p. 189); *Winwalloe* 1935–1939 (Kelly); *Tewinock* 1996 (*TDD*).

In 1878 the parish feast was held on the Sunday on or after St Mark's Day (25 April), with a fair on the Tuesday on or nearest to 27 September (Boase, 1890, col. 1595).

The name Tewynnoc is a hypocoristic or 'pet' form of the name of the Breton saint Winwaloe, who was therefore the patron of the church (under the form Tewynnoc) from at least 1334 until the Reformation (compare Landewednack). The saint's name has continued to be used in variants of the Tewynnoc form down to modern times, apart from a few scholarly deductions of Winwaloe.

Tregony: Augustinian priory

The medieval dedication has not been discovered.

Tregony: parish church

James 1267 (BL, Cotton MS Cleopatra C.vii, f. 129v), 1282 (Chanter I, f. 124v), 1286 (ibid., f. 131v), 1450 (Chanter XI, f. 348v), 1502 (PROB 11/13, f. 162), 1733 (Willis, p. 170), 1742 (Ecton, p. 177), 1782 (Jones, p. 100), 1814 (Lysons, p. 75); *Jacobus* 1846 (Oliver, p. 443); James 1883 (Kelly), 1925 (Henderson, p. 189), 1939 (Kelly).

In 1302 a fair was held on St James' Day (Boase, 1890, col. 1583). In 1867 the parish feast was said to be kept on 25 July (St James' Day) (Polsue, i, 285), but in 1878 the latter was called a fair and the parish feast days stated to be held on the Sunday and Monday nearest 29 September (Boase, 1890, col. 1595).

James since at least 1267.

Tremaine

Capelle . . . Sancti Winwolai 1506 (Chanter XIII, f. 147v). Unknown 1733 (Willis, p. 172), 1742 (Ecton, p. 180), 1782 (Jones, p. 109). *Winwolaus* 1814 (Lysons, p. 307). Unknown 1846 (Oliver, p. 443), 1883 (Kelly). *Winwolaus* 1889 (Kelly), 1925 (Henderson, p. 190), 1939 (Kelly); *Winwalo* 1996 (*TDD*).

In 1878 the parish feast was said to be held on Whit Sunday (Boase, 1890, col. 1595).

The Breton saint Winwaloe from at least 1506 until the Reformation; the dedication was then forgotten but was recovered in 1814.

Treneglos

Gregory 1281 (Oliver, 1846, p. 43). George 1467 (Chanter XII (ii), f. 9v), 1518 (Chanter XIII, f. 75-v). Unknown 1733 (Willis, p. 172), 1742 (Ecton, p. 180), 1782 (Jones, p. 108). Gregory, sometimes George 1846 (Oliver, p. 443). Werburgh (a mistake for Warbstow) 1883–1902 (Kelly). Gregory 1906–1939 (Kelly). Gregory, or George in error 1925 (Henderson, p. 192). Gregory 1996 (*TDD*).

In 1878 the parish feast was said to be held on the first Thursday in August (Boase, 1890, col. 1595).

George, with two references before the Reformation, looks more likely than Gregory with one. The names were sometimes confused (compare Frithelstock and Seaton in Devon), but George is the commoner patron saint. The dedication was forgotten by the 18th century; the two saints were recovered in 1846 but Gregory has become normal.

Tresmere

Nicholas 1385 (15th) (Hull, 1987, p. 88), 1575 (RIC, Henderson, East Cornwall Book, p. 549), 1733 (Willis, p. 172), 1742 (Ecton, p. 180), 1782 (Jones, p. 110). *Winwolaus* (perhaps a mistake for Tremaine) 1846 (Oliver, p. 443). Nicholas or *Winwolaus* 1883–1935 (Kelly). Nicholas 1925 (Henderson, p. 192), 1939 (Kelly), 1996 (*TDD*).

In 1878 no parish feast was held (Boase, 1890, col. 1595).
Nicholas from at least 1385. Oliver introduced the incorrect Winwolaus, *current until the 1930s.*

Trevalga

Petroc 1399 (Chanter IX, f. 13v). Unknown 1733 (Willis, p. 231), 1742 (Ecton, p. 182), 1782 (Jones, p. 113). *Petrocus* 1846 (Oliver, p. 443); Petroc 1883 (Kelly), 1925 (Henderson, p. 193), 1939 (Kelly), 1996 (*TDD*).

In 1878 the parish feast was held on Whit Sunday and formerly also on Whit Tuesday (Boase, 1890, col. 1595).

Petroc from at least 1399 to the Reformation; it was then forgotten but recovered in 1846.

Trewen

Michael 1478 (Worcester, 1969, p 15), 1558 (RIC, Henderson, HC 66, p. 151). Unknown 1733 (Willis, p. 171), 1742 (Ecton, p. 180). Michael 1754 (Ecton, p. 628). Unknown 1782 (Jones, p. 108), 1846 (Oliver, p. 443). Michael 1883 (Kelly), 1925 (Henderson, p. 193), 1939 (Kelly), 1996 (*TDD*).

In 1739 the parish feast was said to be held on the Sunday before Michaelmas Day (29 September) or on that day if a Sunday (MS Willis 41, f. 244). In 1878 the feast was thought to have been formerly held on the Sunday before 10 October, with fairs on 14 May and 10 October (Boase, 1890, col. 1595).

Michael before the Reformation; it was then forgotten, recovered in 1754 but not fully accepted again until the late 19th century.

Truro

Mary 1259 (Chanter I, f. 7v), 1279 (ibid., p. 188), 1400 (*CPL*, v, 376–7), 1462 (Chanter XII (i), ff. 17, 24), 1515 (PROB 11/18, f. 68v), 1733 (Willis, p. 171), 1742 (Ecton, p. 178), 1782 (Jones, p. 102), 1814 (Lysons, p. 312), 1846 (Oliver, p. 443), 1883 (Kelly), 1925 (Henderson, p. 193), 1939 (Kelly), 1996 (*TDD*).

Bishop Bronescombe dedicated the church on 28 September 1259 (Chanter I, f. 7v) and Bishop Grandisson the high altar on 6 November 1328 (Chanter IV, f. 79). In 1878 the parish feast was said to be held on 25 March (the Annunciation of Mary) (Boase, 1890, col. 1596).

Mary since at least 1259.

Truro: Dominican friary

Bishop Bronescombe dedicated the church on 29 September 1259 (Chanter I, f. 7v). *The medieval dedication has not been discovered.*

St Tudy

Ecglostudic, also *Hecglostudic* (place) 1086 (Exon, pp. 186, 471); *ecclesie Sancti Tudi* 1263 (Chanter I, f. 26v); *ecclesia Sancti Tudii* 1291 (Tax.), 1348 (Chanter V, f. 67v), 1389 (Chanter VI, f. 198); *parochia Sancte Ude* (ibid., f. 225v) 1391; *ecclesiam . . . sancti Tudy* 1425 (Chanter XI, f. 39); *ecclesiam . . . Sancti Tudii* 1445 (Chanter X, f. 213v); *ecclesiam . . . Sancti Tudy alias Vdi* 1535 (Chanter XIV, f; 80v); *S. Tedy* c; 1540 (Leland, 1907–10, i, 191); *Udy* 1733 (Willis, p. 173); *Tudye* 1742 (Ecton, p. 181), 1782 (Jones, p. 112); *Uda* or *Tudius* 1846 (Oliver, p. 443); *Tudy* 1883–1939 (Kelly); *Tudius* 1925 (Henderson, p. 195); *Tudy* 1996 (*TDD*).

In 1878 no parish feast was held (Boase, 1890, col. 1596).

Tudic, a Breton male saint said to have been a disciple of Maudith, since at least 1086.

Tywardreath: Benedictine priory

Andrew 1154 x 1189 (Oliver, 1846, pp. 37–8; Andrew the Apostle and *Sancto Austolo* 1173 (ibid., p. 38); Andrew *c.*1200 (Gervase, 1867, ii, 424).
Usually Andrew before the Reformation; Andrew and Austol in 1173.

Tywardreath: parish church

Andrew 1467 (Chanter XII (ii), f. 7), 1472 (ibid., f. 19), 1478 (ibid., f. 84), 1520 (Chanter XIV, f. 6), 1522 (PROB 11/20, f. 229v), 1733 (Willis, p. 171), 1742 (Ecton, p. 177), 1782 (Jones, p. 102), 1846 (Oliver, p. 443), 1883 (Kelly), 1925 (Henderson, p. 195), 1939 (Kelly), 1996 (*TDD*).

In 1878 the parish feast was said to be held on the nearest Sunday to St Andrew's Day, i.e. Advent Sunday (Boasc, 1890, col. 1596).
Andrew since at least 1467.

St Veep

Ecclesia Sancti Vep 1236 x ?1237 (14th) (Barlow, 1996, no. 281); St Veep 1284 (Rowe, 1914–50, i, 181); *ecclesia Sancti Vepi* 1291 (Tax.); church of *Sancto Vepo* 1297 (*Cal. Chancery Rolls*, p. 31); *Vepy* 1340 (*Nonarum*, p. 342); *parochia Sancte Vepe* 1373 (Chanter VII, f. 23v); *ecclesie . . . Sancte Vepe* 1384 (ibid., f. 88); *ecclesiam . . . Sancti Vepi* (Chanter VII (part iii), f. 7v); *ecclesia . . . Sancte Vepe* (Chanter VI, f. 142); *ecclesie Sancti Vepi* 1412 (Chanter IX, f. 138v); *parochia Sancti Vepi* 1415 (Chanter VIII, f. 209v); *ecclesie . . . Sancte Vepe* 1424 (Chanter X, f. 67v); *ecclesie . . . Sancti Vepi* 1436 (ibid., f. 147v); *vicaria S. Vepy* 1453 (Chanter XI, f. 400); *ecclesie . . . Sancte Vepe* 1454 (Chanter X, f. 284); *vicaria Sancte Vepe* 1463 (Chanter XII (i), f. 46); *Veep* 1733 (Willis, p. 174); *Vepe* 1742 (Ecton, p. 183). *Ciricius* and *Juliette* 1754 (Ecton, p. 628). *Vepe* 1782 (Jones, p. 115). *Ciricius* 1786 (Bacon, p. 318). *Vepus* alias *Vepa* 1846 (Oliver, p. 443). *Ciricius* 1883–1926 (Kelly). *Vepus* 1925 (Henderson, p. 197). *Ciricus* and *Julitta* 1935–1939 (Kelly). *Cyricius* 1996 (*TDD*).

Bishop Grandisson dedicated the church, *ecclesiam Sancte Vepe*, and high altar in honour of *Sanctorum Cirici et Juliette* on 1 July 1336 (Chanter IV, f. 201). In 1878 the parish feast was thought to have been held on 1 July, with a fair on the Wednesday before Midsummer Day (Boase, 1890, col. 1596).

The original patron was an otherwise unrecorded Vepe. The unusual degree of confusion about the saint's gender suggests that, by the later middle ages, the name was largely that of a place-name rather than a saint with an active cult. Instead, the cult of Cyricus and Julitta was introduced in 1336, perhaps because it was already established in the nearby priory of St Carrock. Both cults have been acknowledged since the 18th century.

Veryan

Sibillon (saint's name) 10th century (Olson and Padel, 1986, p. 47). *Parochia Sancti Simphoriani* 1278 (PRO, JUST 1/110); *ecclesia . . . Sancti Simphoriani* 1321 (ECA, D&C 995; 3672, p. 143); *Sunphoria* 1419 (Rowe, 1914–50, ii, 135); *ecclesie . . . Sancti Simphoriani* 1494 (Chanter XII (ii), f. 168v); *Seynt Uryan* 1535 (*Valor*, ii, 397); *St. Viriane* 1553 (Snell, *c.*1955, p. 42). *Symphoriana* 1733 (Willis, p. 170). *Uryan* 1742 (Ecton, p. 176). *Symphoriana* 1754 (Ecton, p. 129). *Uryan* alias *Veryan* 1782 (Jones, p. 99). *Symphorianus* 1846 (Oliver, p. 443); Symphorian 1883–1939 (Kelly); *Simphorian* 1925 (Henderson, p. 198); Symphorian 1996 (*TDD*).

In 1878 the parish feast was held on the first Sunday in October (Boase, 1890, col. 1596).

By at least 1278, the church was believed to be under the patronage of the Latin male saint Symphorian; Veryan is a modified form of this. The presence of the name Sibillon *in the 10th-century list of Cornish saints raises the possibility that the patron saint was originally a different figure (Olson and Padel, 1986, p. 47). In the 18th-century, some antiquaries made the saint a female Symphoriana; some modern commentators have also believed the saint to be female and identical with Buryan, but the distinct male Symphorian is perfectly clear in the records.*

Warbstow

De Sancto (sic) Warcherc (place) 1201 (Stenton, 1952, p. 621); *capella Sancte Werburge* 1281 (Oliver, 1846, p. 43); *parochia Sancte Warburge* 1334 (Glasscock, 1975, p. 33); Werburg 1733 (Willis, p. 172), 1742 (Ecton, p. 180), 1782 (Jones, p. 108); *Werburgha* 1846 (Oliver, p. 443); *Werburgh* 1883–1939 (Kelly); Werburga 1925 (Henderson, p. 199); *Werburgh* 1996 (*TDD*).

In 1878 the parish feast was held on the first Thursday in August (Boase, 1890, col. 1596).

Werburg of Chester since at least 1201. The nearest proven pre-Reformation dedication to this saint is in Bristol; that would accord with the view that north Devon and north Cornwall were settled from Somerset (PDN, i, p. xx).

Warleggan

Bartholomew 1434 (Chanter X, f. 122). Unknown 1733 (Willis, p. 174), 1742 (Ecton, p. 183). Bartholomew 1754 (Ecton, p. 628), 1782 (Jones, p. 116), 1846 (Oliver, p. 443), 1883 (Kelly), 1925 (Henderson, p. 199), 1939 (Kelly), 1996 (*TDD*).

Bartholomew from at least 1434 until the Reformation; it was then forgotten but recovered in 1754.

Week St Mary

Ecclesiam Sancte Marie de Wich 1162 x 1170 (Oliver, 1846, p. 41; Oliver, 1854, p. 4); *ecclesia de Wike Sancte Marie* 1291 (Tax.); *Sancte Marie de Wike* 1325 (Chanter II, f. 183v); Mary 1733 (Willis, p. 172), 1742 (Ecton, p. 180), 1782 (Jones, p. 108), 1846 (Oliver, p. 443), 1883 (Kelly), 1925 (Henderson, p. 200), 1939 (Kelly), 1996 (*TDD*).

In 1878 the parish feast was held on the first Sunday after 15 September, and there were four fairs (Boase, 1890, col. 1596).

Mary since at least the late 12th century.

Wendron

Ecclesia Sancte Wendrone 1291 (Tax.), 1310 (Chanter II, f. 48v), 1347 (Chanter III, f. 151; cf. Chanter V, f. 62v); *Wendrona* 1733 (Willis, p. 167); *Wendron* 1742 (Ecton, p. 174), 1782 (Jones, p. 92); *Wendrona* 1846 (Oliver, p. 443); *Gwendron* 1883–1939 (Kelly); *Wendrona* 1925 (Henderson, p. 202); *Wendron* 1996 (*TDD*).

Wendern, a female saint, since at least 1291. In the 16th century she was believed to be a sister of Columb.

St Wenn

Ecclesiam Sancte Wenne 1236 (Luard, 1864, p. 102; cf. p. 111), 1238 (Barlow, 1996, no. 296), 1260 (Chanter I, f. 15), 1291 (Tax.); *ecclesie . . . Sancte Wenne* 1428 (Chanter X, f. 86), 1459 (Chanter XII (i), f. 12); *Wenna* 1733 (Willis, p. 169); *Wenne* 1742 (Ecton,

p. 179), 1782 (Jones, p. 105); *Wenna* 1846 (Oliver, p. 443), 1883 (Kelly), 1925 (Henderson, p. 203), 1939 (Kelly), 1996 (*TDD*).

In 1878 the parish feast was held on the Sunday nearest to 18 October (Boase, 1890, col. 1596).

Wenna, a female saint since at least 1236 (compare Morval).

Werrington (transferred from Exeter to Truro diocese 1877 and from Devon to Cornwall 1966)

Martin 1186 x 1191 (Finberg, 1947, p. 369). *Paternus* 1733 (Willis, p. 172). Unknown 1742 (Ecton, p. 180). *Paternus* 1754 (Ecton, p. 133). Unknown 1782 (Jones, p. 110). Martin 1846 (Oliver, p. 455), 1925 (Henderson, p. 203), 1996 (*TDD*).

In 1878 no parish feast was held (Boase, 1890, col. 1596).

Martin from at least the late 12th century until the Reformation; it was then forgotten. Paternus was a suggestion influenced by the nearby church of North Petherwin; Martin was recovered in 1846.

West Looe

Nicholas 1336 (Chanter IV, f. 200), 1733 (Willis, p. 173). Not in Ecton (1742) or Jones (1782). Nicholas 1814 (Lysons, p. 301). Mary 1846 (Oliver, p. 441). Nicholas 1883 (Kelly), 1925 (Henderson, p. 125), 1939 (Kelly), 1996 (*EDD*).

In 1878 no parish feast was held (Boase, 1890, col. 1592).

Nicholas since at least 1336; Oliver's Mary is probably due to confusion with East Looe.

Whitstone

Nicholas 1309 (Chanter II, f. 42v). Unknown 1733 (Willis, p. 172), 1742 (Ecton, p. 180), 1782 (Jones, p. 109). Nicholas 1814 (Lysons, p. 326), 1846 (Oliver, p. 443). Anne 1883–1939 (Kelly). Nicholas or Anne 1925 (Henderson, p. 204). Anne 1996 (*TDD*).

In 1878 the parish feast was held on Easter Sunday and Monday (Boase, 1890, col. 1596).

Nicholas since at least 1309 until the Reformation; it was then forgotten until it was recovered in 1814. Anne (suggested by a well in the churchyard) has appeared since the 19th century.

St Winnow

Sanwinvec 1086 (DB 2/10); *San Winnuc* 1086 (Exon, p. 183); *parochia Sancte Wennoce* 1201 (Stenton, 1952, p. 345); *ecclesiam Sancti Wynnoci* 1238 (ECA, D&C 1502); *Sancto Winnoco* 1238 (Rowe, 1914–50, i, 35); *ecclesiam Sancti Wynnoci* 1238 (ECA, D&C 1502; Barlow, 1996, no. 255); *apud Sanctum Wynnocum* 1331 (ECA, D&C 2851); *S. Winnous, S. Ginokes, S. Guinows* c.1540 (Leland, 1907–10, i, 206); *Wynnock* 1733 (Willis, p. 174); *Wynnowe* 1742 (Ecton, p. 183), 1782 (Jones, p. 115); *Winnocus* 1846 (Oliver, p. 443); *Winnow* 1883–1939 (Kelly); *Wynnocus* 1925 (Henderson, p. 205); *Winnow* 1996 (*TDD*).

One of the two distinct saints Winnoc or Winwaloe since at least 1086. The saint was usually, but not invariably, recorded as male. Winnoc is an acceptable short form of Winwaloe, who was patron of several churches in Cornwall, whereas the saint whose full name was Winnoc had none for certain (Padel, 1988, p. 180).

Withiel

Clement 1476 (Chanter XII (ii), f. 47v), 1480 (ibid., f. 88v). *Uvel* 1733 (Willis, p. 169); *Uvell* 1742 (Ecton, p. 179), 1782 (Jones, p. 105). Clement 1846 (Oliver, p. 443).

Uvell 1883–1889 (Kelly). Clement 1902–1939 (Kelly), 1925 (Henderson, p. 206), 1996 (*TDD*).

In 1878 the parish feast was held on 23 November (St Clement's Day) (Boase, 1890, col. 1596).

Clement from at least 1476 until the Reformation; it was then forgotten. Uvel(l) arose from a confusion with the parish of St Eval but lasted until the late 19th century, even after Clement was recovered in 1846.

Zennor

Ecclesiam Sancti Sinari . . . apud Sanctam Sinaram 1100 x 1135 (Oliver, 1846, pp. 37–8); *ecclesiam Sancti Sinar* 12th century (Oliver, 1846, p. 39); *ecclesias . . . de Sancta Senara* (Chanter I, f. 44v); *ecclesia Sancte Senare* 1291 (Tax.), 1340 (*Nonarum*, p. 344), 1447 (Chanter X, f. 227); *vicaria Sancti Senari* 1453 (Chanter XI, f. 400); *vicaria Sancte Senare* 1463 (Chanter XII (i), f. 46); *Sener* 1733 (Willis, p. 168); *Sennar* 1742 (Ecton, p. 176), 1782 (Jones, p. 97); *Senara* 1846 (Oliver, p. 443); *Sennar* 1883 (Kelly); *Senara* 1925 (Henderson, p. 207), 1939 (Kelly); *Senera* 1996 (*TDD*).

In 1872 the parish feast was said to be held on the Sunday nearest to 6 May (Polsue, iv, 340), and in 1878 likewise to Old May Day (Boase, 1890, col. 1596).

Senar or Sinar since at least the early 12th century. The saint was twice recorded as a male at that time, but later references to a female saint may better reflect the local tradition; if so, she may be identical with the mother of Budoc in Breton legend.

Church Dedications in Devon

Abbots Bickington

James 1742 (Ecton, p. 149; source, MS Willis 41, f. 230), 1782 (Jones, p. 63), 1846 (Oliver, p. 445), 1996 (*EDD*).

The medieval dedication has not been discovered; James since 1742.

Abbotsham

Ecclesiam Sancte Helene 1193 (Chanter XV, f. 43v; Oliver, 1846, p. 95); *ecclesiam Sancte Elene* 1284 (Chanter I, f. 123; dated by Finberg, 1969, p. 24); *ecclesie . . . Sancte Elene Regi[n]e* 1500 (Chanter XII (ii), Redmayn f. 13); *vicariam . . . Sancte Helene* 1521 (Chanter XIV, f. 8v). Helen 1733 (Willis, p. 157), 1742 (Ecton, p. 148). Unknown *c.*1755 (MS Milles, i, f. 1). Helen 1782 (Jones, p. 46), 1846 (Oliver, p. 444), 1996 (*EDD*).

Helen since at least 1193. Though sometimes supposed to be a Celtic saint, she is equally if not more likely to be the Roman Helen, mother of Constantine.

Abbotskerswell

Mary 1742 (Ecton, p. 151), *c.*1755 (MS Milles, i, f. 307), 1782 (Jones, p. 64), 1846 (Oliver, p. 446), 1996 (*EDD*).

The medieval dedication has not been discovered; Mary since 1742.

Affeton

Peter 1407 (LPL, Reg. Arundel, i, f. 249).

Peter from at least 1407. This parish was united, in effect, to West Worlington in 1439 and subsequently disappeared (Chanter X, ff. 187v–8).

Alphington

Michael 1141 x 1155 (Oliver, 1846, p. 136), 1295 (ECA, D&C 2122), 1546 (Moger, xvi, 5825), 1733 (Willis, p. 153), 1742 (Ecton, p. 152), 1782 (Jones, p. 25), 1846 (Oliver, p. 444); Michael and All Angels 1996 (*EDD*).

Michael since at least the mid 12th century.

Alverdiscott

All Saints 1488 (Chanter XII (ii), f. 102v). Unknown 1742 (Ecton, p. 147). All Saints 1754 (Ecton, p. 627). Peter *c.*1755 (MS Milles, i, f. 5). All Saints 1782 (Jones, p. 44), 1846 (Oliver, p. 444), 1996 (*EDD*).

In 1740–2 the parish feast was variously said to be held a fortnight after Midsummer Day (24 June) and on the Sunday after St Peter's Day (MS Willis 41, ff. 207, 211, 226b).

All Saints before the Reformation; it was probably then forgotten, before being recovered from the 1488 source in 1754. Peter was a conjecture from the feast day.

Alwington

Store of Andrew 1433 x 1434 (DRO, Exeter City Library, DD 39010); Andrew 1437 (Brooking-Rowe, 1901, pp. 166–7), 1742 (Ecton, p. 147; source, MS Willis 41, ff. 211, 230), *c.*1755 (MS Milles, i, f. 7), 1782 (Jones, p. 45), 1846 (Oliver, p. 444), 1996 (*EDD*).

In 1742 and *c.*1755 the parish feast was said to be held on Whit Monday (MS Willis 41, f. 211; MS Milles, i, f. 7).

Andrew since at least 1437.

Arlington

Peter 1495 (NDRO, 50/11/1/4–5). James 1742 (Ecton, p. 159), 1782 (Jones, p. 47), 1846 (Oliver, p. 444), 1996 (*EDD*).

In 1740 and *c.*1742 the parish feast was said to be held on St James' Day (MS Willis 41, ff. 213, 227).

Peter before the Reformation. James, since 1742, is a conjecture based on the parish feast day.

Ashburton

Andrew 1454 (PROB 11/1, f. 75v; Weaver, 1901, p. 165); Andrew the Apostle 1480 (Hanham, 1970, p. 1); Andrew 1733 (Willis, p. 161), 1742 (Ecton, p. 154), *c.*1755 (MS Milles, i, f. 20), 1782 (Jones, p. 67), 1846 (Oliver, p. 444), 1996 (*EDD*).

Andrew since at least 1454.

Ashbury

Mary the Virgin 1329 (Chanter V, f. 8v); Mary 1417 (Chanter IX, f. 181v), 1435 (Chanter X, f. 133v). John the Baptist 1742 (Ecton, p. 156; source, MS Willis 41, f. 225). Mary 1754 (Ecton, p. 627), 1782 (Jones, p. 72), 1846 (Oliver, p. 444), 1939 (Kelly), 1989 (Cherry and Pevsner, p. 134).

In 1740 the parish feast was said to be held on 24 June (St John the Baptist's Day) (MS Willis 41, f. 225).

Mary the Virgin from at least 1329 until the Reformation; it was then forgotten. John the Baptist was a conjecture based on the parish feast day; Mary was recovered in 1754.

Ashcombe

Unknown 1742 (Ecton, p. 152), 1782 (Jones, p. 26). *Nectanus*, with a query 1846 (Oliver, p. 444). Unknown 1873 (Kelly). *Nectanus* 1883 (ibid.); Nectan 1889 (ibid.,), 1912 (Cresswell, 1912, p. 18, quoting the will of John Comin 1544 (modern style)), 1939 (Kelly), 1996 (*EDD*).

Bishop Bronescombe dedicated the church on 22 November 1259 (Chanter I, f. 9v).

The medieval dedication has not been discovered, and it was forgotten after the Reformation. Oliver saw in the 1840s a reference to Nectan as the patron of Ashton, or possibly Ashcombe, church (Oliver, 1846, pp. 444–5). This was probably in the will of John Comin (1544), quoted by Cresswell (1912, p. 18) who believed that it referred to Ashcombe. The will is not now available to be checked. In recent times the Nectan dedication has been ascribed to Ashcombe rather than Ashton, probably because Ashton is thought to have a different dedication whereas Ashcombe's is unknown. Against that must be set the facts that Oliver preferred Ashton and that a Comin family can be traced in Ashton not in Ashcombe. These objections, which are serious, leave Ashcombe without a certain pre-Reformation dedication.

Ashford

Peter 1742 (Ecton, pp. 140, 161; source, MS Willis 41, f. 226b). John the Baptist *c.*1755 (MS Milles, i, f. 22). Peter 1782 (Jones, p. 40), 1846 (Oliver, p. 444), 1996 (*EDD*).

The bishop of Waterford dedicated the church in 1338–9 (Chanter IV, f. 220v). In *c.*1755 the parish feast was said to be held seven days after St Peter's Day (29 June or 1 August) (MS Milles, i, f. 22).

The medieval dedication has not been discovered; usually Peter since 1742.

Ashprington

Unknown 1742 (Ecton, p. 169), *c.*1755 (MS Milles, i, f. 24). David 1782 (Jones, p. 81), 1846 (Oliver, p. 444), 1996 (*EDD*).

The medieval dedication has not been discovered, and it was forgotten after the Reformation. David since 1782, probably because Ecton's 1742 reference mentions him as patron saint of the chapel at Painsford in the parish; this dedication seems then to have been considered as applying to the parish church, though there is no evidence to that effect. David is a rare church saint in Devon.

Ashreigney

James 1742 (Ecton, p. 168; source, MS Willis 41, f. 225v). Unknown *c.*1755 (MS Milles, i, f. 26). James 1782 (Jones, p. 57), 1806 (Polwhele, iii, 415), 1846 (Oliver, p. 445), 1996 (*EDD*).

In 1740 the parish feast was said to be held on 3 August (MS Willis 41, f. 225v), and in *c.*1755 on the Sunday nearest to Lammas Day (1 August) (MS Milles, i, f. 26).

The medieval dedication has not been discovered; James since 1742.

Ashton

Store of John the Baptist 1539 (PROB 11/26, f. 115v). Unknown 1742 (Ecton, p. 146). John the Baptist *c.*1755 (MS Milles, i, 28), 1782 (Jones, p. 19). *Nectanus* 1846 (Oliver, p. 445). John the Baptist 1873 (Kelly), 1939 (ibid.), 1996 (*EDD*).

In 1742 the parish feast was said to be held on the Sunday after the Decollation of John the Baptist (29 August) (MS Willis 41, f. 212), and in *c.*1755 one week after that day (MS Milles, i, 28).

The pre-Reformation evidence here is equivocal. John the Baptist had a store in the church and he appears on the central doors of the chancel screen (Bond and Camm, 1909, ii, 290). These facts, like the parish feast day in 1742, may or may not indicate the patron saint. But Oliver saw in the 1840s a reference to Nectan as the patron of Ashton, or possibly Ashcombe, church (Oliver, 1846, pp. 444–5). This was probably in the will of John Comin (1544), quoted by Cresswell (1912, p. 18) who believed that it referred to Ashcombe. However, Oliver's preference for Ashton requires consideration and a Robert Comyn or Comyng indeed occurs in Ashton parish between 1544 and 1570 (Stoate, 1986, p. 175; DRO, Ashton PR 1/2: burial, 8 March 1570), whereas no Comin is recorded in Ashcombe in the right period. Unfortunately, the Comin will is not available to be checked, so the matter remains an open question (see also Ashcombe, above).

Ashwater

Peter 1504 (Chanter XIII, f. 3v), 1505 (*CPL*, xviii, 349), 1742 (Ecton, p. 148). Unknown *c*.1755 (MS Milles, i, f. 30). Peter 1782 (Jones, p. 61), 1846 (Oliver, p. 445); Peter ad Vincula 1996 (*EDD*).
In 1740 the parish feast was said to be held on 1 August (MS Willis 41, f. 225v).
Peter since at least 1504.

Atherington

Mary 1500 (Chanter XII (ii), Redmayn f. 16v). Laurence 1742 (Ecton, p. 140). Unknown *c*.1755 (MS Milles, i, f. 32). Mary 1763 (Ecton, p. 114), 1782 (Jones, p. 38), 1846 (Oliver, p. 445), 1996 (*EDD*).
In 1740 and *c*.1755 the parish feast was said to be held on the Sunday one week after 1 August (MS Willis 41, f. 230; MS Milles, i, f. 32), and in 1742 on 16 August (MS Willis 41, f. 207).
Mary by at least 1500; it was then forgotten. Laurence was probably a conjecture based on the date of the parish feast day; Mary was recovered in 1763.

Aveton Gifford

Chancel of John the Baptist 1392 (DRO, 158 M/T7). Andrew 1742 (Ecton, p. 171). Unknown *c*.1755 (MS Milles, i, f. 34). Andrew 1782 (Jones, p. 84), 1846 (Oliver, p. 445), 1996 (*EDD*).
Fair on the Nativity of St John Baptist (24 June) 1290 (*CChR 1257–1300*, p. 341).
John the Baptist, perhaps by 1290 and certainly by 1392; Andrew since 1742.

Awliscombe

Mary and Michael 1521 (DRO, ED/AWL/62). Michael 1742 (Ecton, p. 145; source, MS Willis 41, f. 223v), 1782 (Jones, p. 18), 1793 (Polwhele, ii, 328), 1846 (Oliver, p. 445); Michael and All Angels 1996 (*EDD*).
Fair on St Michael's Day 1292 (*CChR 1257–1300*, p. 423). In 1740 the parish feast was said to be held on the Sunday after Michaelmas Day (29 September) (MS Willis 41, f. 223v).
Mary and Michael before the Reformation, of which only the latter has remained in memory or use since 1742.

Axminster

Mary 1195 x 1205 (ECA, D&C 813). John the Baptist 1315 (Chanter II, f. 28v). Mary 1341 (Pole, ii, 153–4, no. 1638). John the Baptist 1414 (PROB 11/2B, f. 252 or 27; see also Wilkin, 1936–7, pp. 257–8), 1490 (PROB 11/9, f. 8v), 1590 (Moger, ix, 2805). Martin 1733 (Willis, p. 153). John the Baptist 1742 (Ecton, p. 150; source, MS Willis 41, f. 223v). Mary 1754 (Ecton, p. 110). John the Baptist *c*.1755 (MS Milles, i, f. 36). Mary 1782 (Jones, p. 22), 1793 (Polwhele, ii, 292). Mary and John the Baptist 1846 (Oliver, p. 445). Mary 1873 (Kelly), 1939 (ibid.), 1996 (*EDD*).
In 1740 the parish feast was said to be held on 24 June (St John the Baptist's Day) (MS Willis 41, f. 223v).
The medieval evidence suggests a double dedication to Mary and John the Baptist. The two saints have caused confusion since the 18th century and Mary alone has been normal since 1782, despite Oliver's attempt to re-establish both patron saints.

Axmouth

Unknown 1742 (Ecton, p. 150), 1782 (Jones, p. 22), 1846 (Oliver, p. 445). Michael 1873 (Kelly), 1939 (ibid.), 1996 (*EDD*).

In 1740 the parish feast was said to be held on 25 April (MS Willis 41, f. 223v). *The medieval dedication has not been discovered, and it was forgotten after the Reformation. The parish feast day was that of St Mark, but he is rarely found as a medieval church patron (despite the reference to Aylesbeare below), and is unlikely here. Michael since the late 19th century, presumably on the grounds that the church belonged in the middle ages to the abbey of Mont St Michel.*

Aylesbeare

Ecclesie Sancti Marci de Aylysbeayre 1516 (DRO, MCR 8–9 Henry VIII, m. 36). Unknown 1742 (Ecton, p. 139). Christopher 1742 (MS Willis 41, f. 211v), 1754 (Ecton, p. 106). Unknown c.1755 (MS Milles, i, f. 3). Christopher 1782 (Jones, p. 7), 1793 (Polwhele, ii, 201). Mary 1846 (Oliver, p. 445), 1996 (*EDD*).

Fair on St Osyth's Day 1239 (*CChR 1225–1257*, p. 243). In 1740 and c.1755 the parish feast was said to be held on Ascension Day (MS Willis 41, f. 223v; MS Milles, i, f. 3).

The reference of 1516 is clearly to Mark, though this saint is uncommon as a patron of religious buildings in medieval England. The dedication was forgotten by the 18th century when Christopher was suggested on unknown grounds (perhaps a painting in the church). The authority for Mary is uncertain; it has, however, been adopted since 1846.

Bampton

Mary c.1200 (Seymour, 1977, p. 161; Dublin, MS E.5.15, f. 49; DRO, 1508M/193). Michael 1448 (*CPL*, x, 145), 1509 (PROB 11/16, f. 185), 1742 (Ecton, p. 167), 1782 (Jones, p. 36), 1793 (Polwhele, ii, 379). Mary 1846 (Oliver, p. 445). Michael 1873 (Kelly), 1939 (ibid.); Michael and All Angels 1996 (*EDD*).

In 1740 the parish feast was said to be held on St Luke's Day (16 October) (MS Willis 41, f. 223v).

Either a double dedication to Mary and Michael, or Mary was superseded by Michael. Despite Oliver's recovery of Mary, Michael has commonly been used alone since 1742.

Barnstaple: Cluniac priory

Mary, Peter and Paul, and Mary Magdalene 1113 x 1119 (Barlow, 1996, no. 12). Mary Magdalene 1157 x 1160 (Round, 1899, p. 460), c.1200 (Gervase, 1867, ii, 424), 1233 (Oliver, 1846, p. 200; Barlow, 1996, no. 228), 1261 (Chanter I, f. 20), 1535 (*Valor*, ii, 354).

Usually Mary Magdalene before the Reformation.

Barnstaple: hospital

The medieval dedication has not been discovered; the conjecture that it was to Mary Magdalene has not been substantiated (Orme and Webster, 1995, p. 215).

Barnstaple: parish church of St Peter

Peter c.1189 x 1196 (Round, 1899, p. 461), 1233 (Oliver, 1846, p. 200; Barlow, 1996, no. 228), 1303 (*CPR 1301–7*, p. 104), 1272 (Chanter I, f. 49), 1352 (Chanter IV, f.

192v), 1360 (Chanter III, f. 32). Peter and Paul 1370 (Chanter and Wainwright, 1900, i, 204). Peter 1411 (*CPL*, vi, 279), 1435 (Chanter XI, f. 118v); Peter the Apostle 1482 (Chanter and Wainwright, 1900, i, 203); Peter 1490 (ibid., p. 130). Peter and Paul 1511 (PRO, C 142/81 no. 325; IPM, Alice Symon), 1539 (Chanter XIV, f. 99), 1733 (Willis, p. 156), 1742 (Ecton, p. 140). Peter *c*.1755 (MS Milles, i, f. 41). Peter and Paul 1782 (Jones, p. 40), 1806 (Polwhele, iii, 404). Peter 1846 (Oliver, p. 445), 1983 (*EDD*). Peter and Mary Magdalene 1987–1996 (ibid.).

Bishop Stapledon dedicated the church, high altar and three others on 9 September 1318 (Chanter II, f. 129). The dedication feast was changed from the morrow of the Nativity of Mary the Virgin (9 September) to St Faith (6 October) 1452 (Chanter XI, f. 384v). In *c*.1755 the parish feasts were said to be held on the Tuesday in Rogation week and 8 September (MS Milles, i, f. 41).

Peter and Paul probably from at least the early 13th century although Peter has been often used alone. Mary Magdalene has been added since 1987.

Beaford

Store of George 1521 (CRO, Henderson, HC 66, p. 165); George 1532 (Cresswell, 1927, p. 7; Murray, xiii, John Gasse). All Saints 1742 (Ecton, p. 168), *c*.1755 (MS Milles, i, f. 43), 1782 (Jones, p. 57). George 1846 (Oliver, p. 445), 1873 (Kelly). All Saints 1883 (ibid.), 1939 (ibid.), 1996 (*EDD*).

In 1742 and *c*.1755 the parish feast was said to be held on Whit Tuesday (MS Willis 41, f. 207; MS Milles, i, f. 43).

George before the Reformation; All Saints usually since 1742, despite Oliver's recovery of George.

Beaworthy

Alban 1742 (Ecton, p. 156; source, MS Willis 41, f. 225). John the Baptist *c*.1755 (MS Milles, i. f. 47). Alban 1782 (Jones, p. 72). Not in Oliver (1846). Alban 1873 (Kelly), 1939 (ibid.), 1996 (*EDD*).

In 1740 the parish feast was said to be held on 22 June (MS Willis 41, f. 225), and in *c*.1755 on the Sunday before 24 June (MS Milles, i, f. 47).

The medieval dedication has not been discovered. Usually Alban since 1742 which (like John the Baptist) may well be a conjecture based on the date of the parish feast. Alban looks an unlikely dedication for a medieval church in Devon.

Beer

Unknown 1742 (Ecton, p. 150), 1782 (Jones, p. 24). Michael 1846 (Oliver, p. 452), 1996 (*EDD*).

The feast was said to be held on the Monday one week after Michaelmas Day *c*.1755 (MS Milles, ii, f. 146).

The medieval dedication has not been discovered. Michael since 1846, perhaps on the basis of the parish feast.

Belstone

Unknown 1742 (Ecton, p. 156), 1782 (Jones, p. 72). Mary 1846 (Oliver, p. 445), 1996 (*EDD*).

In 1740 the parish feast was said to be held on Whit Monday (MS Willis 41, f. 225). *The medieval dedication has not been discovered; Mary since 1846.*

Bere Ferrers

Andrew 1475 (PROB 11/6, f. 173), 1733 (Willis, p. 163), 1742 (Ecton, p. 164), c.1755 (MS Milles, i, f. 49), 1782 (Jones, p. 76), 1846 (Oliver, p. 445), 1996 (*EDD*). Fair on St Andrew's Day 1295 (*CChR 1257–1300*, p. 463). In 1740 the parish feast was said to be held on Shrove Tuesday (MS Willis 41, f. 225).

Andrew, probably since at least 1295, certainly since at least 1475.

Berrynarbor

Grant of land to the church of *Biri* in honour of the blessed apostles Peter and Andrew c.1150 (Budgen and Salzman, 1943, pp. 2–3). Mary Magdalene 1742 (Ecton, p. 159). Peter 1754 (Ecton, p. 116), 1782 (Jones, p. 48), 1846 (Oliver, p. 445), 1996 (*EDD*). In 1740 the parish feast was said to be held on St Peter's Day (MS Willis 41, f. 226b).

Peter and Andrew by the mid 12th century. Peter since the 18th century, either due to a deduction from the feast day or from memory of the medieval dedication.

Berry Pomeroy

Mary 1496 (PROB 11/11, f. 11), 1511 (PROB 11/17, f. 199v), 1733 (Willis, p. 160; source MS Willis 41, f. 223), 1742 (Ecton, p. 151). Unknown c.1755 (MS Milles, i, f. 53). Mary 1782 (Jones, p. 64), 1846 (Oliver, p. 445), 1996 (*EDD*). Fair on St James's Day 1267 (*CChR 1257–1300*, p. 76).

Mary since at least 1496.

Bickington

Nicholas 1547 (Worthy, 1896, p. 157). Unknown 1742 (Ecton, p. 154), c.1755 (MS Milles, i, f. 57), 1782 (Jones, p. 67). Mary 1846 (Oliver, p. 445), 1996 (*EDD*).

Nicholas before the Reformation; it was then forgotten and replaced by Mary in 1846.

Bickleigh (near Plymouth)

Ecclesia Omnium Sanctorum de Bycklegh c.1500 (BL, Add. MS 5665, f. 69v). Unknown 1742 (Ecton, p. 364), c.1755 (MS Milles, i, f. 59), 1782 (Jones, p. 76), 1846 (Oliver, p. 445), 1873 (Kelly). Mary 1883 (Kelly), 1996 (*EDD*).

The reference of c.1500 comes in a certificate by John Berman, apparently parish priest of Bickleigh, that he has called the banns of his parishioner John Forde in the church. No vicar of Bickleigh with this name is known, but the list of vicars is deficient in the late 15th century or Berman could have been a curate. In favour of Bickleigh near Plymouth are the facts that the certificate is copied in a manuscript with Devon associations, that the other Bickleigh had a different patron saint, and that there was a John Forde in the parish in 1524 (Stoate, 1979, p. 156). Provisionally, therefore, All Saints before the Reformation; if so, it was then forgotten. Mary since the late 19th century, perhaps influenced by the other Bickleigh.

Bickleigh (near Tiverton)

Mary 1465 (Chanter XII (i), f. 103-v), 1742 (Ecton, p. 166), 1782 (Jones, p. 33), 1793 (Polwhele, ii, 359), 1846 (Oliver, p. 445), 1996 (*EDD*). In 1740 the parish feast was held three weeks before Michaelmas (perhaps meaning 8 September, the Nativity of Mary) (MS Willis 41, f. 224).

Mary since at least 1465.

Bicton

Trinity 1742 (Ecton, p. 138). Bridget conjectured *c.*1742 (MS Willis 41, f. 220). Unknown *c.*1755 (MS Milles, i, f. 62). Trinity 1782 (Jones, p. 4), 1793 (Polwhele, ii, 222). Mary 1846 (Oliver, p. 445), 1854 (Oliver, p. 68), 1996 (*EDD*).
The medieval dedication has not been discovered. Trinity in the 18th century and Mary since 1846.

Bideford

Fraternity of Mary 1420 (DRO, 314M/F96); Mary 1493 (PROB 11/10, f. 122), 1504 (LPL, Reg. Warham, i, 204); store of St Mary 'of Bideford' 1524 x 1547 (Oliver, 1842, p. 44); Mary 1742 (Ecton, p. 147). Margaret *c.*1755 (MS Milles, i, f. 51). Mary 1782 (Jones, p. 45), 1846 (Oliver, p. 445), 1996 (*EDD*).
Fair on St Margaret's Day 1272 (*CChR 1257–1300*, p. 181). In *c.*1755 the parish feast was said to be held on Ascension Day (MS Milles, i, f. 51).
Mary, probably since at least 1420, certainly since 1493. Margaret in about 1755 was a conjecture from the fair day.

Bigbury

Laurence 1411 (Chanter VIII, f. 321v), 1433 (PRO, C 139/61 no. 48; IPM, Elizabeth Bikebury), 1497 (PROB 11/12, f. 76v), 1742 (Ecton, p. 171), *c.*1755 (MS Milles, i, f. 65), 1782 (Jones, p. 84), 1846 (Oliver, p. 445), 1996 (*EDD*).
Laurence since at least 1411.

Bishop's Nympton

Unknown 1742 (Ecton, p. 162). Holy Ghost *c.*1755 (MS Milles, ii, f. 68). Unknown 1782 (Jones, p. 53). Mary 1846 (Oliver, p. 451), 1996 (*EDD*).
In 1742 the parish feast was said to be held on Whit Sunday or Monday (MS Willis 41, ff. 207, 212), and in *c.*1755 on Whit Sunday (MS Milles, ii, f. 68).
The medieval dedication has not been discovered, and it was forgotten after the Reformation. The Holy Ghost was a conjecture from the date of the parish feast. The authority for Mary is not known, but it has become adopted.

Bishop's Tawton

Peter 1256 (ECA, D&C 1805). John the Baptist 1742 (Ecton, p. 140), Unknown *c.*1755 (MS Milles, ii, f. 188). John the Baptist 1782 (Jones, p. 39). Peter 1846 (Oliver, p. 445), 1873 (Kelly). John the Baptist 1883 (ibid.), 1939 (ibid.), 1996 (*EDD*).
Fair on St Laurence's Day 1398 (*CChR 1341–1427*, p. 375). In 1740 and *c.*1755 the parish feast was said to be held on 24 June (MS Willis 41, f. 226b; MS Milles, ii, f. 188).
Peter before the Reformation; it was then forgotten. John the Baptist was conjectured in 1742 from the parish feast day and has persisted, although Oliver recovered Peter in 1846.

Bishopsteignton

All Saints 1539 (Moger, i, 104), 1544 (ibid., i, 33, 105). Unknown 1742 (Ecton, p. 154). John the Baptist 1754 (Ecton, p. 154), 1782 (Jones, p. 39), 1793 (Polwhele, ii, 149). All Saints 1846 (Oliver, p. 454). John the Baptist 1873 (Kelly), 1939 (ibid.), 1996 (*EDD*).
Fair on St James's Day 1270 (*CChR 1257–1300*, p. 134).
All Saints before the Reformation; it was then forgotten. John the Baptist has been usual since 1754, despite Oliver's recovery of All Saints in 1846.

Bittadon

Peter 1742 (Ecton, p. 161). Unknown *c.*1755 (MS Milles, i, f. 67). Peter 1782 (Jones, p. 51), 1846 (Oliver, p. 445), 1996 (*EDD*).
In 1740 the parish feast was said to be held on the Monday after St Peter's Day (MS Willis 41, f. 226b).
The medieval dedication has not been discovered; Peter since 1742.

Blackawton

Michael 1742 (Ecton, p. 170; source, MS Willis 41, f. 223). Unknown *c.*1755 (MS Milles, i, f. 69). Michael 1782 (Jones, p. 83), 1806 (Polwhele, iii, 484), 1846 (Oliver, p. 445), 1996 (*EDD*).
Bishop Grandisson dedicated the high altar on 5 October 1333 (Chanter IV, f. 170).
The medieval dedication has not been discovered; Michael since 1742.

Blackborough

Allhalowes 1546 (Snell, Devon and Exeter, p. 28); All Saints 1742 (Ecton, p. 156), 1782 (Jones, p. 30), 1793 (Polwhele, ii, 258), 1846 (Oliver, p. 445), 1994 (*EDD*).
All Saints since at least 1546; the church is now closed.

Black Torrington

Barnabas 1740 (MS Willis 41, f. 225). Mary 1742 (Ecton, p. 148), 1782 (Jones, p. 61), 1846 (Oliver, p. 445), 1996 (*EDD*).
In 1740 the parish feast was said to be held on 16 June (MS Willis 41, f. 225).
The medieval dedication has not been discovered. Barnabas was probably a conjecture based on the parish feast day; Mary, on unknown grounds, since 1742.

Blaxton in Tamerton Foliot (formerly Martinstow; now Maristow)

Martin *c.*1193 x 1208 (Bearman, 1994, pp. 167–8), 1335 (Chanter IV, f. 12).
Martin by at least the late 12th century, when the place was described as a church (ecclesia). *It had lost the status of a church by 1291 (Tax.).*

Bondleigh

Mary 1499 (*CPL*, xvii part i, 65), 1505 (*CPL*, xviii, 352–3). Philip 1740 (MS Willis 41, f. 225). James 1742 (Ecton, p. 143), 1782 (Jones, p. 41). Not in Oliver (1846). James 1873 (Kelly), 1939 (ibid.); James the Apostle 1996 (*EDD*).
In 1740 the parish feast was said to be held on 7 May (MS Willis 41, f. 225).
Mary before the Reformation; James since 1742, perhaps a conjecture based on the parish feast day lying close to SS Philip's and James's Day.

Bovey Tracey

Peter and Paul 1401 (Chanter IX, f. 20). Thomas Becket 1742 (Ecton, p. 154), 1782 (Jones, p. 67). Peter, Paul and Thomas Becket 1846 (Oliver, p. 445), 1996 (*EDD*).
Fair on the Translation of Thomas Becket (7 July) 1260 (*CChR 1257–1300*, p. 26).
Peter and Paul before the Reformation; Thomas Becket since 1742, probably a conjecture based on the fair and the Tracey connection. Peter and Paul were recovered in 1846, but Thomas Becket has persisted alongside them.

Bow—see Nymet Tracy

Bradford

All Saints 1337 (*CPR 1334–8*, pp. 516–17; Chanter I, f. 18v), 1352 (*CPR 1350–4*, pp. 314, 330). Philip 1740 (MS Willis 41, f. 225). All Saints 1742 (Ecton, p. 149). Unknown *c*.1755 (MS Milles, i, f. 71). All Saints 1782 (Jones, p. 62), 1846 (Oliver, p. 445), 1996 (*EDD*).

In 1740 the parish feast was said to be held on 26 May (MS Willis 41, f. 225), and in *c*.1755 on Whit Monday (MS Milles, i, f. 71).

All Saints since at least 1337, not always remembered in the 18th century.

Bradninch

Dennys 1562 (PROB 11/46, f. 26), 1587 (Moger, ix, 2845); *Dennis* 1742 (Ecton, p. 157); *Denys* 1782 (Jones, p. 32); *Dennis* 1793 (Polwhele, ii, 252). *Disen* 1831 (Lewis, i, s.n.). *Dionysius* 1846 (Oliver, p. 445), 1883 (Kelly); *Dionysius* or Denis 1889 (Kelly), 1906 (ibid.). *Disen* 1910 (Kelly), 1939 (ibid.), 1996 (*EDD*).

Fair on the feast of St Denis 1208 (*Rotuli Chartarum*, i part i, 183).

Denis (Latin Dionysius), perhaps from as early as 1208, certainly from at least 1562. He was always reckoned to be the patron saint from then until 1831, and usually until the late 19th century. Disen in 1831 was probably a vernacular or misspelt form of Denis or Dionysius, but after 1910 it was interpreted and popularised locally as the name of a distinct Irish saint. There is no evidence even that such a saint existed, let alone that he was the patron saint of Bradninch (Orme, 1992a, pp. 45–7).

Bradstone

Store of Christopher 1469 (DRO, Catalogue of Kelly Deeds, TD 1/3). Matthias 1740 (MS Willis 41, f. 225v). *Nun*, with a query 1742 (Ecton, p. 166). Unknown *c*.1755 (MS Milles, i, f. 73). *Nun* 1782 (Jones, p. 80); *Nonna* 1846 (Oliver, p. 445), 1996 (*EDD*).

Bishop Bronescombe dedicated the church on 2 September 1261 (Chanter I, f. 21). In 1740 the parish feast was said to be held on 3 March (MS Willis 41, f. 225v).

The medieval dedication has not been discovered. Christopher is not found elsewhere in Devon as a church patron, so the reference to him may involve a subsidiary saint cult in the church. Matthias is certainly, and Nun perhaps, a conjecture based on the parish feast day, Nun being very likely due to the learned Browne Willis. He, and later people, have meant the saint nowadays known as Nonn, mother of St David. But Celtic saint dedications are rare in Devon, and the context of the evidence does not encourage the view that she was the medieval patron saint of the church (this withdraws the suggestion previously made in Orme, 1992c, p. 162).

Bradworthy

Peter *c*.1250, *c*.1310 (Seymour, 1977, p. 173; Dublin, MS E.5.15, ff. 52, 55). John the Baptist 1733 (Willis, p. 160). Peter 1740 (MS Willis 41, f. 225v). John the Baptist 1742 (Ecton, p. 149), 1782 (Jones, p. 61). Peter 1846 (Oliver, p. 446), 1873 (Kelly). John the Baptist 1883 (Kelly), 1939 (ibid.), 1996 (*EDD*).

In 1740 the parish feast day was said to be held on 29 June (MS Willis 41, f. 225v).

Peter before the Reformation; it was then almost forgotten. John the Baptist was conjectured in 1733 and has persisted despite Oliver's recovery of Peter in 1846.

Brampford Speke

Peter 1138 x 1160 (BL, Cotton MS Vitellius D.ix, f. 33v), 1366 (Chanter V, f. 152).

Unknown 1742 (Ecton, p. 141). Peter 1754 (Ecton, p. 627), 1782 (Jones, p. 9), 1793 (Polwhele, ii, 53), 1846 (Oliver, p. 446), 1996 (*EDD*).

In 1793 the parish feast was said to be held on the first Sunday after Michaelmas (Polwhele, ii, 53).

Peter since at least the mid 12th century.

Branscombe

Image of Mary the Virgin in the chancel 1307 (ECA, D&C 3673). '*Sanctus Brandwellanus* . . . lies in the church of the township of *Branston*, eight miles from Axminster and four from the south sea' 1478 (Worcester, 1969, p. 124). Winifred 1742 (Ecton, p. 138; source, MS Willis 41, f. 223v), 1782 (Jones, p. 4); 'said to be dedicated to St Winifred' 1793 (Polwhele, ii, 237); Winifred 1846 (Oliver, p. 446), 1996 (*EDD*).

In 1740 and 1793 the parish feast was said to be held on the Monday after St Giles (MS Willis 41, f. 223v; Polwhele, ii, 237).

The medieval dedication is not clear. Churches often had an image of Mary in the chancel, so the reference of 1307 does not prove that she was patron or co-patron of the church though this is possible. The evidence of 1478 was noted down by the anti-quary William Worcester from information given him by John Burges, a Dominican friar in Exeter. The note is not entirely clear or accurate, but if Branston is Branscombe, Brandwell may have been its patron saint: a distinct local figure. A well in Branscombe seems to have been named after Winifred—famous for her well in north Wales—which apparently gave rise to the belief in 1742 that she had been patron of the church. There is, however, no certain medieval church dedication to her in Devon or Cornwall and the case of Manaton (below) urges caution in making this assumption at Branscombe. Two women called Winifred who occur in the parish reg-isters before 1600 are not sufficient to establish the case either (Tapley-Soper and Chick, 1913, pp. 2–3).

Bratton Clovelly

Unknown 1742 (Ecton, p. 155), c.1755 (MS Milles, i, f. 79), 1782 (Jones, p. 70), 1846 (Oliver, p. 446), 1883 (Kelly). Mary 1889 (Kelly), 1996 (*EDD*).

In 1740 and c.1755 the parish feast was said to be held on Whit Tuesday (MS Willis 41, f. 225v; MS Milles, i, f. 79).

The medieval dedication has not been discovered, and it was forgotten after the Reformation. Mary since the 1880s.

Bratton Fleming

Peter and Paul the Apostles of *Bratton* 1524; Bratton Fleming is established by the presence of the Dillon family (PROB 11/23, f. 125). Peter 1742 (Ecton, p. 159), c.1755 (MS Milles, i, 80), 1782 (Jones, p. 48), 1846 (Oliver, p. 446), 1996 (*EDD*).

In 1740 and c.1755 the parish feast was said to be held on St Peter's Day (29 June or 1 August) (MS Willis 41, f. 227; MS Milles, i, 80).

Peter and Paul before the Reformation, shortened to Peter since 1742.

Braunton

Branot (for *Branoc*) 854 (Finberg, 1963, p. 9); *Brannocminster* (place) 855 x 867 (ibid.); *Brancminstre* (place) 973 (ibid., p. 13); *Brauntona* (place) c.1107 (Hull, 1987, p. 2); *Sanctus Barnocus anglice Barnoc* (Worcester, 1969, p. 114); *Brannock*, with a query 1733 (Willis, p. 157). Peter 1740 (MS Willis 41, f. 226b). *Brannock* 1742 (Ecton, p.

159). Unknown *c*.1755 (MS Milles, i, f. 82). *Brannock* 1782 (Jones, p. 48), 1806 (Polwhele, iii, 396), 1846 (Oliver, p. 446), 1996 (*EDD*).

There was allegedly a parish feast on Easter Monday *c*.1620 (Orme, 1992, p. 57). In *c*.1755 the parish feast was said to be held on Whit Monday (MS Milles, i, f. 82).

Brannoc since at least the 9th century, not always remembered in the mid 18th century.

Brendon

Brendon 1742 (Ecton, p. 161); with a query 1754 (Ecton, p. 117). Unknown *c*.1755 (MS Milles, i, f. 86). *Brendon* 1782 (Jones, p. 51); *Brendonus* 1846 (Oliver, p. 446). 'Brendon occurs sometimes as dedicated to St Mary' 1854 (Oliver, p. 68). *Brendonus* 1873 (Kelly); *Brendon* 1883 (ibid.), 1889 (ibid); *Brendan* 1893 (ibid.), 1939 (ibid.); *Brendon* 1996 (*EDD*).

In 1740, 1742 and *c*.1755 the parish feast was said to be held on Whit Tuesday (MS Willis 41, ff. 207, 220, 226b; MS Milles, i, f. 86).

The medieval dedication has not been discovered; usually Brendon since 1742. The place-name Brendon, however, means 'bramble hill' (PND, i, 58–9) or 'broom hill' (Ekwall, 1960, p. 63), so this is not a place named after a saint as might happen in Cornwall. St Brendon or Brendan may well be modern conjectures suggested by the place-name, and Oliver's Mary be the original dedication if he saw early evidence such as wills.

Brentor

Michael 1155 x 1162 (Finberg, 1947, p. 357; Bearman, 1994, pp. 184–5), 1193 (Chanter XV, f. 44; Oliver, 1846, p. 95), 1284 (Chanter I, f. 123; dated by Finberg, 1969, p. 24), 1478 (Worcester, 1969, pp. 10–11), 1733 (Willis, p. 163). John the Baptist 1740 (MS Willis 41, f. 225v). Michael 1742 (Ecton, p. 166), *c*.1755 (MS Milles, i, f. 88), 1782 (Jones, p. 81), 1846 (Oliver, p. 446), 1996 (*EDD*).

Fair on St Michael's Day 1232 (*CChR 1225–57*, p. 157). Bishop Stapledon dedicated the church on 4 December 1319 (Chanter II, f. 145). In 1740 the parish feast was said to be held on 24 June (MS Willis 41, f. 225v), and in *c*.1755 on the Sunday before that day (MS Milles, i, f. 88).

Michael since at least the mid 12th century, John the Baptist being a mistaken conjecture from the parish feast day.

Bridestowe

Bridestov (place) 1086 (DB 16/7); *Brigidestowe* (place) 1259 (Chanter I, f. 8v); store of St Bridget 1451 (Chanter XI, f. 442v); Bridget, with a query 1733 (Willis, p. 163); Bridget 1742 (Ecton, p. 165), 1782 (Jones, p. 78), 1806 (Polwhele, iii, 445); *Brigida* 1846 (Oliver, p. 446); Bridget 1996 (*EDD*).

In 1740 the parish feast was said to be held on Whit Monday (MS Willis 41, f. 225).

Bridget since at least the late 11th century.

Bridford

Thomas Becket 1742 (Ecton, p. 146; source, MS Willis 41, f. 208v), 1782 (Jones, p. 19), 1793 (Polwhele, ii, 76), 1846 (Oliver, p. 446), 1996 (*EDD*).

Bishop Bronescombe dedicated the church on 8 November 1259 (Chanter I, f. 9). In 1742 the parish feast was said to be held on the Sunday after St Thomas Becket's Day (MS Willis 41, ff. 211, 222).

The medieval dedication has not been discovered. Thomas Becket since 1742, perhaps a conjecture based on the parish feast day and (on the analogy of similar conjectures) unlikely to be the original dedication.

Bridgerule

Michael *c.*1170 x 1186 (15th) (Hull, 1987, p. 157), 1448 (Chanter X, f. 240). Unknown 1742 (Ecton, p. 149), *c.*1755 (MS Milles, i, f. 90), 1782 (Jones, p. 63). Bridget 1806 (Polwhele, iii, 433). Michael 1846 (Oliver, p. 446). Bridget 1873 (Kelly), 1939 (ibid.), 1996 (*EDD*).

In 1740 the parish feast was said to be held on Whit Sunday (MS Willis 41, f. 225v), and in *c.*1755 on Whit Monday (MS Milles, i, f. 90).

Michael before the Reformation; it was then forgotten. Bridget is a late invention suggested by the place-name, which actually means 'bridge belonging to Ruald'; this has persisted despite Oliver's recovery of Michael in 1846.

Brixham

Mary 1449 (DRO, Exeter City Library Calendar of Deeds, DD 4519), 1473 (ibid., DD 4524), 1521 (PROB 11/20, f. 130v), 1742 (Ecton, p. 152), *c.*1755 (MS Milles, i, f. 94), 1782 (Jones, p. 65), 1846 (Oliver, p. 446), 1996 (*EDD*).

Mary since at least 1449.

Brixton

Unknown 1742 (Ecton, p. 158), *c.*1755 (MS Milles, i, f. 99), 1782 (Jones, p. 75), 1846 (Oliver, p. 446), 1883 (Kelly). Mary 1889 (Kelly), 1996 (*EDD*).

In 1740 the parish feast was said to be held at Whitsuntide (MS Willis 41, f. 228).

The medieval dedication has not been discovered, and it was forgotten after the Reformation. Mary since the 1880s.

Broadclyst

John the Baptist 1742 (Ecton, p. 138), 1782 (Jones, p. XXX), 1793 (Polwhele, ii, 196), 1846 (Oliver, p. 447), 1996 (*EDD*).

The medieval dedication has not been discovered; John the Baptist since 1742.

Broadhembury

Andrew 1742 (Ecton, p. 157; source, MS Willis 41, f. 223), *c.*1755 (MS Milles, i, f. 258), 1782 (Jones, p. 32), 1793 (Polwhele, ii, 260), 1846 (Oliver, p. 449), 1996 (*EDD*).

Bishop Bronescombe dedicated the church of *Hambiritone* on 3 December 1259 (Chanter I, f. 10). Fair on the Assumption of the Virgin Mary (15 August) 1290 (*CChR 1257–1300*, p. 371). In 1740 the parish feast was said to be held on St Andrew's Day (30 November or 9 May).

The medieval dedication has not been discovered; Andrew since 1742. A place in Broadhembury called Seynt Andrewis wood *is recorded in 1546 (Youings, 1955, p. 88), but this was not the property of the parish church and may have taken its name from a chapel nearby. It is difficult to decide if Andrew in 1742 was a new conjecture based on St Andrew's Wood and on the parish feast day, or whether all the Andrew evidence accurately reflects the medieval dedication.*

Broadhempston

Peter and Paul 1384 (Chanter VII, f. 83v). A request to be buried *in the churche yarde of Saint Peters* 1537 may relate to this church (PROB 11/28, f. 217). Unknown 1742

(Ecton, p. 151), 1782 (Jones, p. 64), 1846 (Oliver, p. 449), 1897 (Kelly). Peter and Paul 1902 (Kelly), 1996 (*EDD*).

Peter and Paul before the Reformation; it was then forgotten, and was not recovered until about 1897–1902.

Broad Nymet

Unknown 1742 (Ecton, p. 143), 1782 (Jones, p. 42), 1846 (Oliver, p. 451). Martin 1883 (Kelly), 1939 (Kelly), 1989 (Cherry & Pevsner, p. 194).

The medieval dedication has not been discovered, and it was forgotten after the Reformation. Martin since the late 19th century.

Broadwoodkelly

Unknown 1742 (Ecton, p. 155), 1782 (Jones, p. 70). All Hallows 1846 (Oliver, p. 446), 1873 (Kelly), 1939 (ibid.); All Saints 1996 (*EDD*).

In 1740 the parish feast was said to be held on 20 May (MS Willis 41, f. 225).

The medieval dedication has not been discovered, and it was forgotten after the Reformation. All Saints since 1846; it is not clear if this was based on medieval evidence.

Broadwoodwidger (transferred from Exeter to Truro diocese 1877, and back again 1922)

Unknown 1742 (Ecton, p. 165), *c.*1755 (MS Milles, i, f. 101), 1782 (Jones, p. 78), 1846 (Oliver, p. 446), 1873 (Kelly). Nicholas 1883 (Kelly), 1996 (*EDD*).

In 1740 the parish feast was said to be held on Easter Monday (MS Willis 41, f. 225v).

The medieval dedication has not been discovered, and it was forgotten after the Reformation. Nicholas since the late 19th century.

Brushford

Unknown 1742 (Ecton, p. 144), 1782 (Jones, p. 43), 1846 (Oliver, p. 446). Mary 1873 (Kelly), 1939 (ibid.), 1996 (*EDD*).

In 1740 the parish feast was said to be held on Easter Sunday (MS Willis 41, f. 225v), and in 1742 on Easter Monday (ibid., f. 207).

The medieval dedication has not been discovered, and it was forgotten after the Reformation. Mary since the late 19th century.

Buckerell

Mary *c.*1200 (ECA, D&C 667). Unknown 1742 (Ecton, p. 157). Mary 1754 (Ecton, p. 112). Unknown *c.*1755 (MS Milles, i, f. 103). Mary 1782 (Jones, p. 32). 'Said to be dedicated to St Mary; rather, perhaps, to St Giles, as the revel is held on the first Sunday in September' 1793 (Polwhele, ii, 275). Mary 1846 (Oliver, p. 446). Unknown 1873 (Kelly). Mary 1883 (Kelly). Mary and Giles 1889 (Kelly), 1939 (ibid.), 1996 (*EDD*).

In 1740 the parish feast was said to be held on 15 September (MS Willis 41, f. 223v), in *c.*1755 on 14 September, if a Sunday, or on the following Sunday (MS Milles, i, f. 103), and in 1793 on the first Sunday in September (see above).

Mary since at least about 1200, to whom Giles was added in 1793 as a conjecture based on the date of the parish feast.

Buckfast: Benedictine, later Savignac and Cistercian, abbey

Mary and Stephen *c.*1143 (Stéphan, 1970, p. 36). Mary 1189 x 1199 (Oliver, 1846, p. 373), *c.*1200 (Gervase, 1867, ii, 423), 1535 (*Valor*, ii, 368).

Usually Mary before the Reformation, Stephen also being mentioned in the mid 12th century.

Buckfastleigh

Fraternity of the Trinity 1487 (PROB 11/8, f. 161; Weaver, 1901, p. 265); Trinity 1518 (PROB 11/19, f. 74), 1539 (Murray, xxv, William Phylyppe), 1742 (Ecton, p. 170). Peter c.1755 (MS Milles, i, f. 105). Trinity 1782 (Jones, p. 81), 1846 (Oliver, p. 446), 1996 (*EDD*).

The dedication feast was changed from 23 May to the Monday after Trinity Sunday in 1451 (Chanter XI, f. 365-v).

Trinity, probably since at least 1451, certainly since at least 1518, with some uncertainty in the mid 18th century.

Buckland: Cistercian abbey

Mary and Benedict 1278 (Oliver, 1846, p. 382), 1485 (*CPR 1485–94*, p. 117); Mary 1535 (*Valor*, ii, 378).

Mary and Benedict before the Reformation, sometimes shortened to Mary.

Buckland Brewer

Ecclesie Sancti Andree de Buklond 1445 may relate to this church or to Buckland Monachorum, below (London, Guildhall Library, MS 9171/4, f. 163v); Andrew of *North Buckland* 1508 (*CPL*, xviii, 578–9). Mary and Benedict 1742 (Ecton, p. 148; source, MS Willis 41, f. 230), 1782 (Jones, p. 46). Mary 1846 (Oliver, p. 446). Mary and Benedict 1873 (Kelly), 1939 (ibid.), 1996 (*EDD*).

Fair on the Assumption of the Virgin Mary (15 August) 1290 (*CChR 1257–1300*, p. 371).

Andrew before the Reformation, North Buckland being an alternative name for Buckland Brewer; it was then forgotten. Mary, usually with Benedict, since 1742, a conjecture which must have arisen through confusion or analogy with Buckland Abbey (see above). There are no grounds for this conjecture; in any case, Buckland Brewer church belonged in the middle ages to Torre Abbey not to Buckland Abbey.

Buckland Filleigh

Mary 1742 (Ecton, p. 168), 1782 (Jones, p. 57), 1806 (Polwhele, iii, 417), 1846 (Oliver, p. 446), 1873 (Kelly), 1939 (ibid.). Mary 1926 (Crockford). Mary and Trinity 1929 (Crockford), 1996 (*EDD*).

In 1740 the parish feast was said to be held on 15 May (MS Willis 41, f. 225).

The medieval dedication has not been discovered. Mary since 1742 to whom Trinity was added in about 1929, on unknown grounds. The latter did not appear in Kelly's Directory.

Buckland in the Moor

Peter 1547 (Worthy, 1896, p. 157). Unknown 1742 (Ecton, p. 154), c.1755 (MS Milles, i, f. 114), 1782 (Jones, p. 67), 1846 (Oliver, p. 446), 1883 (Kelly). Peter 1889 (Kelly), 1996 (*EDD*).

Peter before the Reformation; it was then forgotten until it was recovered in the late 19th century.

Buckland Monachorum

Ecclesie Sancti Andree de Buklond 1445 may relate to this church or to Buckland Brewer, above (London, Guildhall Library, MS 9171/4, f. 163v). *Portam cemeterii Sancti Andree de Bucklonde c.*1490 (DRO, G. Oliver, Précis of Leases, vol. i, note after DD 22558). Trinity 1742 (Ecton, p. 164), 1782 (Jones, p. 76). Andrew 1846 (Oliver, p. 446), 1996 (*EDD*).

Fair on the Nativity of St John the Baptist (24 June) 1318 (*CChR 1300–26*, p. 373). In 1740 and *c.*1755 the parish feast was said to be held on Trinity Monday (MS Willis 41, f. 225; MS Milles, i, f. 112).

The document of c.1490 is not now extant, but it seems to relate to Buckland Monachorum rather than Buckland Brewer because it is a grant by the abbot of Buckland. Andrew therefore before the Reformation; it was then forgotten. Trinity was conjectured in 1742 from the date of the parish feast; Andrew was recovered in 1846.

Buckland Tout Saints

Peter 1483 (*CPL*, xiii (ii), 862). Not in Ecton (1742). Unknown 1782 (Jones, p. 86). All Saints 1846 (Oliver, p. 446), 1883 (Kelly). Peter 1889 (Kelly), 1983 (*EDD*), 1996 (ibid.).

Peter before the Reformation; it was then forgotten. All Saints was suggested by Tout Saints, which is said to refer instead to the family who owned the place (PND, i, 317–18). Peter was recovered in the late 19th century.

Bulkworthy

Unknown 1742 (Ecton, p. 148), 1782 (Jones, p. 46), 1846 (Oliver, p. 446). Michael 1873 (Kelly), 1939 (ibid.), 1996 (*EDD*).

In 1740 the parish church was said to be dedicated to the Ascension, probably indicating that the parish feast was held on Ascension Day (MS Willis 41, f. 230).

The medieval dedication has not been discovered, and it was forgotten after the Reformation. Michael since the late 19th century.

Burlescombe

Mary 1742 (Ecton, p. 167; source, MS Willis 41, f. 223). Unknown 1754 (Ecton, p. 113). Mary 1782 (Jones, p. 36); 'tis conjectured that the church is dedicated to the Blessed Virgin Mary' 1793 (Polwhele, ii, 368); Mary 1846 (Oliver, p. 446), 1996 (*EDD*).

In 1740 and 1793 the parish feast was said to be held on the first Sunday after 8 September (MS Willis 41, f. 223; Polwhele, ii, 368).

The medieval dedication has not been discovered; Mary since 1742.

Burrington

Trinity 1193 (Chanter XV, f. 43v; Oliver, 1846, p. 95). Parish of St Mary of *Borington* 1365 (Pole, i, 105 no. 247). Trinity 1733 (Willis, p. 156), 1742 (Ecton, p. 143), *c.*1755 (MS Milles, i, f. 120a), 1782 (Jones, p. 41), 1846 (Oliver, p. 446), 1996 (*EDD*).

In *c.*1755 the parish feast was said to be held on Trinity Sunday and Monday (MS Milles, i, f. 120a).

Originally Trinity; Mary in 1365 either indicates a double dedication or refers to Tavistock Abbey which owned the parish church. Trinity again since 1733.

Butterleigh

Unknown 1742 (Ecton, p. 157), 1782 (Jones, p. 32), 1846 (Oliver, p. 446), 1883 (Kelly). Matthew 1889 (Kelly), 1939 (ibid.), 1996 (*EDD*).

Bishop Stapledon dedicated the cemetery on 14 April 1318 (Chanter II, f. 145) and the church and high altar on 23 November 1319 (ibid., p. 137). In 1740 the parish feast was said to be held on the Monday after St Matthew's Day (21 September) (MS Willis 41, f. 223v).

The medieval dedication has not been discovered, and it was forgotten after the Reformation. Matthew since the late 19th century, evidently a conjecture from the parish feast day.

Cadbury

Michael 1742 (Ecton, p. 142; source, MS Willis 41, f. 223v), 1782 (Jones, p. 12), 1793 (Polwhele, ii, 45), 1846 (Oliver, p. 446), 1996 (*EDD*).

In 1740 the parish feast was said to be held on the Monday after Michaelmas Day (MS Willis 41, f. 223v).

The medieval dedication has not been discovered; Michael since 1742.

Cadeleigh

Bartholomew 1742 (Ecton, p. 141; source, MS Willis 41, f. 224), 1782 (Jones, p. 9), 1793 (Polwhele, ii, 43). Mary 1846 (Oliver, p. 446). Bartholomew 1873 (Kelly), 1939 (ibid.), 1996 (*EDD*).

In 1740 the parish feast was said to be held on the Sunday after St Bartholomew's Day (24 August) (MS Willis 41, f. 224).

The medieval dedication has not been discovered. Usually Bartholomew since 1742; it is not clear if Oliver's suggestion is based on pre-Reformation evidence.

Calverleigh

Unknown 1742 (Ecton, p. 166), c.1755 (MS Milles, i, f. 120c). Mary 1782 (Jones, p. 33), 1793 (Polwhele, ii, 381), 1846 (Oliver, p. 446), 1996 (*EDD*).

The medieval dedication has not been discovered, and it was forgotten after the Reformation. Mary since 1793.

Canonsleigh: Augustinian priory of canons, changed in about 1284 to canonesses

Mary and John the Evangelist 1161 x 1177 (London, 1965, p. 2). Mary, John the Evangelist and Etheldreda c.1286 (ibid., p. 77). Mary the Virgin and John the Evangelist 1535 (*Valor*, ii, 328).

Originally Mary and John the Evangelist. Etheldreda (the Saxon Aethelthryth) was added in about 1284 when the priory was changed from a house of canons to one of canonesses.

Chagford

Michael 1447 (Chanter X, f. 226), 1475 (*CPL*, xiii (i), 470), 1481 (Osborne, 1979, p. 2), 1517 (Chanter XIII, f. 71), 1557 (Osborne, 1979, p. 185), 1742 (Ecton, p. 146), c.1755 (MS Milles, i, f. 122), 1782 (Jones, p. 19), 1793 (Polwhele, ii, 73). Unknown 1846 (Oliver, p. 446). Mary 1854 (Oliver, p. 68). Michael 1873 (Kelly), 1939 (ibid.), 1996 (*EDD*).

Bishop Bronescombe dedicated the church on 30 July 1261 (Chanter I, f. 20). In

1741–2 the parish feasts were said to be held on Michaelmas Day (29 September) and Whit Monday (MS Willis 41, ff. 211, 222), and in c.1755 on Whit Tuesday and Ascension Day (MS Milles, i, f. 122).
Michael since at least 1447; Oliver's Mary is unexplained.

Challacombe

Trinity 1742 (Ecton, p. 159). Unknown c.1755 (MS Milles, i, f. 138). Trinity 1782 (Jones, p. 48). Unknown 1846 (Oliver, p. 446). Mary 1854 (Oliver, p. 68). Trinity 1873 (Kelly), 1939 (ibid.), 1996 (*EDD*).
In 1740 the parish feast was said to be held on the Monday after Trinity Sunday (MS Willis 41, f. 226b), and in c.1755 on Trinity Sunday (MS Milles, i, f. 138).
The medieval dedication has not been discovered. Usually Trinity since 1742. The reason for Oliver's suggestion of Mary is not known.

Chardstock (transferred from Dorset to Devon 1896, and from Salisbury to Exeter diocese 1978)

Andrew 1405 (Timmins, 1984, p. 13), 1518 (PROB 11/19, f. 125v), 1521 (PROB 11/20, f. 111), 1531 (PROB 11/24, f. 92), 1742 (Ecton, p. 50), 1774 (Hutchins, i, 259), 1996 (*EDD*).
Fair on St Michael's Day 1441 (*CChR 1427–1516*, p. 11).
Andrew since at least 1405.

Charles

John 1517 (PROB 11/18, f. 265); John the Baptist 1742 (Ecton, p. 159); John c.1755 (MS Milles, i, f. 124); John the Baptist 1782 (Jones, p. 48), 1846 (Oliver, p. 446), 1996 (*EDD*).
In 1740 and c.1755 the parish feast was said to be held at or about 24 June (St John the Baptist's Day) (MS Willis 41, f. 227; MS Milles, i, f. 124).
John (probably the Baptist) since at least 1517.

Charleton

Mary 1742 (Ecton, p. 171; source, MS Willis 41, f. 223). Unknown c.1755 (MS Milles, i, f. 126). Mary 1782 (Jones, p. 84). Unknown 1846 (Oliver, p. 446). Mary 1873 (Kelly), 1939 (ibid.), 1996 (*EDD*).
The medieval dedication has not been discovered. Usually Mary since 1742.

Chawleigh

Peter 1357 (DRO, MCR 30–31 Edward III, m. 38). James 1742 (Ecton, p. 144), c.1755 (MS Milles, i, f. 128), 1782 (Jones, p. 42). Unknown 1846 (Oliver, p. 446). James 1873 (Kelly), 1939 (ibid.), 1996 (*EDD*).
The bishop of Waterford dedicated the high altar in 1338–9 (Chanter IV, f. 220v). In c.1755 the parish feast was said to be held on the Monday nearest to St James's Day (25 July) (MS Milles, i, f. 128).
Peter before the Reformation; it was then forgotten. James since 1742, evidently a conjecture based on the date of the parish feast.

Cheldon

Ecclesiam beate Marie de Chyldeladon 1280 x 1281 (PRO, JUST 1/181, m. 13; Whitley, 1913, p. 311); store of Mary 1534 (in what looks like a list of stores of church patron saints) (Moger, x, 3049a); Mary 1742 (Ecton, pp. 163; source, MS

Willis 41, f. 222). Bartholomew *c*.1755 (MS Milles, ii, f. 44). Mary 1782 (Jones, p. 55). Unknown 1846 (Oliver, p. 446). Mary 1873 (Kelly), 1939 (ibid.), 1996 (*EDD*).

In *c*.1755 the parish feast was said to be held on the Sunday nearest to St Bartholomew's Day (24 August) (MS Milles, ii, f. 44).

Mary since at least 1281; Bartholomew was a conjecture based on the date of the parish feast.

Cheriton Bishop

Michael 1445 (*CPL*, ix, 489–90), 1481 (*CPL*, xiii (ii), 736), 1482 (ibid., p. 782). Mary 1742 (Ecton, p. 146; source, MS Willis 41, f. 211), 1782 (Jones, p. 19), 1793 (Polwhele, ii, 63), 1846 (Oliver, p. 446), 1996 (*EDD*).

In 1742 the parish feast was variously said to be held on Whit Sunday and Whit Tuesday (MS Willis 41, ff. 211, 222).

Michael before the Reformation; it was then forgotten. Mary since 1742.

Cheriton Fitzpaine

All Saints 1335 (*CIPM*, vii, 487). Mary 1742 (Ecton, p. 141), *c*.1755 (MS Milles, i, f. 130), 1782 (Jones, p. 10), 1793 (Polwhele, ii, 44). Unknown 1846 (Oliver, p. 446). Mary 1902 (Kelly), 1914 (ibid.). Matthew 1923 (Kelly), 1939 (ibid.), 1996 (*EDD*).

In *c*.1742 and *c*.1755 the parish feast was said to be held on the Sunday after the Nativity of Mary (8 September) (MS Willis 41, f. 222; MS Milles, i, f. 130),

All Saints before the Reformation; it was then forgotten. Usually Mary from 1742 to 1914, a conjecture based on the parish feast day, although this was not accepted by Oliver. Matthew was substituted between about 1914 and 1923.

Chittlehampton

Urith(e), *Uritha* 15th century, sometimes in another latinized form as *Hieritha* 16th century (Orme, 1992c, p. 137–9); *church of Saint Vrithes* 1530 (PROB 11/23, f. 148v); *Uritha* alias *Hiertha* 1733 (Willis, p. 156); Urith 1742 (Ecton, p. 140). Winifred *c*.1755 (MS Milles, i, f. 132). Urith 1782 (Jones, p. 38); *Herygh* or *Hierytha* 1846 (Oliver, p. 446); *Hieritha* 1996 (*EDD*).

In *c*.1755 the parish feast was said to be held on the Monday after St Peter's Day (29 June or 1 August) (MS Milles, i, f. 132).

The church has been dedicated to its own local saint Urith (latinized as Hieritha) since at least the 15th century.

Chivelstone

Mary 1450 (Sharpe, 1889–90, ii, 521). Sylvester 1742 (Ecton, p. 171; source, MS Willis 41, f. 223). Unknown *c*.1755 (MS Milles, i, f. 136). Sylvester 1782 (Jones, p. 85), 1846 (Oliver, p. 447), 1996 (*EDD*).

Mary before the Reformation; Sylvester since 1742, perhaps a conjecture from a parish feast held on 31 December.

Christow

Cristinestowe (place) 1244 (*PND*, ii, 430); *ecclesie . . . Sancte Cristine de Cristawe* 1443 (Chanter XI, f. 510). James 1742 (Ecton, p. 147), 1782 (Jones, p. 21), 1793 (Polwhele, ii, 74). Christina 1846 (Oliver, p. 447). Andrew 1854 (Oliver, p. 68, where Christow is a mistake for Yarnscombe). Christina 1873 (Kelly). James 1883 (Kelly), 1939 (ibid.), 1996 (*EDD*).

In 1742 and 1793 the parish feast was said to be held on the Sunday after St James' Day (25 July) (MS Willis 41, ff. 212, 222; Polwhele, ii, 74).

The authors of PND explained Cristinestowe as meaning 'Christian holy place', but this was apparently in ignorance of the 1443 evidence about Christina. 'Christina's stow' or 'holy place' accords with several other 'stow' place-names in Devon and Cornwall accompanied by the name of a saint. Christina therefore by at least 1244 unless it was a later invention from a place-name meaning something else, in which case by at least 1443. The dedication was forgotten after the Reformation; James since 1742 is evidently a conjecture based on the date of the parish feast. This has persisted, despite Oliver's recovery of Christina in 1846. His Andrew was based on a mistake.

Chudleigh

Store of Mary 1559 (Moger, vii, 2198). Martin 1733 (Willis, p. 153), 1742 (Ecton, p. 153), 1782 (Jones, p. 26), 1793 (Polwhele, ii, 123). Martin and Mary 1846 (Oliver, p. 447). 1873 (Kelly). Martin 1883 (Kelly), 1897 (ibid.). Mary and Martin 1902 (Kelly), 1939 (ibid.), 1996 (EDD).

Fair on St Barnabas' Day 1309 (CChR 1300–26, p. 133). Bishop Bronescombe dedicated the church on 6 November 1259 (Chanter I, f. 9).

Possibly Mary before the Reformation. Martin since 1733, to whom Mary was added by Oliver in 1846 but not with effect locally until about 1902.

Chulmleigh: prebendal and parish church

Mary Magdalene 1279 x 1291 (DRO, Courtenay Cartulary, f. 54), 1297 (Cal. Chancery Rolls, p. 49), 1428 (Chanter X, f. 43); Mary 1468 (Chanter XII (ii), f. 14); Mary Magdalene 1733 (Willis, p. 156), 1742 (Ecton, p. 144), c.1755 (MS Milles, i, f. 134), 1782 (Jones, p. 42), 1846 (Oliver, p. 447), 1996 (EDD).

In c.1755 the parish feast was said to be held on St Mary Magdalene's Day (22 July) (MS Milles, i, f. 134).

Mary Magdalene since at least the late 13th century.

Churchstanton (transferred from Devon to Somerset 1896, and from Exeter to Bath and Wells diocese 1971)

Mary 1532 (PROB 10/5; will of William Richarddes). Paul 1742 (Ecton, p. 145), 1782 (Jones, p. 17), 1793 (Polwhele, ii, 336), 1846 (Oliver, p. 447), 1893 (Kelly).

Mary before the Reformation; Paul since 1742.

Churchstow

Mary 1380 (Chanter VI, f. 79v), 1506 (Chanter XIII, f. 6v; PROB 11/15, f. 93v), 1742 (Ecton, p. 172; source, MS Willis 41, f. 223), c.1755 (MS Milles, i, f. 140), 1782 (Jones, p. 86), 1846 (Oliver, p. 447), 1996 (EDD).

Mary since at least 1380.

Churston Ferrers

Unknown 1742 (Ecton, p. 152), c.1755 (MS Milles, i, f. 142), 1782 (Jones, p. 67), 1846 (Oliver, p. 447), 1873 (Kelly), 1939 (ibid.). Christ Church 1947 (Crockford), 1961 (ibid.). Mary 1967 (ibid.), 1996 (EDD).

The medieval dedication has not been discovered, and it was forgotten after the Reformation. Christ was introduced in about the 1940s, before Mary was adopted in the 1960s.

Clannaborough

Feast of Petroc an important day *c*.1266 (DRO, Exeter City Library, DD 43106); Petroc 1470 (Chanter XII (ii), ff. 18v, 66v). Unknown 1742 (Ecton, p. 144), *c*.1755 (MS Milles, i, f. 144). Petroc 1763 (Ecton, p. 115), 1782 (Jones, p. 42), 1846 (Oliver, p. 447), 1996 (*EDD*).

Petroc probably by at least about 1266, certainly by 1470; it was forgotten after the Reformation until it was recovered in 1763.

Clawton

Barnabas 1740 (MS Willis 41, f. 225v). Unknown 1742 (Ecton, p. 149), *c*.1755 (MS Milles, i, f. 146), 1782 (Jones, p. 63), 1846 (Oliver, p. 447), 1889 (Kelly). Leonard 1897 (Kelly), 1983 (*EDD*), 1996 (ibid.).

In 1740 the parish feast was said to be held on 16 June (MS Willis 41, f. 225v).

The medieval dedication has not been discovered, and it was forgotten after the Reformation. Barnabas was evidently a conjecture from the parish feast day. Leonard since the late 19th century.

Clayhanger

John the Baptist 1546 (Moger, vi, 1812). Unknown 1742 (Ecton, p. 166). Peter 1754 (Ecton, p. 113), 1782 (Jones, p. 33), 1846 (Oliver, p. 447), 1996 (*EDD*).

In 1740 the parish feast day was said to be held five weeks after Whit Sunday (MS Willis 41, f. 223v).

John the Baptist before the Reformation (the patrons of the church were the knights of St John of Jerusalem); it was then forgotten. Peter since 1754, perhaps a conjecture based on the parish feast day.

Clayhidon

Andrew 1490 (PROB 11/10, f. 90, two entries), 1504 (PROB 11/14, f. 192v), 1510 (PROB 11/17, f. 2), 1742 (Ecton, p. 145), 1782 (Jones, p. 17), 1793 (Polwhele, ii, 337), 1846 (Oliver, p. 447), 1996 (*EDD*).

Andrew since at least 1490.

Clovelly

Mary the Virgin and All Saints 1393 (*CPL*, iv, 462). All Saints 1471 (Chanter XII (ii), f. 95; *CPL*, xii, 822), *c*.1530 (Moger, xv, 5412a; Murray, xxv, Henry Plympton), 1742 (Ecton, p. 147). Holy Ghost *c*.1742 (MS Willis 41, f. 210). All Saints with a query 1754 (Ecton, p. 115). Holy Ghost *c*.1755 (MS Milles, i, f. 153). All Saints 1782 (Jones, p. 45), 1846 (Oliver, p. 447), 1996 (*EDD*)..

Fair on All Saints' Day 1290 (*CChR 1257–1300*, p. 351). In 1742 the parish feast was said to be held on Whit Monday or Tuesday (MS Willis 41, ff. 207, 210, 219) and in *c*.1755 on Whit Monday (MS Milles, i, f. 153).

Mary and All Saints before the Reformation, also abbreviated to the latter. All Saints alone since 1742, the Holy Ghost being a mistaken conjecture from the parish feast day.

Clyst Gabriel: hospital

Gabriel 1309 (Oliver, 1846, p. 295; Orme and Webster, 1995, pp. 217–22).

Gabriel, borrowed from a nearby chapel at Bishop's Court established by Bishop Bronescombe (compare Stoke Gabriel).

Clyst Honiton

Unknown 1742 (Ecton, p. 139), *c.*1755 (MS Milles, i, f. 149), 1782 (Jones, p. 8), 1846 (Oliver, p. 447). Michael 1873 (Kelly), 1939 (ibid.); Michael and All Angels 1983 (*EDD*), 1996 (ibid.).

The medieval dedication has not been discovered, and it was forgotten after the Reformation. Michael since the late 19th century.

Clyst Hydon

Mary 1470 (Chanter XII (ii), Reg. Bothe f. 62), 1508 (*CPL*, xviii, 578–9). Andrew 1742 (Ecton, p. 156), 1782 (Jones, p. 30), 1793 (Polwhele, ii, 266), 1846 (Oliver, p. 447). Mary 1854 (Oliver, p. 68). Andrew 1873 (Kelly), 1939 (ibid.), 1996 (*EDD*).

Mary before the Reformation; it was then forgotten. Andrew was conjectured in 1742, which has persisted despite Oliver's recovery of Mary in 1854.

Clyst St George

George 1327 (*PND*, ii, 585), 1477 (Chanter XII (ii), f. 36), 1733 (Willis, p. 151), 1742 (Ecton, p. 138), 1782 (Jones, p. 5), 1793 (Polwhele, ii, 205), 1846 (Oliver, p. 447), 1996 (*EDD*).

In 1745 the parish feast was said to be held on St George's Day (23 April) (MS Willis 41, ff. 243a-b).

George since at least 1327.

Clyst St Lawrence

Laurence 1203–4 (*CuRR, 1201–3*, p. 176), 1261 (Chanter I, f. 21), 1733 (Willis, p. 154), 1742 (Ecton, p. 156), *c.*1755 (MS Milles, i, f. 150b), 1782 (Jones, p. 30), 1793 (Polwhele, ii, 267), 1846 (Oliver, p. 447), 1996 (*EDD*).

In *c.*1755 the parish feast was said to be held on 10 August (St Laurence's Day) (MS Milles, i, f. 150b), and in 1793 on the Sunday after St Laurence's Day (Polwhele, ii, 267).

Laurence since at least the early 13th century.

Clyst St Mary

Mary 1242 (*Book of Fees*, ii, 763), 1283 (Chanter I, f. 119v), 1733 (Willis, p. 151), 1742 (Ecton, p. 138), *c.*1755 (MS Milles, i, f. 151), 1782 (Jones, p. 5), 1846 (Oliver, p. 447), 1996 (*EDD*).

No parish feast was said to be held in 1745 (MS Willis 41, ff. 243a-b).

Mary since at least 1242.

Cockington

George and Mary 1469 (Seymour, 1977, p. 248; Dublin, MS E.5.15, ff. 107–8). Unknown 1742 (Ecton, p. 152), *c.*1755 (MS Milles, i, f. 155), 1782 (Jones, p. 66). George and Mary 1846 (Oliver, p. 447), 1996 (*EDD*).

George and Mary before the Reformation; they were then forgotten but recovered in 1846.

Coffinswell

Bartholomew 1164 (14th) (ECA, D&C 1407; Barlow, 1996, no. 82). Unknown 1742 (Ecton, p. 152), *c.*1755 (MS Milles, i, f. 157), 1782 (Jones, p. 66), 1846 (Oliver, p. 447). Bartholomew 1854 (Oliver, p. 68), 1996 (*EDD*).

Bartholomew before the Reformation; it was then forgotten until it was recovered in 1854.

Colaton Raleigh

Church of St Michael *Coleton* 1329 (*CIPM*, vii, 188). John the Baptist 1742 (Ecton, p. 138), *c.*1755 (MS Milles, i, f. 163), 1782 (Jones, p. 5), 1793 (Polwhele, ii, 224), 1846 (Oliver, p. 447), 1996 (*EDD*).

In *c.*1755 the parish feast was said to be held on Ascension Day (MS Milles, i, f. 163), *The reference of 1329 occurs in a document which centres on Thorncombe. Colyton is nearer geographically, but a mention of* Kyngeston *(together with the dedication evidence about Colyton) indicates Colaton Raleigh. Michael therefore before the Reformation; it was then forgotten. John the Baptist since 1742.*

Coldridge (also Coleridge)

Mary 1742 (Ecton, p. 144), 1782 (Jones, p. 44), 1846 (Oliver, p. 447). Matthew 1873 (Kelly), 1939 (ibid.), 1996 (*EDD*).

In *c.*1742 the parish feast was said to be held on 8 September (Nativity of Mary) (MS Willis 41, f. 222).

The medieval dedication has not been discovered. Mary after 1742, replaced by Matthew in the late 19th century.

Colebrooke

Mary *c.*1300 (ECA, D&C 3672, p. 185). Andrew 1418 (Chanter VIII, f. 331v), 1496 (PROB 11/11, f. 179v), 1742 (Ecton, p. 141), 1782 (Jones, p. 10). Mary, Andrew, or Thomas Becket 1793 (Polwhele, ii, 36). Andrew 1846 (Oliver, p. 447), 1996 (*EDD*).

In 1793 the parish feast was said to be held on the Monday after 7 July (Polwhele, ii, 36).

Apparently a double dedication to Mary and Andrew before the Reformation (compare Colyton); usually Andrew alone since 1742. Thomas Becket was evidently a conjecture based on the parish feast day.

Colyton

St Andrew's Day an important feast in 1194 x 1206 (Barlow, 1996, no. 193). Andrew 1216–17 (ECA, D&C 3672, p. 35), 1225 (ibid., p. 37), 1228 (ibid., p. 46), *c.*1270 (ECA, D&C 818), *c.*1280 (ECA, D&C 821). Mary 1301 (ECA, D&C 3673). St Michael *Coleton* occurs 1329 in a document centring on Thorncombe (*CIPM*, vii, 188); Colyton is nearer geographically, but a reference to *Kyngeston* and the other dedication evidence about Colyton make Colaton Raleigh more likely. Andrew 1507 (PROB 11/16, f. 63), 1520 in the will of John Bagwell of *Colitone*—a family traceable in Colyton (PROB 11/20, f. 124v), 1558 (PROB 11/41, f. 197v), 1733 (Willis, p. 153), 1742 (Ecton, p. 150), *c.*1755 (MS Milles, i, f. 159), 1782 (Jones, p. 23), 1793 (Polwhele, ii, 312), 1846 (Oliver, p. 447), 1996 (*EDD*).

Fair granted on St Michael's Day 1207 (DRO, Courtenay Cartulary, f. 78). In 1740 the parish feast was said to be held on St Andrew's Day (MS Willis 41, f. 223v).

Andrew probably since at least about 1200, but the Mary reference suggests a double dedication before the Reformation (compare Colebrooke).

Combeinteignhead

Fraternity of Mary 1445 (Chanter XI, f. 512). Unknown 1742 (Ecton, p. 153), 1782 (Jones, p. 26), 1846 (Oliver, p. 447), 1983 (*EDD*). All Saints 1986 (ibid.), 1996 (ibid.).

Bishop Bronescombe dedicated two altars in the church on 10 November 1259 (Chanter I, f. 9) and the bishop of Waterford the high altar on 3 September 1339 (Chanter IV, f. 226).
Possibly Mary before the Reformation; it was then forgotten. All Saints since 1986.

Combe Martin

Peter ad Vincula 1740 (MS Willis 41, f. 226b); Peter 1742 (Ecton, p. 159). Unknown *c.*1755 (MS Milles, i, f. 172). Peter 1782 (Jones, p. 48), 1846 (Oliver, p. 447), 1996 (*EDD*).
The medieval dedication has not been discovered; Peter since 1742. Images of Peter and Paul appear on the doors of the chancel screen (Bond and Camm, 1909, ii, 308).

Combe Raleigh

Nicholas 1260 (Chanter I, f. 14v), 1313 (Chanter II, f. 199v). Erasmus 1742 (Ecton, p. 145; source, MS Willis 41, f. 223v). Nicholas 1754 (Ecton, p. 627). Unknown *c.*1755 (MS Milles, i, f. 174). Nicholas 1782 (Jones, p. 17), 1846 (Oliver, p. 447), 1996 (*EDD*).
In 1740 the parish feast was said to be held on the Sunday after 3 May (MS Willis 41, f. 223v).
Nicholas before the Reformation; it was then forgotten until it was recovered in 1754. Erasmus was evidently a conjecture based on the parish feast day.

Combpyne

Unknown 1742 (Ecton, p. 151), 1782 (Jones, p. 25), 1846 (Oliver, p. 447). Mary 1873 (Kelly), 1939 (ibid.), 1996 (*EDD*).
The medieval dedication has not been discovered, and it was forgotten after the Reformation. Mary since the late 19th century.

Cookbury

Bishop Stapledon dedicated the chapel on 9 August 1315 to John the Baptist and the Seven Maccabees (Chanter II, f. 107v). Unknown 1742 (Ecton, p. 149). John the Baptist 1754 (Ecton, p. 119), 1782 (Jones, p. 62). John the Baptist and the Seven Maccabees 1846 (Oliver, p. 447), 1996 (*EDD*).
In 1740 the parish feast was said to be held on 19 May (MS Willis 41, f. 225), and in 1806 in the week before Whit Sunday (Polwhele, iii, 434).
John the Baptist and the Seven Maccabees before the Reformation; it was then forgotten until he was recovered in 1754 and they in 1846.

Cornwood

Michael 1303 (*Inquisitions . . . relating to Feudal Aids*, i, 353). Unknown 1742 (Ecton, p. 157). Michael 1754 (Ecton, p. 123), 1782 (Jones, p. 73), 1846 (Oliver, p. 447); Michael and All Angels 1996 (*EDD*)..
Bishop Grandisson dedicated the church on 19 June 1336 (the feast of SS Gervase and Prothasius) (Chanter IV, f. 200), an event still commemorated in 1438 (Chanter XI, ff. 159-v).
Michael before the Reformation; it was then forgotten until it was recovered in 1754.

Cornworthy: Augustinian priory of canonesses

Mary 1535 (*Valor*, ii, 366).
Mary by 1535; the dedication is not usually mentioned in earlier documents.

Cornworthy: parish church

Peter 1742 (Ecton, p. 170; source, MS Willis 41, f. 223). Unknown *c.*1755 (MS Milles, i, f. 178). Peter 1782 (Jones, p. 83), 1846 (Oliver, p. 447), 1996 (*EDD*).
The medieval dedication has not been discovered; Peter since 1742.

Coryton

Andrew 1462 (Chanter XII (i), ff. 24, 85). James 1742 (Ecton, p. 165; source, MS Willis 41, f. 225v). Unknown *c.*1755 (MS Milles, i, f. 176). Andrew 1763 (Ecton, p. 124), 1782 (Jones, p. 79), 1846 (Oliver, p. 447), 1996 (*EDD*).

Bishop Bronescombe dedicated the church on 1 September 1261 (Chanter I, f. 21). In 1740 the parish feast was said to be held on 28 July (MS Willis 41, f. 225v), and in *c.*1755 on the Sunday after Easter (MS Milles, i, f. 176).

Andrew before the Reformation; it was then forgotten. James was evidently a conjecture from the parish feast day; Andrew was recovered in 1763.

Cotleigh

Ecclesia Sancti Petroci apud Cottelegh iuxta Honyton 1293 (CRO, ME 595, m. 4). Mary 1548 (Moger, xi, 3573). Unknown 1742 (Ecton, p. 150), *c.*1755 (MS Milles, i, f. 180), 1782 (Jones, p. 23), 1846 (Oliver, p. 447). Michael 1873 (Kelly), 1939 (ibid.), 1996 (*EDD*).

In 1740 and *c.*1755 the parish feast was said to be held on Whit Tuesday (MS Willis 41, f. 223v; MS Milles, i, f. 180).

Petroc in 1293; Mary either superseded him or was the joint patron saint, as at South Brent. Both were forgotten after the Reformation; Michael since the late 19th century.

Countisbury

Rent-charge payable by the vicar of Countisbury to Forde Abbey for the site of the church of St Pancras *c.*1220 x *c.*1240 (Forde Abbey Cartulary, charter no. 440, kindly communicated by Mr S. Hobbs). Unknown 1742 (Ecton, p. 161), *c.*1755 (MS Milles, i, f. 182), 1782 (Jones, p. 52). John the Baptist 1787 (Jones supplement, p. 3). Unknown 1846 (Oliver, p. 447). John the Baptist 1873 (Kelly), 1889 (ibid.). John the Evangelist 1897 (Kelly), 1939 (ibid.), 1983 (*EDD*), 1996 (ibid.).

In 1742 the parish feast was said to be held on the Monday week before Ascension Day (MS Willis 41, f. 207) and in 1740 and *c.*1755 a month after Easter (MS Willis 41, f. 226b; MS Milles, i, f. 182).

Apparently Pancras before the Reformation, which was forgotten afterwards. John the Baptist usually from 1787 to 1889, then changed to John the Evangelist.

Cowick: Benedictine priory and earlier parish church

Andrew *c.*1190 (DRO, W 1258/G6/46), *c.*1200 (Gervase, 1867, ii, 423), 1261 (Chanter I, f. 18v), 1412 (Chanter IX, f. 287).

Andrew before the Reformation. The priory church (founded by 1137) seems originally to have served as the parish church of the parish of Cowick (now usually known as St Thomas). Later, the chapel of St Thomas became the parish church (see below).

Cowick (alias St Thomas Exeter): later parish church

Thomas the Martyr *c.*1190 (DRO, W 1258/G6/46); Thomas *c.*1215 (ECA, D&C 2513; Troup, 1923, p. 47); Thomas the Martyr 1412 (Chanter VIII, f. 317), 1537 (DRO, QS 47/1 m 5); Thomas the Martyr, corrected to the Apostle 1733 (Willis, pp. 154, 230). Thomas the Apostle 1745 (MS Willis 41, ff. 243a-b); Thomas the Apostle, originally Thomas the Martyr 1846 (Oliver, p. 454); Thomas the Apostle 1996 (*EDD*). The church, having moved its site, was dedicated on 4 October 1412 (Chanter IX, ff. 287–8).

In the 12th century, the priory church of St Andrew Cowick (see above) appears to have served as the parish church of the parish of Cowick (or St Thomas Exeter as now usually known). The church of St Thomas was originally a chapel in the parish, built near Exe Bridge soon after the canonisation of Thomas Becket in 1173 and dedicated to him. In about the 13th century, it became the parish church of Cowick and was moved to its present location in Cowick Street in the early 15th century, the new building being dedicated in 1412. At or after the Reformation, the dedication was changed to Thomas the Apostle.

Creacombe

Mary 1422 (Chanter XI, f. 49). Michael 1742 (Ecton, p. 163; source, MS Willis 41, f. 222), 1782 (Jones, p. 55). Mary 1846 (Oliver, p. 447), 1873 (Kelly). Michael 1883 (Kelly), 1939 (ibid.); Michael and All Angels 1996 (*EDD*).

Mary before the Reformation; it was then forgotten. Michael was proposed in 1742 and has persisted despite Oliver's recovery of Mary in 1846.

Crediton: collegiate and parish church

Mary, alleged date 934 x 953 in later document (Davidson, 1878, p. 237). Holy Cross and Mary 1237 (ibid., p. 240). Holy Cross 1386 (Chanter VI, f. 154v), 1405 (Chanter VIII, f. 304v), 1508 (*CPL*, xviii, 600), 1535 (*Valor*, ii, 324). 'The olde chirch (i.e. the pre–1050 cathedral) was dedicate to S. Gregory' *c.*1540 (Leland, 1907–10, i, 239). Renamed 'in honour of Christ' 1547 (*CPR 1547*–8, p. 44). Holy Cross 1733 (Willis, p. 153), 1742 (Ecton, p. 153), 1782 (Jones, p. 26), 1793 (Polwhele, ii, 92), 1846 (Oliver, p. 447). Holy Cross and Mary 1996 (*EDD*).

Probably a double dedication to Mary and Holy Cross since early times. There is no early evidence of a dedication to Gregory. In 1547 the church was renamed in honour of Christ, but this was not remembered or regarded in later times.

Crediton: Trinitarian hospital

Laurence 1249 (Reichel, 1912–39, i, 254–6; Orme and Webster, 1996, pp. 222–4).
Laurence before the Reformation.

Cruwys Morchard

All Saints 1538 (Murray, xi, Richard Elston). Holy Cross 1742 (Ecton, p. 161), 1782 (Jones, p. 52). All Hallows 1846 (Oliver, p. 447). Holy Cross 1873 (Kelly), 1939 (ibid.), 1996 (*EDD*).

In *c.*1742 the parish feast was said to be held on the second Sunday after 8 September (MS Willis 41, f. 222).

All Saints before the Reformation; it was then forgotten. Holy Cross since 1742, suggested either by the name of the parish—taken from its medieval owners the Crues family—or by the date of the parish feast day which fell close to Holy Cross

Day (14 September). Oliver rediscovered the pre-Reformation dedication, but the 18th-century one has persisted.

Cullompton

Mary 13th century (BL, Cotton MS Vitellius D.ix, f. 42-v); churchyard of Our Lady of Cullompton 1518 (PROB 11/19, f. 50v); Mary 1742 (Ecton, p. 156; source, MS Willis 41, f. 223). Andrew 1754 (Ecton, p. 627). Mary *c*.1755 (MS Milles, i, f. 165). Andrew 1782 (Jones, p. 31). Mary 1793 (Polwhele, ii, 254), 1846 (Oliver, p. 447). Andrew 1873 (Kelly), 1939 (ibid.), 1996 (*EDD*).

Fair on St John the Baptist's Day 1257 (*CChR 1257–1300*, p. 2). The dedication festival was changed from the vigil of St Andrew (29 November) to the Monday after Michaelmas in 1435 (Chanter XI, f. 117), and moved back to 29 November in 1450 (ibid., ff. 347v–8). In 1740 the parish feast was said to be held on the Sunday after the Nativity of Mary (8 September) (MS Willis 41, f. 223).

Mary by at least the 13th century. This was recovered from the 1518 source by Willis in 1742, and remained current until 1846. Andrew was conjectured in 1754 from the date of the dedication festival which, in truth, tells us nothing about the patron saint. It has been dominant, however, since 1873.

Culmstock

All Saints 1504 (PROB 11/14, f. 169), 1529 (PROB 11/27, f. 201v), *c*.1530 (Moger, xv, 5412a). Mary 1740 (MS Willis 41, f. 223). All Saints 1742 (Ecton, p. 167). Mary 1754 (Ecton, p. 627). Unknown *c*.1755 (MS Milles, i, f. 186). Mary 1782 (Jones, p. 36). All Saints 1846 (Oliver, p. 447), 1996 (*EDD*).

In 1740 the parish feast was said to be held on the Sunday after the Nativity of Mary (8 September) (MS Willis 41, f. 223).

Usually All Saints since at least 1504; Mary was evidently a conjecture from the parish feast day.

Dalwood (transferred from Dorset to Devon 1832–44, and from Salisbury to Exeter diocese 1836)

Peter 1742 (Ecton, p. 51), 1774 (Hutchins, i, 323), 1996 (*EDD*).

The medieval dedication has not been discovered; Peter since 1742.

Dartington

Mary 1500 (Chanter XII (ii), Redmayn f. 18). Thomas Becket 1742 (Ecton, p. 170). Mary 1782 (Jones, p. 82), 1806 (Polwhele, iii, 481), 1846 (Oliver, p. 447), 1996 (*EDD*),

Usually Mary since at least 1500; Ecton's Thomas Becket is one of a several such unfounded conjectures about this saint, perhaps based on the date of a parish feast day.

Dartmouth: St Clement—see Townstall

Dartmouth: St Petrox

Petroc 1332 (Chanter IV, f. 152), 1344 (Watkin, 1945, p. 283), 1438 (Chanter XI, f. 168). *Seint Patrike c*.1540 (Leland, 1907–10, v, 230). Petroc 1545 (Youings, 1955, p. 69). 1733 (Willis, p. 164), 1742 (Ecton, p. 171). Not in Jones (1782). Petroc 1787 (Jones supplement, p. 4), 1846 (Oliver, p. 452), 1996 (*EDD*).

Petroc since at least 1332.

Dartmouth: St Saviour alias Trinity

The chapel of the Trinity, first mentioned in 1370 (Watkin, 1955, p. 285), was dedicated by Bishop Brantingham on 13 October 1372 (Chanter VI, ff. 30v–32). It is later referred to variously as Trinity 1416 (Chanter VIII, f. 226v), St Saviour 1416 (Watkin, 1935, pp. 98–9), St Saviour 1441 (Chanter XI, f. 233v), Trinity 1451 (ibid., f. 359), St Saviour 1521 (PROB 11/20, f. 130v), St Saviour 1535 (*Valor*, ii, 365). St Saviour 1733 (Willis, p. 164), 1742 (Ecton, p. 170), 1782 (Jones, p. 83). Not in Oliver (1846). St Saviour 1873 (Kelly), 1939 (ibid.), 1996 (*EDD*).

Trinity or St Saviour since at least 1370. Trinity churches were sometimes popularly known as Christ Church or St Saviour, because Christ was the most familiar or most prominently represented person of the Trinity.

Dawlish

Image of Gregory by the high altar 1301 (ECA, D&C 3673); Gregory 1448 (Chanter XI, f. 303-v). Unknown 1742 (Ecton, p. 153). Gregory 1754 (Ecton, p. 111). Unknown *c*.1755 (MS Milles, i, f. 188). Gregory 1782 (Jones, p. 26), 1793 (Polwhele, ii, 152), 1846 (Oliver, p. 447), 1996 (*EDD*).

In 1741 the parish feast was said to be held on Easter Monday but formerly on Good Friday (MS Willis 41, ff. 208v, 241).

Gregory before the Reformation; it was then forgotten, but was recovered in 1754.

Dean Prior

George 1479 (Chanter XII (ii), f. 88). Mary 1742 (Ecton, p. 170). George 1763 (Ecton, p. 125). Mary 1782 (Jones, p. 82). George 1787 (Jones supplement, p. 4), 1846 (Oliver, p. 447); George the Martyr 1996 (*EDD*).

Bishop Stapledon reconciled the church on 22 February 1323 (Chanter II, f. 174).

George before the Reformation; it was then forgotten. Usually Mary between 1742 and 1782, although George was recovered in 1763.

Denbury

Mary 1193 (Chanter XV, f. 43v; Oliver, 1846, p. 95), 1237 (Evans, 1960, p. 162), 1280 x 1281 (PRO, JUST 1/181, m. 21d; Whitley, 1913, p. 312), 1733 (Willis, p. 160), 1742 (Ecton, p. 151), *c*.1755 (MS Milles, i, f. 190c), 1782 (Jones, p. 64), 1846 (Oliver, p. 447), 1996 (*EDD*).

Fair on the Nativity of the Virgin Mary (8 September) 1286 (*CChR 1257–1300*, pp. 331, 352). Bishop Stapledon dedicated the church and high altar on 27 August 1318 (Chanter II, f. 128v). In *c*.1755 the fair was said to be held on 7–8 September (MS Milles, i, f. 190c).

Mary since at least 1193.

Diptford

Unknown 1742 (Ecton, p. 170), *c*.1755 (MS Milles, i, f. 192), 1782 (Jones, p. 82). Mary 1787 (Jones supplement, p. 4), 1846 (Oliver, p. 447), 1996 (*EDD*).

Bishop Grandisson dedicated the high altar on 14 June 1336 (Chanter IV, f. 200).

The medieval dedication has not been discovered, and it was forgotten after the Reformation. Mary since 1787.

Dittisham

George 1363 (DRO, Exeter City Library, DD 60707), 1430 (Jacob, ii, 502), 1507 (*CPL*, xviii, 553), 1508 (PROB 11/17, f. 60), 1742 (Ecton, p. 170), *c.*1755 (MS Milles, i, f. 194), 1782 (Jones, p. 82), 1846 (Oliver, p. 447), 1996 (*EDD*).

Bishop Grandisson dedicated the church on 4 October 1333 (Chanter IV, f. 170).

George since at least 1363.

Dodbrooke

Thomas Becket 1355 (Chanter V, f. 105); Thomas 1419 (Chanter VIII, f. 333v). Mary Magdalene 1742 (Ecton, p. 172). Thomas Becket 1754 (Ecton, p. 627). Unknown *c.*1755 (MS Milles, i, f. 196). Thomas Becket 1782 (Jones, p. 86); Thomas 1846 (Oliver, p. 447); Thomas Becket 1873 (Kelly), 1939 (ibid.), 1996 (*EDD*).

Fair on St Mary Magdalene's Day 1257 (*CChR 1225–57*, p. 456). In 1740 the parish feast was said to be held on the second Wednesday before Easter (MS Willis 41, f. 223).

Thomas Becket before the Reformation; it was then forgotten until it was recovered in 1754.

Doddiscombsleigh

Michael 1464 (Chanter XII (i), ff. 23v, 98), 1742 (Ecton, p. 146), *c.*1755 (MS Milles, i, f. 198), 1782 (Jones, p. 20), 1793 (Polwhele, ii, 83), 1846 (Oliver, p. 447), 1996 (*EDD*).

In 1742 and *c.*1755 the parish feast was said to be held on the Sunday and Monday after Michaelmas (MS Willis 41, ff. 211, 222; MS Milles, i, f. 198).

Michael since at least 1464.

Dolton

Edmund 1742 (Ecton, p. 168). Unknown *c.*1755 (MS Milles, i, f. 200). Edmund 1782 (Jones, p. 58), 1846 (Oliver, p. 447), 1996 (*EDD*).

In 1740 and *c.*1755 the parish feast was said to be held on Whit Sunday (MS Willis 41, f. 225v; MS Milles, i, f. 200).

The medieval dedication has not been discovered; Edmund since 1742.

Dotton

David 1259 (Chanter I, f. 11). Mary the Virgin 1532 (DRO, 96M/81/1), 1543 (Youings, 1955, p. 31).

This was either a double dedication to Mary and David, or else Mary superseded David due to the acquisition of the church in the 13th century by Dunkeswell Abbey, dedicated to Mary. The church effectively ceased to be parochial in the later middle ages.

Dowland

John the Baptist 1740 (MS Willis 41, f. 226a). Unknown 1742 (Ecton, p. 169). Conjectured to be John the Baptist *c.*1755 (MS Milles, i, f. 201). Unknown 1782 (Jones, p. 60), 1846 (Oliver, p. 447), 1910 (Kelly). Peter 1914 (Kelly), 1996 (*EDD*).

In 1740 the parish feast was said to be held on the Monday before 24 June (St John the Baptist's Day) (MS Willis 41, f. 226a), and in *c.*1755 on the Sunday nearest to that day (MS Milles, i, f. 201).

The medieval dedication has not been discovered, and it was forgotten after the Reformation. John the Baptist in the 18th century was probably a scholarly conjecture from the parish feast day, which does not seem to have received local support. Peter since about 1910–14.

Down St Mary

Mary 1332 (Chanter V, f. 20), 1413 (Chanter VIII, f. 189v), 1733 (Willis, p. 151), 1742 (Ecton, p. 141), 1782 (Jones, p. 10), 1793 (Polwhele, ii, 40), 1846 (Oliver, p. 447), 1996 (*EDD*).
Mary since at least 1332.

Drewsteignton

Trinity 1742 (Ecton, p. 146), 1782 (Jones, p. 20), 1793 (Polwhele, ii, 69), 1846 (Oliver, p. 454). 'Dedicated, probably, to All Hallows' 1854 (Oliver, p. 68). Trinity 1873 (Kelly), 1996 (ibid.), (*EDD*).

In 1742 the parish feast was said to be held on Trinity Sunday (MS Willis 41, ff. 211, 222).

The medieval dedication has not been discovered; Trinity since 1742. The basis for Oliver's suggestion of All Saints is not clear.

Dunchideock

Michael 1308 (Chanter II, f. 35v). Trinity 1740 (MS Willis 41, f. 241). Unknown 1742 (Ecton, p. 153). Trinity 1754 (Ecton, p. 111), 1793 (Polwhele, ii, 115), 1782 (Jones, p. 26), 1846 (Oliver, p. 448), 1889 (Kelly). Michael 1897 (Kelly), 1939 (ibid.); Michael and All Angels 1996 (*EDD*).

In 1741 the parish feast was variously said to be held on Easter Monday and on the day after Trinity Sunday (MS Willis 41, ff. 241, 208v).

Michael before the Reformation; it was then forgotten. Trinity was evidently a conjecture based on the parish feast day; Michael was recovered in the late 19th century.

Dunkeswell: Cistercian abbey

Mary 1206 (Oliver, 1846, pp. 395–6), 1242 (Chanter I, f. 19; Barlow, 1996, no. 243), 1497 (*CPL*, xvii part i, 8), 1535 (*Valor*, ii, 304).
Mary, as usual with Cistercian houses.

Dunkeswell: parish church

Unknown 1742 (Ecton, p. 145). Nicholas 1754 (Ecton, p. 109). Patrick *c*.1755 (MS Milles, i, f. 206). Nicholas 1782 (Jones, p. 18). Patrick 1793 (Polwhele, ii, 333). Nicholas 1846 (Oliver, p. 448), 1996 (*EDD*). Well of St Patrick 1940–1 (Binnall, p. 123).

Bishop Bronescombe dedicated the church of Old Dunkeswell on 5 December 1259 (Chanter I, f. 10). In 1740 the parish feast was said to be held on the Sunday after St Luke's Day (18 October) (MS Willis 41, f. 223), and in *c*.1755 on St Patrick's Day (17 March, unless Patrick was a dialect form of Petroc, in which case 4 June) (MS Milles, i, f. 206).

The medieval dedication has not been discovered. Patrick is not found for certain as a medieval parish-church dedication in Devon or Cornwall, so if the 18th-century writers and the well tradition really refer to Patrick, the attribution looks unlikely with regard to the middle ages. Petroc was often spelt as Patrick, however, and if that is the meaning it would be a likely pre-Reformation dedication, although any such tradition was not strong enough to prevent Nicholas being suggested in and after 1754. The latter suggestion can be ruled out for the pre-Reformation period since it was based on the date when the church was dedicated, which had nothing to do with the patron saint of the church.

Dunsford

Mary 1742 (Ecton, p. 146), 1782 (Jones, p. 20), 1793 (Polwhele, ii, 80), 1846 (Oliver, p. 448), 1996 (*EDD*).

Bishop Bronescombe dedicated the church on 29 July 1261 (Chanter I, f. 20). In 1742 the parish feast was said to be held on the Sunday after the Nativity of Mary (8 September) (MS Willis 41, ff. 211v, 222).

The medieval dedication has not been discovered. Mary since 1742.

Dunterton

All Saints 1513 (Chanter XIII, f. 49). Peter 1742 (Ecton, p. 165; source MS Willis 41, f. 225v). Unknown *c.*1755 (MS Milles, i, f. 208). Peter 1782 (Jones, p. 79). All Saints 1786 (Bacon, p. 124), 1846 (Oliver, p. 448), 1996 (*EDD*).

In 1740 the parish feast was said to be held on 29 June (MS Willis 41, f. 225v).

All Saints before the Reformation; it was then forgotten. Peter was evidently a conjecture based on the parish feast day; All Saints was recovered in 1786.

East Allington

Andrew 1742 (Ecton, p. 171; source, MS Willis 41, f. 223), *c.*1755 (MS Milles, i, f. 9), 1782 (Jones, p. 85), 1806 (Polwhele, iii, 466), 1846 (Oliver, p. 444), 1996 (*EDD*).

Bishop Grandisson dedicated the high altar on 6 October 1333 (Chanter IV, f. 170).

The medieval dedication has not been discovered; Andrew since 1742.

East Anstey

Michael 1742 (Ecton, p. 162; source, MS Willis 41, f. 223), *c.*1755 (MS Milles, i, f. 14), 1782 (Jones, p. 53), 1846 (Oliver, p. 444), 1996 (*EDD*).

In 1740 and *c.*1755 the parish feast was said to be held on the Sunday after Michaelmas (MS Willis 41, f. 223; MS Milles, i, f. 14).

The medieval dedication has not been discovered; Michael since 1742.

East Buckland

Michael 1472 (PRO, C 140/41 no. 39; IPM, Martin Fortescue), 1742 (Ecton, p. 159), 1782 (Jones, p. 49). Guy 1846 (Oliver, p. 446). Michael 1873 (Kelly), 1939 (ibid.), 1996 (*EDD*).

In 1740 the parish feast was said to be held on Michaelmas Day (29 September) (MS Willis 41, f. 227).

Michael since at least 1472. Oliver's conjecture of Guy was based on the occurrence of the place-name as Boklanda Gwidonis *in 1186 x 1191 (DRO, ED/PP/8; Oliver, 1846, p. 138), but this must represent the name of an owner of the place since a saint would have been distinguished with the title* Sanctus.

East Budleigh

All Saints 1201 (*Rotuli Chartarum*, i part i, 95), 1229 x 1230 (*Calendarium*, 1803, p. 45), 1417 (PROB 11/2B, f. 327 or 102), 1520 (PROB 11/20, f. 124v), 1742 (Ecton, p. 139; source, MS Willis 41, f. 220). Unknown *c.*1755 (MS Milles, i, f. 116). All Saints 1782 (Jones, p. 7), 1793 (Polwhele, ii, 220), 1846 (Oliver, p. 446), 1996 (*EDD*).

In 1740 the parish feast was said to be held on Good Friday (MS Willis 41, f. 223v).

All Saints since at least 1201.

East Down

John the Baptist 1742 (Ecton, p. 160). John *c.*1755 (MS Milles, i, f. 202). John the Baptist 1782 (Jones, p. 49), 1806 (Polwhele, iii, 399), 1846 (Oliver, p. 447), 1996 (*EDD*).

In 1740 the parish feast was said to be held on 24 June (St John the Baptist's Day) (MS Willis 41, f. 226b), and in *c.*1755 on that day and St Peter's Day (29 June or 1 August) (MS Milles, i, f. 202).

The medieval dedication has not been discovered; John the Baptist since 1742.

East Ogwell

Gregory 1555 (Murray, xxv, Roger Peter). Unknown 1742 (Ecton, p. 153). Bartholomew 1754 (Ecton, p. 111), *c.*1755 (MS Milles, ii, f. 79), 1782 (Jones, p. 27), 1793 (Polwhele, ii, 133), 1846 (Oliver, p. 451), 1873 (Kelly), 1939 (ibid.), 1996 (*EDD*).

Gregory before the Reformation; it was then forgotten. Bartholomew since 1754.

East Portlemouth

Church of *Sancti Winwolai* 1450 (Sharpe, 1889–90, ii, 521); *rectoriam . . . parochie Sancti Onolai* 1541 (Chanter XIV, f. 103); *Twinnels* 1742 (Ecton, p. 171; source, MS Willis 41, f. 223); *Winnell c.*1755 (MS Milles, ii, f. 116a). *Onelaus* 1782 (Jones, p. 85), 1806 (Polwhele, iii, 475); *Onolaus* 1846 (Oliver, p. 452). *Onesilaus* 1873 (Kelly), 1883 (ibid.). *Onolaus* 1889 (Kelly), 1897 (ibid.). *Winwaloe* 1902 (Kelly), 1939 (ibid.); *Winwalloe Onocaus* (*sic*) 1996 (*EDD*).

Fairs at SS Peter and Paul (29 June) and St Peter ad Vincula (1 August) 1280 (*CChR 1257–1300*, p. 225).

Winwaloe since at least 1450, of which Onolaus is a variant. There were five or six parish churches dedicated to this saint in Cornwall.

East Putford

Philip and James the Less 1740 (MS Willis 41, f. 230). Unknown 1742 (Ecton, p. 148), 1782 (Jones, p. 46), 1846 (Oliver, p. 452), 1873 (Kelly), 1939 (ibid.), 1989 (Cherry and Pevsner, p. 350).

The medieval dedication has not been discovered, and was apparently forgotten after the Reformation. Philip and James appears in 1740, but this is unlikely to have been based on popular tradition or documentary evidence because it does not appear in any later source. It may have been a conjecture from a parish feast on or around 1 May.

East Teignmouth

Michaheles ciricean 1044 (Davidson, 1883, p. 293; Hooke, 1994, p. 204); Michael *c.*1540 (Leland, 1907–10, i, 225), 1733 (Willis, p. 153), 1742 (Ecton, p. 153), 1782 (Jones, p. 26), 1793 (Polwhele, ii, 147), 1846 (Oliver, by 454), 1996 (*EDD*).

Fair on St Michael's Day 1253 (*CChR 1225–57*, p. 428).

Michael since at least the 11th century.

East Worlington

Mary 1502 (*CPL*, xvii part i, 535–6; Chanter XII (ii), Arundell f. 8); store of Mary 1534 (Moger, x, 3049a); Mary 1733 (Willis, p. 158), 1742 (Ecton, p. 162); Mary the Virgin postulated *c.*1755 (MS Milles, ii, f. 243); Mary 1782 (Jones, p. 53), 1846 (Oliver, p. 455), 1996 (*EDD*).

In *c*.1755 the parish feast was said to be held on the Sunday after the Assumption of Mary (15 August) (MS Milles, ii, f. 243).

Mary since at least 1502.

Egg Buckland

Edward 1161 x 1184 (Bodleian, MS James 23, p. 159), 1441 (Chanter X, f. 196v). Unknown 1742 (Ecton, p. 164), *c*.1755 (MS Milles, i, f. 108), 1782 (Jones, p. 76). Edward 1846 (Oliver, p. 446), 1996 (*EDD*).

Edward before the Reformation, the early date of the first reference making the Martyr more likely than the Confessor. This was forgotten by the 18th century but was recovered in 1846.

Eggesford

A request to be buried before *imaginem crucifixi Omnium Sanctorum in ecclesia de Eggisford* 1504 appears to be a confused reference to a dedication to All Saints (PROB 11/14, f. 82v). Unknown 1742 (Ecton, p. 145), 1782 (Jones, p. 44), 1846 (Oliver, p. 448). All Saints 1873 (Kelly), 1939 (ibid.), 1996 (*EDD*).

In 1740 the parish feast was said to be held on Easter Sunday (MS Willis 41, f. 225v), and in 1742 on Easter Tuesday (ibid., ff. 207, 222).

Probably All Saints before the Reformation; it was then forgotten until it was recovered in recent times through knowledge of the 1504 reference.

Ermington

Peter and Paul 1402 (Chanter IX, ff. 275–8). Peter 1494 (C 142/10 no. 12; IPM, William Stonor). Peter and Paul 1557 (Chanter 855A, f. 311v). Peter 1742 (Ecton, p. 158; source, MS Willis 41, f. 223). Unknown *c*.1755 (MS Milles, i, f. 18). Peter 1782 (Jones, p. 73), 1846 (Oliver, p. 448), 1897 (Kelly). Peter and Paul 1902 (Kelly), 1996 (*EDD*).

Fair on St John the Baptist's Day 1304 (*CChR 1300–26*, p. 40). The feast of dedication was held on 5 February in 1402 (Chanter IX, ff. 275–8). In 1740 the parish feast was said to be held on 2 February (MS Willis 41, f. 223).

Peter and Paul since at least 1402, sometimes shortened to or understood as Peter alone. Both have been recognised again since about 1902.

Exbourne

Mary 1329 (Chanter IV, f. 116), 1331 (ibid., ii, 628), 1436 (Chanter XI, ff. 126v–7). Trinity 1742 (Ecton, p. 155). Mary 1754 (Ecton, p. 627), 1782 (Jones, p. 70), 1806 (Polwhele, iii, 438), 1846 (Oliver, p. 448), 1996 (*EDD*).

In 1740 the parish feast was said to be held on the Monday after Trinity Sunday (MS Willis 41, f. 225).

Mary before the Reformation; it was then forgotten. Trinity was evidently a conjecture based on the parish feast day; Mary was recovered in 1754.

Exeter: St Alexius hospital

Alexius *c*.1170 (Orme and Webster, 1996, pp. 231–3)

Alexius; the hospital was united with that of St John in 1238–9.

Exeter: All Hallows on the Walls

All Saints 1194 x 1204 (ECA, D&C 2923; Barlow, 1996, no. 190), *c*.1215 (ECA, D&C 2513; Troup, 1923, p. 47), 1291 (Tax.).

All Saints since at least about 1200.

Exeter: All Hallows Goldsmith Street

All Saints c.1215 (ECA, D&C 2513; Troup, 1923, p. 47), 1291 (Tax.).
All Saints since at least about 1215.

Exeter: castle chapel (prebendal church)

Mary 1486 (*CPR 1485–94*, p. 28). Trinity 1546 (Snell, no date, p. 16).
Perhaps a double dedication to Mary and the Trinity, unless the latter superseded the former.

Exeter: cathedral

Mary and Peter 925 x 939 (Finberg, 1963, p. 10). Mary 925 x 939, 937 (ibid.), 1019 (ibid., p. 14). Peter 1069 (*Regesta*, i, 8). Peter and Mary 1136 (ECA, D&C 2036). Mary and Peter 1200 (ECA, D&C 2080). Peter c.1215 (ECA, D&C 2513; Troup, 1923, p. 47). Mary and Peter 1224 x 1235 (ECA, D&C 2084; Barlow, 1996, no. 248). Peter and Paul 1448 (Chanter XI, f. 510v). Peter 1535 (*Valor*, ii, 292).

Bishop Grandisson dedicated the high altar to Mary the Virgin and the apostles Peter and Paul on 18 December 1328 (Chanter IV, f. 102).

Mary and Peter by the 10th century, Peter eventually predominating and having Paul associated with him by 1328.

Exeter: St Cuthbert

Capella Sancti Cuthberti 1194 x 1204 (ECA, D&C 2923; Barlow, 1996, no. 190); *kapellis . . . Sancti Cudberti* c.1215 (ECA, D&C 2513; Troup, 1923, p. 47).
Cuthbert by 1200. The parish was united with St Paul in 1284 (ECA, D&C 2111; Troup, 1923, p. 52).

Exeter: St David

David 1194 x 1204 (ECA, D&C 2923; Barlow, 1996, no. 190), 1224 x 1225 (ECA, D&C 2084; Barlow, 1996, no. 248).
David since at least about 1200.

Exeter: Dominican friary

Bishop Bronescombe dedicated the church on 26 November 1259 (Chanter I, f. 9v).
Possibly Mary, who was represented on the seal of the house (Little and Easterling, 1927, p. 50).

Exeter: St Edmund

Edmund c.1215 (ECA, D&C 2513; Troup, 1923, p. 47), 1291 (Tax.).
Edmund since at least about 1215, i.e. the king and martyr.

Exeter: St Edward—see St Mary Steps

Exeter: Franciscan friary

Chapel of Mary and Francis, on the first site of the friary, 1434 (Little and Easterling, pp. 59–60).
Possibly Mary and Francis, if the chapel on the first site of the friary preserved the dedication.

Exeter: St George

George *c*.1215 (ECA, D&C 2513; Troup, 1923, p. 47), 1291 (Tax.).
George since at least about 1215.

Exeter: St James, Cluniac priory

Jacobescherche (place) 1086 (DB 52/50); James 1142 (*Regesta*, iii, 241–2), *c*.1200
(Gervase, 1867, ii, 423), 1304 (Chanter II, f. 85v).
James, presumably the Great, before the Reformation.

Exeter: St James, parish church (South Street)

James 1194 x 1204 (ECA, D&C 2923; Barlow, 1996, no. 190), *c*.1215 (ECA, D&C
2513; Troup, 1923, p. 47), 1291 (Tax.).
*James the Apostle by about 1200. The parish is last mentioned in 1384 (LPL,
Reg. Courtenay, f. 107), and was eventually united with Trinity.*

Exeter: St John Arches

John *c*.1215 (ECA, D&C 2513; Troup, 1923, p. 47), 1291 (Tax.).
*John since at least about 1215, probably the Baptist since he was more common as
a patron saint than the Evangelist. Moreover, this church was often called St John
Bow to distinguish it from the hospital church of St John the Baptist, which suggests
that they shared the same patron saint.*

Exeter: St John hospital

John 1184 x 1185 (Orme and Webster, 1995, p. 233); John the Baptist 1240 (in later
document) (Oliver, 1846, p. 302).
Bishop Grandisson dedicated the high altar on 12 November 1336 (Chanter IV, f. 204v),
and the nave and cemetery for burials on 16 September 1351 (Chanter III, f. 168v).
John the Baptist: probably from the 1180s, a common hospital dedication.

Exeter: St Katharine almshouse

Chapel dedicated to Our Lady *c*.1450–60; Katharine 15th century (Orme and
Webster, 1995, pp. 244–5).
Possibly originally dedicated to Mary, but later generally designated to Katharine.

Exeter: St Kerrian

Capella Sancti Kerani 1194 x 1204 (ECA, D&C 2923; Barlow, 1996, no. 190); *kapellis
. . . Sancti Kierani c*.1215 (ECA, D&C 2513; Troup, 1923, p. 47); *capella Sancti Kerani*
1291 (Tax.), 1332 (Chanter IV, f. 151v); *Sancti Kyerani* 1398 (Chanter VIII, f. 302v);
Sancti Kyrany, also *Sancti Kyrani Episcopi* 15th century (Hingeston-Randolph, 1886, p.
480, quoting St Kerrian parish documents); *ecclesiam . . . Sancti Kierani* 1438 (Chanter
X, f. 165v); *St. Kirrians* 1733 (Willis, p. 150).
*Dedicated by about 1200 to a saint who, by 1337, was considered to be identical
with Ciarán of Saighir (Dalton and Doble, 1909–41, i, pp. xxxii-iii, 216, 344).
Alternatively, he may have been the patron saint of St Keverne (Cornwall), who was
also reinterpreted as Ciarán.*

Exeter: St Laurence

Laurence *c*.1215 (ECA, D&C 2513; Troup, 1923, p. 47), 1291 (Tax.).
Laurence since at least about 1215.

Exeter: St Leonard

Avice *de Sancto Leonardo* (name) 1146 x 1149 (Bearman, 1994, p. 78); *capellam Sancti Leonardi* 1161 x 1184 (DRO, Exeter City Library, DD 6664); Leonard *c*.1215 (ECA, D&C 2513; Troup, 1923, p. 47), 1291 (Tax.).
Leonard since at least the mid 12th century.

Exeter: St Martin

Christ, Holy Cross, Mary and Martin 1065 (DRO, Exeter City Archives, Book 53A, f. 36; Troup, 1923, p. 9). Martin 1194 x 1204 (ECA, D&C 2923; Barlow, 1996, no. 190), *c*.1215 (ECA, D&C 2513; Troup, 1923, p. 47), 1291 (Tax.).
The church was dedicated on 6 July 1065 (DRO, Exeter City Archives, Book 53A, f. 36). In 1409 Bishop Stafford transferred the dedication feast to the Sunday after the translation of Thomas Becket (7 July) (ibid., f. 77v).
Originally there were four patrons, usually summarised as Martin since at least 1065.

Exeter: St Mary Arches

Mary *c*.1215 (ECA, D&C 2513; Troup, 1923, p. 47), 1291 (Tax.).
In 1231 x 1232 the dedication feast was held on the eve of Trinity Sunday; this was still the case in 1390 (DRO, Exeter City Archives, St Mary Arches, 33A/PF 2 add, 6 add).
Mary since at least about 1215.

Exeter: St Mary Major

Mary 1194 x 1204 (ECA, D&C 2923; Barlow, 1996, no. 190), *c*.1215 (ECA, D&C 3513; Troup, 1923, p. 47), 1284 (Chanter I, f. 123), 1291 (Tax.).
Bishop Grandisson dedicated the high altar on 6 November 1336 (Chanter IV, f. 204v).
Mary since at least about 1200.

Exeter: St Mary Minor

Mary 1194 x 1204 (ECA, D&C 2923; Barlow, 1996, no. 190), *c*.1215 (ECA, D&C 2513; Troup, 1923, p. 47).
Mary by about 1200. This church stood close to St Mary Major, with which its parish was united in about 1285 (Orme, 1991a, pp. 164, 169 note 5).

Exeter: St Mary Steps

Edward *c*.1215 (ECA, D&C 2513; Troup, 1923, p. 47); this was evidently the church later known as St Mary Steps (Orme, 1991a, p. 164). Mary 1262 (DRO, Courtenay Cartulary, f.60-v), 1291 (Tax.), 1294 (ECA, D&C 2121).
This was either a double dedication to Mary and Edward, or else he was superseded by her. Edward, at this date, would have been the Martyr not the Confessor.

Exeter: St Mary Magdalene hospital

Mary Magdalene 1161 x 1184 (DRO, ED/MAG/1; Barlow, 1996, no. 98; Orme and Webster, 1995, pp. 226–31).
Mary Magdalene before the Reformation.

Exeter: St Nicholas, Benedictine priory

Nicholas 1106 (*Regesta*, ii, 59), *c*.1200 (Gervase, 1867, ii, 423), 1291 (Tax.), 1535 (*Valor*, ii, 313).
Nicholas before the Reformation.

Exeter: St Olave

Olave king and martyr 1057 x 1065 (Kemble, 1839–48, iv, 264 (no. 926); Finberg, 1963, p. 15). Mary, Thomas the Apostle and Olave 1063 (Kemble, 1839–48, iv, 160 (no. 814); Finberg, 1963, p. 16). *Olaf* 1086 (DB 9/2); Olave 1072 x 1103 (13th) (Barlow, 1996, no. 4); Olave king and martyr *c*.1180 (Searle, 1980, p. 80); Olave *c*.1215 (ECA, D&C 2513; Troup, 1923, p. 47); 1291 (Tax.).

Olaf of Norway by the mid 11th century (compare Poughill, Cornwall), with co-patrons Mary and Thomas the Apostle in 1063.

Exeter: St Pancras

Pancras *c*.1215 (ECA, D&C 2513; Troup, 1923, p. 47), 1291 (Tax.).
Pancras since at least about 1215.

Exeter: St Paul

Paul *c*.1215 (ECA, D&C 2513; Troup, 1923, p. 47), 1291 (Tax.).
Paul since at least about 1215.

Exeter: St Petroc

Petroc 1194 x 1204 (ECA, D&C 2923; Barlow, 1996, no. 190), *c*.1215 (ECA, D&C 2513; Troup, 1923, p. 47), 1291 (Tax.); *Petrox* 1742 (Ecton, p. 143).

In 1528 the dedication festival was changed from St Mary Magdalene's Day (22 July) to the Sunday before St Margaret the Virgin's Day (20 July) (Chanter XV, f. 81v).
Petroc since at least about 1200.

Exeter: St Roche hospital

Roche 1506, 1511. Mary the Virgin, the Eleven Thousand Virgins and Roche 1521 (Orme, 1989, pp. 153–9; Orme and Webster, 1995, pp. 247–8).
Probably a triple dedication, as in the reference of 1521, but usually known as Roche alone.

Exeter: St Sidwell

Satiuola (saint's name) 11th century (Orme, 1992c, p. 171); *ecclesias . . . Sancte Sativole* 1152 (Chanter 1001; Oliver, 1861, p. 9); *capella Sancte Sativole* 1194 x 1204 (ECA, D&C 2923; Barlow, 1996, no. 190); *kapellis . . . beate Sativole c*.1215 (ECA, D&C 2513; Troup, 1923, p. 47); *ecclesia Sancte Sativole* 1291 (Tax.); *Sancta Sativola virgo* 1478 (Worcester, 1969, p. 124); *Satiola* or *Saviola*, alias *Sydwell* 1733 (Willis, pp. 150, 230); *Sativola* or Sidwell 1742 (Ecton, p. 142).
Sidwell or Sativola, a female saint local to the place, since at least the 11th century.

Exeter: St Stephen

Stephen *c*.1107, 1123 (*Regesta*, ii, 72, 185), 1146 (Blake, 1981, p. 309), *c*.1215 (ECA, D&C 2513; Troup, 1923, p. 47), 1291 (Tax.).
Stephen since at least about 1107.

Exeter: St Thomas—see Cowick

Exeter: Trinity

Trinity 1194 x 1204 (ECA, D&C 2923; Barlow, 1996, no. 190), *c*.1215 (ECA, D&C 2513; Troup, 1923, p. 47), 1291 (Tax.).

In 1442 the dedication festival was observed on 30 September (Chanter XI, f. 240). *Trinity since at least about 1200.*

Exeter: Wynard's almshouse

God's House, with chapel dedicated to Trinity 1436 (Orme and Webster, 1995, p. 242).

Either God's House (but this was a common synonym for the word 'hospital') or Trinity; in practice the dedication was rarely used.

Exminster

Martin 1400 (Chanter VIII, f. 301v), 1446 (Chanter X, f. 222v), 1471 (Chanter XII (ii), f. 18), 1497 (PROB 11/11, f. 70), 1742 (Ecton, p. 153), 1782 (Jones, p. 27), 1793 (Polwhele, ii, 109), 1846 (Oliver, p. 448), 1996 (*EDD*).

Martin since at least 1400.

Exmouth

St Saviour 1349 (ECA, D&C 1148). Trinity 1412 (Chanter VIII, f. 160v). A church of St Mary the Virgin was planned 1414 (*CPL*, vi, 509). Not in Ecton (1742). Trinity 1745 (MS Willis 41, ff. 243a-b). Unknown 1782 (Jones, p. 8). Margaret 1787 (Jones supplement, p. 2). Trinity 1846 (Oliver, p. 448), 1996 (*EDD*).

Trinity (apparently also called St Saviour, compare Dartmouth) since at least 1349.

Farringdon

Petroc 1401 (DRO, J.F. Chanter, Register of Institutions, p. 20, quoting an undiscovered reference in LPL), 1516 (DRO, MCR 8–9 Henry VIII, m. 36). Unknown 1742 (Ecton, p. 138), c.1755 (MS Milles, i, f. 212), 1782 (Jones, p. 5), 1846 (Oliver, p. 448). Barnabas 1873 (Kelly), 1902 (ibid.). Petroc and Barnabas 1906 (Kelly), 1939 (ibid.), 1996 (*EDD*).

Petroc before the Reformation; it was then forgotten. Barnabas was invented in the late 19th century, Petroc being restored in tandem with him soon after 1900.

Farway

Michael c.1135 x 1155 (Bearman, 1994, pp. 183–4); Michael the Archangel 1505 (*CPL*, xviii, 346); Michael 1558 (PROB 11/42A, f. 128v), 1742 (Ecton, p. 150), c.1755 (MS Milles, i, f. 214), 1782 (Jones, p. 23), 1793 (Polwhele, ii, 308), 1846 (Oliver, p. 448); Michael and All Angels 1996 (*EDD*).

In c.1755 the parish feast was said to be held on the Tuesday after Michaelmas (MS Milles, i, f. 214).

Michael since at least about 1150.

Feniton

Andrew 1502 (Canterbury Cathedral, Reg. F, f. 171), c.1503 (PROB 11/13, f. 185), 1733 (Willis, p. 154), 1742 (Ecton, p 157). Laurence c.1755 (MS Milles, i, f. 216). Andrew 1782 (Jones, p. 31), 1793 (Polwhele, ii, 276), 1846 (Oliver, p. 448), 1996 (*EDD*).

In 1740 the parish feast was said to be held on the Sunday after 1 August (MS Willis 41, f. 223v), and in c.1755 one week after 1 August (MS Milles, i, f. 216). In 1793 it was said to be held on the first Sunday in August (Polwhele, ii, 276).

Andrew since at least about 1503, Laurence being evidently a conjecture from the parish feast day.

Filleigh

Mary 1472 (PRO, C 140/41 no. 39; IPM, Martin Fortescue), 1517 (PROB 11/18, f. 265, where Filleigh is misspelt *Fylby*). Paul 1742 (Ecton, p. 140; source, MS Willis 41, f. 226b), 1782 (Jones, p. 39), 1846 (Oliver, p. 448), 1996 (*EDD*).
Mary before the Reformation; it was then forgotten. Paul since 1742.

Forde: Cistercian Abbey (transferred from Devon to Dorset and from Exeter to Salisbury diocese 1836)

Mary 1161 x 1184 (15th) (Barlow, 1996, no. 105), *c*.1200 (Gervase, 1867, ii, 423), 1493 (*CPL,* xvii part i, 22), 1507 (*CPL,* xviii, 554), 1535 (*Valor,* ii, 299).
Mary, as usual with Cistercian houses.

Fremington

Peter 1742 (Ecton, p. 140; source MS Willis 41, f. 226b), *c*.1755 (MS Milles, i, f. 220), 1782 (Jones, p. 39). All Saints 1846 (Oliver, p. 448). Peter 1873 (Kelly), 1939 (ibid.), 1996 (*EDD*).
In *c*.1755 the parish feast was said to be held on the Monday after St Peter's Day (29 June or 1 August) (MS Milles, i, f. 220).
The medieval dedication has not been discovered; Peter since 1742. It is not clear if Oliver's suggestion is based on early documentary evidence.

Frithelstock: Augustinian priory

Mary and Gregory 1341 (Oliver, 1846, p. 220). George, bishop 1535 (*Valor,* ii, 335).
Mary and Gregory before the Reformation. George was probably a mistake, a confusion of the two saints which is paralleled elsewhere.

Frithelstock: parish church

Mary and Gregory 1742 (Ecton, p. 148). Said to be St Gregory (on the basis of the priory dedication) *c*.1755 (MS Milles, i, f. 222). Mary and Gregory 1782 (Jones, p. 47). Gregory 1846 (Oliver, p. 448). Mary and Gregory 1873 (Kelly), 1939 (ibid.), 1996 (*EDD*).
In 1740 and *c*.1755 the parish feast was said to be held on the second Sunday after Easter (MS Willis 41, f. 230; MS Milles, i, f. 222).
The medieval dedication has not been discovered; Mary and Gregory since 1742. This is based on the assumption that the parish church had the same dedication as the nearby priory.

Georgeham

George 1322–3 (Pole, i, 181, no. 1904), 1356 (*PND,* i, 43), 1362 (Chanter V, f. 134v), 1374 (Chanter VII, f. 31v), 1430 (Jacob, ii, 478), 1742 (Ecton, p. 160), *c*.1755 (MS Milles, i, f. 224), 1782 (Jones, p. 49), 1846 (Oliver, p. 448), 1996 (*EDD*).
In *c*.1755 the parish feast was said to be held 'after St George's Day' (MS Milles, i, f. 224).
George since at least 1323.

George Nympton (alias Nymet St George)

George 1281 (*PND,* ii, 348), 1291 (Tax.), 1312 (Chanter II, f. 67), 1733 (Willis, p. 158), 1742 (Ecton, p. 162), 1782 (Jones, p. 53), 1846 (Oliver, p. 451), 1996 (*EDD*).
George since at least 1281.

Germansweek

Wyke Germyn (place) 1458 (*PND*, i, 183); German 1733 (Willis, p. 162); *Week St Germans* 1742 (Ecton, p. 156). Unknown *c*.1755 (MS Milles, i, f. 226). *Week St. Germans* 1782 (Jones, p. 72); *Germans* 1846 (Oliver, p. 448); German 1996 (*EDD*).

In 1740 the parish feast was said to be held on the Monday after Trinity Sunday (MS Willis 41, f. 225v).

German since at least 1458, possibly German of Auxerre.

Gidleigh

Peter *c*.1742 (MS Willis 41, f. 222). Trinity 1742 (Ecton, p. 147), 1782 (Jones, p. 21), 1793 (Polwhele, ii, 71), 1846 (Oliver, p. 448), 1996 (*EDD*).

In 1742 the parish feast was said to be held on Trinity Sunday (MS Willis 41, ff. 211, 222).

The medieval dedication has not been discovered; usually Trinity since 1742. It is not clear why Peter was suggested.

Gittisham

Image of Michael 1407 (Chanter VIII, f. 312v); Michael 1500 (PROB 11/12, f. 30). Unknown 1742 (Ecton, p. 150), *c*.1755 (MS Milles, i, f. 230), 1782 (Jones, p. 23), 1846 (Oliver, p. 448), 1873 (Kelly), 1939 (ibid.). Michael 1900 (Crockford), 1940 (ibid.). Gregory 1983–1986 (*EDD*). Michael 1987–1996 (ibid.).

Michael before the Reformation; it was then forgotten. Michael was recovered by 1900 (but not in Kelly's Directory). Gregory was evidently a directory mistake through confusion with Goodleigh, and was not in use locally (information from the Revd. James Trevelyan).

Goodleigh

Gregory 1450 (Chanter XI, f. 337v). George 1459 (*CPL*, xi, 533). Gregory the Pope 1504 (LPL, Reg. Warham, i, f. 206). Store of Gregory (probably relating to Goodleigh) 1538 (DRO, 1148M/Wills 1; Murray, i, John Ackeland). Unknown 1742 (Ecton, p. 160). Peter 1754 (Ecton, p. 116). Unknown *c*.1755 (MS Milles, i, f. 234). Peter 1782 (Jones, p. 49). Gregory 1787 (Jones supplement, p. 3), 1846 (Oliver, p. 448), 1996 (*EDD*).

In 1742 the parish feast was said to be held on the Monday a fortnight after Michaelmas Day (29 September) (MS Willis 41, f. 207), in 1740 on the Monday one week after St Peter's Day (ibid., f. 227), in *c*.1742 on the Monday a fortnight after St Peter's Day (ibid., f. 220), and in *c*.1755 on the Monday after St Peter's Day (29 June or 1 August) (MS Milles, i, f. 234).

Gregory before the Reformation, George in 1459 being probably a mistake for Gregory (compare Frithelstock Priory). This was forgotten by the 18th century when Peter was conjectured on the basis of the parish feast, until Gregory was recovered in 1787.

Great Torrington: hospital

Trinity, John the Evangelist and John the Baptist 1400 (*CPL 1396–1404*, p. 270; Orme and Webster, 1995, p. 248).

The dedication of this short-lived hospital is mentioned only on this occasion.

Great Torrington: parish church

Michael 1342 (*CIPM*, viii, 259), 1353 (Putnam, 1938, p. 81), 1482 (*CPL*, xiii (ii), 747), 1742 (Ecton, p. 169), *c*.1755 (MS Milles, ii, f. 207), 1782 (Jones, p. 59). Giles 1806 (Polwhele, iii, 413). Michael 1846 (Oliver, p. 454), 1996 (*EDD*).

In *c*.1755 fairs were held on St George's Day (23 April), Midsummer Day (24 June), and Michaelmas Day (29 September) (MS Milles, ii, f. 207).

Michael since at least 1342.

Haccombe

Blaise 1335 (*CPR 1334–8*, pp. 183, 197), 1406 (Chanter VIII, ff. 120, 309); store of St Blaise 1445 (Chanter XI, f. 512); *Blaze* 1742 (Ecton, p. 153), 1782 (Jones, p. 27), 1793 (Polwhele, ii, 139); *Blase* 1846 (Oliver, p. 448); Blaise 1996 (*EDD*).

Bishop Grandisson dedicated the church and two altars on 19 July 1328 (Chanter IV, f. 53).

Blaise since at least 1335.

Halberton

Andrew 1489 (*CPL*, xv, 210), 1508 (PROB 11/16, f. 185v); Andrew the Apostle 1513 (Chanter XIII, f. 52v); Andrew 1513 (PROB 11/17, ff. 187–8; Weaver, 1903, p. 169), 1516 (Chanter XIII, f. 65), 1546 (Moger, ii, 264), 1547 (ibid., vi, 1689), 1733 (Willis, p. 155), 1742 (Ecton, p. 167), 1782 (Jones, p. 36). 'The parishioners say it is dedicated to St Bartholomew' 1793 (Polwhele, ii, 362). Andrew 1846 (Oliver, p. 448), 1996 (*EDD*).

In 1740 the parish feast was said to be held on St Bartholomew's Day (24 August) (MS Willis 41, f. 224). In 1752 this was changed to the Monday before St Bartholomew's Day, still observed in 1793 (Polwhele, ii, 362).

Andrew since at least 1489, Bartholomew being a conjecture based on the parish feast day.

Halwell (near Harberton)

Offerings were made on St Leonard's Day *c*.1240 (ECA, D&C 1012; Oliver, 1861, pp. 418–19); Leonard 1574 (PRO, C 142/168 no. 36), 1742 (Ecton, p. 170; source, MS Willis 41, f. 223), *c*.1755 (MS Milles, i, f. 278), 1782 (Jones, p. 82). Peter and Paul 1846 (Oliver, p. 448). Leonard 'in a deed of April 15, 1474' 1854 (Oliver, p. 68), 1996 (*EDD*).

Leonard probably since at least about 1240. Oliver withdrew his alternative suggestion in 1854.

Halwill (or Halwell, near Hatherleigh)

Peter 1161 x 1184 (Weaver, 1909, p. 159). Unknown 1742 (Ecton, p. 149), *c*.1755 (MS Milles, i, f. 236), 1782 (Jones, p. 82). Peter 1846 (Oliver, p. 449), 1873 (Kelly). Peter and James 1883 (Kelly), 1983 (*EDD*), 1996 (ibid.).

In *c*.1755 the parish feast was said to be held on Whit Sunday (MS Milles, i, f. 236).

Peter before the Reformation; it was then forgotten until it was recovered in 1846. The reason for the addition of James is not clear.

Harberton

Offerings were made on St Andrew's Day *c*.1240 (ECA, D&C 1012; Oliver, 1861, pp. 418–19); Andrew 1409 (ECA, D&C 1021), 1511 (PROB 11/17, f. 20v), 1514 (PROB

11/17, f. 265), 1742 (Ecton, p. 170), c.1755 (MS Milles, i, f. 238), 1782 (Jones, p. 82), 1846 (Oliver, p. 448), 1996 (*EDD*).
Andrew: probably since at least about 1240, certainly since at least 1409.

Harford

George the Martyr 1555 (DRO, Enrolled Deeds, QS 47/9, m. 14). Unknown 1742 (Ecton, p. 158), 1782 (Jones, p. 74), 1846 (Oliver, p. 448). Patrick (a mistake for Harpford) 1854 (Oliver, p. 68). Unknown 1873 (Kelly), 1889 (ibid.). Patrick 1893 (Kelly). Petroc 1902 (Kelly), 1996 (*EDD*).
George before the Reformation; it was then forgotten. Patrick arose through Oliver confusing Harford with Harpford (see the next entry). Patrick has been legitimately explained as Petroc, but the evidence simply does not belong to this parish.

Harpford

Patrick (probably meaning Petroc) 1537 (Oliver, 1854, p. 38, where Harford should read Harpford). Unknown 1742 (Ecton, p. 138), c.1755 (MS Milles, i, f. 240), 1782 (Jones, p. 6). Gregory 1787 (Jones supplement, p. 2), 1793 (Polwhele, ii, 226), 1846 (Oliver, p. 449), 1996 (*EDD*). Well of St Petroc 1940–1 (Binnall, p. 123)
Probably Petroc before the Reformation, this saint's name being sometimes spelt as Patrick. There is no medieval evidence for churches in Devon or Cornwall being dedicated to Patrick. The well evidence supports that of the 1537 document. After the Reformation the dedication was forgotten, and Gregory was substituted in the late 18th century (very likely through adopting the dedication date of Venn Ottery church, see below). Oliver rediscovered the medieval dedication but thought it referred to Harford, and his mistake has hitherto gone unnoticed.

Hartland: Augustinian abbey

Nectan 12th century (Grosjean, 1953, pp. 397–8); Nectan c.1200 (Gervase, 1867, ii, 423), 1243 (Chanter I, f. 22; Barlow, 1996, no. 266); Mary and Nectan 1535 *(Valor,* ii, 333).
Mary and Nectan before the Reformation, often abbreviated to the latter.

Hartland: parish church

Nistenestoch (place) 1086 (DB 45/3); Nectan 1508 (Chanter XIII, f. 159), 1513 (PROB 11/17, f. 186v), 1546 (Youings, 1955, p. 75), 1733 (Willis, p. 157), 1742 (Ecton, p. 142). Holy Ghost c.1755 (MS Milles, i, f. 242). Nectan 1782 (Jones, p. 47), 1846 (Oliver, p. 449), 1996 (*EDD*).
Fair on St Nectan's Day 1281 (*CChR 1257–1300*, p. 253). In c.1742 and c.1755 the parish feast was said to be held on St James' Day (25 July) (MS Willis 41, f. 220; MS Milles, i, f. 242).
Nectan since at least the 11th century.

Hatherleigh

John the Baptist 1174 x 1184 (Finberg, 1947, p. 366; Barlow, 1996, no. 135), 1193 (Chanter XV, f. 43v; Oliver, 1846, p. 95). Mary early 13th century (DRO, 312M/TY198). John the Baptist 1284 (Chanter I, f. 123; dated by Finberg, 1969, p. 24). Store of St Mary of Hatherleigh 1348 and subsequently (DRO, 312M/TY213). John the Baptist 1399 (*CPR 1396–9*, p. 556), 1530 (Chanter XIV, f. 47v), 1733 (Willis, p. 161), 1742 (Ecton, p. 155), c.1755 (MS Milles, i, f. 247), 1782 (Jones, p. 70), 1846 (Oliver, p. 449), 1994 (*EDD*).

In 1740 the parish feast was said to be held on 24 June (St John the Baptist's Day) (MS Willis 41, f. 225v).

Apparently a double dedication to Mary and John the Baptist until the Reformation (compare Axminster); only the Baptist has survived in use since 1733.

Hawkchurch (transferred from Dorset to Devon 1896, but remaining in Salisbury diocese)

All Saints 1558 (Murray, 2nd series, John Sampson), 1584 (Moger, i, 63). John the Baptist 1742 (Ecton, p. 49). John the Baptist, All Saints and Peter 'at different periods' 1774 (Hutchins, ii, 299). John 1989 (Cherry and Pevsner, p. 475).

All Saints before the Reformation. John the Baptist was conjectured in 1742 from the will of John Hembury, vicar of Axminster and rector of Hawkchurch, dated 1490 (PROB 11/9, f. 8v), but the reference relates to Axminster; it has, however, persisted.

Heanton Punchardon

Augustine 1488 (*CPL*, xiii (ii), 746), 1518 (PROB 11/21, f. 35v); *Austine* 1573 (Moger, vi, 1907); *Austin* 1733 (Willis, p. 157), 1742 (Ecton, p. 160), 1782 (Jones, p. 49). Trinity *c*.1755 (MS Milles, i, f. 253). Augustine 1846 (Oliver, p. 449), 1996 (*EDD*).

In *c*.1755 the parish feast was said to be held on Trinity Sunday and Monday (MS Milles, i, f. 253).

Augustine (of which Austin is an English form) since at least 1488. The parish today does not identify which Saint Augustine is meant, and knows of no tradition to that effect (information from the Revd John Dykes, the rector).

Heavitree

Michael 1153 (Chanter 1001; Oliver, 1861, p. 19), 1194 x 1204 (ECA, D&C 2923; Barlow, 1996, no. 190), 1490 (ECA, D&C 472), 1544 (Moger, xii, 3852), 1742 (Ecton, p. 142), 1782 (Jones, p. 13), 1846 (Oliver, p. 449); Michael and All Angels 1996 (*EDD*).

Michael since at least 1153.

Hemyock

Mary 1461 (Chanter XII (i), f. 14v), 1474 (ibid., (ii), f. 23v). George 1742 (Ecton, p. 145). Peter 1754 (Ecton, p. 109), *c*.1755 (MS Milles, i, f. 260), 1782 (Jones, p. 17). Mary 1786 (Bacon, p. 256). George or Mary 1793 (Polwhele, ii, 335). Mary 1846 (Oliver, p. 449), 1996 (*EDD*).

In 1740 the parish feast was said to be held on the Sunday after St George's Day (23 April) (MS Willis 41, f. 223), and in *c*.1755 on the Sunday after Holy Rood Day (3 May or 14 September) (MS Milles, i, f. 260).

Mary before the Reformation; it was then forgotten. Various other conjectures were made in the 18th century, including George on the basis of the parish feast day. Mary was recovered in 1786.

Hennock

Mary 1492 (Chanter XII (ii), Redmayn f. 26v), 1742 (Ecton, p. 155), 1782 (Jones, p. 69), 1846 (Oliver, p. 449), 1996 (*EDD*).

In 1742 the parish feast was said to have been moved, about 15 or 16 years previously, from the Monday after Lammas Day (1 August) to the first Monday in September (MS Willis 41, f. 218).

Mary since at least 1492.

Highampton

Holy Cross 1742 (Ecton, p. 156). Unknown c.1755 (MS Milles, i, f. 256). Holy Cross 1782 (Jones, p. 72), 1846 (Oliver, p. 449), 1996 (*EDD*).

In 1740 the parish feast was said to be held on 12 September (MS Willis 41, f. 225), and in c.1755 on the nearest Sunday to Holy Cross Day (14 September) (MS Milles, i, f. 256).

The medieval dedication has not been discovered; Holy Cross since 1742.

High Bickington

Mary 1514 (Chanter XIII, f. 54). Bartholomew 1742 (Ecton, p. 140; source, MS Willis 41, f. 230), c.1755 (MS Milles, i, f. 55). Mary 1763 (Ecton, p. 114), 1782 (Jones, p. 38), 1846 (Oliver, p. 445), 1996 (*EDD*)

In 1740 the parish feast was said to be held on the fourth Sunday after 24 June (MS Willis 41, f. 230).

Mary before the Reformation; it was then forgotten. Bartholomew in the mid 18th century until Mary was recovered in 1763.

High Bray

All Saints 1511 (*CPL*, xix (forthcoming), no. 498), 1517 (PROB 11/18, f. 265), 1524 (PROB 11/23, f. 54), 1733 (Willis, p. 158), 1742 (Ecton, p. 160). Holy Ghost conjectured c.1755 (MS Milles, i, f. 84). All Saints 1782 (Jones, p. 49), 1846 (Oliver, p. 449), 1996 (*EDD*).

In c.1755 the parish feast was said to be held on Whit Monday (MS Milles, i, f. 84).

All Saints since at least 1511.

Highweek

All Saints 1427 (*CPL*, vii, 519). Unknown 1742 (Ecton, p. 154). Mary 1742 (Ecton, p. 121), corrected to All Saints (ibid., p. 627). Unknown c.1755 (MS Milles, i, f. 270). All Saints 1782 (Jones, p. 68), 1846 (Oliver, p. 449), 1996 (*EDD*).

The chapel was dedicated or rededicated on 19 April 1428, the dedication feast being ordered to be held in future on the second Sunday after Easter (Chanter X, ff. 10v–11). In 1741 the parish feast was said to be held on the first Monday in July (MS Willis 41, f. 219).

All Saints before the Reformation; it was then forgotten until it was recovered in 1754.

Hittisleigh

Unknown 1742 (Ecton, p. 147). Andrew 1742 (MS Willis 41, ff. 211, 212; the latter reference was said to be based on 'ancient writings'), 1754 (Ecton, p. 110), 1782 (Jones, p. 21), 1793 (Polwhele, ii, 67), 1846 (Oliver, p. 449), 1996 (*EDD*).

In 1742 the parish feast was said to be held on the Monday before Ascension Day (MS Willis 41, f. 211).

The medieval dedication has not been discovered; Andrew since at least 1742. This looks likely to be the original dedication, in view of the alleged documentary evidence and because it was evidently not a conjecture from the parish feast day.

Hockworthy

Unknown 1742 (Ecton, p. 167), 1782 (Jones, p. 36), 1846 (Oliver, p. 449). Simon and Jude 1873 (Kelly), 1939 (ibid.), 1996 (*EDD*).

In *c.*1742 the parish feast was said to be held on the Sunday after Easter Day (MS Willis 41, ff. 213, 223).

The medieval dedication has not been discovered, and it was forgotten after the Reformation. Simon and Jude since the late 19th century.

Holbeton

All Saints 1742 (Ecton, p. 158), 1782 (Jones, p. 74), 1846 (Oliver, p. 449), 1996 (*EDD*).

Bishop Grandisson dedicated the church, high altar and another altar on 18 June 1336 (Chanter IV, f. 200).

The medieval dedication has not been discovered; All Saints since 1742.

Holcombe Burnell

Nicholas 1150, *c.*1180 (*Calendar of Wells MSS*, i, 19–20). Unknown 1742 (Ecton, p. 146), *c.*1755 (MS Milles, i, f. 272). John the Baptist 1782 (Jones, p. 20), 1793 (Polwhele, ii, 82), 1846 (Oliver, p. 449), 1996 (*EDD*).

In 1742 the parish feast was said to be held on the Sunday after St John the Baptist's Day (24 June) (MS Willis 41, ff. 211v, 212, 242), and in *c.*1755 on the Monday afterwards (MS Milles, i, f. 272).

Nicholas before the Reformation; it was then forgotten. John the Baptist since the 18th century, evidently a conjecture based on the parish feast day.

Holcombe Rogus

Mary 1206 (Holmes and Weaver, 1894, pp. 170–1). All Saints *c.*1530 (Moger, xv, 5412a). Unknown 1742 (Ecton, p. 167). Mary 1754 (Ecton, p. 113), corrected to All Saints (ibid., p. 627). Unknown *c.*1755 (MS Milles, i, f. 274). All Saints 1782 (Jones, p. 36), 1793 (Polwhele, ii, 371), 1846 (Oliver, p. 449), 1996 (*EDD*).

Fair on All Saints' Day 1343 (*CChR 1341–1427*, p. 24). In 1740 the parish feast was said to be held on Whit Sunday (MS Willis 41, f. 223) and in *c.*1755 on Whit Monday (MS Milles, i, f. 274).

Probably a double dedication to Mary and All Saints before the Reformation (compare Clovelly). This was forgotten after the Reformation. Both Mary and All Saints were rediscovered in 1754, causing confusion; All Saints alone since 1782.

Hollacombe

Petroc 1456 (Chanter XII (i), f. 3v), 1467 (ibid., (ii), f. 9v), 1492 (ibid., f. 118). David 1742 (Ecton, p. 149; source, MS Willis 41, f. 225v), 1782 (Jones, p. 63). Petroc 1786 (Bacon, p. 263), 1846 (Oliver, p. 449), 1996 (*EDD*).

In 1740 the parish feast was said to be held on 1 March (St David's Day) (MS Willis 41, f. 225v).

The church belonged to St Petroc's, Bodmin by 1066 (DB 51/15). Petroc since at least 1456 until the Reformation, when the dedication was forgotten. David was evidently a conjecture from the parish feast day; Petroc was recovered in 1786.

Holne

Unknown 1742 (Ecton, p. 170), 1782 (Jones, p. 82). Mary 1846 (Oliver, p. 449), 1996 (*EDD*).

The medieval dedication has not been discovered; it was then forgotten. Mary since 1846; she appears on the central doors of the chancel screen (Bond and Camm, 1909, ii, 321).

Holsworthy

Store of Peter (apparently chief store of the church) 1418 (Chanter VIII, f. 331v); Peter 1740 (MS Willis 41, f. 225v). Peter and Paul 1742 (Ecton, p. 149), 1782 (Jones, p. 62), 1846 (Oliver, p. 449), 1996 (*EDD*).
In 1740 the parish feast was said to be held on 29 June (MS Willis 41, f. 225v).
Probably Peter before the Reformation, possibly with Paul if Ecton's information or conjecture is accurate. Peter and Paul since 1742.

Honeychurch

Mary 1466 (Chanter XII (ii), ff. 7, 60v). Store of All Saints 1548 (PROB 11/31, f. 299). James 1742 (Ecton, p. 156; source, MS Willis 41, f. 225), 1782 (Jones, p. 72). Mary 1786 (Bacon, p. 274), 1846 (Oliver, p. 449), 1996 (*EDD*).
In 1740 the parish feast was said to be held on 28 July (MS Willis 41, f. 225).
Mary before the Reformation, possibly with All Saints (compare Clovelly and Holcombe Rogus). This was forgotten by 1742, when James was conjectured on the basis of the parish feast day. Mary was recovered in 1786.

Honiton: hospital

Margaret 1374 (Chanter VI, f. 54; Orme and Webster, 1995, pp. 249–50).
Margaret before the Reformation.

Honiton: parish church

Michael 1406 (Chanter VIII, f. 307), 1431 (*CPL*, viii, 332), 1487 (Chanter XII (ii), f. 98), 1501 (PROB 11/13, f. 157v; Weaver, 1903, p. 25), 1539 (Chanter XIII, f. 99v); store of Michael 1546 (Moger, xi, 3567); Michael 1547 (ibid., xiii, 4250), 1742 (Ecton, p. 150), *c.*1755 (MS Milles, i, f. 282 verso), 1782 (Jones, p. 23), 1793 (Polwhele, ii, 281), 1846 (Oliver, p. 449), 1996 (*EDD*).
In 1740 the parish feast was said to be held on the Sunday after Michaelmas Day (29 September) (MS Willis 41, f. 223v), and in *c.*1755 on the Monday with a procession on Ascension Day (MS Milles, i, f. 282 verso).
Michael since at least 1406.

Horwood

Michael the Archangel 1386 (LPL, Reg. Courtenay, f. 222v), 1468 (Chanter XII (ii), ff. 13), 1476 (ibid., f. 38v), 1493 (PROB 11/10, f. 76), 1512 (Chanter XIII, f. 48); Michael 1742 (Ecton, p. 140; source, MS Willis 41, f. 226b). Philip and James *c.*1755 (MS Milles, i, f. 286). Michael 1782 (Jones, p. 40), 1846 (Oliver, p. 449), 1996 (*EDD*).
In *c.*1755 the parish feast was said to be held on 1 May (MS Milles, i, f. 286).
Michael since at least 1386, except in 1755 when Philip and James the Less were conjectured on the basis of the parish feast day.

Huish

Stephen 1444 (Chanter XI, f. 256). Philip and James the Less 1740 (MS Willis 41, f. 225v). James 1742 (Ecton, p. 169). Unknown *c.*1755 (MS Milles, i, f. 264). James 1782 (Jones, p. 60), 1846 (Oliver, p. 449), 1873 (Kelly), 1939 (ibid.). James the Less 1983 (*EDD*), 1996 (ibid.).
In 1740 the parish feast was said to be held on 29 May (MS Willis 41, f. 225v).
Stephen before the Reformation; it was then forgotten. Philip and James the Less were conjectured in 1740, a dedication subsequently reduced to James the Less alone.

Huntsham

Unknown 1742 (Ecton, p. 166). Mary c.1755 (MS Milles, i, f. 290). Unknown 1782 (Jones, p. 33), 1846 (Oliver, p. 449), 1889 (Kelly). All Saints 1897 (Kelly), 1939 (ibid.), 1983 (*EDD*), 1996 (ibid.).

In 1740 the parish feast was said to be held on the Sunday before Whit Sunday (MS Willis 41, f. 223v).

The medieval dedication has not been discovered, and it was forgotten after the Reformation. Mary once in the mid 18th century; All Saints since about 1897. The basis of these dedications is not clear.

Huntshaw

Mary Magdalene 1742 (Ecton, p. 140). Unknown c.1755 (MS Milles, i, f. 288). Mary Magdalene 1782 (Jones, p. 39), 1846 (Oliver, p. 449), 1996 (*EDD*).

In 1742 the parish feast was said to be on the Sunday after St James' Day (25 July) (MS Willis 41, f. 207), and in c.1755 a month after Midsummer Day (24 June) (MS Milles, i, f. 288).

The medieval dedication has not been discovered; Mary Magdalene since 1742.

Huxham

Unknown 1742 (Ecton, p. 138), 1782 (Jones, p. 6), 1846 (Oliver, p. 449). Mary 1873 (Kelly), 1939 (ibid.), 1996 (*EDD*).

The medieval dedication has not been discovered, and it was forgotten after the Reformation. Mary since the late 19th century.

Iddesleigh

Store of Mary 1536, apparently the chief of six stores in the church, none of which was dedicated to James (NDRO, Iddesleigh, PW 1). Philip and James the Less 1740 (MS Willis 41, f. 226a). James 1742 (Ecton, p. 168). Unknown c.1755 (MS Milles, i, f. 292). James 1782 (Jones, p. 58), 1846 (Oliver, p. 449), 1996 (*EDD*).

In 1740 the parish feast was said to be held on Whit Tuesday (MS Willis 41, f. 226a), and in c.1755 on Whit Sunday (MS Milles, i, f. 292).

Mary seems likely before the Reformation; it was then forgotten. Philip and James is probably a conjecture from some local observance of 1 May, and James by himself may stem from that although he has presumably come to be regarded as James the Great.

Ide

Unknown 1742 (Ecton, p. 154). *Ide* 1754 (Ecton, p. 627); Ida 1782 (Jones, p. 29), 1846 (Oliver, p. 449), 1996 (*EDD*).

The medieval dedication has not been discovered, and it was forgotten after the Reformation. Ide or Ida since 1754. It is probably an attempt, originating in the mid 18th century, to explain the name of the parish as that of a saint and thereby to provide a patron for the church (compare Brendon). Such a conjecture would be reasonable in Cornwall, where parishes are often named after a saint without the addition of any other word or element, but that does not happen in Devon. Rather, the name of the parish appears to be that of a river (PND, ii, 497).

Ideford

Martin 1511 (*CPL*, xix (forthcoming), no. 671), 1569 (Moger, vii, 2193). Mary 1741 (MS Willis 41, ff. 217, 219). Unknown 1742 (Ecton, p. 154). Mary 1754 (Ecton, p.

121); Mary the Virgin *c*.1755 (MS Milles, i, f. 210); Mary 1782 (Jones, p. 68). Mary and Martin 1846 (Oliver, p. 449). Mary 1873 (Kelly), 1939 (ibid.), 1996 (*EDD*).

In 1742 and *c*.1755 the parish feast was said to be held on the first Monday after 8 September (MS Willis 41, ff. 217, 219; MS Milles, i, f. 210).

Martin before the Reformation; it was then forgotten. Mary usually since 1741, despite Oliver's recovery of Martin in 1846.

Ilfracombe

Image of Mary the Virgin mentioned in church (not necessarily patron saint) 1309 (Chanter II, f. 42v). Trinity 1742 (Ecton, p. 161), *c*.1755 (MS Milles, i, f. 294), 1782 (Jones, p. 51), 1846 (Oliver, p. 449), 1996 (*EDD*).

Fair at Holy Trinity 1272 (*CChR 1257–1300*, p. 181), 1279 (ibid., p. 211). In 1740 the parish feast was said to be held on the Monday after Trinity Sunday (MS Willis 41, f. 226b), and in *c*.1755 on Trinity Sunday (MS Milles, i, f. 294).

The medieval dedication has not been discovered: possibly Mary. Trinity since 1742.

Ilsington

Michael 1479 (Chanter XII (ii), f. 87), 1531 (Moger, iii, 662); store of Michael 1532 (ibid., xviii, 6598). Unknown 1742 (Ecton, p. 154). Michael 1763 (Ecton, p. 121), 1782 (Jones, p. 68), 1846 (Oliver, p. 449), 1996 (*EDD*).

Michael before the Reformation; it was then forgotten but recovered in 1763.

Instow

Lohannestov for *Iohannestov* (place) 1086 (DB 24/26); John the Baptist 1476 (Chanter XII (ii), f. 38v), 1486 (*CIPM, Henry VII*, i, 64), 1501 (Chanter XII (ii), Redmayn f. 22v). Justus 1733 (Willis, p. 156), 1742 (Ecton, p. 140). John *c*.1755 (MS Milles, i, f. 299). John the Baptist 1763 (Ecton, p. 114), 1782 (Jones, p. 40), 1846 (Oliver, p. 449), 1996 (*EDD*).

In *c*.1755 the parish feast was said to be held on the day after St Peter's Day (29 June or 1 August) (MS Milles, i, f. 299).

Dedicated to a Saint John by 1086. A 12th-century reference to a John as a (Celtic) child of Brychan and brother of Nectan of Hartland may refer to this saint (Orme, 1992c, pp. 45, 49, although a contrary argument is put forward there), because John Leland transcribed in c.1540 a list of west-country saints, apparently of 12th- or 13th-century origin, which refers to a Saint John beheaded and lying in a church near the River Torridge opposite a chapel similarly dedicated (Oxford, Bodleian Library, MS Top. Gen. c.2, p. 369; Orme, 1995a, pp. 10–13). Instow lies by the Torridge and there was a chapel of St John at Appledore opposite. Any such belief in a distinct Saint John of Instow, however, seems to have disappeared by 1476 when the church was understood to be dedicated to the Baptist. This tradition in turn was weak by the 18th century, and was fully recovered only in 1763.

Inwardleigh

Unknown 1742 (Ecton, p. 155), 1782 (Jones, p. 71), 1846 (Oliver, p. 449), 1873 (Kelly), 1939 (ibid.). Petroc 1983 (*EDD*), 1996 (ibid.).

In 1740 the parish feast was aid to be held on Whit Tuesday (MS Willis 41, f. 225).

The medieval dedication has not been discovered, and it was forgotten after the Reformation. Petroc in recent times.

Ipplepen

Andrew 1499 (Chanter XII (ii), Redmayn f. 9v), 1503 (*CPL*, xvii part i, 618), 1513 (PROB 11/17, ff. 187–8; Weaver, 1903, p. 169). John the Baptist 1742 (Ecton, p. 152), 1782 (Jones, p. 66). Andrew 1846 (Oliver, p. 449), 1996 (*EDD*).

Fair on St Andrew's Day 1317 (*CChR 1300–26*, p. 359). Bishop Stapledon dedicated the high altar on 3 May 1318 (Chanter II, f. 126v).

Andrew before the Reformation; it was then forgotten and replaced by John the Baptist until it was recovered in 1846.

Jacobstowe

James 1331 (Chanter IV, f. 34), 1733 (Willis, p. 162), 1742 (Ecton, p. 156), 1782 (Jones, p. 71), 1846 (Oliver, p. 449), 1996 (*EDD*).

In 1740 the parish feast was said to be held on the Monday after St James' Day (25 July) (MS Willis 41, f. 225).

James since at least 1331.

Kelly

Mary 1391 (Chanter VII, f. 127). Mark 1740 (MS Willis 41, f. 225v). Luke *c.*1742 (ibid., f. 210). Unknown 1742 (Ecton, p. 165). Mary 1754 (Ecton, p. 627). Unknown *c.*1755 (MS Milles, i, f. 301). Mary 1782 (Jones, p. 79), 1846 (Oliver, p. 449), 1996 (*EDD*).

Bishop Bronescombe dedicated the church on 24 October 1259 (Chanter I, f. 8v). In 1740 the parish feast was said to be held on 28 April (MS Willis 41, f. 225v).

Mary before the Reformation; it was then forgotten until it was recovered in 1754.

Kenn

Andrew 1141 x 1155 (Oliver, 1846, p. 136), 1503 (*CPL*, xvii part i, 588), 1506 (*CPL*, xviii, 395), 1733 (Willis, p. 154), 1742 (Ecton, p. 153), 1782 (Jones, p. 27), 1793 (Polwhele, ii, 183), 1846 (Oliver, p. 449), 1996 (*EDD*).

Andrew since at least about 1150.

Kennerleigh

Clement 1334 (ECA, D&C 3521, p. 262). Unknown 1742 (Ecton, p. 142). John the Baptist *c.*1742 (MS Willis 41, f. 222), 1754 (Ecton, p. 108). Unknown 1782 (Jones, p. 12). John the Baptist 1787 (Jones supplement, p. 3), 1793 (Polwhele, ii, 41). Clement 1846 (Oliver, p. 449). John the Baptist 1873 (Kelly), 1939 (ibid.), 1996 (*EDD*).

In *c.*1742 the parish feast was said to be held on the Sunday after Midsummer Day (MS Willis 41, f. 222).

Clement before the Reformation; it was then forgotten. John the Baptist since about 1742, evidently a conjecture from the date of the parish feast, despite Oliver's recovery of Clement in 1846.

Kentisbeare

Mary 1308 (Chanter II, f. 37r), 1510 (*CPL*, xix (forthcoming), no. 366), 1543 (PROB 11/30, f. 73v), 1742 (Ecton, p. 157), 1782 (Jones, p. 31), 1793 (Polwhele, ii, 258), 1846 (Oliver, p. 449), 1996 (*EDD*).

Bishop Bronescombe dedicated three altars in the church with the cemetery on 9 December 1259 (Chanter I, f. 10). In 1793 the parish feast was said to be held on Whit Wednesday and Thursday (Polwhele, ii, 258).

Mary since at least 1308.

Kentisbury

Unknown 1742 (Ecton, p. 160). Holy Ghost c.1755 (MS Milles, i, f. 303). Unknown 1782 (Jones, p. 49), 1846 (Oliver, p. 449), 1889 (Kelly). Thomas 1897 (Kelly), 1939 (ibid.), 1996 (*EDD*).

In 1740, 1742 and in c.1755 the parish feast was said to be held on Whit Tuesday (MS Willis 41, ff. 207, 213, 226b; MS Milles, i, f. 303).

The medieval dedication has not been discovered, and it was forgotten after the Reformation. The Holy Ghost is an unlikely suggestion based on the parish feast. Thomas since the late 19th century.

Kenton

Andrew 1476 (DRO, MCR 17–18 Edward IV, m. 7). All Saints 1742 (Ecton, p. 153). Andrew c.1755 (MS Milles, i, f. 305). All Saints 1782 (Jones, p. 27). 'All Saints or, according to some accounts, . . . St Patrick' 1793 (Polwhele, ii, 165). All Saints 1846 (Oliver, p. 449), 1996 (*EDD*).

Andrew before the Reformation, still remembered in about 1755. In 1742, however, All Saints was conjectured and has persisted ever since.

Kerswell: Cluniac priory

Mary c.1206 (Holmes and Weaver, 1894, pp. 170, 175–6).
Mary before the Reformation.

Kilmington

Giles 1548 (Moger, vi, 1858), 1742 (Ecton, p. 150), 1782 (Jones, p. 22), 1793 (Polwhele, ii, 294), 1846 (Oliver, p. 449), 1996 (*EDD*).

In 1740 the parish feast was said to be held on 11 June (MS Willis 41, f. 223v).
Giles since at least 1548.

Kingsbridge

Edmund king and martyr 1309 (DRO, Exeter City Library, DD 33227); Edmund 1316 (DRO, 215M/T22). Chapel of Our Saviour 1379 (DRO, Exeter City Library, DD 33248). Store of St Saviour and St Edmund 1385 (ibid., DD 33252). Cemetery of Edmund the king 1388 (ibid., DD 33254); chapel of Edmund king and martyr 1410 (ibid., DD 33265a); store of Edmund 1427 (Chanter XI, f. 500); Edmund the king 1440 (ibid., f. 210); store of Edmund 1506 (DRO, 215M/T51); Edmund 1529 (DRO, 215M/T58), 1733 (Willis, p. 164), 1742 (Ecton, p. 172), c.1755 (MS Milles, i, f. 311), 1782 (Jones, p. 86), 1846 (Oliver, p. 449); Edmund king and martyr 1996 (*EDD*).

In 1740 the parish feast was said to be held on 20 July (MS Willis 41, f. 223).

Normally Edmund of Bury, king and martyr, since at least 1309. The reference of 1379 may be to a separate chapel, but that of 1385 raises the possibility that there was a double dedication to the Saviour and Edmund, of which only the latter was commonly used.

Kingskerswell

Mary 1477 (ECA, D&C 2885). Unknown 1742 (Ecton, p. 142), c.1755 (MS Milles, i, f. 309), 1782 (Jones, p. 66), 1846 (Oliver, p. 446). Mary 1873 (Kelly), 1939 (ibid.), 1996 (*EDD*).

Fair on St Giles' Day 1268 (*CChR 1257–1300*, p. 89).
Mary before the Reformation; it was then forgotten until restored in recent times.

King's Nympton

Mary 1490 (*CIPM, Henry VII,* i, 234). James 1742 (Ecton, p. 162; source, MS Willis 41, f. 227), 1782 (Jones, p. 53), 1846 (Oliver, p. 451); James the Apostle 1996 (*EDD*). In 1740 the parish feast was said to be held on Whit Sunday (MS Willis 41, f. 227).
Mary before the Reformation; James (presumably the Great) since 1742.

Kingsteignton

Mary 1742 (Ecton, p. 154). Michael 1754 (Ecton, p. 121). Unknown *c.*1755 (MS Milles, ii, f. 201). Michael 1782 (Jones, p. 68), 1846 (Oliver, p. 454), 1996 (*EDD*). Bishop Stapledon dedicated the high altar on 1 May 1318 (Chanter II, f. 126v). In 1741 the parish feast was said to be held on Michaelmas Day (29 September) (MS Willis 41, ff. 217, 219).
The medieval dedication has not been discovered. Mary in 1742, replaced by Michael since 1754—the latter possibly a conjecture from the parish feast day.

Kingston

James the Apostle 1402 (Chanter IX, f. 275), 1457 (PROB 11/4, f. 93). Not in Ecton (1742). Unknown 1754 (Ecton, p. 123), *c.*1755 (MS Milles, i, f. 313), 1782 (Jones, p. 75). James the Apostle 1846 (Oliver, p. 449). James the Less 1996 (*EDD*).
James the Apostle before the Reformation; it was then forgotten and recovered in 1846. The Apostle seems more likely to mean James the Great, since James the Less was usually coupled with Philip; the latter therefore appears to be a modern revision.

Kingswear

Thomas Becket 1173 x 1196 (DRO, 312M/TY24), 1742 (Ecton, p. 152), *c.*1755 (MS Milles, i, f. 315), 1782 (Jones, p. 67), 1846 (Oliver, p. 449), 1996 (*EDD*).
An early dedication to Thomas Becket, apparently remembered ever since.

Knowstone

Peter 1742 (Ecton, p. 162; source, MS Willis 41, f. 222), *c.*1755 (MS Milles, i, ff. 317–18), 1782 (Jones, p. 53). Andrew 1846 (Oliver, pp. 204, 449). Peter 1873 (Kelly), 1939 (ibid.), 1996 (*EDD*).
In *c.*1755 the parish feast was said to be held on the Sunday one week after St Peter's Day (29 June or 1 August) (MS Milles, i, ff. 317–18).
The medieval dedication has not been discovered for certain, but Oliver's Andrew may well have been based on pre-Reformation documentary evidence such as a will and is plausible. If that view is correct, Peter would be a conjecture from the parish feast day.

Lamerton

Peter 1284 (Chanter I, f. 123; dated by Finberg, 1969, p. 24), 1733 (Willis, p. 163), 1742 (Ecton, p. 165). Unknown *c.*1755 (MS Milles, ii, f. 1). Peter 1782 (Jones, p. 79), 1846 (Oliver, p. 449), 1996 (*EDD*).
In 1740 the parish feast was said to be held on 30 June (MS Willis 41, f. 225v).
Peter since at least 1284.

Landcross

A reference to the church of Our Lady *Lancas* 1517 in a group of bequests to north Devon churches must relate to Landcross (PROB 11/18, f. 265). Trinity 1742 (Ecton,

p. 148; source, MS Willis 41, f. 230), 1782 (Jones, p. 46), 1846 (Oliver, p. 449), 1996 (*EDD*).
Mary before the Reformation; Trinity since 1742.

Landkey

Landechei (place) 1166 (*PND*, ii, 341), meaning 'the church of thy Cei'. Paul 1346 (*CPR 1345–8*, p. 210), 1538 (DRO, 1148M/Wills 1; Murray, i, John Ackeland). Our Saviour 1740 (MS Willis 41, f. 226b). Trinity 1742 (Ecton, p. 161). Unknown *c.*1755 (MS Milles, ii, f. 3). Trinity 1782 (Jones, p. 41). Paul 1846 (Oliver, p. 449), 1996 (*EDD*).
Originally Cei, a saint who is probably identifiable with the Celtic St Kea and a rare example of a Devon dedication that is probably pre-Saxon. Paul by 1346 until the Reformation, then forgotten. Trinity in the 18th century, perhaps a conjecture from a parish feast day, until Paul was recovered in 1846.

Langtree

All Saints 1509 (*CPL*, xix (forthcoming), no. 280), 1546 (DRO, Exeter City Library, DD 30091). Unknown 1742 (Ecton, p. 168), 1782 (Jones, p. 58), 1846 (Oliver, p. 450), 1996 (*EDD*).
In 1740 the parish feast was said to be held on Easter Sunday (MS Willis 41, f. 230), and in 1742 on Easter Monday (ibid., f. 207).
All Saints before the Reformation. It was then forgotten and, unusually, no alternative patron was adopted.

Lapford

All Saints 1494 (Hull, 1987, p. 217). Thomas Becket 1742 (Ecton, p. 144), 1782 (Jones, p. 43), 1846 (Oliver, p. 450), 1996 (*EDD*).
In *c.*1742 the parish feast was said to be held on St Thomas Becket's Day (MS Willis 41, f. 222).
All Saints before the Reformation; Thomas Becket since 1742, evidently a conjecture based on the parish feast day.

Lew Trenchard

Unknown 1742 (Ecton, p. 165). Peter *c.*1742 (MS Willis 41, f. 210), 1782 (Jones, p. 79), 1846 (Oliver, p. 450), 1996 (*EDD*).
Bishop Bronescombe dedicated the church on 2 August 1261 (Chanter I, f. 20v). In 1740 the parish feast was said to be held on 9 June (MS Willis 41, f. 225v).
The medieval dedication has not been discovered; Peter since about 1742.

Lifton

Andrew 1353 (*CIPM*, x, 50). Mary 1742 (Ecton, p. 165; source, MS Willis 41, f. 225v). Unknown *c.*1755 (MS Milles, ii, f. 13). Mary 1782 (Jones, p. 79), 1846 (Oliver, p. 450), 1996 (*EDD*).
In 1740 the parish feast was said to be held on 4 February (MS Willis 41, f. 225v).
Andrew before the Reformation; Mary since 1742, perhaps a conjecture from the parish feast day (close to the Purification of Mary).

Littleham (near Bideford)

Swithin 1365 (Chanter V, f. 152), 1399 (Chanter IX, f. 13), 1402 (ibid., f. 22v), 1486 (*CIPM, Henry VII*, i, 65). Unknown 1742 (Ecton, p. 147). Swithin 1754 (Ecton,

p. 627). Unknown *c*.1755 (MS Milles, ii, f. 19). Swithin 1782 (Jones, p. 45), 1846 (Oliver, p. 450), 1996 (*EDD*).
Bishop Stapledon dedicated the church on 17 October 1319 (Chanter II, f. 144). In *c*.1742 and *c*.1755 the parish feast was said to be held on Ascension Day (MS Willis 41, f. 220; MS Milles, ii, f. 19).
Swithin before the Reformation; it was then forgotten until it was recovered in 1754.

Littleham (near Exmouth)

Andrew 1414 (*CPL*, vi, 508). Unknown 1742 (Ecton, p. 139). Michael 1745 (MS · Willis 41, ff. 243a-b). Trinity 1754 (Ecton, p. 107). Unknown *c*.1755 (MS Milles, ii, f. 17). Trinity 1782 (Jones, p. 8), 1793 (Polwhele, ii, 217). Margaret and Andrew 1846 (Oliver, p. 450). Margaret 1873 (Kelly). Margaret and Andrew 1883 (Kelly), 1939 (ibid.). Margaret 1996 (*EDD*).
Andrew before the Reformation; it was then forgotten. Trinity was presumably influenced by, or a confusion with, the chapel in Exmouth dependent on Littleham. Oliver evidently saw a medieval record of Andrew (probably not that of 1414), but his reason for Margaret (an unlikely pairing with Andrew) is not clear. Yet Margaret has proved more popular than the verifiable Andrew.

Little Hempston

Michael 1277 (DRO, 312M/TY91); store of Michael 1537 (PROB 11/28, f. 217). John the Baptist 1742 (Ecton, p. 151), 1782 (Jones, p. 64), 1846 (Oliver, p. 449), 1996 (*EDD*).
Michael before the Reformation; John the Baptist since 1742.

Little Torrington

Mary 1486 (*CIPM, Henry VII*, i, 65). Unknown 1742 (Ecton, p. 169). Ascension conjectured *c*.1755 (MS Milles, ii, f. 209). Unknown 1782 (Jones, p. 59). Giles 1846 (Oliver, p. 454), 1996 (*EDD*).
The bishop of Waterford dedicated the high altar in 1338–9 (Chanter IV, f. 220v). In 1742 the parish feast was said to be held on Ascension Day (MS Willis 41, f. 207), and in *c*.1755 on that day and the previous Sunday (MS Milles, ii, f. 209).
Mary before the Reformation; it was then forgotten. Oliver's proposal of Giles in 1846 was a mistake for St Giles in the Wood, but it has persisted.

Loddiswell

Translation of St Thomas the Martyr (7 July) an important festival 1413 (Chanter X, ff. 288–90v). Michael 1742 (Ecton, p. 171; source, MS Willis 41, f. 223), *c*.1755 (MS Milles, ii, f. 21), 1782 (Jones, p. 85), 1846 (Oliver, p. 450); Michael and All Angels 1996 (*EDD*).
Possibly Thomas Becket before the Reformation; Michael since 1742.

Loxbeare

Unknown 1742 (Ecton, p. 167), 1782 (Jones, p. 37), 1846 (Oliver, p. 450), 1873 (Kelly), 1939 (ibid.). Michael and All Angels 1983 (*EDD*), 1996 (*EDD*).
The medieval dedication has not been discovered, and it was forgotten after the Reformation. Michael in recent years.

Loxhore

Michael 1742 (Ecton, p. 160); Michael and All Angels *c*.1755 (MS Milles, ii, f. 24); Michael 1782 (Jones, p. 50), 1846 (Oliver, p. 450); Michael and All Angels 1996 (*EDD*).

In 1740 and *c*.1755 the parish feast was said to be held on Michaelmas Day (MS Willis 41, f. 227; MS Milles, ii, f. 24).
The medieval dedication has not been discovered. Michael since 1742.

Luffincott

James 1474 (Chanter XII (ii), f. 29v). Michael 1742 (Ecton, p. 149; source, MS Willis 41, f. 225v), Unknown *c*.1755 (MS Milles, ii, f. 26). James 1763 (Ecton, p. 120), 1782 (Jones, p. 63), 1846 (Oliver, p. 450).
In 1740 the parish feast was said to be held on 29 September (Michaelmas Day) (MS Willis 41, f. 225v).
James before the Reformation; it was then forgotten. Michael was evidently a conjecture from the parish feast day; James was recovered in 1763.

Lundy

Mary 1254 (*CPR 1247–58*, p. 378). *Elena* 1325 (Chanter II, f. 184v); *Helena* 1353 (Chanter V, f. 101v), 1355 (ibid., f. 105); *ecclesiam . . . Sancte Elene* 1384 (LPL, Reg. Courtenay, f. 107v). Not in Ecton (1742) or Jones (1782). Helen 1846 (Oliver, p. 450).
Possibly a double dedication: Mary and Helen, only the latter being used after 1325. Helen is sometimes considered Celtic, but there is no apparent reason why she should not be the Roman saint, mother of Constantine.

Luppitt

Mary 1327 (Bodleian, MS Top. Devon d.5, f. 81), 1469 (Chanter XII (ii), f. 15v), 1742 (Ecton, p. 145), 1782 (Jones, p. 18); Mary but Michael postulated 1793 (Polwhele, ii, 331); Mary 1846 (Oliver, p. 450), 1996 (*EDD*).
In 1740 the parish feast was said to be held on 13 September (MS Willis 41, f. 223v), and in 1793 on the Sunday before or after Michaelmas Day (29 September) (Polwhele, ii, 331).
Mary since at least 1327, Michael being evidently a conjecture from the parish feast day.

Lustleigh

Unknown 1742 (Ecton, p. 154; source, MS Willis 41, f. 218). John the Baptist 1754 (Ecton, p. 121), 1782 (Jones, p. 68), 1846 (Oliver, p. 450), 1996 (*EDD*).
In 1742 the parish feast was said to be held on St John the Baptist's Day (MS Willis 41, f. 218).
The medieval dedication has not been discovered. John the Baptist since 1754.

Lydford

Petroc 1237 (*CPR 1232–47*, p. 189), 1733 (Willis, p. 163). Bartholomew 1740 (MS Willis 41, f. 225v). Petroc 1742 (Ecton, p. 165), 1782 (Jones, p. 79), 1846 (Oliver, p. 450), 1996 (*EDD*).
Bishop Bronescombe dedicated the church on 3 August 1261 (Chanter I, f. 20v). Fair on St Petroc's Day 1267 (*CChR 1257–1300*, p. 84), 1269 (ibid., p. 131). In 1740 the parish feast was said to be held on 24 August (MS Willis 41, f. 225v).
Petroc since at least 1237, Bartholomew being a mistaken conjecture from the parish feast day.

Lympstone

Dedicated in honour of the Nativity of the Virgin Mary 24 September 1409 (Chanter VIII, f. 90v); Mary 1742 (Ecton, p. 138), 1782 (Jones, p. 6), 1793 (Polwhele, ii, 212), 1846 (Oliver, p. 450); Nativity of Mary 1996 (*EDD*).
For the dedication feast, see above. In 1793 the parish feast was said to be held on the Wednesday after St Swithin's Day (2 or 15 July) (Polwhele, ii, 212).
Nativity of Mary since at least 1409.

Lynton

Unknown 1742 (Ecton, p. 161). John the Baptist *c.*1755 (MS Milles, ii, f. 15). Unknown 1782 (Jones, p. 52). Mary 1786 (Bacon, p. 282), 1846 (Oliver, p. 450), 1996 (*EDD*).
In 1740 and *c.*1755 the parish feast was said to be held on the Monday after St John the Baptist's Day (24 June) (MS Willis 41, f. 226b; MS Milles, ii, f. 15).
The medieval dedication has not been discovered, and it was forgotten after the Reformation. John the Baptist was conjectured in 1755, evidently on the basis of the parish feast day, and Mary was successfully proposed on unknown grounds in 1786.

Malborough

Peter 1450 (Sharpe, 1889–90, ii, 521), 1464 (London, Guildhall Library, MS 9171/5, f. 359). Unknown 1742 (Ecton, p. 171), *c.*1755 (MS Milles, ii, f. 28), 1782 (Jones, p. 84). All Saints 1806 (Polwhele, iii, 475). Unknown 1846 (Oliver, p. 450). All Saints 1873 (Kelly), 1939 (ibid.), 1996 (*EDD*).
In *c.*1755 the parish feast was said to be held on Shrove Tuesday (MS Milles, ii, f. 28).
Peter before the Reformation; it was then forgotten. All Saints since 1806, from a mere guess that several churches in this part of Devon had that dedication.

Mamhead

Thomas 1741 (MS Willis 41, f. 241). Unknown 1742 (Ecton, p. 154). Thomas the Apostle 1754 (Ecton, p. 111), 1782 (Jones, p. 28); Thomas 1846 (Oliver, p. 450), 1919 (Kelly); Thomas the Martyr 1923 (Kelly), 1939 (ibid.); Thomas the Apostle 1996 (*EDD*).
No parish feast was said to be held in 1741 (MS Willis 41, f. 241).
The medieval dedication has not been discovered. Thomas since 1741, usually interpreted as the Apostle, although Thomas the Martyr ought to mean Thomas Becket.

Manaton

George 1486 (*CPL*, xv, 104), 1503 (*CPL*, xvii part i, 588), 1506 (*CPL*, xviii, 395). *Wenefrid* 1742 (Ecton, p. 154; source, alleged popular tradition, MS Willis 41, f. 222), 1782 (Jones, p. 68); Winifred 1846 (Oliver, p. 450), 1996 (*EDD*).
In *c.*1742 no parish feast was said to be held (MS Willis 41, f. 222).
George from at least 1486 until the Reformation; it was then forgotten. Winifred since 1742, based on an evidently erroneous popular tradition.

Mariansleigh

Marinelegh (place) 1238 (*PND*, ii, 382). *Seyntemarilegh* (place) 1242 (ibid.). *Marinelegh* (place) 1291 (Tax.); *ecclesie . . . Sancte Marine alias Marnelegh* 1444 (Chanter XI, f. 260). Thomas Becket 1740 (MS Willis 41, f. 227). Unknown 1742 (Ecton, p.

164). Mary 1754 (Ecton, p. 118); Mary the Virgin *c*.1755 (MS Milles, ii, f. 37); *Anstey St. Mary's* alias *Mariansleigh* 1782 (Jones, p. 56). *Marina* 1846 (Oliver, p. 450). Mary 1873 (Kelly), 1939 (ibid.), 1996 (*EDD*).

In *c*.1755 the parish feast was said to be held on the Sunday after St Thomas Becket's Day (7 July) (MS Milles, ii, f. 37).

The original dedication seems to have been to Mary, but the use of the form Marian in the place-name gave rise to a belief by 1444 that the saint was Marina. The latter was forgotten after the Reformation. Thomas Becket was conjectured from the parish feast day, but Mary was restored again from 1754, despite Oliver's preference for Marina.

Maristow—see Blaxton

Marldon

John the Baptist 1439 (PRO, C 139/68; IPM, Otho Gilbert), 1493 (Chanter XII (ii), f. 166v), 1504 (LPL, Reg. Warham, i, f. 206), 1536 (Murray, xxv, Alison Peter). Unknown 1742 (Ecton, p. 151), *c*.1755 (MS Milles, ii, f. 32), 1782 (Jones, p. 65). John the Baptist 1846 (Oliver, p. 450), 1996 (*EDD*).

John the Baptist before the Reformation; it was then forgotten until it was recovered in 1846.

Marsh Barton in Alphington: Augustinian priory

Mary 1219 x 1227 (DRO, Courtenay Cartulary, ff. 234v–135), 1335 (Chanter IV, f. 12), 1445 (Chanter XI, f. 452).

Mary before the Reformation.

Martinhoe

Martin 1742 (Ecton, p. 161). The Ascension of Our Lord and Saviour *c*.1755 (MS Milles, ii, f. 34). Martin 1782 (Jones, p. 51), 1846 (Oliver, p. 450), 1996 (*EDD*).

The bishop of Waterford dedicated the church in 1338–9 (Chanter IV, f. 220v). In 1740, 1742 and *c*.1755 the parish feast was said to be held on Ascension Day (MS Willis 41, ff. 207, 220, 226b; MS Milles, ii, f. 34).

The medieval dedication has not been discovered; usually Martin since 1742. The medieval name of the parish, however, was Matingeho which became Martinhoe only by the 18th century, making it likely that Martin originated as a conjecture in that period (PND, i, 65–6).

Martinstow—see Blaxton

Marwood

Michael 1476 (*CPL*, xiii (ii), 491), 1514 (Chanter XIII, f. 54). Trinity 1742 (Ecton, p. 160). Unknown *c*.1755 (MS Milles, ii, f. 35). Michael 1763 (Ecton, p. 117), 1782 (Jones, p. 50), 1846 (Oliver, p. 450); Michael and All Angels 1996 (*EDD*).

Fair on St Michael's Day 1293 (*CChR 1257–1300*, p. 433). In 1740 the parish feast was said to be held on the Monday after Trinity Sunday (MS Willis 41, f. 226b), and in *c*.1755 on the following Thursday (MS Milles, ii, f. 35).

Michael before the Reformation; it was then forgotten. Trinity in 1742, evidently a conjecture based on the parish feast day, Michael being recovered in 1763.

Marystow

Ecclesiam Sancte Marie de Sideham 1186 x 1188 (DRO, ED/PP/9; Barlow, 1996, no. 168); Mary 1266 (Chanter I, f. 34v), 1475 (Chanter XII (ii), f. 35), 1733 (Willis, p. 163), 1742 (Ecton, p. 165), 1782 (Jones, p. 80), 1846 (Oliver, p. 450), 1996 *(EDD)*.

In 1740 the parish feast was said to be held on 9 February (MS Willis 41, f. 225v).

Mary since at least the late 12th century, Sideham *being an earlier name of the parish.*

Marytavy

Mary 1270 (Chanter I, f. 46), 1312 (Reichel, 1912–39, ii, 134), 1733 (Willis, p. 163), 1742 (Ecton, p. 164), *c.*1755 (MS Milles, ii, f. 176), 1782 (Jones, p. 77), 1846 (Oliver, p. 453), 1996 *(EDD)*.

In 1740 the parish feast was said to be held on 6 February (MS Willis 41, f. 225).

Mary since at least 1270.

Meavy

Unknown 1742 (Ecton, p. 165). Peter 1754 (Ecton, p. 124), *c.*1755 (MS Milles, ii, f. 46), 1782 (Jones, p. 78), 1846 (Oliver, p. 450), 1996 *(EDD)*.

In 1740 the parish feast was said to be held on the Monday after St Peter's Day (29 June or 1 August) (MS Willis 41, f. 228), and in *c.*1755 on the Sunday nearest St Peter's Day (MS Milles, ii, f. 46).

The medieval dedication has not been discovered, and it was forgotten after the Reformation. Peter since 1754.

Meeth

Michael 1312 (Chanter II, f. 79v). John the Baptist 1742 (Ecton, p. 168; source, MS Willis 41, f. 225v), 1782 (Jones, p. 58). Michael 1846 (Oliver, p. 450); Michael and All Angels 1996 *(EDD)*.

In 1740 the parish feast was said to be held two weeks after Whit Sunday (MS Willis 41, f. 225v).

Michael before the Reformation; it was then forgotten. John the Baptist was conjectured in the 18th century; Michael was recovered in 1846.

Membury

Laurence 1556 (PROB 11/40, f. 127), 1558 (ibid., f. 179), 1742 (Ecton, p. 150). Laurence 1754 (Ecton, p. 110), replaced by John the Baptist (ibid., p. 627). John the Baptist 1782 (Jones, p. 22), 1793 (Polwhele, ii, 285), 1846 (Oliver, p. 450), 1996 *(EDD)*.

Bishop Stapledon dedicated the cemetery on 22 July 1316 (Chanter II, f. 113).

Laurence before the Reformation, known to Browne Willis in 1742 though not necessarily remembered locally. The change to John the Baptist in 1754 coincided with the change of John the Baptist to Mary as the presumed patron saint of Membury's mother church, Axminster. Confused by Axminster's two medieval patrons, Mary and John the Baptist, learned opinion may have decided that the latter related to Membury.

Merton

All Saints *c.*1483 (PROB 11/8, f. 196v). Matthias 1740 (MS Willis 41, f. 225v). Martin with a query 1742 (Ecton, p. 168). All Saints 1763 (Ecton, p. 119), 1782 (Jones,

p. 58). Martin 1846 (Oliver, p. 450). All Saints 1873 (Kelly), 1939 (ibid.), 1996 *(EDD)*. In 1740 and 1742 the parish feast was said to be held on Easter Tuesday (MS Willis 41, ff. 207, 225v).

All Saints before the Reformation; this was then forgotten. Martin was conjectured in 1742, probably because the place-name was then spelt Martin. All Saints was recovered in 1763, but Martin continued to be current until the late 19th century.

Meshaw

Store of Mary 1534 (in what looks like a list of stores of church patron saints) (Moger, x, 3049a). John the Baptist 1742 (Ecton, p. 163; source MS Willis 41, f. 227), *c.*1755 (MS Milles, ii, f. 44), 1782 (Jones, p. 56), 1846 (Oliver, p. 450), 1873 (Kelly), 1939 (ibid.). John 1996 *(EDD)*.

In *c.*1755 the parish feast was said to be held on the Sunday after St John the Baptist's Day (24 June or 29 August) (MS Milles, ii, f. 44).

Probably Mary before the Reformation; John the Baptist since 1742, perhaps a conjecture from the parish feast day.

Milton Abbot

Ecclesiam Sancti Constantini confessoris 1193 (Chanter XV, f. 43v; Oliver, 1846, p. 95). *Ecclesiam Sanctorum Constantini et Egidii* 1284 (Chanter I, f. 123; dated by Finberg, 1969, p. 24). *Ecclesie . . . Sancti Constantini confessoris* 1521 (Chanter XIV, f. 8v); *Sancti Constantini* 1527 (ibid., f. 33v); Constantine 1733 (Willis, p. 163), 1740 (Ecton, p. 166), *c.*1755 (MS Milles, ii, f. 49), 1782 (Jones, p. 80), 1806 (Polwhele, iii, 443). *Constantinus* and *Eligius* 1846 (Oliver, p. 450). Constantine 1873 (Kelly), 1939 (ibid.), 1996 *(EDD)*.

In 1740 the parish feast was said to be held on Easter Tuesday (MS Willis 41, f. 225v).

Constantine since at least 1193, with Giles once mentioned as a co-patron. Finberg proposed that Constantine was a Celtic saint but the Roman Emperor is equally likely: compare Abbotsham, which also belonged to Tavistock, dedicated to Helen, the name of Constantine's mother (Finberg, 1950–1, pp. 225–6). Finberg further suggested that the Giles dedication may really have applied to the chapel of Leigh in Milton Abbot parish (ibid.). Oliver in 1846 confused Giles (Egidius) with Loye (Eligius).

Milton Damerel

Trinity 1742 (Ecton, p. 149; source, MS Willis 41, f. 230), 1782 (Jones, p. 62), 1846 (Oliver, p. 450), 1996 *(EDD)*.

In 1806 the parish feast was said to be held on the Sunday after Trinity Sunday (Polwhele, iii, 435).

The medieval dedication has not been discovered. Trinity since 1742.

Modbury: Benedictine priory and parish church

George 1187 x 1190 (Barlow, 1996, no. 172), *c.*1200 (Gervase, 1867, ii, 423); George the Martyr 1438 *(CFR 1437–45*, p. 46). Store of the High Cross and Mary 1505, apparently the chief store of the church (DRO, 269A/PW 1–7). *Terre beate ecclesie Marie de Modbury* 1555 (DRO, Enrolled Deeds, QS 47/10, m. 1d). George 1742 (Ecton, p. 158; source, MS Willis 41, f. 223). Unknown *c.*1755 (MS Milles, ii, f. 50d). George 1782 (Jones, p. 74). Peter 1846 (either because the priory belonged to the French abbey of St Pierre-sur-Dives or because of a medieval reference to the aisle of St Peter in the church) (Oliver, pp. 298, 451). Peter, erroneously called George 1873 (Kelly), 1883 (ibid.). George 1889 (Kelly), 1939 (ibid.), 1996 *(EDD)*.

In 1740 the parish feast was said to be held on St George's Day (23 April) (MS Willis 41, f. 223).

The pre-Reformation references suggest a double dedication to Mary and George. Usually George alone since 1742; Oliver's Peter was probably based on a misunderstanding but was influential until the 1880s, when George was recovered.

Molland

Laurence, with a query 1742 (Ecton, p. 162). Mary 1754 (Ecton, p. 627). Laurence c.1755 (MS Milles, ii, f. 52v). Mary 1782 (Jones, p. 53), 1846 (Oliver, p. 451), 1996 (*EDD*).

In 1740 the parish feast was said to be held a week after 1 August (MS Willis 41, f. 227), and in c.1755 on the Sunday after St Laurence's Day (10 August) (MS Milles, ii, f. 52 verso).

The medieval dedication has not been discovered. Laurence in the 18th century and Mary (on unknown grounds) since 1754.

Monkleigh

George 1519 (*LPFD*, iii part i, 60), 1520 (PRO, C 142/53 no. 3, m. 5; IPM, Anne St Leger), 1530 (PROB 11/24, f. 157v), 1733 (Willis, p. 157), 1742 (Ecton, p. 147), 1782 (Jones, p. 45), 1846 (Oliver, p. 451), 1996 (*EDD*).

The church is mentioned as not yet dedicated in 1421 (Chanter XI, f. 11).

George since at least 1519.

Monk Okehampton

Peter the Apostle 1170 x 1186 (Finberg, 1947, p. 364); Peter 1193 (Chanter XV, f. 44; Oliver, 1846, p. 95). Unknown 1742 (Ecton, p. 155), c.1755 (MS Milles, ii, f. 84), 1782 (Jones, p. 71), 1846 (Oliver, p. 451). All Saints 1873 (Kelly), 1939 (ibid.), 1996 (*EDD*).

In 1740 and c.1755 the parish feast was said to be held on Whit Sunday (MS Willis 41, f. 225; MS Milles, ii, f. 84).

Peter before the Reformation; it was then forgotten. All Saints since the late 19th century.

Monkton

Mary Magdalene 1228 (ECA, D&C 3672, p. 46). Unknown 1742 (Ecton, p. 150). Mary Magdalene 1763 (Ecton, p. 110). Unknown 1782 (Jones, p. 23). Mary Magdalene 1793 (Polwhele, ii, 283), 1846 (Oliver, p. 451), 1996 (*EDD*).

Mary Magdalene before the Reformation; it was then forgotten until it was recovered in 1763.

Morchard Bishop

Peter and Paul 1355 (PRO, JUST 1/192, m 16). Mary 1742 (Ecton, p. 141); Mary the Virgin c.1755 (MS Milles, ii, f. 54); Mary 1782 (Jones, p. 10), 1793 (Polwhele, ii, 41), 1846 (Oliver, p. 451), 1996 (*EDD*).

In c.1742 and c.1755 the parish feast was said to be held on the Sunday after 8 September (MS Willis 41, f. 222; MS Milles, ii, f. 54).

Peter and Paul before the Reformation; the dedication was then forgotten. Mary since 1742.

Morebath

George 1526 (Binney, 1904, p. 3), 1742 (Ecton, p. 167; source, MS Willis 41, f. 223), 1782 (Jones, p. 37); 'it is called St George's church' 1793 (Polwhele, ii, 376); George 1846 (Oliver, p. 451), 1996 (*EDD*).

In *c.*1742 the parish feast was said to be held on the Sunday after St Bartholomew's Day (24 June) but, sixty or seventy years previously, two or three weeks earlier (MS Willis 41, ff. 213; cf. f. 223).

George since at least 1526.

Moreleigh

Offerings were made on All Saints' Day *c.*1240 (ECA, D&C 1012; Oliver, 1861, pp. 418–19). Mary Magdalene 1742 (Ecton, p. 172). Unknown *c.*1755 (MS Milles, ii, f. 56). Mary Magdalene 1782 (Jones, p. 86). All Saints 1786 (Bacon, p. 299), 1846 (Oliver, p. 451), 1996 (*EDD*).

Fair on St Mary Magdalene's Day 1316 (*CChR 1300–26*, p. 306). Bishop Grandisson dedicated the high altar on 13 June 1336 (Chanter IV, f. 200).

Probably All Saints before the Reformation; this was then forgotten. Mary Magdalene on the basis of the fair; All Saints was recovered in 1786.

Moretonhampstead

Andrew 1742 (Ecton, p. 155), 1782 (Jones, p. 68), 1846 (Oliver, p. 451), 1996 (*EDD*).

Fair on St Margaret's Day 1270 (*CChR 1257–1300*, p. 157), and also on St Andrew's Day 1334 (*CChR 1327–41*, p. 312). In *c.*1742 the parish feast was said to be held on St Andrew's Day (30 November or 9 May) (MS Willis 41, f. 222).

The medieval dedication has not been discovered; Andrew since 1742. This may well be the medieval dedication in view of the fair evidence, the parish feast day, and the frequency of this dedication in Devon.

Mortehoe

Mary 1309 (*CPR 1307–13*, p. 108), 1566 (Moger, xiv, 4850), 1742 (Ecton, p. 161). Unknown *c.*1755 (MS Milles, ii, f. 58). Mary 1782 (Jones, p. 51), 1846 (Oliver, p. 451), 1996 (*EDD*).

In 1740 the parish feast was said to be held on the Monday after Whit Monday (MS Willis 41, f. 226b), and in *c.*1755 on Whit Tuesday (MS Milles, ii, f. 58).

Mary since at least 1309.

Musbury

Michael the Archangel 1545 (PROB 11/30, f. 333), 1546 (Moger, i, 135), 1548 (PROB 11/32, f. 43), 1550 (PROB 11/33, f. 152v); Michael 1742 (Ecton, p. 150; source, MS Willis 41, f. 223v), 1782 (Jones, p. 23), 1793 (Polwhele, ii, 298), 1846 (Oliver, p. 451), 1996 (*EDD*).

In 1740 the parish feast was said to be held on the Sunday after Michaelmas Day (29 September) (MS Willis 41, f. 223v).

Michael since at least 1545.

Nether Exe

Unknown 1742 (Ecton, p. 142), 1782 (Jones, p. 12), 1846 (Oliver, p. 451), 1873 (Kelly), 1939 (ibid.). John the Baptist 1983 (*EDD*), 1996 (ibid.).

The medieval dedication has not been discovered, and it was forgotten after the Reformation. John the Baptist in recent times.

Newenham: Cistercian abbey

Trinity and Mary 1245 x 1257 (Oliver, 1846, pp. 360, 361), 1535 (*Valor*, ii, 301). The abbey was dedicated to Mary on 18 April (Worcester, 1969, p. 122).

Trinity and Mary, shortened to Mary; Mary was the usual dedication of Cistercian abbeys.

Newton Abbot

Leonard 1350 (Chanter V, f. 91), 1742 (Ecton, p. 152), 1782 (Jones, p. 66), 1846 (Oliver, p. 451), 1996 (*EDD*).

Fair on St Leonard's Day 1269 (*CChR 1257–1300*, p. 131).

Leonard, possibly since at least 1269, certainly since at least 1350.

Newton Ferrers

Holy Cross 1742 (Ecton, p. 158), *c*.1755 (MS Milles, ii, f. 64, citing Ecton), 1782 (Jones, p. 74), 1846 (Oliver, p. 451), 1996 (*EDD*).

The medieval dedication has not been discovered. Holy Cross since 1742.

Newton Poppleford

Luke 1330 (*CPR 1330–4*, p. 29). Not in Ecton (1742). Unknown 1754 (Ecton, p. 107). Luke 1846 (Oliver, pp. 445, 451), 1996 (*EDD*).

Luke since at least 1330.

Newton St Cyres

Nywetone Sancti Ciricii (place) 1338 (Chanter IV, ff. 206v–7); *Neuton Sancti Cirici* 1400 (Chanter VIII, f. 35v); store of *St. Cire* 1546 (Worthy, 1896, p. 2); *Newton St. Ciricks* 1733 (Willis, p. 151); *Newton Sancti Cerici* 1742 (Ecton, p. 141); *Newton St. Cyr* 1782 (Jones, p. 10). *Siricius* archbishop of Canterbury 1793 (Polwhele, ii, 30). Cyrus and *Julitta* 1846 (Oliver, p. 451); Cyr and Julitta 1996 (*EDD*).

Cyricus (alias Cyriac or Cyr) since at least 1338; Julitta is not recorded before 1846.

Newton St Petrock

Petroc 1317 (Chanter II, f. 119), 1458 (Chanter XII (i), f. 8v), 1468 (ibid., (ii), f. 13v), 1733 (Willis, p. 159), 1742 (Ecton, p. 169), 1782 (Jones, p. 58), 1846 (Oliver, p. 451), 1996 (*EDD*).

The church belonged to St Petroc's, Bodmin by 1086 (DB 51/16). Petroc since at least 1317.

Newton Tracey

Thomas Becket 1742 (Ecton, p. 141; source, MS Willis 41, f. 226b). Unknown *c*.1755 (MS Milles, ii, f. 66). Thomas Becket 1782 (Jones, p. 40), 1846 (Oliver, p. 451), 1996 (*EDD*).

In *c*.1755 the parish feast was said to be held on the Monday before Midsummer Day (24 June) (MS Milles, ii, f. 66).

The medieval dedication has not been discovered. Thomas Becket since 1742, probably suggested by the Tracey connection. Caution is needed in assuming that the Becket dedication goes back earlier, in view of the other parishes where such a claim runs counter to pre-Reformation evidence.

Northam

Our Lady of Northam is mentioned as a principal saint or image 1532 (Moger, xx, 7213–4). Margaret 1742 (Ecton, p. 148; source, MS Willis 41, f. 230). Unknown c.1755 (MS Milles, ii, f. 75). Margaret 1782 (Jones, p. 46), 1846 (Oliver, p. 451). Mary 1873 (Kelly). Margaret 1883 (Kelly), 1939 (ibid.), 1996 (*EDD*).

Fair on the Decollation of St John Baptist (29 August) 1252 (*CChR 1225–57*, p. 408). *The medieval dedication has not been discovered for certain, but Mary is possible. Usually Margaret since 1742.*

North Bovey

John the Baptist 1343 (*CPR 1343–5*, pp. 37, 55); John 1742 (Ecton, p. 155; source, MS Willis 41, f. 222), 1782 (Jones, p. 69); John the Baptist 1846 (Oliver, p. 445), 1996 (*EDD*).

In c.1742 no parish feast was said to be held (MS Willis 41, f. 222). *John the Baptist since at least 1343, perhaps with some uncertainty as to which John in the 18th century.*

North Huish

Unknown 1742 (Ecton, p. 158), c.1755 (MS Milles, i, f. 266), 1782 (Jones, p. 74), 1846 (Oliver, p. 449), 1883 (Kelly). Mary, with a query 1889 (Kelly), 1939 (ibid.).

Bishop Grandisson dedicated the church and high altar of *Hywishe*, either North or South Huish, on 15 June 1336 (Chanter IV, f. 200). *The medieval dedication has not been discovered, and it was forgotten after the Reformation. Mary since the late 19th century.*

Northleigh

Unknown 1742 (Ecton, p. 150). 'Supposed St James' c.1755 (MS Milles, ii, f. 5). Unknown 1782 (Jones, p. 24). Giles conjectured 1793 (Polwhele, ii, 306). Unknown 1846 (Oliver, p. 450). Giles 1873 (Kelly), 1939 (ibid.), 1996 (*EDD*).

In c.1755 the parish feast was said to be held on St James' Day (25 July) (MS Milles, ii, f. 5), and in 1793 on the first Monday in September (Polwhele, ii, 306). *The medieval dedication has not been discovered, and it was forgotten after the Reformation. James and Giles were both proposed between about 1755 and 1793 on the basis of the parish feast day, of whom Giles was eventually adopted.*

North Lew

All Hallows of *Liu* 1219: probably North Lew, in view of the presence of the Wanford family based nearby at Black Torrington (Reichel, 1912–39, i, 55). Thomas Becket 1742 (Ecton, p. 155; source, MS Willis 41, f. 225), c.1755 (MS Milles, ii, f. 11), 1782 (Jones, p. 71), 1846 (Oliver, p. 450), 1996 (*EDD*).

In 1740 the parish feast was said to be held on 13 July (MS Willis 41, f. 225), and in c.1755 on the Sunday after St Thomas Becket's Day (7 July) (MS Milles, ii, f. 11). *All Saints before the Reformation; Thomas Becket since 1742, evidently a conjecture based on the parish feast day.*

North Molton

All Saints 1482 (*CPL*, xiii (ii), 747), 1742 (Ecton, p. 163). Unknown c.1755 (MS Milles, ii, f. 60). All Saints 1782 (Jones, p. 56), 1806 (Polwhele, iii, 395), 1846 (Oliver, p. 451), 1996 (*EDD*).

Fair on All Saints' Day 1270 (*CChR 1257–1300*, p. 150). In 1740 the parish feasts were said to be held on the first Tuesday in May and 1 November (All Saints' Day) (MS Willis 41, f. 2267). In *c.*1755 the 'Holywell wake' was on Ascension Day (MS Milles, ii, f. 60).
All Saints, perhaps since at least 1270, certainly since at least 1482.

North Petherwin—see under Cornwall

North Tawton

Peter 1181 (BL, Cotton MS Vitellius D.ix, ff. 37v–38). Peter and Paul 1292 (*CPL*, i, 547). Peter 1368 (*CPL*, iv, 67), 1479 (Chanter XII (ii), f. 87); Peter the Apostle 1492 (Harper-Bill, 1991, p. 88); Peter 1742 (Ecton, p. 144). Unknown *c.*1755 (MS Milles, ii, f. 190a). Peter 1782 (Jones, p. 43), 1846 (Oliver, p. 453), 1996 (*EDD*).
In *c.*1742 the parish feast was said to be held on St Peter's Day (MS Willis 41, f. 222).
Peter and Paul before the Reformation, sometimes shortened to Peter which has become normal since 1742.

Nymet Rowland

Bartholomew 1742 (Ecton, p. 145), 1782 (Jones, p. 44), 1846 (Oliver, p. 451), 1996 (*EDD*).
In *c.*1742 the parish feast was said to be held on St Bartholomew's Day (24 August) (MS Willis 41, f. 222).
The medieval dedication has not been discovered; Bartholomew since 1742.

Nymet St George—see George Nympton

Nymet Tracey

Image of Mary in the chancel 1537 (PROB 11/27, f. 107). Bartholomew 1742 (Ecton, p. 144), 1782 (Jones, p. 43). Martin 1846 (Oliver, p. 451). Bartholomew 1996 (*EDD*).
Fair on St Martin's Day 1259 (*CChR 1257–1300*, p. 19). In *c.*1742 the parish feast was said to be held on Whit Sunday (MS Willis 41, f. 222).
The medieval dedication has not been discovered for certain, but Martin or Mary are possible. Usually Bartholomew since 1742.

Oakford

Peter 1503 (PROB 11/13, f. 249), 1742 (Ecton, p. 162), *c.*1755 (MS Milles, ii, f. 77), 1782 (Jones, p. 53), 1846 (Oliver, p. 451), 1996 (*EDD*).
In 1740 the parish feast was said to be held on the first Sunday in July (MS Willis 41, f. 223v), and in *c.*1755 on the Monday after 29 June (MS Milles, ii, f. 77).
Peter since at least 1503.

Offwell

Store of Mary 1545 (Murray, xxxii, John Stowe). Unknown 1742 (Ecton, p. 150). Mary 1782 (Jones, p. 24), 1793 (Polwhele, ii, 321). Unknown 1846 (Oliver, p. 451). Mary 1873 (Kelly), 1939 (ibid.), 1996 (*EDD*).
For the parish feast in *c.*1755, see Widworthy.
Possibly Mary before the Reformation, if the 1545 store was the chief store of the church and if the 1782 reference was based on tradition or documents. It was not known in the mid 18th century, however, and Mary is certain only from 1782.

Okehampton: hospital

Magdalene (place) 1316, 1375 (Orme and Webster, 1995, p. 252).
The hospital was probably dedicated to Mary Magdalene; it seems to have disappeared by the late 14th century.

Okehampton: parish church

All Saints 1362 (DRO, 3248A/11/31), 1448 (*CPL*, x, 145), 1497 (*CPL*, xvi, 528), 1733 (Willis, p. 162), 1742 (Ecton, p. 156), *c*.1755 (MS Milles, ii, f. 82), 1782 (Jones, p. 71). James (a mistake for the chapel in the town centre) 1846 (Oliver, p. 451). All Saints 1873 (Kelly), 1939 (ibid.), 1996 (*EDD*).
Bishop Bronescombe dedicated the church on 31 July 1261 (Chanter I, f. 20v). In 1740 the parish feast was said to be held on 3 May (MS Willis 41, f. 225).
All Saints since at least 1362.

Oldridge

Unknown 1742 (Ecton, p. 154), 1782 (Jones). Not in Oliver (1846). Unknown 1902 (Kelly), 1939 (ibid.). Thomas 1983 (*EDD*), 1996 (ibid.).
The medieval dedication has not been discovered, and it was forgotten after the Reformation. Thomas in recent times, perhaps because the parish was for several centuries part of St Thomas parish, Cowick; if so, Thomas should now be Thomas the Apostle.

Otterton: Benedictine priory and parish church

Michael early 13th century (Oliver, 1846, p. 252 no. 9), 1546 (Moger, xiii, 4400; xv, 5081), 1547 (ibid., xx, 7148), 1558 (ibid., xix, 6811), 1742 (Ecton, p. 138). Unknown *c*.1755 (MS Milles, ii, f. 86). Michael 1782 (Jones, p. 6), 1793 (Polwhele, ii, 231), 1846 (Oliver, p. 451). Thomas the Apostle postulated as the original dedication 1928 'as the hill from the churchyard going south is still called S. Thomas's Hill' (Grimaldi, 1928, p. 7). Michael 1996 (*EDD*).
In 1740 the parish feast was said to be held on Whit Monday (MS Willis 41, f. 223v), and *c*.1755 on that day and on Michaelmas Day (29 September) (MS Milles, ii, f. 86).
The church belonged to the abbey of Mont-St-Michel in France by 1086 (DB 11/1). Michael since at least the early 13th century, which rules out Grimaldi's suggestion.

Ottery St Mary: parish and collegiate church

Mary *c*.1200 (Gervase, 1867, ii, 424), 1269 (Chanter I, f. 43), 1733 (Willis, p. 151), 1742 (Ecton, p. 139), *c*.1755 (MS Milles, ii, f. 88), 1782 (Jones, p. 8), 1793 (Polwhele, ii, 244), 1846 (Oliver, p. 451), 1996 (*EDD*).
Bishop Bronescombe dedicated the church on 4 December 1259 (Chanter I, f. 10). In 1740 the parish feast was said to be held on 15 August (Assumption of Mary) (MS Willis 41, f. 228v), and in *c*.1755 the fair to be held on the same day (MS Milles, ii, f. 88).
The church belonged to St Mary's, Rouen by 1066 (DB 10/1); Mary since at least about 1200.

Paignton

Peter and Paul 1488 (*CPL*, xiii (ii), p. 746), 1538 (Moger, xi, 3718), 1543 (Oliver, 1840, i, 172), 1548 (Murray, xxv, Juliane Peter). Store of Peter 1549 (Moger, iv, 1191).

Peter and Paul 1553 (Murray, xxv, Joan Peter). John the Baptist 1742 (Ecton, p. 151). Peter c.1755 (MS Milles, ii, f. 93-v). John the Baptist 1782 (Jones, p. 65), 1846 (Oliver, p. 451), 1996 (EDD).
Fair at Holy Trinity 1295 (CChR 1257–1300, p. 460). In c.1755 the parish feast was said to be held on Whit Tuesday (MS Milles, ii, f. 93-v).
Peter and Paul before the Reformation, sometimes shortened to Peter which was still remembered in about 1755. John the Baptist has been conjectured since 1742, however, possibly through confusion with Marldon, a chapelry of Paignton; oddly, Oliver's 1840 reference did not get into his book of 1846.

Pancrasweek

Pancradeswike (place) 1198 (Reichel, 1912–39, i, 9; Seymour, 1977, p. 171; Dublin, MS E.5.15, f. 52). Pancras 1291 (Reichel, 1912–39, ii, 53), 1403 (Chanter VIII, f. 68), 1450 (Chanter XI, f. 335), 1535 (Valor, ii, 387), 1733 (Willis, p. 160), 1742 (Ecton, p. 149), c.1755 (MS Milles, ii, f. 96), 1782 (Jones, p. 61), 1806 (Polwhele, iii, 436), 1846 (Oliver, p. 452), 1996 (EDD).
In 1740 the parish feast was said to be held on Trinity Sunday (MS Willis 41, f. 225v), and in c.1755 on the following Monday (MS Milles, ii, f. 96),
Pancras since at least 1198.

Parkham

Unknown 1742 (Ecton, p. 147). James 1754 (Ecton, p. 115). Unknown c.1755 (MS Milles, ii, f. 99). James 1782 (Jones, p. 45), 1846 (Oliver, p. 452), 1996 (EDD).
In 1740 the parish feast was said to be held on Easter Sunday (MS Willis 41, f. 230), while in 1742 and c.1755 feasts were said to be held on Easter Monday and St James' Day (25 July) (ibid., ff. 207, 220; MS Milles, ii, f. 99).
The medieval dedication has not been discovered; James since 1754.

Parracombe

Pedrecumbe (place) 1086 (DB 20/3; PND, i, 67). Unknown 1742 (Ecton, p. 160), c.1755 (MS Milles, ii, f. 98), 1782 (Jones, p. 50), 1846 (Oliver, p. 452), 1883 (Kelly). Helen 1889 (Kelly), 1897 (ibid.). Peter 1902 (Kelly), 1910 (ibid.). Petroc 1914 (Kelly), 1939 (ibid.), 1989 (Cherry & Pevsner, p. 624).
In 1740, 1742 and c.1755 the parish feast was said to be held on Whit Monday (MS Willis 41, ff. 207, 220, 226b; MS Milles, ii, f. 98).
Place-name experts interpret Pedrecumbe as 'valley with an enclosure' (PND, i, 67) or 'pedlars' valley' (Ekwall, 1960, p. 358), rather than 'Petroc's valley'. The church dedication has not otherwise been discovered before the Reformation, and was then forgotten. Since the late 19th century three saints have been proposed: Helen (perhaps on the analogy of Abbotsham and Lundy), Peter (suggested by the place-name), and finally Petroc (likewise, with the added attraction of Celtic romance). This all relates to the old church in Parracombe; the new church is Christ Church 1996 (EDD).

Payhembury

Mary 1516 (Chanter XIII, f. 65). James 1742 (Ecton, p. 157; source, MS Willis 41, f. 223). Mary 1763 (Ecton, p. 112), 1782 (Jones, p. 31). James or Mary 1793 (Polwhele, ii, 268). Mary 1846 (Oliver, p. 452), 1996 (EDD).
In 1740 the parish feast was said to be held on the Sunday after St James' Day (25 July) (MS Willis 41, f. 223).

Mary before the Reformation; James in 1742, evidently a conjecture based on the date of the parish feast day. Mary was recovered in 1763.

Peters Marland

Peter Merlaunde (place) 1242 (Reichel, 1912–39, i, 183). Peter 1247 (ibid., p. 228), 1733 (Willis, p. 159). *Petermerland* 1742 (Ecton, p. 169). Peter 1754 (Ecton, p. 119), 1782 (Jones, p. 60), 1846 (Oliver, p. 452), 1996 (*EDD*).
Peter since at least 1242.

Petertavy

Ecclesie de Peterestavi (place) 1276 (Chanter I, f. 75v); Peter 1297 (*CPR 1292–1301*, p. 281), 1318 (Chanter II, f. 128), 1377 (Chanter VII, f. 52), 1733 (Willis, p. 163), 1742 (Ecton, p. 164), *c*.1755 (MS Milles, ii, f. 179), 1782 (Jones, p. 77), 1806 (Polwhele, iii, 466), 1846 (Oliver, p. 453), 1996 (*EDD*).
In 1740 the parish feast was said to be held on the Monday after St Peter's Day (29 June or 1 August) (MS Willis 41, f. 225), and in *c*.1755 on the Sunday after (MS Milles, ii, f. 179),
Peter since at least 1276.

Petrockstow

Petrochestov (place) 1086 (DB 6/1); *Petrochestovam* (place) 1150 (Barlow, 1996, no. 29); *Padricstowe* (place) 1291 (Tax.); *Patrikestowe* (place) 1311 (Chanter II, f. 65. Petroc 1345 (Chanter V, f. 53v), 1349 (ibid., f. 73). *Patrokystowe* (place) 1366 (ibid. iii, 1499); *Patrickestawe* (place) 1401 (Chanter VIII, f. 58v). Petroc 1475 (*CPL*, xiii (i), 470). *Patrikstowe* (place) 1535 (Valor, ii, 369). *Stowe Sancti Petroci* (place) 1537 (Chanter XIV, f. 87); Petroc 1733 (Willis, p. 159), 1742 (Ecton, p. 169), 1782 (Jones, p. 59), 1846 (Oliver, p. 452), 1996 (*EDD*).
In 1740 the parish feast was said to be held on Whit Sunday (MS Willis 41, f. 225).
Petroc since at least 1086.

Pilton: Benedictine priory and parish church

Mary 1261 (Chanter I, f. 18v), 1421 (Chanter X, f. 32v), 1535 (*Valor*, ii, 355). James 1740 (MS Willis 41, f. 226b). Margaret 1742 (Ecton, p. 141). Unknown *c*.1755 (MS Milles, ii, f. 101). Margaret 1782 (Jones, p. 40). Mary 1846 (Oliver, p. 452), 1996 (*EDD*).
In *c*.1755 the parish feast was said to be held on St James' Day (25 July) (MS Milles, ii, f. 101).
Mary before the Reformation, then forgotten. Usually Margaret during the 18th century, perhaps in mistake for the hospital (below); Mary was recovered in 1846.

Pilton: hospital

Margaret 1189 (Orme and Webster, 1995, p. 252).
Margaret before the Reformation.

Pinhoe

Michael 1359 (Chanter V, f. 120v). Unknown 1742 (Ecton, p. 139). Michael *c*.1755 (MS Milles, ii, f. 103). Unknown 1782 (Jones, p. 6). Michael 1787 (Jones supplement, p. 2), 1793 (Polwhele, ii, 186), 1846 (Oliver, p. 452); Michael and All Angels 1996 (*EDD*).

In 1745 the parish feast was said to be held on Michaelmas Day (29 September) (MS Willis 41, ff. 243a-b), and in c.1755 on the Monday after (MS Milles, ii, f. 103). *Michael since at least 1359.*

Plymouth: Carmelite friary

The dedication has not been discovered, but friaries of this order were usually dedicated to Mary.

Plymouth: Charles church

Charles Church 1641 (Bracken, 1931, p. 142). St. Charles 1733 (Willis, p. 162); King Charles the Martyr 1742 (Ecton, p. 157), 1782 (Jones, p. 73); Charles king and martyr 1846 (Oliver, p. 446).

The church (authorized in 1641) was named after the contemporary monarch Charles I, simply as a compliment; later, after his death, it was regarded as dedicated to his memory (compare Falmouth).

Plymouth: Franciscan friary

The dedication has not been discovered.

Plymouth: hospital

Trinity and Mary Magdalene 1374 (Chanter VI, f. 52v); God's House 1546 (Orme and Webster, 1995, p. 254).

Trinity and Mary Magdalene; God's House is probably simply a synonym for 'hospital'.

Plymouth: Sutton

Andrew 1137 (17th) (Barlow, 1996, no. 23), 1161 x 1173 (17th) (ibid., no. 120), 1375 (DRO, MCR 48–49 Edward III, m. 47); Andrew the Apostle 1447 (Chanter XI, f. 509v); Andrew 1465 (Chanter XII (i), f. 27v), 1487 (*Catalogue of Ancient Deeds*, iii, 498), 1507 (ibid., p. 438), 1733 (Willis, p. 162), 1742 (Ecton, p. 158), 1782 (Jones, p. 74), 1846 (Oliver, p. 444), 1996 (*EDD*).
Andrew since at least 1137.

Plympton: Augustinian priory and parish church

Peter 1086 (DB 29/10), 1121 (17th) (Barlow, 1996, no. *19). Peter and Paul 1186 x 1188 (ibid., no. 168), c.1200 (Gervase, 1867, ii, 424), 1385 (Chanter VI, f. 146-v), 1437 (Chanter XI, f. 139v–40), 1535 (*Valor*, ii, 375).
Peter (and probably Paul) since at least 1086, sometimes shortened to Peter.

Plympton: hospital

Margaret 1436 (Chanter XI, f. 135v); *Mawdelyn* 1546 (Orme and Webster, 1995, p. 256).
Despite the reference to Margaret in 1436, medieval allusions to the hospital, like that of 1546, are usually to Mary Magdalene.

Plympton St Mary: parish church

Mary 1333 (Chanter IV, f. 170), 1335 (ibid., f. 12), 1352 (Oliver, 1846, p. 142), 1385 (Chanter VI, f. 146-v), 1437 (Chanter XI, f. 139v–40), 1538 (DRO, DD 22891), 1733 (Willis, p. 162), 1742 (Ecton, p. 159); Mary the Virgin c.1755 (MS Milles, ii, f. 106); Mary 1782 (Jones, p. 75), 1846 (Oliver, p. 452), 1996 (*EDD*).
Bishop Stapledon dedicated the church on 29 October 1311 (Chanter II, f. 65).
Mary since at least 1333.

Plympton St Maurice

Thomas 1335 (Chanter IV, f. 12), 1438 (Chanter XI, f. 153), c.1539 (Oliver, 1846, p. 133). *Morys* 1538 (DRO, DD 22889); 'Thomas *Beket*, but now the church there is of *S. Mauricius*, knight and martyr' c.1540 (Leland, 1907–10, i, 216); *Saynt Moris chappell* 1546 (Snell, *Devon and Exeter*, p. 42); Maurice 1733 (Willis, p. 162), 1742 (Ecton, p. 159). Thomas c.1755 (MS Milles, ii, f. 108). Maurice 1782 (Jones, p. 75). Peter and Paul 1782 (in mistake for the priory) (Jones supplement, p. 4). Maurice, formerly Thomas Becket, 1846 (Oliver, p. 452); Maurice 1996 (*EDD*).
Originally Thomas Becket; changed in about 1538 to Maurice.

Plymstock

All Saints 1538 (DRO, DD 22890). Mary and All Saints 1742 (Ecton, p. 159), 1782 (Jones, p. 75). All Saints (Oliver, p. 452). Mary and All Saints 1873 (Kelly), 1939 (ibid.), 1996 (*EDD*).
All Saints before the Reformation, possibly with Mary as co-patron if the later evidence is traditional. Mary and All Saints usually since 1742.

Plymtree

John the Baptist 1742 (Ecton, p. 157). Mary the Virgin conjectured c.1755, from the possibility of Easter Monday (the date of the parish feast) falling on Lady Day (MS Milles, ii, f. 110). John the Baptist 1782 (Jones, p. 31), 1793 (Polwhele, ii, 264), 1846 (Oliver, p. 452), 1996 (*EDD*).
In 1740 the parish feast was said to be held on Easter Sunday (MS Willis 41, f. 223), and in c.1755 on Easter Monday (MS Milles, ii, f. 110).
The medieval dedication has not been discovered. John the Baptist since 1742; the image of Mary appears on the central doors of the chancel screen (Bond and Camm, 1909, ii, 343).

Polsloe: Benedictine priory for women

Katherine c.1200 (Gervase, 1867, ii, 424), 1534 (Oliver, 1846, p. 164); Katherine the Virgin 1535 (*Valor*, ii, 315).
Katherine before the Reformation.

Poltimore

Mary 1527 (PROB 11/22, f. 278v), 1733 (Willis, p. 151), 1742 (Ecton, p. 139), 1782 (Jones, p. 6), 1793 (Polwhele, ii, 189), 1846 (Oliver, p. 452), 1996 (*EDD*).
In 1740 the parish feast was said to be held on the Sunday after 8 September (Nativity of Mary) (MS Willis 41, f. 223v).
Mary since at least 1527.

Poughill

Mary 1742 (Ecton, p. 141). Michael c.1755 (MS Milles, ii, f. 118). Mary 1782 (Jones, p. 10). 1793 (Polwhele, ii, 42). Michael 1846 (Oliver, p. 452); Michael and All Angels 1996 (*EDD*).
In c.1742 and 1793 the parish feast was said to be held on the Sunday after Michaelmas Day (29 September) (MS Willis 41, f. 222; Polwhele, ii, 42), and in c.1755 on the Monday afterwards (MS Milles, ii, f. 118).
The medieval dedication has not been discovered. Both Mary and Michael occur in the 18th century, of which the latter has triumphed.

Powderham

Clement 1487 (*CPR 1485–94*, p. 173), 1513 (Chanter XIII, f. 49v), 1547 (Moger, viii, 2450). Unknown 1742 (Ecton, p. 153). Clement *c.*1755 (MS Milles, ii, f. 120), 1782 (Jones, p. 27), 1793 (Polwhele, ii, 179), 1846 (Oliver, p. 452), 1996 (*EDD*).

Bishop Bronescombe dedicated the church on 24 November 1259 (Chanter I, f. 9v). In *c.*1755 a procession was held on Ascension Day (MS Milles, ii, f. 120).

Clement since at least 1487.

Puddington

Thomas Becket 1742 (Ecton, p. 162), 1782 (Jones, p. 54). Thomas the Apostle 1846 (Oliver, p. 452). Thomas Becket 1873 (Kelly), 1939 (ibid.), 1996 (*EDD*).

In *c.*1742 the parish feast was said to be held on the Sunday after St Thomas Becket's Day (7 July) (MS Willis 41, f. 222).

The medieval dedication has not been discovered. Usually Thomas Becket since 1742, perhaps a conjecture on the basis of the parish feast and (as in other such cases) doubtfully true of earlier times.

Pyworthy

All Saints 1449 (PROB 11/3, f. 288). Swithin 1742 (Ecton, p. 149; source, MS Willis 41, f. 225v). Unknown *c.*1755. Swithin 1782 (Jones, p. 62), 1846 (Oliver, p. 452), 1996 (*EDD*).

In 1740 the parish feast was said to be held on 15 July (St Swithin's Day) (MS Willis 41, f. 225v), and in *c.*1755 on St Swithin's Day, if a Thursday, or the following Thursday (MS Milles, ii, f. 124).

All Saints before the Reformation; Swithin since 1742, evidently a conjecture from the parish feast day.

Rackenford

All Saints 12th century (BL, Cotton MS Vitellius D.ix, f. 81). Trinity 1742 (Ecton, p. 162; source, MS Willis 41, f. 222). All Saints 1754 (Ecton, p. 627), 1782 (Jones, p. 54), 1846 (Oliver, p. 452), 1996 (*EDD*).

Fair on All Saints' Day 1235 (*CChR 1225–57*, p. 193).

All Saints before the Reformation; it was probably then forgotten. Trinity in 1742; All Saints was recovered in 1754.

Rattery

Mary 1203 (Seymour, 1977, p. 247; Dublin, MS E.5.15, f. 86), 1354 (Chanter V, f. 103), 1543 (Youings, 1955, p. 29). Unknown 1742 (Ecton, p. 170), 1782 (Jones, p. 82), 1846 (Oliver, p. 452), 1914 (Kelly). Mary 1923 (Kelly), 1996 (*EDD*).

Mary before the Reformation; it was then forgotten and recovered in 1914–23.

Revelstoke

Peter 1421 x 1432 (Chanter X, f. 22v). Unknown 1742 (Ecton, p. 158), 1782 (Jones, p. 74). Peter 1846 (Oliver, p. 452), 1996 (*EDD*).

Peter before the Reformation; it was then forgotten until it was recovered in 1846.

Rewe

All Saints 1504 (PROB 11/14, f. 167v; Weaver, 1903, p. 62). Mary 1742 (Ecton, p. 157), 1782 (Jones, p. 31), 1793 (Polwhele, ii, 249), 1846 (Oliver, p. 452), 1996 (*EDD*).

In 1740 the parish feast was said to be held on the Sunday after 8 September (Nativity of Mary) (MS Willis 41, f. 224).

All Saints before the Reformation; Mary since 1742, evidently a conjecture based on the parish feast day.

Ringmore

Unknown 1742 (Ecton, p. 171), *c.*1755 (MS Milles, ii, f. 126), 1782 (Jones, p. 85). All Hallows 1846 (Oliver, p. 452), 1996 (*EDD*).

The medieval dedication has not been discovered, and it was forgotten after the Reformation. All Saints since 1846.

Roborough

Peter 1742 (Ecton, p. 169; source, MS Willis 41, f. 230), *c.*1755 (MS Milles, ii, f. 128), 1782 (Jones, p. 59), 1846 (Oliver, p. 452), 1996 (*EDD*).

In *c.*1755 the parish feast was said to be held on the Sunday after St Peter's Day (29 June or 1 August) (MS Milles, ii, f. 128).

The medieval dedication has not been discovered. Peter since 1742.

Rockbeare

Martin 1316 (Chanter II, f. 209), 1474 (PROB 11/6, f. 103). Mary 1742 (Ecton, p. 139), 1782 (Jones, p. 8). Mary, but Nicholas conjectured, 1793 (Polwhele, ii, 198). Mary 1846 (Oliver, p. 452), 1873 (Kelly), 1939 (ibid.). Mary 1900 (Crockford). Mary and Andrew 1906 (ibid.), 1996 (*EDD*).

Martin before the Reformation; Mary since 1742. Andrew was added, on uncertain grounds, soon after 1900, but this did not appear in Kelly's Directory.

Romansleigh

Reymundesle (place) 1228 (Reichel, 1912–39, i, 106); *Romenedesleghe, Romundesleghe* 1282 (Chanter I, f. 116); *Romandeslegh* 1464 (Chanter XII (i), f. 21v). Rumon 1733 (Willis, p. 158). Roman 1740 (MS Willis 41, f. 227). Rumon 1742 (Ecton, p. 162). Mary the Virgin *c.*1755, because the church was dedicated at about the time of her Nativity (MS Milles, ii, f. 132). Rumon 1782 (Jones, p. 54), 1846 (Oliver, p 452), 1996 (*EDD*).

In *c.*1755 the parish feast was said to be held on the first Sunday and Monday in September (MS Milles, ii, f. 132).

The church belonged to Tavistock Abbey, so Rumon has been reasonably deduced since 1742. However, the medieval forms of the name—together with the other Tavistock churches dedicated to Constantine, Eustace and Helen—might make possible a Saint Romanus.

Rose Ash

All Saints 1512 (*CPL*, xix (forthcoming), no. 742). James 1740 (MS Willis 41, f. 227). Peter 1742 (Ecton, p. 162). James the Great *c.*1755 (MS Milles, ii, f. 130v). Peter 1782 (Jones, p. 52), 1846 (Oliver, p. 452), 1996 (*EDD*).

In *c.*1755 the parish feast was said to be held held on the Sunday and Monday after St James' Day (25 July) (MS Milles, ii, f. 130v).

All Saints before the Reformation; it was then forgotten. James was evidently a conjecture from the parish feast day, and Peter possibly too since the feast day was close to his feast on 1 August.

Rousdon

Pancras 1158 x ?1160 (14th) (Barlow, 1996, no. 66), 1169 (ibid., no. 116), 1282 (Chanter I, f. 120), 1309 (Chanter II, f. 38v), 1407 (Chanter IX, f. 96), 1511 (Chanter XIII, f. 44), 1531 (Chanter XIV, f. 57), 1535 (*Valor*, ii, 302), 1733 (Willis, p. 153), 1742 (Ecton, p. 151), 1782 (Jones, p. 25), 1846 (Oliver, p. 452).
Pancras since at least about 1160.

St Budeaux

Bucheside (place) 1086 (DB 39/18); *Bottockishide* (place) 1335 (Chanter IV, f. 12); *Budokyshyde* (place) 1441 (Chanter XI, f. 226). Budoc 1520 (*PND*, i, 236), 1535 (*Valor*, ii, 373, 377); *S. Budok c*.1540 (Leland, 1907–10, i, 212); *St. Budos* 1733 (Willis, p. 162); *St. Budeaux* 1742 (Ecton, p. 158); *Bude c*.1755 (MS Milles, i, f. 118). *Budock* 1782 (Jones, p. 74); *Budocus* 1846 (Oliver, p. 446); Budeaux 1996 (*EDD*).
In *c*.1755 the church was believed to have been dedicated or consecrated on the feast of St Augustine (MS Milles, i. f. 118).
PND (i, 236–7) explains St Budeaux as named from the saint Budoc, and nearby Budshead as 'Budoc's hide of land'. If so, Budoc since at least 1086.

St Giles in the Wood

Giles 1329 (PRO, C 143/207/19), 1535 (*Valor*, ii, 353), 1733 (Willis, p. 159), 1742 (Ecton, p. 169), 1782 (Jones, p. 59), 1846 (Oliver, p. 448), 1996 (*EDD*).
The feast of dedication was changed from the morrow of St Giles (2 September) to the Sunday after 15 September (Chanter XI, f. 190-v).
Giles since at least 1329.

St Giles on the Heath (transferred from Exeter to Truro diocese 1877)

Giles 1194 x 1206 (Finberg, 1947, p. 373), 1291 (Tax.), 1496 x 1501 (Chanter XII (ii), Redmayn f. 30v), *c*.1755 (MS Milles, i, f. 228), 1733 (Willis, p. 172), 1742 (Ecton, p. 180), 1782 (Jones, p. 109), 1846 (Oliver, p. 448), 1996 (TDD).
In 1740, the parish feast was said to be held on 7 September (MS Willis 41, f. 225v), in *c*.1755 on the Sunday after St Giles' Day (1 September) (MS Milles, i, f. 228), and in 1878 on the Sunday after 18 July with a fair on the following day (Boase, 1890, col. 1589).
Giles since at least about 1200.

St Marychurch

Mary 1050 x 1072 (Earle, 1888, p. 249); *aecclesiam S' Mariae* 1086 (DB 2/8, 15/42); *Sainctemariecherche* (place) 1148 (14th) (Barlow, 1996, no. 32); Mary 1269 (ECA, D&C 1408; 3625, f. 100), 1733 (Willis, p. 160), 1742 (Ecton, p. 152), *c*.1755 (MS Milles, ii, f. 41), 1782 (Jones, p. 66), 1846 (Oliver, p. 450), 1996 (*EDD*).
The bishop of Waterford dedicated the high altar in 1338–9 (Chanter IV, f. 220v).
Mary since at least the 11th century.

St Nicholas—see Shaldon

St Thomas by Exeter—see Cowick

Salcombe

John the Baptist 1420 (Chanter XI, f. 1v), 1539 (Chanter XV, f. 81). Not in Ecton (1742), Jones (1782). John the Baptist 1846 (Oliver, p. 452). Trinity 1873 (Kelly), 1939 (ibid.), 1996 (*EDD*).

John the Baptist before the Reformation and in 1846; Trinity in recent years.

Salcombe Regis

Peter 1742 (Ecton, p. 139; source, MS Willis 41, f. 223v). Unknown *c*.1755 (MS Milles, ii, f. 134). Peter 1782 (Jones, p. 8). Peter and Mary 1786 (Bacon, p. 246). Mary 1793 (Polwhele, ii, 236), 1846 (Oliver, p. 452). Peter 1873 (Kelly). Peter and Mary 1883 (Kelly), 1939 (ibid.), 1996 (*EDD*).

The medieval dedication has not been discovered. Peter since 1742, to whom Mary was added in 1786, on unknown grounds.

Sampford Courtenay

Store of Andrew 1483 (PROB 11/7, f. 127v); Andrew 1539 (PROB 11/26, f. 118), 1733 (Willis, p. 162). Peter 1740 (MS Willis 41, f. 225). Unknown 1742 (Ecton, p. 156). Andrew 1754 (Ecton, p. 122). Unknown *c*.1755 (MS Milles, ii, f. 138). Andrew 1782 (Jones, p. 71), 1806 (Polwhele, iii, 438), 1846 (Oliver, p. 452), 1996 (*EDD*).

In 1740 the parish feast was said to be held on 30 June (MS Willis 41, f. 225), and in *c*.1755 on the Sunday after St Peter's Day (29 June or 1 August) (MS Milles, ii, f. 138).

Andrew since at least 1483, not always remembered in the 18th century but recovered in 1754.

Sampford Peverell

John the Baptist 1742 (Ecton, p. 167). Unknown *c*.1755 (MS Milles, ii, f. 140). John the Baptist 1782 (Jones, p. 34), 1793 (Polwhele, ii, 365), 1846 (Oliver, p. 452), 1996 (*EDD*).

Bishop Bronescombe dedicated the church on 10 December 1259 (Chanter I, f. 10). Bishop Stapledon dedicated the church of *Saunforde*, identified by Hingeston-Randolph with Sampford Peverell, on 12 April 1318 (Chanter II, f. 126v). Fairs were granted on the feasts of the Annunciation of the Virgin (25 March) 1335 (*CChR 1327–41*, p. 344) and on St Alphege (19 April) and St John the Baptist (29 August) 1487 (*CPR 1485–94*, pp. 171–2). In *c*.1755 the parish feast was said to be held held on the Sunday after 29 August (MS Milles, ii, f. 140).

The medieval dedication has not been discovered; John the Baptist since 1742.

Sampford Spiney

Unknown 1742 (Ecton, p. 165), *c*.1755 (MS Milles, ii, f. 142), 1782 (Jones, p. 78), 1846 (Oliver, p. 452). Mary 1873 (Kelly), 1939 (ibid.), 1996 (*EDD*).

In 1740 the parish feast was said to be held on Whit Tuesday (MS Willis 41, f. 225).

The medieval dedication has not been discovered, and it was forgotten after the Reformation. Mary since about 1873.

Sandford

Swithin 1351 (Putnam, 1938, p. 65), 1437 (Chanter XI, f. 142v-3), 1524 (Chanter XV, f. 35v), 1543 and frequently to 1554 (Moger, i, 66; viii, 2524; xiv, 4738–40), 1547 (Youings, 1955, p. 96), 1590 (Murray, x, Thomas Dowriche). Unknown 1742 (Ecton, p. 142). Swithin *c*.1742 (MS Willis 41, f. 222), *c*.1755 (MS Milles, ii, f. 136), 1782 (Jones, p. 12), 1793 (Polwhele, ii, 38), 1846 (Oliver, p. 452), 1996 (*EDD*).

In *c*.1755 the parish feast was said to be held on the Sunday after St Swithin's Day (2 or 15 July) (MS Milles, ii, f. 136).
Swithin since at least 1351.

Satterleigh

Peter *c*.1742 (MS Willis 41, f. 248a). Unknown 1742 (Ecton, p. 163). Peter 1754 (Ecton, p. 118). Unknown *c*.1755 (MS Milles, ii, f. 144). Peter 1782 (Jones, p. 56), 1846 (Oliver, p. 452), 1996 (*EDD*).

In 1740 the parish feast was said to be held on Whit Sunday (MS Willis 41, f. 227).

The medieval dedication has not been discovered. Peter since about 1742, possibly a local tradition since it was not apparently a conjecture from a parish feast day.

Seaton

George 1349 (Chanter V, f. 77), 1546 (Moger, v, 1277), 1547 (ibid., xi, 3353; xx, 7141). Gregory 1742 (Ecton, p. 150); Gregory with a query 1754 (Ecton, p. 110). Unknown *c*.1755 (MS Milles, ii, f. 146). Gregory 1782 (Jones, p. 24), 1793 (Polwhele, ii, 304), 1846 (Oliver, p. 452). George 1854 (Oliver, p. 68). Gregory 1873 (Kelly), 1939 (ibid.), 1996 (*EDD*).

Fair on St Gregory's Day 1280 (*CChR 1257–1300*, p. 200). In *c*.1755 the parish feast was said to be held held on Whit Tuesday (MS Milles, ii, f. 146).

George before the Reformation; Gregory since 1742 on the basis of the fair, despite the recovery of George in 1854.

Shaldon (St Nicholas)

Nicholai de Pola 1186 x 1188 may refer to this chapel (DRO, ED/PP/9; Barlow, 1996, no. 168). Image of Nicholas in the chapel of Ringmore 1445 (Chanter XI, f. 512). Nicholas 1733 (Willis, p. 154), 1742 (Ecton, p. 154), 1782 (Jones, p. 28), 1793 (Polwhele, ii, 145), 1846 (Oliver, p. 451), 1996 (*EDD*).

Nicholas, perhaps since the late 12th century, certainly since at least 1445.

Shaugh Prior

Edward 1538 (DRO, DD 22887). Unknown 1742 (Ecton, p. 159), *c*.1755 (MS Milles, ii, f. 148), 1782 (Jones, p. 75). Edward 1846 (Oliver, p. 452), 1996 (*EDD*).

Edward before the Reformation; it was then forgotten until it was recovered in 1846. If the Edward dedication is an early one, as at Egg Buckland and Exeter, it is likely to refer to the Martyr; if late medieval, the Confessor is more likely.

Shebbear

Michael 13th century (Dublin, MS E.5.15, f. 116), 1422 (PRO, C 139/8 no. 78; IPM, Christina Cary). Unknown 1742 (Ecton, p. 169), 1782 (Jones, p. 60). Michael 1846 (Oliver, p. 453), 1996 (*EDD*).

In 1358 the parishioners of Sheepwash were ordered to attend Shebbear church annually on the feast of St Michael in Monte Tumba (16 October) (Chanter III, f. 210v). In 1740 the parish feast was said to be held on 13 April (MS Willis 41, f. 225), and in 1742 on the second Monday after Easter (ibid., f. 207).

Michael before the Reformation; it was then forgotten until it was recovered in 1846.

Sheepstor

Unknown 1742 (Ecton, p. 164), 1782 (Jones, p. 76), 1846 (Oliver, p. 453), 1939 (Kelly). Well of St Leonard 1940–1 (Binnall, p. 125). Leonard 1983 (*EDD*), 1996 (ibid.).

In 1740 the parish feast was said to be held at Whitsuntide (MS Willis 41, f. 228).

Possibly Leonard before the Reformation, if the well evidence is traditional; the dedication was then forgotten. Leonard in recent years.

Sheepwash

Laurence 13th century (Seymour, 1977, p. 188; Dublin, MS E.5.15, f. 116), 1358 (Chanter III, f. 210v), 1742 (Ecton, p. 169), 1782 (Jones, p. 60), 1846 (Oliver, p. 453), 1996 (*EDD*).

Fair on St Laurence's Day 1230 (*CChR 1225–57*, p. 125). In 1740 the parish feast was said to be held on 27 May (MS Willis 41, f. 225).

Laurence since at least the 13th century.

Sheldon

James 1740 (MS Willis 41, f. 223). Unknown 1742 (Ecton, p. 145). James 1754 (Ecton, p. 109), 1782 (Jones, p. 18), 1793 (Polwhele, ii, 334), 1846 (Oliver, p. 453). James the Greater 1996 (*EDD*).

Bishop Bronescombe dedicated the church on 7 December 1259 (Chanter I, f. 10). In 1740 the parish feast was said to be held on the Sunday after St James' Day (25 July) (MS Willis 41, f. 223).

The medieval dedication has not been discovered; James since 1740.

Sherford

Martin 1457 (Chanter XII (i), f. 36), 1742 (Ecton, p. 171; source, MS Willis 41, f. 223), *c.*1755 (MS Milles, ii, f. 151), 1782 (Jones, p. 85), 1846 (Oliver, p. 453), 1996 (*EDD*).

Martin since at least 1457.

Shillingford St George

George 1398 (Chanter IX, f. 9v), 1475 (Pole, i, 18 no. 207). Unknown 1742 (Ecton, p. 154). George 1782 (Jones, p. 28), 1793 (Polwhele, ii, 112), 1846 (Oliver, p. 453), 1996 (*EDD*).

No parish feast was said to be held in 1741 (MS Willis 41, f. 241).

George since at least 1398.

Shirwell

Peter 1742 (Ecton, p. 160; source, MS Willis 41, f. 226b). Mary *c.*1755 (MS Milles, ii, f. 153). Peter 1782 (Jones, p. 50), 1846 (Oliver, p. 453), 1996 (*EDD*).

In *c.*1755 the parish feast was said to be held on Whit Monday (MS Milles, ii, f. 153).

The medieval dedication has not been discovered; usually Peter since 1742.

Shobrooke

Peter 1499 (*CPL*, xvii part i, 91); store and bead-roll of Peter 1536 (PROB 11/27, f. 69v). Unknown 1742 (Ecton, p. 141). Thomas Becket *c.*1755 (MS Milles, ii, f. 155). Unknown 1782 (Jones, p. 11), 1846 (Oliver, p. 453). Laurence 1873 (Kelly). Swithin 1882 (Kelly), 1939 (ibid.), 1996 (*EDD*).

In *c.*1755 the parish feast was said to be held on the Monday before St Thomas Becket's Day, with procession on Ascension Day (MS Milles, ii, f. 155). *Peter before the Reformation; it was then forgotten. Thomas Becket was suggested in about 1755, on the basis of the feast day; Laurence appears briefly in the late 19th century, replaced in about 1880 by Swithin—perhaps borrowed from nearby Sandford.*

Shute

Michael *c.*1225 (ECA, D&C 3672, p. 44); Michael the Archangel 1494 (PROB 11/10, f. 163v; DRO, MCR 10–11 Henry VII, m. 29; DRO, 123M/TB538B); Michael 1508 (PROB 11/17, f. 12). Peter 1742 (Ecton, p. 150). Michael 1763 (Ecton, p. 110). Peter 1782 (Jones, p. 23), 1793 (Polwhele, ii, 317). Michael 1846 (Oliver, p. 453), 1996 (*EDD*).

Michael before the Reformation; usually Peter in the 18th century, although Michael was recovered in 1763.

Sidbury

Michael 1498 (PROB 11/11, f. 171v). Giles 1742 (Ecton, p. 139; source, MS Willis 41, f. 223v), *c.*1755 (MS Milles, ii, f. 160b), 1782 (Jones, p. 7), 1793 (Polwhele, ii, 239), 1846 (Oliver, p. 453), 1873 (Kelly), 1939 (ibid.). Peter and Giles 1983 (*EDD*). Giles and Peter 1996 (ibid.).

Fair on the Nativity of Mary (8 September) 1291 (*CChR 1257–1300*, p. 403). In 1740 and 1793 the parish feast was said to be held on St Giles' Monday (MS Willis 41, f. 223v; Polwhele, ii, 239), and in *c.*1755 the beginning of September was locally known as 'Gilesmass' (MS Milles, ii, f. 160b).

Michael before the Reformation; Giles since 1742, evidently a conjecture on the basis of the parish feast day. In truth, Giles was the original dedication of nearby Sidmouth. Peter has been added in recent times.

Sidmouth

Giles 1310 (Chanter II, f. 52v), 1433 (DRO, Exeter City Archives, Misc. Rolls, 4, m 3), 1547 (Moger, xv, 5278). Nicholas 1733 (Willis, p. 151). Giles 1740 (MS Willis 41, f. 223v). Nicholas 1742 (Ecton, p. 139), 1782 (Jones, p. 7). 'St Nicholas, or probably St Giles' 1793 (Polwhele, ii, 234). Giles 1846 (Oliver, p. 453). Nicholas 1873 (Kelly), 1939 (ibid.). Nicholas and Giles 1983 (*EDD*), 1996 (ibid.).

In 1740 and 1793 the parish feast was said to be held on St Giles' Monday (MS Willis 41, f. 223v; Polwhele, ii, 234).

Giles before the Reformation. It was still remembered in the 18th century, when Nicholas—a new conjecture—came to prominence, largely through the printed directories. Giles has been fully restored only recently, and even then demoted to second place.

Silverton

Image of Mary in the chancel 1478 (Chanter XII (ii), f. 126); Mary 1504 (LPL, Reg. Warham, i, f. 206v; PROB 11/14, f. 167v; Weaver, 1903, p. 62), 1733 (Willis, p. 154). Laurence 1740 (MS Willis 41, f. 223v). Mary 1742 (Ecton, p. 157), 1782 (Jones, p. 31), 1793 (Polwhele, ii, 250), 1846 (Oliver, p. 453), 1996 (*EDD*).

In 1740 the parish feast was said to be held on 24 June (MS Willis 41, f. 223v). *Mary since at least 1504.*

Slapton: collegiate church

Mary 1369 (*CPR 1367–70*, pp. 299, 322), 1374 (Chanter VI, f. 54v), 1534 (Oliver, 1846, p. 322).

Mary before the Reformation.

Slapton: parish church

James 1310 (Chanter II, f. 53), 1411 (Chanter VIII, f. 317v), 1534 (Oliver, 1846, p. 322), 1544 (Yallop, 1959, p. 138). Mary 1733 (Willis, p. 165). James 1740 (MS Willis 41, f. 223). Mary 1742 (Ecton, p. 172), 1782 (Jones, p. 86). James 1846 (Oliver, p. 453); James the Greater 1996 (*EDD*).

Bishop Stapledon dedicated the high altar on 16 May 1318 (Chanter II, f. 127). In 1740 the parish feast was said to be held on 24 June (MS Willis 41, f. 223).

James before the Reformation. It was still remembered in the 18th century, but the printed directories substituted Mary through confusion with the nearby collegiate church until James was restored in 1846.

Sourton

Thomas Becket 1742 (Ecton, p. 165; source, MS Willis 41, f. 225), 1782 (Jones, p. 78). Unknown 1846 (Oliver, p. 453). Thomas Becket 1854 (Oliver, p. 68), 1996 (*EDD*).

In 1740 the parish feast was said to be held on 14 July (this is one week after St Thomas Becket's Day) (MS Willis 41, f. 225).

The medieval dedication has not been discovered. Thomas Becket since 1742, perhaps a conjecture based on the parish feast day. Caution is needed in assuming that this represents the medieval dedication, in view of several other cases where a Becket claim in 1742 runs counter to pre-Reformation evidence.

South Brent

Petroc and Mary the Virgin 1436 (Chanter XI, f. 134). Petroc 1469 (*CPL*, xii, 717). Patrick 1538 (DRO, DD 22558; Exeter City Library, DD 22824), 1742 (Ecton, p. 170; source, MS Willis 41, f. 223), 1782 (Jones, p. 81). Petroc 1846 (Oliver, p. 446), 1996 (*EDD*).

Fair on St Michael's Day 1353 (*CChR 1341–1427*, p. 130). Bishop Lacy consecrated the principal altar on 11 September 1436 (Chanter XI, f. 134). In 1740 the parish feast was said to be held on 29 September (Michaelmas Day) (MS Willis 41, f. 223).

Petroc and Mary before the Reformation (Petroc was sometimes spelt as, or confused with, Patrick). Patrick in the 18th century, and Petroc alone since 1846.

South Huish

Unknown 1742 (Ecton, p. 171), c.1755 (MS Milles, i, f. 268), 1782 (Jones, p. 84). All Saints 1806 (Polwhele, iii, 475). Unknown 1846 (Oliver, p. 449). Andrew 1873 (Kelly), 1939 (ibid.).

Bishop Grandisson dedicated the church and high altar of *Hywishe*, either North or South Huish, on 15 June 1336 (Chanter IV, f. 200).

The medieval dedication has not been discovered, and it was forgotten after the Reformation. All Saints arose from a rather unconvincing conjecture in 1806 that several adjoining churches were so dedicated; Andrew since the late 19th century.

Southleigh

All Saints 1307 (DRO, 123M/TB397). Laurence 1742 (Ecton, p. 150; source, MS Willis 41, f. 223v). Unknown *c*.1755 (MS Milles, ii, f. 7). Laurence 1782 (Jones, p. 24), 1793 (Polwhele, ii, 306), 1846 (Oliver, p. 450), 1996 (*EDD*).
All Saints before the Reformation; Laurence since 1742, perhaps a conjecture from a parish feast day.

South Milton

Unknown 1742 (Ecton, p. 171), *c*.1755 (MS Milles, ii, f. 50b), 1782 (Jones, p. 84). All Saints 1806 (Polwhele, iii, 475). Unknown 1846 (Oliver, p. 451). All Saints 1996 (*EDD*).
The medieval dedication has not been discovered, and it was forgotten after the Reformation. All Saints since 1806.

South Molton

Church of St Syth *Molton* 1517, in a will which evidently relates to South Molton church (PROB 11/18, f. 265; Orme, 1995b, pp. 249–50). Mary 1733 (Willis, p. 158). Mary the Virgin 1740 (MS Willis 41, f. 227). Mary 1742 (Ecton, p. 164). Mary Magdalene 1754 (Ecton, p. 118). Mary the Virgin *c*.1755 (MS Milles, ii, f. 62). Mary Magdalene 1782 (Jones, p. 57). Mary 1806 (Polwhele, iii, 392). Mary Magdalene 1846 (Oliver, p. 451), 1996 (*EDD*).

Fairs on the Assumption of the Virgin (15 August) 1246 (*CChR 1225–57*, p. 307) and on St John the Baptist's Day (24 June) 1490 (*CChR 1427–1516*, p. 269). The dedication festival was moved from the second Sunday in Lent to 10 October in 1417 (Chanter VIII, f. 234v), and was still observed on 10 October in the early sixteenth century (Orme, 1991b, p. 347).

Syth in 1517. Syth is usually the English form of Zita, an Italian saint who was popular in England at the end of the middle ages (Sutcliffe, 1993, pp. 83–9), but if this is the identification here, she must have replaced or been added to an earlier patron since South Molton church existed by Domesday (1086). Alternative possibilities are that (a) Syth is an abbreviated form of Osith, a Saxon woman saint of Chich in Essex, to whom no other church in Devon is known to be dedicated; (b) Syth is a variant form of the male saint Cyr or Cyricus, who owned two other ancient churches in Devon (compare Weaver, 1890, pp. 172–3); (c) the will-maker of 1517 confused a popular image of St Syth in the church with the patron saint. More information is needed. By the 18th century, Mary the Virgin appears (perhaps suggested by the fair day); she was superseded by Mary Magdalene between 1754 and 1846.

South Pool

Siriacus 1450 (Sharpe, 1889–90, ii, 521); *ecclesiam . . . Sancti Ciriaci martyris* 1459 (Chanter XII (i), f. 11). *Ecclesiam Sancte Cecilie de Southpool* 1508 (PROB 11/16, f. 58v). A bequest to *St Sykeke* of Poule 1530 looks like a mistranscription of Ciriac (PROB 11/28, f. 126). Swithin 1740 (MS Willis 41, f. 223). *Caecilia* 1742 (Ecton, p. 170). Unknown *c*.1755 (MS Milles, ii, f. 112). *Caecilia* 1782 (Jones, p. 85). *Cyriac* 1786 (Bacon, p. 298). Nicholas and *Cyriacus* the martyr 1846 (Oliver, p. 452); Nicholas and Cyriac 1996 (*EDD*).

Bishop Stapledon dedicated the church, high altar and three others on 24 August 1318 (Chanter II, f. 128v).

Two clear references before the Reformation to Cyricus (alias Cyriac) against one for Cecily suggest that the latter is a mistake; it would be an unusual dedication, whereas Cyricus is fairly common. In the 18th century Cecily was revived, probably on the basis of the reference of 1508, but Cyricus has been dominant since 1786 with the addition of Nicholas (on grounds which are unknown).

South Tawton

Andrew 1517 (DRO, MCR 8–9 Henry VIII, m. 48), 1525 (DCRSL, Transcript of Registers of South Tawton, vol ii, quoting original document f. 84v), 1555 (ibid., quoting f. 97v), 1742 (Ecton, p. 146), 1782 (Jones, p. 20), 1793 (Polwhele, ii, 66), 1846 (Oliver, p 453), 1996 (*EDD*).

In 1742 the parish feast was variously said to be held on the Sunday after St Thomas Becket's Day (7 July) and on Whit Monday (MS Willis 41, ff. 211v, 222).

Andrew since at least 1517.

Sowton

Michael 1337 (Chanter V, f. 37), 1445 (*CPL*, ix, 478), 1733 (Willis, p. 150), 1742 (Ecton, p. 138). Unknown *c*.1755 (MS Milles, ii, f. 160d). Michael 1782 (Jones, p. 5), 1793 (Polwhele, ii, 185), 1846 (Oliver, p. 453); Michael and All Angels 1996 (*EDD*).

Michael since at least 1337.

Spreyton

An inscription in the church commemorating its rebuilding in 1451 includes prayers to Nicholas and Edward the Martyr (Polwhele, ii, 64). Michael 1742 (Ecton, p. 147; source, MS Willis 41, f. 222), *c*.1755 (MS Milles, ii, f. 160f), 1782 (Jones, p. 21), 1793 (Polwhele, ii, 64), 1846 (Oliver, p. 453), 1996 (*EDD*).

In *c*.1742 and *c*.1755 the parish feast was said to be held held on the Sunday before Midsummer Day (24 June) (MS Willis 41, f. 222; MS Milles, ii, f. 160f).

Possibly Nicholas or Edward the Martyr before the Reformation; Michael since 1742.

Staverton

Paul mentioned as patron of the church (but not necessarily the only patron) 1314 (Chanter II, f. 84v). Peter 1368 (DRO, 158M/T3; Webster, 1989, p. 182). Store of Peter and Paul 1479 (ECA, D&C 2379), 1548 (Worthy, 1896, p. 158). George 1742 (Ecton, p. 151). Unknown *c*.1755 (MS Milles, ii, f. 160h). George 1782 (Jones, p. 65), 1806 (Polwhele, iii, 486). Paul 1846 (Oliver, p. 453), 1923 (Kelly). *Paul de Lyon* 1926 (Kelly), 1939 (ibid.); *Paul de Leon* 1983 (*EDD*), 1996 (ibid.).

Peter and Paul before the Reformation; they were then forgotten. George in the 18th century, until Paul was recovered in 1846. The vicar, E.D. Drake-Brockman (1922–57), introduced Paul de Leon on the romantic and speculative grounds popular in the 1920s but there is no historical basis for a connection with that saint (ECA, Drake-Brockman papers).

Stockland (transferred from Dorset to Devon 1832–44, and from Salisbury to Exeter diocese 1836)

Michael 1443 (Jacob, ii, 625), 1742 (Ecton, p. 49), 1774 (Hutchins, i, 323); Michael and All Angels 1996 (*EDD*).

Fair on the Assumption of the Virgin Mary 1252 (*CChR 1225–57*, p. 414).

Michael since at least 1443.

Stockleigh English

Unknown 1742 (Ecton, p. 142). Mary 1754 (Ecton, p. 107), 1782 (Jones, p. 11), 1793 (Polwhele, ii, 46), 1846 (Oliver, p. 453), 1996 (*EDD*). In *c.*1742 no parish feast was said to be held (MS Willis 41, f. 222).
The medieval dedication has not been discovered; Mary since 1754.

Stockleigh Pomeroy

Mary 1742 (Ecton, p. 142), 1782 (Jones, p. 11), 1793 (Polwhele, ii, 45), 1846 (Oliver, p. 453), 1996 (*EDD*).
Bishop Bronescombe dedicated the church on 23 July 1261 (Chanter I, f. 20). In *c.*1742 the parish feast was said to be held on the Monday before 24 August (MS Willis 41, f. 222).
The medieval dedication has not been discovered; Mary since 1742.

Stoke Canon

Image of Mary Magdalene at the high altar 1301 (ECA, D&C 3673). Unknown 1742 (Ecton, p. 139). Bartholomew 1754 (Ecton, p. 107). Mary Magdalene 1763 (Ecton, p. 107). Unknown 1782 (Jones, p. 9). Mary Magdalene 1793 (Polwhele, ii, 189), 1846 (Oliver, p. 453), 1996 (*EDD*).
In 1740 the parish feast was said to be held on the Sunday after St Bartholomew's Day (24 August) (MS Willis 41, f. 223v).
Mary Magdalene before the Reformation, because only the images of the patron saint and the Virgin Mary would have stood by the high altar; it was then forgotten. Bartholomew was a conjecture from the parish feast day. The recovery of Mary Magdalene in 1763 was probably based on the reference of 1301.

Stoke Damarel

Unknown 1742 (Ecton, p. 164), 1782 (Jones, p. 77), 1846 (Oliver, p. 453), 1883 (Kelly). Andrew 1889 (Kelly), 1939 (ibid.), 1996 (*EDD*).
The medieval dedication has not been discovered, and it was forgotten after the Reformation. Andrew since the late 19th century, perhaps on the analogy of St Andrew's, the chief church of Plymouth, since Stoke Damarel held that position in Devonport.

Stoke Fleming

Ecclesia Sancti Ermondi 1364 (PRO, C 135/183 no. 3; *CIPM*, xi, 470); *ecclesiam . . . Sancti Ermundi* 1419 (Chanter IX, f. 202). Peter 1742 (Ecton, p. 151; source, MS Willis 41, f. 223). Edmund *c.*1755 (MS Milles, ii, f. 160j). Peter 1782 (Jones, p. 65), 1846 (Oliver, p. 453). Edmund 1854 (Oliver, p. 68). Peter 1873 (Kelly), 1939 (ibid.), 1996 (*EDD*).
The two medieval references indicate a dedication to a St Ermund or Ermond, a distinct and apparently unique local saint (Orme, 1995a, pp. 10–13). This was largely forgotten after the Reformation—hence Peter in 1742, which has generally endured since. Of the two references to Edmund, the first may preserve a misunderstood tradition of Ermund; the second was based on a belief that the reference of 1419 should be read as Edmund. The reference of 1364 was not known until recent times.

Stoke Gabriel

Philip de Stokes Gabriele (personal name) 1276 (Chanter I, f. 73). Gabriel 1281 (ibid., p. 356), 1291 (Tax.), 1309 (Chanter II, f. 44), 1500 (Chanter XII (ii), Redmayn f. 15v), 1515 (Chanter XIII, f. 60), 1733 (Willis, p. 161), 1742 (Ecton, p. 152). Unknown *c.*1755 (MS Milles, ii, f. 161). Gabriel 1782 (Jones, p. 66). Mary and Gabriel 1846 (Oliver, p. 453). Gabriel 1873 (Kelly), 1939 (ibid.), 1996 (*EDD*).

Gabriel since at least 1276, probably due to Bishop Bronescombe of Exeter, a devotee of this cult (Hingeston-Randolph, 1889, p. xvi). The reason for Oliver's Mary is not clear.

Stokeinteignhead

Andrew 1354 (*CPR 1354–8*, pp. 147–8), 1418 (Chanter VIII, f. 333v), 1742 (Ecton, p. 153), 1782 (Jones, p. 28), 1793 (Polwhele, ii, 143), 1846 (Oliver, p. 453), 1996 (*EDD*).

Fair on St Bartholomew's Day 1310 (*CChR 1300–26*, p. 137). Bishop Grandisson dedicated the high altar on 14 May 1336 (Chanter IV, f. 198v).

Andrew since at least 1354.

Stokenham

Ecclesiam Sancti Michaelis de Hurdestok 1280 x 1281 (PRO, JUST 1/181, m. 23d). *Ecclesia Sancti Humberti* (or *Huniberti*) *Confessoris* 1343 (PRO, C 135/72 no. 2; *CIPM*, viii, 347–8). Barnabas 1742 (Ecton, p. 171; source, MS Willis 41, f. 223). Ambrose *c.*1755 (MS Milles, ii, f. 165). Barnabas 1782 (Jones, p. 85). Michael 1846 (Oliver, p. 453); Michael and All Angels 1996 (*EDD*).

In 1740 the parish feast was said to be held on Easter Tuesday (MS Willis 41, f. 223), and in *c.*1755 on Good Friday (MS Milles, ii, f. 165).

Hurdestok *in 1280–1 is an alternative name for Stokenham, but the source (an Assize Roll) uses the word* ecclesia *(church) to mean parish churches and chapels indiscriminately, so this reference may be to a chapel in the parish. The reference to Humbert does relate to the church, and therefore carries weight. There were several continental saints named Humbert, but none seems a strong candidate to be patron of this church which was evidently ancient and probably had the status of a minster in Anglo-Saxon times. The name* Hunbeorht *occurs several times in Anglo-Saxon sources, being borne by clergy and laity and was latinized in one instance as Humbertus, so the saint may have been English and even unique to Stokenham as was Ermund in the neighbouring parish of Stoke Rivers. The medieval dedication was perhaps faintly remembered in the Ambrose of c.1755, but was generally forgotten by that time, being replaced by Barnabas (a typical 18th-century conjecture) and later by Michael (perhaps suggested by the reference of 1280–1).*

Stoke Rivers

A reference to the church of Our Lady *Stoke* 1517 in a group of bequests to north Devon churches must relate to Stoke Rivers (PROB 11/18, f. 265). Bartholomew 1742 (Ecton, p. 160). Unknown *c.*1755 (MS Milles, ii, f. 163). Bartholomew 1782 (Jones, p. 50). Unknown 1846 (Oliver, p. 453). Holy Ascension 1873 (Kelly). Bartholomew 1883 (Kelly), 1939 (ibid.), 1996 (*EDD*).

In 1740, 1742 and *c.*1755 the parish feast was said to be held on Ascension Day (MS Willis 41, ff. 207, 220, 227; MS Milles, ii, f. 163).

Mary before the Reformation; Bartholomew was suggested in 1742 and was eventually adopted. Holy Ascension was a guess from the parish feast day.

Stoodleigh

Margaret 1373 (Chanter VII, f. 23v), 1742 (Ecton, p. 162; source, MS Willis 41, f. 224), c.1755 (MS Milles, ii, f. 170b), 1782 (Jones, p. 54), 1846 (Oliver, p. 453), 1996 (*EDD*).

In 1740 and c.1755 the parish feast was said to be held on the Sunday after St Margaret's Day (20 July) (MS Willis 41, f. 224; MS Milles, ii, f. 170b).

Margaret since at least 1373.

Stowford

Unknown 1742 (Ecton, p. 166), c.1755 (MS Milles, ii, f. 169), 1782 (Jones, p. 80), 1846 (Oliver, p. 453), 1873 (Kelly). John the Baptist 1883 (Kelly), 1939 (ibid.). John 1983 (*EDD*), 1996 (ibid.).

In 1740 the parish feast was said to be held on Easter Tuesday (MS Willis 41, f. 225v), and in c.1755 on Easter Day (MS Milles, ii, f. 169).

The medieval dedication has not been discovered, and it was forgotten after the Reformation. John the Baptist since the late 19th century, although curiously the Baptist is not identified in modern directories.

Sutcombe

Andrew 1342 (*CIPM*, viii, 259), 1479 (Chanter XII (ii), f. 87), 1742 (Ecton, p. 149), 1782 (Jones, p. 62), 1846 (Oliver, p. 453), 1996 (*EDD*).

Andrew since at least 1342.

Swimbridge

Store of James 1443 (Brooking-Rowe, 1901, p. 169; Murray, ix, Thomas Dabernon), 1538 (DRO, 1148M/Wills 1), 1544 (Moger, vii, 1989), 1545 (ibid., x, 2956); James 1742 (Ecton, p. 141; source, MS Willis 41, f. 226b), c.1755 (MS Milles, ii, f. 171), 1782 (Jones, p. 41), 1842 (Oliver, p. 6); James the Apostle 1846 (Oliver, p. 453), 1996 (*EDD*).

In c.1755 the parish feast was said to be held on 25 July (MS Milles, ii, f. 171).

James since at least 1443. The earliest references are merely to the store of the saint, but the context of them suggests that the store of James was the principal store of the church and therefore that of the patron saint.

Sydenham Damerel

Store of Mary 1437 (DRO, 158M/T6); Mary 1733 (Willis, p. 163), 1742 (Ecton, p. 166). Unknown c.1755 (MS Milles, ii, f. 159). Mary 1782 (Jones, p. 80), 1846 (Oliver, p 453), 1996 (*EDD*).

In 1740 the parish feast was said to be held on 26 December (MS Willis 41, f. 225v.

Possibly Mary before the Reformation, but medieval evidence sometimes adduced about the church of St Mary of Sideham actually relates to Marystowe. This may have affected the belief in Mary which has been manifest since 1733.

Talaton

James 1742 (Ecton, p. 157; source MS Willis 41, f. 223), 1782 (Jones, p. 32), 1793 (Polwhele, ii, 272), 1846 (Oliver, p. 453); James the Apostle 1996 (*EDD*).

In 1740 the parish feast was said to be held on the Sunday before St James' Day (25 July) (MS Willis 41, f. 223).

The medieval dedication has not been discovered; James since 1742.

Tamerton Foliot

Mary 1292 (*CPL*, i, 549), 1351 (Chanter V, f. 96), 1378 (Stevens, 1962–4, pp. 45, 49), 1742 (Ecton, p. 164). Unknown *c*.1755 (MS Milles, ii, f. 174). Mary 1782 (Jones, p. 77), 1846 (Oliver, p. 453), 1996 (*EDD*).
Fair on St Denis' Day 1270 (*CChR 1257–1300*, p. 148). Bishop Stapledon dedicated the church, high altar and three others on 22 August 1318 (Chanter II, f. 128v). In *c*.1755 the parish feast was said to be held in July (MS Milles, ii, f. 174).
Mary since at least 1292.

Tavistock: Benedictine abbey

Mary 981 (Finberg, 1969, 279–80), *c*.1103 (*Regesta*, ii, 29). Rumon ?1154 x ?1160 (13th) (Barlow, 1996, no. 70). Mary and Rumon 1186 x 1190 (ibid., no. 174). Mary *c*.1200 (Gervase, 1867, ii, 423). Mary and Rumon 1225 (Barlow, 1996, no. 291), 1535 (*Valor*, ii, 381).
Bishop Stapledon dedicated the church and two altars on 21 August 1318 (Chanter II, f. 128v); the dedication was still remembered in 1478 (Worcester, 1969, pp. 112–13).
Mary from the late 10th century, and also Rumon by at least the mid 12th.

Tavistock: hospital

Mary Magdalene 1341 (Orme and Webster, 1995, pp. 259–60). Mary and Theobald 1478 (ibid., p. 260).
The two references might be reconciled if that of 1341 was incorrect (hospitals were often dedicated to or popularly called after the Magdalene), or if the Mary of 1478 was the Magdalene and Theobald the secondary patron. Alternatively, the dedication may have changed.

Tavistock: parish church

Ecclesiam Sancti Eustachii 1284 (Chanter I, f. 123; dated by Finberg, 1969, p. 24); *ecclesia . . . Sancti Eustacii* 1368 (DRO, 158M/T3; Webster, 1989, p. 180); *ecclesie . . . Sancti Eustachii* 1534 (Chanter XIV, f. 74v); *Eustache* 1733 (Willis, p. 164), 1742 (Ecton, p. 166), *c*.1755 (MS Milles, ii, f. 180b), 1782 (Jones, p. 80); *Eustachius* 1846 (Oliver, p. 453), 1996 (*EDD*).
Bishop Stapledon dedicated the church on 21 May 1318 (Chanter II, f. 127). In 1740 the parish feast was said to be held on 28 August (close to St Rumon's Day) (MS Willis 41, f. 225).
Eustace (of which Eustachius is a Latin form) since at least 1284.

Tawstock

'Church of Saint *Petris* of *Tawestok*' 1503 (Canterbury Cathedral Archives, Reg. F, f. 197v); Peter 1733 (Willis, p. 156), 1742 (Ecton, p. 140), *c*.1755 (MS Milles, ii, p. 181), 1782 (Jones, p. 39), 1846 (Oliver, p. 453), 1996 (*EDD*).
The dedication festival was kept on 8 January in the fifteenth century (Orme, 1991b, p. 347). In *c*.1755 the parish feast was said to be held on Whit Sunday (MS Milles, ii, f. 181).
Peter since at least 1503. Tawestok must be Tawstock, not Tavistock, in view of the church dedication of the latter and because the will-maker in 1503 also left a bequest to the hospital at Pilton.

Tedburn St Mary

Mary 1364 (*CIPM*, xi, 470), 1413 (Pole, ii, 343 no. 3138), 1475 (*CPL*, xiii (i), 381), 1521 (Chanter XIII, f. 10v), 1733 (Willis, p. 152), 1742 (Ecton, p. 146), 1782 (Jones, p. 20), 1793 (Polwhele, ii, 59), 1846 (Oliver, p. 454), 1996 (*EDD*).

In 1742 the parish feast was variously said to be held on the Sunday after the Assumption of Mary (15 August) and the Monday fortnight after Lammas Day (1 August) (MS Willis 41, ff. 211v, 222).

Mary since at least 1364.

Teigngrace

Peter and Paul the Apostles 1410 (Chanter IX, f. 108). Unknown 1742 (Ecton, p. 155). John the Baptist 1754 (Ecton, p. 121), corrected to Mary (ibid., p. 627). Mary 1782 (Jones, p. 69). Peter and Paul 1786 (Bacon, p. 272), 1846 (Oliver, p. 454), 1996 (*EDD*).

Peter and Paul before the Reformation; they were then forgotten but were recovered in 1786.

Teignmouth: hospital

[Mary] Magdalene 1469–70 (Orme and Webster, 1995, p. 261).
Mary Magdalene, a common hospital dedication.

Templeton

Margaret (site not located, but see next entry) 1428 (Chanter XI, f. 15v), 1439 (ibid., f. 191-v), 1742 (Ecton, p. 167; source, MS Willis 41, f. 224), 1782 (Jones, p. 34), 1793 (Polwhele, ii, 381), 1846 (Oliver, p. 454), 1996 (*EDD*).

In 1740 the parish feast was said to be held on the Sunday after St Margaret's Day (20 July) (MS Willis 41, f. 224).

Margaret since at least 1428.

Tetcott

Trinity 1428 (Chanter X, f. 85v). Holy Cross 1742 (Ecton, p. 149). Unknown c.1755 (MS Milles, ii, f. 190e). Holy Cross 1782 (Jones, p. 63). All Saints and Trinity 1846 (Oliver, p. 454). Holy Cross 1996 (*EDD*).

The bishop of Waterford dedicated the church and cemetery in 1338–9 (Chanter IV, f. 220v). In 1740 the parish feast was said to be held on 3 May (Invention of the Holy Cross) (MS Willis 41, f. 225v).

Trinity before the Reformation; Holy Cross since 1742, evidently a conjecture from the parish feast day. It has persisted despite Oliver's recovery of Trinity in 1846; his reason for All Saints is not clear.

Thelbridge

Store of Mary 1534 (in what looks like a list of stores of church patron saints) (Moger, x, 3049a). David 1742 (Ecton, p. 163; source, MS Willis 41, f. 222). Michael c.1755 (MS Milles, i, f. 190a). David 1782 (Jones, p. 54), 1846 (Oliver, p. 454), 1996 (*EDD*).

In c.1755 the parish feast was said to be held held at Michaelmas (MS Milles, i, f. 190a).

Probably Mary rather than David before the Reformation; David is a rare patron saint in Devon. David nevertheless since 1742; Michael was a conjecture based on the parish feast day.

Thornbury

Peter 1491 (PROB 11/8, f. 320), 1740 (MS Willis 41, f. 230v). Paul 1740 (ibid., f. 225). Peter 1742 (Ecton, p. 149), c.1755 (MS Milles, ii, f. 193), 1782 (Jones, p. 62), 1846 (Oliver, p. 454), 1996 (*EDD*).
The bishop of Waterford dedicated the church in 1338–9 (Chanter IV, f. 220v). In 1740 the parish feast was said to be held on 5 July (MS Willis 41, f. 225), and in c.1755 on the Sunday after St Peter's Day (29 June) (MS Milles, ii, f. 193).
Peter (possibly with Paul) since at least 1491.

Thorncombe (transferred from Devon to Dorset and from Exeter to Salisbury diocese 1836)

Andrew 1329 (*CIPM*, vii, 188). Mary 1530 (PROB 11/23, f. 133), 1533 (PROB 11/25, f. 95), 1733 (Willis, p. 153), 1742 (Ecton, p. 151). Andrew c.1755 (MS Milles, ii, f. 195). Mary 1782 (Jones, p. 24), 1793 (Polwhele, ii, 287), 1846 (Oliver, p. 454).
In c.1755 the parish feast was said to be held on Easter Tuesday (MS Milles, ii, f. 195).
Probably a double dedication to Mary and Andrew before the Reformation (compare Colyton). Andrew was still remembered in about 1755, but Mary has normally been used alone since 1733.

Thorverton

Thomas Becket 1742 (Ecton, p. 142; source, MS Willis 41, f. 223v), 1782 (Jones, p. 11), 1793 (Polwhele, ii, 51), 1846 (Oliver, p. 454), 1996 (*EDD*).
In 1740 the parish feast was said to be held on the Monday after St Thomas Becket's Day (7 July) (MS Willis 41, f. 223v).
The medieval dedication has not been discovered; Thomas Becket since 1742, likely to be a conjecture from the date of the parish feast day. The church must be older than Becket's time, and other 18th-century statements that he was the patron saint of churches in Devon can often be disproved from pre-Reformation evidence.

Throwleigh

Unknown 1742 (Ecton, p. 146). Holy Ghost conjectured 1793 (Polwhele, ii, 70). Unknown 1782 (Jones, p. 21), 1846 (Oliver, p. 454). Mary 1873 (Kelly), 1939 (ibid.), 1996 (*EDD*).
In 1742 the parish feast was variously said to be held on Whit Sunday and Whit Tuesday (MS Willis 41, ff. 211, 222), and in 1793 on Whit Sunday (MS Willis 41, f. 211; Polwhele, ii, 70).
The medieval dedication has not been discovered, and it was forgotten after the Reformation. The Holy Ghost was conjectured from the date of the parish feast; Mary, on unknown grounds, since about 1873.

Thrushelton

George 1742 (Ecton, p. 165; source, MS Willis 41, f. 225v), 1782 (Jones, p. 80), 1806 (Polwhele, iii, 445), 1846 (Oliver, p. 454), 1996 (*EDD*).
In 1740 the parish feast was said to be held on 23 April (St George's Day) (MS Willis 41, f. 225v).
The medieval dedication has not been discovered; George since 1742. The date of the parish feast, out of the usual run of summer festivals, may possibly indicate that this was the original dedication.

Thurlestone

Unknown 1740 (Ecton, p. 172), *c*.1755 (MS Milles, ii, f. 199-v), 1782 (Jones, p. 86), 1846 (Oliver, p. 454), 1902 (Kelly). All Saints 1906 (Kelly), 1939 (ibid.), 1996 (*EDD*). In *c*.1755 there were fairs on Midsummer Day (24 June) and St Peter's Day (29 June or 1 August) (unless a Sunday, in which case the Monday after) (MS Milles, ii, f. 199-v). *The medieval dedication has not been discovered, and it was forgotten after the Reformation. All Saints since the early 20th century.*

Tiverton: prebendal and parish church

Peter and Paul 1447 (LPL, Reg. Stafford, f. 148), 1492 (PROB 11/10, f. 77), 1493 (ibid.), 1508 (*CPL*, xviii, 596), 1524 (PROB 11/21, f. 202v). Peter 1524 (ibid., f. 223v). Peter and Paul 1539 (PROB 11/27, f. 226v), 1542 (Moger, xvi, 5676). Peter 1546 (Worthy, 1896, p. 1; Moger, xi, 3571). Peter and Paul 1586 (DRO, Moger, xxi, 7615). Peter 1733 (Willis, p. 155), 1742 (Ecton, p. 167), 1782 (Jones, p. 34), 1793 (Polwhele, ii, 353). Peter and Paul 1846 (Oliver, p. 454). Peter 1996 (*EDD*). *Peter and Paul before the Reformation, often shortened to Peter, especially after 1742 since there is now a separate church of St Paul.*

Topsham

Margaret 1152 (Chanter 1001; Oliver, 1861, p. 9), 1194 x 1204 (ECA, D&C 2923; Barlow, 1996, no. 190), 1295 (ECA, D&C 2122), 1474 (ECA, D&C 2369), 1514 (PROB 11/17, f. 260v), 1733 (Willis, p. 151). Unknown 1742 (Ecton, p. 139), 1782 (Jones, p. 9). Margaret 1787 (Jones supplement, p. 3), 1846 (Oliver, p. 454), 1996 (*EDD*).

Fair on St Margaret's Day 1257 (*CChR 1257–1300*, p. 2). The dedication feast was changed from the Friday after Easter to 3 July in 1436 (Chanter XI, f. 128). In 1745 the parish feast was said to be held on St Margaret's Day (20 July) (MS Willis 41, ff. 243a-b). *Margaret since at least 1152.*

Torbryan

Trinity 1742 (Ecton, p. 152), *c*.1755 (MS Milles, ii, f. 203), 1782 (Jones, p. 65), 1846 (Oliver, p. 454). In *c*.1755 the parish feast was said to be held on Trinity Monday (MS Milles, ii, f. 203). *The medieval dedication has not been discovered; Trinity since 1742. The image of Mary appears on the central doors of the chancel screen (Bond and Camm, ii, 355).*

Tormohun

Petroc 1485 (PROB 11/18, f. 242); *Patroce c*.1544 (DRO, 48/13/2/3/2, p. 1); *Patroce* (or *Patrocc*) 1545 (ibid., p. 5); *Petricke* 1566 (ibid., p. 26). Unknown 1742 (Ecton, p. 152), *c*.1755 (MS Milles, ii, f. 205), 1782 (Jones, p. 67). Saviour 1846 (Oliver, p. 454), 1989 (Cherry & Pevsner, p. 851). *Petroc since at least 1485, sometimes spelt like Patrick before the Reformation. It was later forgotten and eventually replaced by the Saviour in 1846, on the mistaken assumption that the parish church had the same dedication as the nearby abbey of Torre.*

Torre: Premonstratensian abbey

Saviour c.1196 (Seymour, 1977, pp. 82, 85, 95; Dublin, MS E.5.15, ff. 4–5, 9, 10), c.1200 (Gervase, 1867, ii, 423), 1502 (*CPL*, xvii part i, 455), 1535 (*Valor*, ii, 361). In the 13th century the dedication was sometimes referred to as Holy Trinity (Seymour, 1977, pp. 85, 119, 130; Dublin, MS E.5.15, ff. 11, 25, 33, 92–3).
Saviour, also known as Holy Trinity (compare Dartmouth).

Totnes: Benedictine priory and parish church

Clerici S' Mariae 1086 (DB 17/58); Mary c.1087 (DRO, 312M/TY1), 1143 (Barlow, 1996, no. 49). Mary Magdalene c.1200 (Gervase, 1867, ii, 423). Mary 1377 (Chanter VII, f. 48v), 1432 (Chanter XI, f. 502), 1464 (Chanter XII (i), f. 26), 1484 (W.S.W., 1851, p. 308), 1493 (Harper-Bill, 1991, p. 89), 1733 (Willis, p. 164), 1742 (Ecton, p. 170), 1782 (Jones, p. 83), 1846 (Oliver, p. 454), 1996 (*EDD*).
Bishop Bronescombe dedicated the conventual church of St Mary Totnes on 17 November 1259 (Chanter I, f. 9). In 1740 the parish feast was said to be held on 1 May (MS Willis 41, f. 223).
Mary since at least 1086; Mary Magdalene, in an early list of religious houses, may have arisen from a confusion with Barnstaple Priory or with the Totnes hospital.

Totnes: hospital

Mary Magdalene 13th century, 1307 (Orme and Webster, 1995, p. 263).
Mary Magdalene, a common hospital dedication.

Totnes: Trinitarian hospital of Warland

Holy Ghost and Katherine 1271 (Orme, 1987, pp. 41–8; Orme and Webster, 1995, p. 265).
Holy Ghost and Katherine; the house was dissolved in 1509.

Townstall

Clement 1231 (Watkin, 1935, p. 279), mid 13th century (Seymour, 1977, p. 205; Dublin, MS E.5.15, f. 67), 1430 (Watkin, 1935, p. 110), 1733 (Willis, p. 164), 1742 (Ecton, p. 170), c.1755 (MS Milles, ii, f. 211), 1782 (Jones, p. 83). Mary Magdalene 1846 (Oliver, p. 454). Clement 1873 (Kelly), 1939 (ibid.), 1996 (*EDD*).
Bishop Stapledon dedicated the high altar on 14 May 1318 (Chanter II, f. 127).
Clement since at least 1231; Oliver's suggestion must therefore be mistaken.

Trentishoe

Peter 1742 (Ecton, p. 161). James conjectured c.1755 (MS Milles, ii, f. 215). Peter 1782 (Jones, p. 51), 1846 (Oliver, p. 454), 1996 (*EDD*).
In 1740 the parish feast was said to be held on the Monday before 1 August (St Peter's Day) (MS Willis 41, f. 226b), in c.1742 on the Monday after St James' Day (25 July) (MS Willis 41, f. 220), and in c.1755 on the Sunday after that day (MS Milles, ii, f. 215).
The medieval dedication has not been discovered; Peter since 1742.

Trusham

Unknown 1742 (Ecton, p. 153), 1782 (Jones, p. 28). All Saints 1846 (Oliver, p. 454). Michael 1873 (Kelly), 1939 (ibid.); Michael and All Angels 1983 (*EDD*), 1996 (ibid.)
Bishop Bronescombe dedicated the church on 21 November 1259 (Chanter I, f. 9).

The medieval dedication has not been discovered, and it was forgotten after the Reformation. All Saints in 1846, on unknown grounds; Michael since the late 19th century.

Twitchen

Peter 1742 (Ecton, p. 164), 1782 (Jones, p. 57), 1806 (Polwhele, iii, 395), 1846 (Oliver, p. 454), 1996 (*EDD*).
In 1740 the parish feast was said to be held on the first Sunday after St Peter's Day (MS Willis 41, f. 227).
The medieval dedication has not been discovered; Peter since 1742.

Uffculme

Mary 1534 (PROB 11/25, f. 227v). Peter 1733 (Willis, p. 155). Mary 1742 (Ecton, p. 167), 1782 (Jones, p. 35), 1793 (Polwhele, ii, 361), 1846 (Oliver, p. 454), 1996 (*EDD*).
Fairs on SS Peter's and Paul's Day (29 June) and St Peter ad Vincula (1 August) 1267 (*CChR 1257–1300*, p. 80). In 1740 the parish feast was said to be held on the Sunday after St Bartholomew's Day (24 August) (MS Willis 41, f. 223)
Mary since at least 1534; Peter in 1733 on the basis of the fairs.

Ugborough

Unknown 1742 (Ecton, p. 158), 1782 (Jones, p. 75), 1846 (Oliver, p 454), 1873 (Kelly), 1939 (ibid.). Peter 1983 (*EDD*), 1996 (ibid.).
Bishop Stapledon dedicated the high altar on 28 October 1311 (Chanter II, f. 65) and the church on 21 February 1323 (ibid., f. 174).
The medieval dedication has not been discovered, and it was forgotten after the Reformation. Peter in recent times.

Uplowman

Peter and Paul the Apostles 1508 (*CPL*, xviii, 600). Peter 1742 (Ecton, p. 167), 1782 (Jones, p. 35), 1793 (Polwhele, ii, 366), 1846 (Oliver, p. 454), 1996 (*EDD*).
Bishop Stapledon dedicated the church and cemetery on 13 April 1318 (Chanter II, f. 126v).
Peter and Paul before the Reformation; Peter alone since 1742.

Uplyme

Peter 1391 (Chanter VII, f. 122). Peter and Paul 1446 (*CPL*, ix, 485); Blessed Apostles Peter and Paul 1466 (PROB 11/5, f. 117v); Peter and Paul 1499 (PROB 11/11, f. 274v). Peter 1505 (PROB 11/14, f. 317). Peter and Paul 1742 (Ecton, p. 151). Unknown *c.*1755 (MS Milles, ii, f. 218). Peter and Paul 1782 (Jones, p. 24), 1793 (Polwhele, ii, 299), 1846 (Oliver, p 454). Peter 1854 (Oliver, p. 68). Peter and Paul 1996 (*EDD*).
In *c.*1755 the parish feast was said to be held on Easter Monday (MS Milles, ii, f. 218).
Peter and Paul since at least 1391, sometimes shortened to Peter alone.

Upottery

Mary *c.*1240 (ECA, D&C 3672, p. 196), 1359 (*CIPM*, x, 432), 1505 (PROB 11/14, f. 316). Unknown 1742 (Ecton, p. 145), *c.*1755 (MS Milles, ii, f. 220b). Mary 1782 (Jones, p. 18), 1793 (Polwhele, ii, 332), 1846 (Oliver, p. 454), 1996 (*EDD*).
Mary before the Reformation; it was then forgotten until it was recovered in 1782.

Upton Hellions

The high altar was dedicated in honour of the Assumption of the Virgin Mary 1409 (Chanter VIII, f. 90v). Mary 1742 (Ecton, p. 142), 1782 (Jones, p. 11). Nicholas 1787 (Jones supplement, p. 3), 1793 (Polwhele, ii, 47). Mary 1846 (Oliver, p. 454), Mary 1996 (*EDD*).

The dedication festival was changed from 7 December to 10 December in 1409 (Chanter VIII, f. 92).

Assumption of Mary from 1409 until the Reformation; Mary alone since 1742, except for a preference for Nicholas in the late 18th century.

Upton Pyne

Unknown 1742 (Ecton, p. 142), 1782 (Jones, p. 11). Mary 1846 (Oliver, p. 454), 1996 (*EDD*).

Bishop Grandisson dedicated the church and three altars on 26 September 1328 (Chanter IV, f. 69v).

The medieval dedication has not been discovered, and it was forgotten after the Reformation. Mary since 1846.

Venn Ottery

Unknown 1742 (Ecton, p. 138). Gregory 1754 (Ecton, p. 627). Unknown *c.*1755 (MS Milles, i, f. 218), 1782 (Jones, p. 6). Gregory 1846 (Oliver, p. 451), 1996 (*EDD*).

In 1410 Bishop Stafford changed the dedication feast from the feast of St Gregory the Pope (perhaps 12 March) to 10 December (Chanter VIII f. 99).

The medieval dedication has not been discovered, and it was forgotten after the Reformation. Gregory since 1754 on the basis of the dedication feast, which tells us nothing about the original patron saint.

Virginstow (transferred from Exeter to Truro diocese 1877)

Virginestowe (place) 1174 x 1183 (*PND*, i, 212). *Ecclesiam . . . Sancte Brigide virginis* 1521 (Chanter XIV, f. 9v). Mary 1742 (Ecton, p. 166; source, MS Willis 41, f. 225v); Virgin Mary *c.*1755 (MS Milles, ii, f. 217). Bridget 1763 (Ecton, p. 124), 1782 (Jones, p. 81); Bridget the Virgin 1846 (Oliver, p. 454); Bridget 1996 (TDD).

In 1740 the parish feast was said to be held on 6 February (MS Willis 41, f. 225v); in 1878 it was believed to have been formerly held on St Bridget's Day (1 February) (Boase, 1890, col. 1596).

Bridget before the Reformation; Mary in the mid 18th century, a conjecture based either on the word 'Virgin' or on the date of the parish feast (close to the Purification of Mary). Bridget was recovered in 1763.

Walkhampton

Mark 1740 (MS Willis 41, f. 225). Unknown 1742 (Ecton, p. 164), *c.*1755 (MS Milles, ii, f. 221a), 1782 (Jones, p. 77), 1846 (Oliver, p. 454), 1983 (*EDD*). Mary 1986 (*EDD*), 1996 (ibid.).

In 1740 the parish feast was said to be held on 26 April (MS Willis 41, f. 225).

The medieval dedication has not been discovered, and it was forgotten after the Reformation. Mark was evidently a conjecture from the parish feast day, and is unlikely as a medieval church dedication (but see Aylesbeare). Mary only since about 1986.

Warkleigh

John 1742 (Ecton, p. 163; source, MS Willis 41, f. 227). Giles c.1742 (MS Willis 41, f. 248a). Unknown c.1755 (MS Milles, ii, f. 223). John 1782 (Jones, p. 54), 1846 (Oliver, p. 454), 1996 (*EDD*).

The medieval dedication has not been discovered. *John usually since 1742, presumably the Baptist. The bases of this and of Giles are unclear.*

Washfield

Matthew 1740 (MS Willis 41, f. 224). Mary 1742 (Ecton, p. 167), 1782 (Jones, p. 35), 1846 (Oliver, p. 454), 1996 (*EDD*).

In 1740 the parish feast was said to be held on the Sunday after St Matthew's Day (MS Willis 41, f. 224).

The medieval dedication has not been discovered. *Mary since 1742, on unknown grounds—possibly traditional or documentary—because it is evidently not a conjecture based on the parish feast day.*

Washford Pyne

Peter 1742 (Ecton, p. 163), 1782 (Jones, p. 56), 1846 (Oliver, p. 454), 1996 (*EDD*).

In c.1742 the parish feast was said to be held on the Sunday after St Peter's Day (MS Willis 41, f. 222).

The medieval dedication has not been discovered; *Peter since 1742.*

Weare Giffard

Trinity 1472 (PRO, C 140/41 no. 39; IPM, Martin Fortescue). Unknown 1742 (Ecton, p. 148). Trinity 1754 (Ecton, p. 115), 1782 (Jones, p. 46), 1846 (Oliver, p. 454), 1996 (*EDD*).

In 1740 the parish feast was said to be held on Easter Sunday (MS Willis 41, f. 230v), and in 1742 on Easter Monday (MS Willis 41, ff. 207, 211).

Trinity usually since at least 1472.

Welcombe

Seynt Nichtons (place) 1478 (Worcester, 1969, p. 26); *capelle . . . Sancti Nectani* 1508 (Chanter XIII, f. 159); Nectan 1742 (Ecton, p. 148; source, MS Willis 41, f. 225v), c.1755 (MS Milles, ii, f. 225), 1782 (Jones, p. 47), 1846 (Oliver, p. 455), 1996 (*EDD*).

In 1508 the feast of dedication was ordered to be held on the Sunday after Michaelmas Day (29 September) (Chanter XIII, f. 159). In 1740 the parish feast was said to be held on Whit Tuesday (MS Willis 41, f. 225v), and in c.1755 on Whit Monday (MS Milles, ii, f. 225).

Nectan since at least 1478.

Wembury

Werburgh 1742 (Ecton, p. 159), 1782 (Jones, p. 75), 1846 (Oliver, p. 445), 1996 (*EDD*).

The medieval dedication has not been discovered. *Werburg of Chester in 1742, perhaps suggested by the place-name which actually has nothing to do with Werburg (PND, i, 260).*

Wembworthy

Michael 1493 (Chanter XII (ii), f. 166). Unknown 1742 (Ecton, p. 144), c.1755 (MS Milles, ii, f. 229). Michael 1763 (Ecton, p. 115), 1782 (Jones, p. 43). Unknown 1846 (Oliver, p. 455). Michael 1873 (Kelly), 1939 (ibid.), 1996 (*EDD*).

In 1740 the parish feast was said to be held on Whit Sunday (MS Willis 41, f f. 225v, 248a), and in 1742 and c.1755 on Whit Monday (ibid., f. 207; MS Milles, ii, f. 229).

Michael before the Reformation; it was then forgotten but was recovered in 1763.

Werrington—see under Cornwall

West Alvington

All Saints 1742 (Ecton, p. 171); All Saints with a query 1754 (Ecton, p. 125). Unknown c.1755 (MS Milles, i, f. 11). All Saints 1782 (Jones, p. 84), 1806 (Polwhele, iii, 475), 1846 (Oliver, p. 444), 1996 (*EDD*).

Fair on St Michael's Day 1272 (*CChR 1257–1300*, p. 181).

The medieval dedication has not been discovered; All Saints since 1742.

West Anstey

Petroc 1304 (ECA, D&C 1924). Mary 1733 (Willis, p. 158). Trinity 1742 (Ecton, p. 163; source, MS Willis 41, f. 223). Petroc 1754 (Ecton, p. 118). Unknown c.1755 (MS Milles, i, f. 16). Petroc 1782 (Jones, p. 56), 1846 (Oliver, p. 444), 1996 (*EDD*).

Bishop Stapledon dedicated the church, high altar and two others on 12 November 1319 (Chanter II, f. 145). In 1740 the parish feast was said to be held on the Sunday after Trinity Sunday (MS Willis 19, f. 223).

Petroc before the Reformation; it was then forgotten. Mary and Trinity were suggested in the 18th century, the latter evidently a conjecture from the parish feast day. Petroc was recovered in 1754.

West Buckland

Peter 1488 (Chanter XII (ii), f. 102), 1517 (PROB 11/18, f. 265). Maurice 1742 (Ecton, p. 160). Matthew c.1755 (MS Milles, i, f. 110). Peter 1763 (Ecton, p. 117), 1782 (Jones, p. 50), 1846 (Oliver, p. 446), 1996 (*EDD*).

In 1740, 1742 and c.1755 the parish feast was said to be held on St Matthew's Day (21 September) (MS Willis 41, ff. 207, 220, 227; MS Milles, i, f. 110).

Peter before the Reformation; it was then forgotten. Maurice and Matthew were conjectured from the parish feast day; Peter was recovered in 1763.

West Down

Doune Sancti Kalixti (place) 1329 (Chanter IV, f. 131v). Trinity 1742 (Ecton, p. 161). Unknown c.1755 (MS Milles, i, f. 204). Trinity 1782 (Jones, p. 52). Unknown 1846 (Oliver, p. 448). Trinity 1902 (Kelly), 1914 (ibid.). Calixtus 1923 (Kelly), 1996 (*EDD*).

In 1740 the parish feast was said to be held on the Monday after Trinity Sunday (MS Willis 41, f. 226b), and in c.1742 and c.1755 on the Monday two weeks after Whit Sunday (ibid., f. 220; MS Milles, i, f. 204).

Calixtus before the Reformation; it was then forgotten. Trinity in the late 19th century, until Calixtus was restored between about 1914 and 1923.

Westleigh

Peter 1740 (MS Willis 41, f. 226b). Unknown 1742 (Ecton, p. 141). Peter 1754 (Ecton, p. 627), c.1755 (MS Milles, ii, f. 9), 1782 (Jones, p. 40), 1846 (Oliver, p. 450). Petroc 1854 (perhaps a misunderstanding of ECA 2143, which mentions Westleigh church with no dedication and West Anstey with that of Petroc; Oliver, p. 68). Peter 1873 (Kelly), 1939 (ibid.), 1996 (*EDD*).

In c.1755 the parish feast was said to be held on Trinity Sunday (MS Milles, ii, f. 9). *The medieval dedication has not been discovered; Peter since 1740.*

West Ogwell

Unknown 1742 (Ecton, p. 154), c.1755 (MS Milles, ii, f. 80b), 1782 (Jones, p. 29), 1846 (Oliver, p. 451).

The medieval dedication has not been discovered, and it was forgotten after the Reformation.

West Putford

Unknown 1742 (Ecton, p. 149). 'Mary, I guess' c.1755 (MS Milles, ii, f. 122). Unknown 1782 (Jones, p. 63), 1846 (Oliver, p. 452), 1897 (Kelly). Stephen, with a query 1902 (Kelly); Stephen 1983 (*EDD*), 1996 (*EDD*).

In 1740 the parish feast was said to be held on the fourth Sunday after Easter (MS Willis 41, f. 230v), and in c.1755 on the first Sunday after Easter (MS Milles, ii, f. 122). *The medieval dedication has not been discovered, and it was forgotten after the Reformation. Stephen gradually during the 20th century.*

West Teignmouth

The alleged reference to James 1275 cannot be found (Hingeston-Randolph, 1889, p. 270). James 1329 (Chanter IV, f. 109), 1448 (Chanter XI, f. 514v); church of *S. Jacobi* c.1540 (Leland, 1907-10, i, 225); James 1742 (Ecton, p. 154), 1782 (Jones, p. 29), 1846 (Oliver, p. 454), 1996 (*EDD*).

James since at least 1329.

West Worlington

Store of Petroc 1534 (in what looks like a list of stores of church patron saints) (Moger, x, 3049a). Mary 1733 (Willis, p. 159); Mary the Virgin 1742 (Ecton, p. 163); Mary 1754 (Ecton, p. 118), c.1755 (MS Milles, ii, f. 245), 1752 (Jones, p. 55), 1846 (Oliver, p 455), 1996 (*EDD*).

In c.1755 the parish feast was said to be held on the Sunday after the Assumption of Mary (15 August). The same information was given for East Worlington, which certainly had a medieval dedication to Mary, and this may have influenced a conjecture of Mary for West Worlington (MS Milles, ii, f. 245).

Probably Petroc before the Reformation; Mary since 1733, perhaps influenced by East Worlington.

Whimple

Mary 1742 (Ecton, p. 139), 1782 (Jones, p. 7), 1793 (Polwhele, ii, 191), 1846 (Oliver, p. 455), 1996 (*EDD*).

In 1740 the parish feast was said to be held on 14 September (which is Holy Cross Day) (MS Willis 41, f. 223v).

The medieval dedication has not been discovered; Mary since 1742.

Whitchurch

Andrew 1304 (*CPL*, v, 426), 1351 (Chanter IV, f. 173v). Michael 1742 (Ecton, p. 165; source, MS Willis 41, f. 225). Andrew 1754 (Ecton, p. 124). Michael *c.*1755 (MS Milles, ii, f. 232). Andrew 1782 (Jones, p. 77), 1846 (Oliver, p. 455), 1996 (*EDD*).

In 1740 the parish feast was said to be held on 29 September (Michaelmas Day) (MS Willis 41, f. 225).

Andrew before the Reformation; Michael in the mid 18th century, evidently a conjecture from the parish feast day. Andrew was recovered in 1754.

Whitestone

Unknown 1742 (Ecton, p. 146). 'The ancient people of this parish do all agree that the church is dedicated to St Catherine, virgin and martyr' 1742 (MS Willis 41, f. 212); Catharine 1754 (Ecton, p. 110); Katharine 1782 (Jones, p. 21); Catharine 1793 (Polwhele, ii, 57); Catharine, virgin martyr 1846 (Oliver, p. 455); Catherine 1996 (*EDD*).

In 1742 no parish feast was said to be held (MS Willis 41, f. 212).

The medieval dedication has not been discovered, and it was forgotten after the Reformation. Katherine may well be the original dedication in view of the alleged popular tradition and because it was not a conjecture from a feast day, but it would be an unusual church dedication in Devon.

Widecombe in the Moor

Henry *persona Sancti Pancrasii c.*1223 probably relates to this church (Hingeston-Randolph, 1894–9, iii, 1599); Pancras 1283 (ECA, D&C 3672, p. 244; Oliver, 1861, pp. 425, 427); store of Pancras 1531 (Moger, xviii, 6598). John the Baptist 1742 (Ecton, p. 155). Pancras 1754 (Ecton, p. 122), 1782 (Jones, p. 69), 1846 (Oliver, p. 445), 1996 (*EDD*).

Pancras before the Reformation; it was then forgotten. John the Baptist in 1742; Pancras was recovered in 1754.

Widworthy

Ecclesia Sancti Cuthberti de Wodworth 1504 (PROB 11/14, f. 174); Cuthbert 1742 (Ecton, p. 151), *c.*1755 (MS Milles, ii, f. 234), 1782 (Jones, p. 25), 1793 (Polwhele, ii, 319), 1846 (Oliver, p. 455), 1996 (*EDD*).

In *c.*1755 the parish feast—in Offwell or Widworthy, it is not clear which—was kept on the second Monday in September (MS Milles, ii, f. 234).

The reference of 1504 occurs in the brief will of John Hillary, which contains no evidence of locality except for a small bequest to Exeter Cathedral. This suggests a Devon context, and although Widworthy is never recorded being spelt as Wodworth, *no better identification can be suggested and the spelling may be a mistake. Cuthbert can therefore be provisionally proposed as the pre-Reformation patron, pending adverse evidence. The reference of 1742 was based on that of 1504 so that it does not represent an independent tradition, but it has been accepted ever since.*

Willand

Mary 1499 (PROB 11/12, f. 33), 1503 (*CPL*, xvii part i, 539), 1547 (Moger, iv, 1201), 1549 (ibid., i, 133; iii, 840), 1742 (Ecton, p. 168), 1782 (Jones, p. 37), 1793 (Polwhele, ii, 360), 1846 (Oliver, p. 455), 1996 (*EDD*).

In 1740 the parish feast was said to be held on the Sunday after the Nativity of Mary (8 September) (MS Willis 41, f. 223).
Mary since at least 1499.

Winkleigh

All Saints 1453 (PROB 11/4, f. 20), 1524 (PROB 11/23, f. 125). Thomas Becket 1740 (MS Willis 41, f. 225v). All Saints 1742 (Ecton, p. 169), 1782 (Jones, p. 59), 1846 (Oliver, p. 455), 1996 (*EDD*).
Bishop Grandisson dedicated the high altar on 17 November 1333 (Chanter IV, f. 172v). In 1740 the parish feast was said to be held on 13 July (MS Willis 41, f. 225v).
All Saints since at least 1453, Thomas Becket being a mistaken conjecture from the feast day.

Witheridge

Store of George 1534 (in what looks like a list of stores of church patron saints) (Moger, x, 3049a). John the Baptist 1742 (Ecton, p. 163; source, MS Willis 41, f. 222). George *c.*1755 (MS Milles, ii, f. 239). John the Baptist 1782 (Jones, p. 55), 1846 (Oliver, p. 455), 1996 (*EDD*).
Fair on St John Baptist's Day 1248 (*CChR 1225–57*, p. 336). The dedication feast was changed from 4 March to 16 July in 1404 (Chanter VIII, f. 73). In *c.*1755 the parish feast was said to have been formerly held on the Sunday after St George's Day (MS Milles, ii, f. 239).
Probably George before the Reformation, still faintly remembered in about 1755. John the Baptist usually since 1742, however, on the basis of the fair.

Withycombe Raleigh

John the Baptist 1414 (*CPL*, vi, 508), 1487 (Harper-Bill, 1991, p. 87; Brooking-Rowe, 1901, p. 173), 1547 (Moger, viii, 2420; xxii, 7950), 1549 (ibid., xx, 7079). Unknown 1742 (Ecton, p. 139). John the Baptist 1745 (MS Willis 41, ff. 243a-b). Unknown *c.*1755 (MS Milles, ii, f. 236), 1782 (Jones, p. 9). John the Baptist 1792 (Polwhele, ii,, 213). Michael 1846 (Oliver, p. 455). John 1996 (*EDD*).
In 1745 the parish feast was said formerly to have been held on 24 June, but to have been discontinued (MS Willis 41, ff. 243a-b). In *c.*1755 the parish procession was said to be held on Ascension Day (MS Milles, ii, f. 236).
John the Baptist since at least 1414, although this was not always remembered during the 18th century. Oliver's Michael must be an error.

Wolborough

Mary 1494 (PROB 11/10, f. 122), 1526 (PROB 11/22, f. 84v), 1538 (new style) (Oliver, 1840, ii, 201), 1742 (Ecton, p. 152), 1782 (Jones, p. 66). James 1786 (Bacon, p. 267). Mary 1846 (Oliver, p. 455), 1996 (*EDD*).
Mary since at least 1494, except for the suggestion of James in 1786.

Woodbury

Swithin 1534 (PROB 11/25, f. 50), 1733 (Willis, p. 230), 1742 (Ecton, p. 139), *c.*1755 (MS Milles, ii, f. 240b), 1782 (Jones, p. 9), 1846 (Oliver, p. 455), 1996 (*EDD*).
Fair on St Swithin's Day 1286 (*CChR 1257–1300*, p. 328). In 1745 the parish feast was said to be held on St Swithin's Day (2 or 15 July) (MS Willis 41, ff. 243a-b).
Swithin, probably since at least 1286, certainly since at least 1534.

Woodland

John the Baptist 1527 (DRO, 2660 A/PW 1, pp. 49–7), 1539 (Chanter XV, f. 81v), 1550 (DRO, Woodland, PW 1, p. 13). Unknown 1742 (Ecton, p. 152), 1782 (Jones, pp. 66–7). John the Baptist 1846 (Oliver, p. 445), 1996 (*EDD*).

John the Baptist before the Reformation; it was then forgotten until it was recovered in 1846.

Woodleigh

Mary 1742 (Ecton, p. 172; source, MS Willis 41, f. 223). Unknown *c.*1755 (MS Milles, ii, f. 241). Mary 1782 (Jones, p. 86), 1846 (Oliver, p. 455), 1996 (*EDD*).

The medieval dedication has not been discovered; Mary since 1742.

Woolfardisworthy East

Trinity 1742 (Ecton, p. 163), 1782 (Jones, p. 55), 1846 (Oliver, p. 455), 1902 (Kelly). Mary 1906 (Kelly), 1939 (ibid.), 1996 (*EDD*).

Bishop Bronescombe dedicated the church on 28 July 1261 (Chanter I, f. 20). No parish feast was said to be held in *c.*1742 (MS Willis 41, f. 222).

The medieval dedication has not been discovered. Trinity from 1742 until 1902, Mary since about 1906. She may have been suggested by the will of John Ufflete (1416), requesting burial in the chapel of St Mary Woolfardisworthy (DRO, 1926B/W/W20c). As Woolfardisworthy was a church not a chapel in 1416, this is more likely to refer to a chapel in the parish (or Lady chapel in the church) than to the church itself.

Woolfardisworthy West

Trinity 1740 (MS Willis 41, f. 230v). Unknown 1742 (Ecton, p. 148), 1782 (Jones, p. 47), 1846 (Oliver, p. 455). 'Dedicated to All Hallows' 1854 (Oliver, p. 68). Trinity 1873 (Kelly), 1919 (ibid.). All Hallows 1923 (Kelly), 1939 (ibid.). Trinity 1983 (*EDD*), 1996 (ibid.).

The medieval dedication has not been discovered for certain, and appears to have been forgotten after the Reformation. Trinity occurs in Willis' notes, but not in Ecton to which he contributed. Oliver's reference of 1854 is simply to Woolfardisworthy, without stating which of the two, but presumably meant West because in his eyes East already had a dedication. It could be based on a pre-Reformation source such as a will, All Saints being a common medieval dedication, unless it is a mistake for nearby Clovelly. Since 1873, Trinity and All Saints have alternated, at least in directories; confusion with Woolfardisworthy East may have been a factor here.

Woolford

The church is mentioned in 1206 (Oliver, 1846, p. 396), but was later united with Dunkeswell; no dedication is known.

Yarcombe

John the Baptist 1497 (*CPL*, xvi, 423), 1505 (*CPL*, xviii, 346). Peter 1742 (Ecton, p. 145). John the Baptist 1754 (Ecton, p. 109), 1782 (Jones, p. 18). Peter 1787 (Jones supplement, p. 3), 1793 (Polwhele, ii, 332). John the Baptist 1846 (Oliver, p. 445), 1996 (*EDD*).

Bishop Stapledon dedicated the high altar on 17 October 1311 (Chanter II, f. 64).

John the Baptist before the Reformation; it was then forgotten. Peter was conjectured in 1742 and accepted for some time, despite the recovery of John the Baptist in 1754.

Yarnscombe

Andrew 1412 (Chanter IX, f. 141v), 1532 (Oliver, 1846, p. 308; 1854, p. 38, where Christow should read Yarnscombe; Murray, xxiii, Richard Newcombe). Thomas Becket 1742 (Ecton, p. 141). Andrew 1754 (Ecton, p. 627), c.1755 (MS Milles, ii, f. 247), 1782 (Jones, p. 41), 1846 (Oliver, p. 455), 1996 (*EDD*).

In 1740 the parish feast was said to be held on the third Sunday after 24 June (MS Willis 41, f. 230v), in 1742 on the Monday after 7 July (ibid., f. 207), and in c.1755 on 21 July (MS Milles, ii, f. 247).

Andrew usually since at least 1412. Thomas Becket was probably a conjecture from the parish feast day.

Yealmpton

Bartholomew 1421 x 1432 (Chanter X, f. 22v); store of St Bartholomew 1521 (PROB 11/20, f. 152v). Unknown 1742 (Ecton, p. 158). Bartholomew 1763 (Ecton, p. 123), 1782 (Jones, p. 74), 1846 (Oliver, p. 455), 1996 (*EDD*).

Bartholomew before the Reformation; it was then forgotten but was recovered in 1763.

Zeal Monachorum

Peter 1430 (Chanter X, f. 95v), 1742 (Ecton, p. 144; source, MS Willis 41, f. 222). Peter and Paul c.1755 (MS Milles, ii, f. 249). Peter 1782 (Jones, p. 43), 1846 (Oliver, p. 455), 1996 (*EDD*).

Fair on St Calixtus' Day 1299 (*CChR 1257–1300*, p. 479). In c.1742 the parish feast was said to be held on St Peter's Day (MS Willis 41, f. 222), and in c.1755 on the Sunday after SS Peter's and Paul's Day (29 June) (MS Milles, ii, f. 249).

Peter, possibly with Paul, before the Reformation, but only Peter has normally been in use since 1742.

BIBLIOGRAPHY

1 UNPRINTED SOURCES

Aberystwyth, National Library of Wales

    MS NLW 22253A (Missal from Cornwall)

Barnstaple, North Devon Record Office

    Iddesleigh, PW 1 (Churchwardens' accounts)
    50/11/1/4–5 (Chichester of Arlington)

Cambridge, King's College

    MS SMM/2 (St Michael's Mount)

Canterbury, Cathedral Archives

    Sede Vacante Wills, Register F

Dublin, Trinity College

    MS E.5.15 (Torre Abbey cartulary)

Exeter, Cathedral Archives

    D&C 472 (Heavitree)
    D&C 600 (Altarnun)
    D&C 667 (Buckerel)
    D&C 813 (Colyton and Monkton)
    D&C 818 (Colyton)
    D&C 821 (Colyton)
    D&C 995 (Veryan)
    D&C 1012 (Harberton)
    D&C 1021 (Harberton)
    D&C 1148 (Exmouth)
    D&C 1381 (Breage)
    D&C 1397 (Gerrans)
    D&C 1408 (St Marychurch)
    D&C 1502 (St Winnow)

D&C 1805 (Bishop's Tawton)
D&C 1924 (West Anstey)
D&C 2036 (Bampton)
D&C 2080 (Exeter Cathedral's churches, Devon and Cornwall)
D&C 2111 (St Cuthbert, Exeter)
D&C 2125 (Bodmin Priory's churches in Cornwall)
D&C 2143 (Westleigh and West Anstey)
D&C 2369 (Will of William Langlegh)
D&C 2379 (Will of John Baryn)
D&C 2513 (Peter of Palerna's grant to Exeter churches)
D&C 2885 (Kingskerswell)
D&C 2923 (Henry Marshal's list of Exeter churches)
D&C 3625 (Statutes)
D&C 3672 (General cartulary)
Drake-Brockman papers

Exeter, Devon Record Office

48/13/2/3/2 (Cockington wills)
96M/Box 93/17 (Lease of Dotton)
123M (Petre deeds)
158 M/T3, T6, T7 (Damarel charters)
215M (Kingsbridge feoffees' deeds)
269A/PW1–7 (Modbury churchwardens' accounts)
312M (Hole deeds)
314M (Luxmoore deeds)
1148M (Acland deeds)
1508M (Courtenay of Powderham deeds)
2660 A/PW 1 (Woodland Churchwardens' Accounts)
3248A (Okehampton borough deeds)
Ashton parish registers (microfilms), PR 1/1
Bedford (Russell) deeds, W 1258/G6/46
Chanter I (Episcopal registers of Walter Bronescombe and Peter Quinil)
    (For printed editions, see Hingeston-Randolph, Robinson, below)
Chanter II (Episcopal register of Walter Stapledon)
    (For a printed edition, see Hingeston-Randolph, below)
Chanter III (Episcopal register of John Grandisson, vol. i)
    (For a printed edition, see Hingeston-Randolph, below)
Chanter IV (Episcopal register of John Grandisson, vol. ii)
    (For a printed edition, see Hingeston-Randolph, below)
Chanter V (Episcopal register of John Grandisson, vol. iii)
    (For a printed edition, see Hingeston-Randolph, below)
Chanter VI (Episcopal register of Thomas Brantingham, vol i)
    (For a printed edition, see Hingeston-Randolph, below)
Chanter VII (Episcopal register of Thomas Brantingham, vol. ii)
    (For a printed edition, see Hingeston-Randolph, below)
Chanter VIII (Episcopal register of Edmund Stafford, vol. i)
    (For a printed edition, see Hingeston-Randolph, below)
Chanter IX (Episcopal register of Edmund Stafford, vol. ii)
    (For a printed edition, see Hingeston-Randolph, below)

Chanter X (Episcopal register of Edmund Lacy, vol. i)
  (For a printed edition, see Hingeston-Randolph, below)
Chanter XI (Episcopal register of Edmund Lacy, vol. ii)
  (For a printed edition, see Dunstan below)
Chanter XII (i) (Episcopal register of George Neville)
Chanter XII (ii) (Episcopal registers, 1465–1504)
Chanter XIII (Episcopal register of Hugh Oldham)
Chanter XIV (Episcopal register of John Veysey, vol. i)
Chanter XV (Episcopal register of John Veysey, vol. ii)
Chanter 1001 (Bull of Eugenius III, 1153)
Chanter 1063–4 (Documents of St Agnes, Cornwall)
Chanter 855A (Consistory court depositions)
Chanter, J.F. A Register of Institutions . . . Sede Vacante (1924)
Courtenay of Powderham Cartulary
Enrolled Deeds, QS 47
Exeter City Archives, Book 53A (Cartulary of St John's Hospital)
Exeter City Archives, Deeds, 31,931
Exeter City Archives, Mayor's Court Rolls
Exeter City Archives, Miscellaneous Rolls, 4
Exeter City Archives, St Mary Arches, 332A/PF 2 add.
Exeter City Deeds, Awliscombe: ED/AWL/62
Exeter City Deeds, Plympton: ED/PP/8–9
Exeter City Library, Calendar of Deeds and Documents
Kelly Deeds, Catalogue of
Moger, Olive. 'Copies of Transcripts from Wills and other Records' (collected
  c.1921–41), 21 vols
Oliver, George. Précis of Leases etc. . . . from Powderham Castle, vol. i

Exeter, Devon and Cornwall Record Society Library (in Exeter, West Country Studies
Library)

Transcripts of Inquisitions Post Mortem
Transcript of Parish Registers and Churchwardens' Accounts of South Tawton
Transcript of Sir William Pole's Extracts from Deeds, Charters and Grants relating
  to Devon and Somerset, c.1616, 3 vols

Exeter, West Country Studies Library

Moger, Olive. 'Copies of Transcripts from Wills and other Records' (collected
  c.1921–41), 21 vols
Murray, Sir Oswyn. 'Transcripts of Wills', 41 vols

Forde Abbey, Somerset

Cartulary of Forde Abbey

Lanhydrock House, Cornwall

FS 2/32/1/42 (Lanhydrock Atlas)

London, British Library

Additional MS 5,665 (Musical anthology)
Additional MS 29,762 (William Hals, History of Cornwall)
Cotton MS Cleopatra A.vii (Cartulary of Tewkesbury Abbey)
Cotton MS Cleopatra C.vii (Register of Merton Priory)
Cotton MS Vitellius D.ix (Cartulary of St Nicholas Priory, Exeter)
Harley MS 3300 (Formulary from Exeter diocese)

London, Lambeth Palace Library

The Register of Walter Reynolds
The Register of William Courtenay
The Register of Thomas Arundel, 2 vols
The Register of John Stafford
The Register of John Kempe
The Register of John Morton, 2 vols
The Register of William Warham, 2 vols

London, Guildhall Library

MSS 9171/1–10 (Commissary Court wills)

London, Public Record Office

C 1 (Early Chancery proceedings)
C 53 (Charter rolls)
C 132–142 (Inquisitions post mortem)
C 143 (Inquisitions ad quod damnum)
CP 25 (Feet of fines)
E 179 (Exchequer, K.R., Subsidy rolls)
JUST 1 (Assize rolls)
PROB 10 (Individual wills)
PROB 11 (Registers of wills proved in the Prerogative Court of Canterbury)
SC 2 (Court Rolls)

Oxford, Bodleian Library

MS Bodley 572 (Miscellany, with mass of St German)
MS James 23 (Notes of charters of Plympton Priory)
MS Top. Devon b.1–2 (Questions sent by Jeremiah Milles, precentor of Exeter
    Cathedral, to incumbents of Devon parishes in c.1755, 2 vols)
MS Top. Devon d.5 (Cartulary of Newenham Abbey)
MS Top. Gen. c.2 (John Leland, Collectanea)
MS Willis 25, 41, 64, 80 (Browne Willis's collections, church dedications and parish
    feasts, Cornwall and Devon)

Truro, Cornwall County Record Office
AR 1/108 (Arundell charter)
AR 1/248 (Arundell charter)

AR 24/21 (Will of Gilbert Begett)
AR 50/1 (Lamford charter)
DDP 7/5/1 (A&B) (Antony parish, transcript of churchwardens' accounts; originals
    lost)
DDP 167/5/1 (North Petherwin parish, churchwardens' accounts)
DDP 322/1–3 (Camborne parish, churchwardens' accounts)
ME 595–6 (Bodrigan Cartulary and Charles Henderson's transcript)

Truro, Royal Institution of Cornwall, Courtney Library

HC 66 (Charles Henderson, transcripts of Cornish wills)
Charles Henderson, East Cornwall Book (1924)
Charles Henderson, Ecclesiastical Antiquities

2 PRINTED SOURCES

(a) Primary Sources Cited in the Gazetteer

Asser. *Asser's Life of King Alfred*, ed. Stevenson, W.H., new ed. (Oxford, 1959).

Bacon, John. *Liber Regis vel Thesaurus Rerum Ecclesiasticarum* (London, 1786).

Barlow, Frank. (ed.) *English Episcopal Acta*, xi: *Exeter 1046–1184* (London, 1996).
    This contains documents nos 1–142a.

Barlow, Frank. (ed.) *English Episcopal Acta*, xii: *Exeter 1186–1257* (London, 1996).
    This contains documents nos 143–327.

Bates, E.H. (ed.) *Two Cartularies of the Benedictine Abbeys of Muchelney and Athelney*,
    Somerset Record Society, xiv (1899).

Bearman, Robert. (ed.) *Charters of the Redvers Family and the Earldom of Devon
    1090–1217*, Devon and Cornwall Record Society, new series, xxxvii (1994).

Binnall, P.B.G. 'Holy Wells in Devonshire', *Devon & Cornwall Notes & Queries*, xxi
    (1940–1), pp. 121–6.

Binney, J. Erskine. (ed.) *The Accounts of the Wardens of the Parish of Morebath, Devon,
    1520–1573* (Exeter, Devon Notes & Queries, 1904).

Birch, Walter de Gray. *Cartularium Saxonicum*, 3 vols (London, 1885–93).

Blake, D.W. 'An Original Bull of Pope Eugenius III, 7th February, 1146', *Devon &
    Cornwall Notes & Queries*, xxxiv part viii (1981), pp. 307–11.

Boase, G.C. *Collectanea Cornubiensia: A Collection of Biographical and Topographical
    Notes Relating to the County of Cornwall* (Truro, 1890).

Bond, Frederick Bligh, and Camm, Bede. *Roodscreens and Roodlofts*, 2 vols (London,
    1909).

Book of Fees, The, 3 vols (London, Public Record Office, 1923).

Bracken, C.W. *A History of Plymouth and her Neighbours* (Plymouth, 1931).

Brooking-Rowe, J. 'Tenth Report of the Committee on Devonshire Records',
    Devonshire Association Transactions, xxxiii (1901), pp. 139–86.

Budgen, W., and Salzman, L.F. (edd.) *The Wiltshire, Devonshire and Dorsetshire Portion
    of the Lewes Cartulary*, Sussex Record Society (1943).

Calendar of Various Chancery Rolls, A.D. 1277–1326 (London, Public Record Office,
    1912).

Calendar of Fine Rolls, 22 vols (London, Public Record Office, 1911–63).

Calendar of Inquisitions Miscellaneous, in progress (London, Public Record Office, 1916-).

Calendar of Inquisitions Post Mortem, in progress (London, Public Record Office, 1904-).

Calendar of Inquisitions Post Mortem, Henry VII, 3 vols (London, Public Record Office, 1898–1956).

Calendar of Letters and Papers, Foreign and Domestic, Henry VIII, 21 vols and addenda (London, 1864–1932).

Calendar of the Manuscripts of the Dean and Chapter of Wells, vol i (London, Historical Manuscripts Commission, 1907).

Calendar of Papal Letters, in progress (London, Public Record Office, and Dublin, Irish Historical Manuscripts Commission, 1894-).

Calendar of Patent Rolls, in progress (London, Public Record Office, 1891-).

Calendarium Rotulorum Chartarum (London, Record Commission, 1803).

Catalogue of Ancient Deeds, 6 vols (London, Public Record Office, 1890–1915).

Chanter, J.F. *A Register of Institutions . . . relating to the Diocese of Exeter . . . "Sede Vacante".* Typescript, 1924; copies in Exeter, Devon Record Office, and Exeter, Devon and Cornwall Record Society Library.

Cherry, Bridget, and Pevsner, Nikolaus. *Devon,* The Buildings of England, 2nd ed. (London, 1989).

Close Rolls, 14 vols (London, Public Record Office, 1902–38).

Cresswell, Beatrix F. *Notes on the Churches of the Deanery of Kenn* (Exeter, 1912).

Cresswell, Beatrix F. *Beaford Folk and their Neighbours* (No place, 1927).

Crockford's Clerical Dictionary (London, 1860, in progress).

Curia Regis Rolls, in progress (London, Public Record Office, 1923-).

Davidson, J.B. 'On Some Ancient Documents Relating to Crediton Minster', *Devonshire Association Transactions,* x (1878), pp. 236–54.

Davidson, J.B. 'On Some Anglo-Saxon Charters at Exeter', *Journal of the British Archaeological Association,* xxxix (1883), pp. 259–303.

Doble, G.H. (ed.) *Pontificale Lanaletense,* Henry Bradshaw Society, lxxiv (1936).

Domesday Book, vol. ix: *Devon,* ed. Thorn, Caroline and Frank, 2 vols (Chichester, 1985).

Domesday Book, vol. x: *Cornwall,* ed. Thorn, Caroline and Frank (Chichester, 1979).

Domesday-Book: Additamenta (London, Record Commission, 1816). The Exeter Domesday text.

Dugdale, William. *Monasticon Anglicanum,* ed. Caley, J., Ellis, H., and Bandinel, B., 6 vols in 8 (London, 1817–30).

Earle, J. *A Hand-Book of the Land Charters, and other Saxonic Documents* (Oxford, 1888).

Ecton, John. *Liber Valorum et Decimarum* (London, 1711).

Ecton, John. *Liber Valorum et Decimarum,* 2nd ed. (London 1723).

Ecton, John. *Liber Valorum et Decimarum,* 3rd ed. (London, 1728).

Ecton, John. *Thesaurus Rerum Ecclesiasticarum* (London, 1742).

Ecton, John. *Thesaurus Rerum Ecclesiasticarum,* 2nd ed. (London, 1754).

Ecton, John. *Thesaurus Rerum Ecclesiasticarum,* 3rd ed. (London, 1763).

Ekwall, Eilert. *The Concise Oxford Dictionary of Place-Names,* 4th ed. (Oxford, 1960).

Ewert, A. (ed.) *The Romance of Tristran by Beroul,* 2 vols (Oxford, 1939–70).

Exeter Diocesan Directory (Exeter, 1996).

Fawtier, R. (ed.) *La Vie de Saint Samson* (Paris, 1912).

Finberg, H.P.R. 'Some Early Tavistock Charters', *English Historical Review,* lxii (1947), pp. 352–77.

Finberg, H.P.R. 'Church Dedications in Devon', *Devon & Cornwall Notes & Queries,* xxiv (1950–1), pp. 225–6.

Finberg, H.P.R. *The Early Charters of Devon and Cornwall*, 2nd ed. (Leicester, 1963).

Finberg, H.P.R. *Tavistock Abbey: a Study in the Social and Economic History of Devon*, 2nd ed. (Newton Abbot, 1969).

Gervase of Canterbury. *The Historical Works of Gervase of Canterbury*, ed. Stubbs, W., 2 vols (London, Rolls Series, 1867).

Glasscock, Robin E. (ed.) *The Lay Subsidy of 1334* (London, British Academy, Records of Social and Economic History, new series, ii, 1975).

Gover, J.E.B., Mawer, A., and Stenton, F.M. *The Place-Names of Devon*, 2 vols, Cambridge, English Place-Name Society, vols viii-ix (1931–2)

[Grimaldi, E.C.] *Some Notes on the History of Otterton* (No place, 1928).

Grosjean, P. 'Vie de S. Rumon, Vie . . . de S. Nectan', *Analecta Bollandiana*, lxxi (1953), pp. 359–414).

Grosjean, P. 'Vies et Miracles de S. Petroc', *Analecta Bollandiana*, lxxiv (1956), pp. 131–88.

Hanham, Alison. (ed.) *Churchwardens' Accounts of Ashburton, 1479–1580*, Devon and Cornwall Record Society, new series, xv (1970).

Harper-Bill, C. (ed.) *The Register of John Morton, Archbishop of Canterbury, 1486–1500*, vol. ii, Canterbury and York Society, lxxv (1991).

Henderson, Charles. 'The Dedication of Landulph Church', *Truro Diocesan Gazette* (June, 1929).

Henderson, Charles. 'Holy Trinity Chapel at St Day', *Devon & Cornwall Notes & Queries*, xvii (1932–3), pp. 349–53.

Henderson, Charles. 'The Ecclesiastical History of the 109 Parishes of West Cornwall', *Journal of the Royal Institution of Cornwall*, new series, ii (1953–6), pp. 1–210; iii (1957–60), pp. 211–382, 383–497.

Hingeston-Randolph, F.C. (ed.) *The Register of Edmund Stafford* (London and Exeter, 1886)

Hingeston-Randolph, F.C. (ed.) *The Registers of Walter Bronescombe and Peter Quivil, Bishops of Exeter* (London and Exeter, 1889)

Hingeston-Randolph, F.C. (ed.) *The Register of Walter de Stapeldon, Bishop of Exeter* (London and Exeter, 1892)

Hingeston-Randolph, F.C. (ed.) *The Register of John de Grandisson, Bishop of Exeter*, 3 vols (London and Exeter, 1894–9)

Hingeston-Randolph, F.C. (ed.) *The Register of Thomas de Brantyngham, Bishop of Exeter*, 2 vols (London and Exeter, 1901–6)

Hingeston-Randolph, F.C. (ed.) *The Register of Edmund Lacy, Bishop of Exeter*, 2 vols (London and Exeter, 1909–15). The second volume is now superseded by the edition of Dunstan, G.R., above.

Holmes, T. Scott, and Weaver, F.W. (edd.) *Two Cartularies of . . . Bruton and . . . Montacute*, Somerset Record Society, viii (1894).

Hooke, Della. *Pre-Conquest Charter-Bounds of Devon and Cornwall* (Woodbridge, 1994).

Hutchins, J. *The History and Antiquities of the County of Dorset*, 2 vols (London, 1774).

Hull, P.L. (ed.) *The Cartulary of St Michael's Mount*, Devon and Cornwall Record Society, new series, v (1962).

Hull, P.L. (ed.) *The Cartulary of Launceston Priory*, Devon and Cornwall Record Society, new series, xxx (1987).

Inquisitions and Assessments relating to Feudal Aids, 6 vols (London, Public Record Office, 1899–1920).

Jacob, E.F. (ed.) *The Register of Henry Chichele, Archbishop of Canterbury 1414–1443*, 4 vols (Oxford, 1938–47).

[Jones, W.] *Thesaurus Ecclesiasticus Provincialis; or, A Survey of the Diocese of Exeter* (Exeter, 1782); with *Supplement* (Exeter, 1787).

Kelly's Directory of Cornwall (London, 1856–1939)

Kelly's Directory of Devonshire (London, 1873–1939)

Kemble, J.M. (ed.) *Codex Diplomaticus Aevi Saxonici*, 6 vols (London, 1839–48).

Liebermann, F. (ed.) *Die Heiligen Englands; angelsÑchsisch und lateinisch* (Hannover, 1889).

Leland, John. *The Itinerary of John Leland*, ed. Smith, Lucy Toulmin, 5 vols (London, 1907–10).

Lewis, Samuel. *A Topographical Dictionary of England*, 4 vols (London, 1831).

Little, A.G., and Easterling, R.C. *The Franciscans and Dominicans of Exeter*, (Exeter, History of Exeter Research Group, Monograph iii, 1927).

London, Vera C.M. (ed.) *The Cartulary of Canonsleigh Abbey: A Calendar*, Devon and Cornwall Record Society, new series, viii (1965).

Luard, H.R. (ed.) *Annales Monastici*, vol. i (London, Rolls Series, 1864).

Lysons, D. and S. *Topographical and Historical Account of the County of Cornwall*, Magna Britannia, vol. iii (London, 1814).

Moulton, H.R. *Palaeography, Genealogy and Topography . . . Selections from the Collection of H.R. Moulton* (London, [1929]).

Nonarum Inquisitiones (London, Record Commission, 1807).

Oliver, George. 'Wills from the Families of Denys, Chamond, and Arundell', *Collectanea Topographica et Genealogica*, iv (1837), pp. 169–177.

Oliver, George. *Ecclesiastical Antiquities in Devon*, vols i-ii (Exeter, 1840).

Oliver, George. *Ecclesiastical Antiquities in Devon*, vol. iii (Exeter and London, 1842).

Oliver, George. *Monasticon Dioecesis Exoniensis*, with supplement (Exeter and London, 1846).

Oliver, George. *Additional Supplement to the Monasticon Dioecesis Exoniensis* (Exeter, 1854).

Oliver, George. *Lives of the Bishops of Exeter and a History of the Cathedral* (Exeter, 1861).

Olson, B. Lynette, and Padel, O.J. 'A Tenth-Century List of Cornish Parochial Saints', *Cambridge Medieval Celtic Studies*, xii (1986), pp. 33–71.

Orme, Nicholas. 'Warland Hospital, Totnes and the Trinitarian Friars in Devon', *Devon & Cornwall Notes & Queries*, xxxvi part ii (1987), pp. 41–8.

Orme, Nicholas. 'A Letter of Saint Roche', *Devon & Cornwall Notes & Queries*, xxxvi part v (1989), pp. 153–9.

Orme, Nicholas. 'The Charnel Chapel of Exeter Cathedral', *Medieval Art and Architecture at Exeter Cathedral*, ed. Kelly, Francis (London, 1991a), pp. 162–171.

Orme, Nicholas. 'Two Early Prayer-Books from North Devon', *Devon & Cornwall Notes & Queries*, xxxvi (1991b), pp. 345–50.

Orme, Nicholas. 'Denis not Disen: the real Patron Saint of Bradninch, Devon', *Devon & Cornwall Notes & Queries*, xxxvii part ii (1992a), pp. 45–7.

Orme, Nicholas. 'Saint Conet: a Cornish Saint', *Devon & Cornwall Notes & Queries*, xxxvii part ii (1992b), pp. 55–8.

Orme, Nicholas. (ed.) *Nicholas Roscarrock's Lives of the Saints: Cornwall and Devon*, Devon and Cornwall Record Society, new series, xxxv (1992c).

Orme, Nicholas. 'Two Unusual Devon Saints', *The Devon Historian*, li (October, 1995a), pp. 10–13.

Orme, Nicholas. 'Church Dedications in North Devon', *Devon & Cornwall Notes & Queries*, xxxvii part viii (1995b), pp. 249–50.

Orme, Nicholas, and Padel, Oliver. 'The Medieval Leper-house at 'Lamford', Cornwall', *Historical Research*, lxviii (1995), pp. 102–7.

Orme, Nicholas, and Webster, Margaret. *The English Hospital 1070–1570* (New Haven and London, 1995).

Osborne, F.M. *The Church Wardens' Accounts of St. Michael's Church, Chagford 1480–1660* (Chagford, 1979).

Padel, O.J. 'Cornish Names of Parish Churches', *Cornish Studies*, iv/v (1976–7), pp. 15–17.

Padel, O.J. 'Two New Pre-Conquest Charters for Cornwall', *Cornish Studies*, vi (1978), pp. 20–7.

Padel, O.J. *Cornish Place-Name Elements*, English Place-Name Society, lvi/lvii (1985).

Padel, O.J. *A Popular Dictionary of Cornish Place-Names* (Penzance, 1988).

Picken, W.M.M. 'The Patron Saints of Poundstock and Helland Churches', *Devon & Cornwall Notes & Queries*, xxiii (1947–9), pp. 342–3.

Picken, W.M.M. 'St German of Cornwall's Day', *Devon & Cornwall Notes & Queries*, xxvii (1956–8), pp. 103–7.

Picken, W.M.M. 'The 'Landochou' Charter', in Hoskins, W.G., *The Westward Expansion of Wessex* (Leicester, University of Leicester, Department of English Local History, Occasional Papers, xiii, 1960), pp. 36–44.

[Polsue, J.] *A Complete Parochial History of the County of Cornwall*, 4 vols (Truro and London, 1867–72).

Polwhele, R. *The History of Devonshire*, 3 vols (London, 1793–1806).

Potts, R. (ed.) *A Calendar of Cornish Glebe Terriers 1673–1735*, Devon and Cornwall Record Society, new series, xix (1974).

Putnam, Bertha H. (ed.) *Proceedings before the Justices of the Peace in the Fourteenth and Fifteenth Centuries: Edward III to Richard II* (London, 1938).

Regesta Regum Anglo-Normannorum, ed. Davis, H.W.C., and others, 4 vols (Oxford, 1913–59).

Reichel, O.J., Prideaux, F.B., and Tapley-Soper, H. (eds.) *Devon Feet of Fines*, 2 vols, Devon and Cornwall Record Society (1912–39).

Robinson, O.F. (ed.) *The Register of Walter Bronescombe Bishop of Exeter 1258–1280*, vol. i, Canterbury and York Society, lxxxii (1995).

Rositzke, Harry August. (ed.) *The C-Text of the Old English Chronicles* (Bochum-Langendreer, 1940; reprinted, New York and London, 1967).

Rotuli Chartarum, ed. Hardy, T.D., vol. i. part i (London, Record Commission, 1837).

Rotuli Litterarum Patentium, ed. Hardy, T.D., vol i, part i (London, Record Commission, 1835).

Round, J.H. (ed.) *Calendar of Documents Preserved in France Illustrative of the History of Great Britain and Ireland*, vol i: *A.D. 918–1206* (London, 1899).

Rowe, Joseph Hambly. (ed.) *Cornwall Feet of Fines*, 2 vols, Devon and Cornwall Record Society (1914–50).

Searle, Eleanor. (ed.) *The Chronicle of Battle Abbey* (Oxford, 1980).

Seymour, Deryck. *Torre Abbey* (Exeter, 1977).

Sharpe, R.R. *Calendar of Wills Proved and Enrolled in the Court of Husting, London, A.D.1258–A.D.1688*, 2 vols (London, 1889–90).

Snell, L.S. *Documents towards a History of the Reformation in Cornwall: i, The Chantry Certificates for Cornwall* (Exeter, c.1953).

Snell, L.S. *Documents towards a History of the Reformation in Cornwall: ii, The Edwardian Inventories of Church Goods for Cornwall* (Exeter, c.1955).

Snell, L.S. *Documents towards a History of the Reformation in Devon: The Chantry Certificates for Devon and the City of Exeter* (Exeter, no date).

Stenton, Doris Mary. (ed.) *The Great Roll of the Pipe for the Sixth Year of King Richard the First*, Pipe Roll Society, xliii, new series v (1928).

Stenton, Doris Mary. (ed.) *The Great Roll of the Pipe for the Tenth Year of King Richard the First*, Pipe Roll Society, xlvii, new series ix (1928).

Stenton, Doris Mary. (ed.) *Pleas before the King or his Justices, 1198–1202*, vol. ii, Selden Society, lxviii (1952).

Stéphan, J. *A History of Buckfast Abbey from 1018 to 1968* (Bristol, 1970).

Stevens, J. 'The Newnham Cartulary', *Devon & Cornwall Notes & Queries*, xxix (1962–4), pp. 41–50.

Stoate, T.L. (ed.) *Devon Lay Subsidy Rolls 1524–7* (Almondsbury, 1979).

Stoate, T.L. (ed.) *Cornwall Subsidies in the Reign of Henry VIII* (Almondsbury, 1985).

Stoate, T.L. (ed.) *Devon Lay Subsidy Rolls 1543–5* (Almondsbury, 1986).

Tapley-Soper, H., and Chick, E. *The Register of . . . the Parish of Branscombe, Devon, 1539–1812*, Exeter, Devon and Cornwall Record Society, 1913.

Taylor, Thomas. *St Michael's Mount* (Cambridge, 1932).

Thesaurus Ecclesiasticus Provincialis—see Jones, W.

Timmins, T.C.B. (ed.) *The Register of John Chandler, Dean of Salisbury 1404–17*, Wiltshire Record Society, xxxix (1984).

Torr, V.J. 'Exeter Diocese in 1563', *Devon & Cornwall Notes & Queries*, xxx (1965–7), pp. 43–50, 75–82, 115–17.

Troup, Frances Rose-. *Lost Chapels of Exeter* (Exeter, 1923).

Truro Diocesan Directory (Truro, 1996).

Valor Ecclesiasticus tempore Henrici VIII auctoritate regia institutus, ed. Caley, J., 6 vols (London, Record Commission, 1810–24).

W., W.S. 'Testamentary Documents Relating to Property at Totnes, Devon', *Archaeological Journal*, viii (1851), pp. 307–12.

Watkin, Hugh R. *Dartmouth*, vol. i: *Pre-Reformation* (Exeter, Devonshire Association, Parochial Histories of Devonshire, vol. v [1935]).

Weaver, F.W. (ed.) *Wells Wills* (London, 1890).

Weaver, F.W. (ed.) *Somerset Medieval Wills (1383–1500)*, Somerset Record Society, xvi (1901).

Weaver, F.W. (ed.) *Somerset Medieval Wills (Second Series) 1501–1530*, Somerset Record Society, xix (1903).

Weaver, F.W. (ed.) *A Cartulary of Buckland Priory in the County of Somerset*, Somerset Record Society, xxv (1909).

Webster, Margaret. 'John Dabernon and his Will (1368)', *Devon & Cornwall Notes & Queries*, xxxvi part iv (1989), pp. 176–84.

Whitley, H. Michell. 'Sanctuary in Devon', *Devonshire Association Transactions*, xlv (1913), pp. 302–13.

Wilkin, W.H. 'Axminster Church—the Dedication', *Devon & Cornwall Notes & Queries*, xix (1936–7), pp. 257–8.

Wilkins, David. *Concilia Magnae Britanniae et Hiberniae*, 4 vols (London, 1737).

Willis, Browne. *Parochiale Anglicanum* (London, 1733).

Worcester, William. *Itineraries*, ed. Harvey, J.H. (Oxford, 1969).

Worthy, Charles. *Devonshire Wills* (London, 1896).

Yallop, H.J. 'Slapton College', *Devonshire Association Transactions*, xci (1959), pp. 138–48.

Youings, Joyce. *Devon Monastic Lands: Calendars of Particulars for Grants 1536–1558*, Devon and Cornwall Record Society, new series, i (1955).

(b) Other Primary Sources

Barnes, R., Oliver, G., and Jones, P. (edd.) *Liber Pontificalis of Edmund Lacy, Bishop of Exeter* (Exeter, 1846).

Bede's Ecclesiastical History of the English People, ed. Colgrave, B., and Mynors, R.A.B. (Oxford, 1991).

The Clergy List (London, 1841–1917).

Conner, Patrick W. *Anglo-Saxon Exeter: a Tenth-century Cultural History* (Woodbridge, 1993).

Cranmer, Thomas. *Miscellaneous Writings and Letters*, ed. Cox, J.E., Parker Society (1846).

Cuming, G.J. *A History of Anglican Liturgy* (London, 1969).

Dalton, J.N., and Doble, G.H. (edd). *Ordinale Exon*, 4 vols, Henry Bradshaw Society, xxxvii-viii, lxiii, lxxix (1909–41).

Doble, G.H. (ed.) *Pontificale Lanaletense*, Henry Bradshaw Society, lxxiv (1936).

Frere, W.H. (ed.) *Pontifical Services illustrated from miniatures of the XVth and XVIth Centuries*, 2 vols, Alcuin Club Collections, iii-iv (1901).

[Greenwell, W. (ed.)] *The Pontifical of Egbert, Archbishop of York*, Surtees Society, xxvii (1853).

Haddan, A.W., and Stubbs, W. (edd.) *Councils and Ecclesiastical Documents relating to Great Britain and Ireland*, 3 vols (Oxford, 1869–73).

[Henderson, W.G. (ed.)] *Liber Pontificalis Chr. Bainbridge Archiepiscopi Eboracensis*, Surtees Society, lxi (1875).

Hooker, Richard. *The Laws of Ecclesiastical Polity*, 2 vols (London, 1907, reprinted 1963).

Hughes, P.L., and Larkin, J.F. (edd.) *Tudor Royal Proclamations*, 3 vols (New Haven and London, 1964–9).

Legg, J. Wickham. (ed.) *English Orders for Consecrating Churches in the Seventeenth Century*, Henry Bradshaw Society, xli (1911).

Lyndwood, William. *Provinciale* (Oxford, 1679).

Masters, Betty R., and Ralph, Elizabeth. (edd.) *The Church Book of St Ewen's, Bristol 1454–1584*, Bristol and Gloucestershire Archaeological Society, Records Section, vi (1967).

Powicke, F.M., and Cheney, C.R. (edd.) *Councils and Synods II: A.D.1205–1313*, 2 vols (Oxford, 1964).

Procter, F., and Frere, W.H. *A New History of the Book of Common Prayer* (London, 1902).

Riley, Athelstan. (ed.) *Pontifical Services*, vol. iv: *illustrated from woodcuts of the XVIth century*, Alcuin Club Collections, xii (1908).

Taxatio Ecclesiastica Angliae et Walliae auctoritate P. Nicholai IV, [ed. Astle, T., Ayscough, S., and Caley, J.] (London, Record Commission, 1802).

Warren, F.E. (ed.) *The Leofric Missal* (Oxford, 1883).

Whitelock, D., Brett, M., and Brooke, C.N.L. (edd.) *Councils and Synods I: A.D.871–1204*, 2 vols (Oxford 1981).

Wilson, H.A. (ed.) *The Pontifical of Magdalen College*, Henry Bradshaw Society, xxxix (1910).

Wordsworth, John. *On the Rite of Consecration of Churches, especially in the Church of England . . . with the form of prayer and order of ceremonies in use in the diocese of Salisbury*, The Church Historical Society, lii (London, 1899).

(c) Modern Secondary Studies

Acta Sanctorum, 64 vols (Antwerp, 1643-, in progress).

Analecta Bollandiana: revue critique d'hagiographie (Brussels, 1882-, in progress).

Arnold-Forster, Frances. *Studies in Church Dedications, or England's Patron Saints*, 3 vols (London, 1899).

Bibliotheca Sanctorum, 13 vols (Rome, 1961-70).

Binns, Alison. *Dedications of Monastic Houses in England and Wales 1066-1216* (Woodbridge, 1989).

Blair, John. 'Minster Churches in the Landscape', in *Anglo-Saxon Settlements*, ed. Hooke, Della (Oxford, 1988), pp. 35-58.

Blair, John. (ed.) *Minsters and Parish Churches: the local Church in Transition, 950-1200* (Oxford, 1988)

Blair, John, and Sharpe, Richard. (edd.) *Pastoral Care before the Parish* (Leicester, 1992).

Bond, Francis. *Dedications and Patron Saints of English Churches* (London, 1914). There is a bibliography of general and local studies on pp. xii-xiii.

Bowen, E.G. *The Settlements of the Celtic Saints in Wales* (Cardiff, 1954).

Butler, Alban. *Butler's Lives of the Saints*, ed. Thurston, Herbert, and Attwater, Donald, 4 vols (London, 1956).

Butler, L. 'Church Dedications and the Cults of Anglo-Saxon Saints in England', in *The Anglo-Saxon Church: Papers on History, Architecture and Archaeology in Honour of Dr H.M. Taylor*, ed. Butler, L., and Morris, R., (London, Council of British Archaeological Research, Report xxx, 1985), pp. 44-50.

Cambridge, Eric, and Rollason, David. 'The Pastoral Organization of the Anglo-Saxon Church: a Review of the 'Minster Hypothesis', *Early Medieval Europe*, iv (1995), pp. 87-104.

Catling, Robert Mason, and Rogers, J.P. *G.H. Doble: a Memoir and a Bibliography* (Exeter, [1949]).

Chadwick, Owen. 'The Evidence of Dedications in the Early History of the Welsh Church', in Chadwick, H.M., and Nora K. *Studies in Early British History* (Cambridge, 1953), pp. 173-88.

Cox, J.C. *Churchwardens' Accounts from the Fourteenth Century to the Close of the Seventeenth Century* (London, 1913).

Cresswell, Beatrix F. *Exeter Churches* (Exeter, 1908).

Davies, Wendy. *An Early Welsh Microcosm: Studies in the Llandaff Charters* (London, 1978).

Delehaye, H. 'Loca Sanctorum', *Analecta Bollandiana*, xlviii (1930), pp. 5-64.

Doble, G.H. For a bibliography of his writings, see Catling, Robert Mason, above.

Doble, G.H. 'The Cornish Saints Series', 48 pamphlets (Truro and other places, 1924-1946).

Doble, G.H. *The Saints of Cornwall*, ed. Attwater, Donald, 5 vols (Truro, 1960-70). This is a reprint of some of Doble's pamphlets in the 'Cornish Saints' and 'Cornish Parish Histories' series. While a useful anthology, it omits much important information from the original pamphlets which should be consulted for preference.

Duchesne, L., *Christian Worship* (London, 1931).

Duffy, Eamon. *The Stripping of the Altars: Traditional Religion in England c.1400-c.1580* (New Haven and London, 1992)

Farmer, D.H., *The Oxford Dictionary of Saints*, 2nd ed. (Oxford, 1987).

Finberg, H.P.R. 'Church Dedications in Devon', *Devon & Cornwall Notes & Queries*, xxiv (1950-1), pp. 225-6.

Förster, M. *Zur Geschichte des Reliquienkultus in Altengland* (Munich, 1943).

Graham, T.H.B. and Collingwood, W.G., 'Patron Saints of the Diocese of Carlisle', *Transactions of the Cumberland and Westmorland Antiquarian and Archaeological Society*, new series, xxv (1925), pp. 1–27.

Gransden, Antonia. 'The Question of the Consecration of St Edmund's Church', in *Church and Chronicle in the Middle Ages: Essays Presented to John Taylor*, ed. Wood, Ian, and Loud, G.A. (London, 1991), pp. 59–86.

Henderson, Charles G., *The Cornish Church Guide and Parochial History of Cornwall* (Truro, 1925).

Henderson, Charles G. 'The Ecclesiastical History of the 109 Parishes of West Cornwall', *Journal of the Royal Institution of Cornwall*, new series, ii (1953–6), pp. 1–210; iii (1957–60), pp. 211–382, 383–497. Pagination is independent of the rest of these volumes.

Henken, Elissa R. *The Welsh Saints: a Study in Patterned Lives* (Woodbridge, 1992).

Hutton, Ronald. *The Rise and Fall of Merry England: The Ritual Year 1400–1700* (Oxford and New York, 1994).

Hutton, Ronald. *Stations of the Sun: a History of the Ritual Year in Britain* (Oxford and New York, 1996).

Kerslake, T. 'The Celt and the Teuton in Exeter', *The Archaeological Journal*, xxx (1873), pp. 211–225.

Kirk, K.E. *Church Dedications of the Oxford Diocese* (Oxford, 1946).

Knowles, D., and Hadcock, R.N. *Medieval Religious Houses: England and Wales*, 2nd ed. (London, 1971).

Leclerq, H. 'Patron', in *Dictionnaire d'Archéologie Chrétienne et de Liturgie*, ed. Cabrol, F., and Leclerq, H., 15 vols (Paris, 1924–53), xiii part ii, cols. 2513–2524.

Levison, W. *England and the Continent in the Eighth Century* (Oxford, 1946).

Levison, W., 'Medieval Church-Dedications in England: some Problems', *Transactions of the Archaeological and Antiquarian Society of Durham and Newcastle upon Tyne*, x (1946), pp. 57–79.

Linnell, C.L.S. *Norfolk Church Dedications*, (York, Borthwick Institute of Historical Research: St Anthony's Hall Publications, xxi, 1962).

Loth, J. 'Les noms des saints bretons', *Revue celtique*, xxix (1908), pp. 222–48, 270–311; xxx (1909), pp. 121–55, 282–320, 395–403.

Mackinlay, James Murray. *Ancient Church Dedications in Scotland*, 2 vols (Edinburgh, 1910–14).

Miller, Molly. *The Saints of Gwynedd* (Woodbridge, 1979).

Muncey, R.W. *A History of the Consecration of Churches and Churchyards* (Cambridge, 1939).

Northeast, Peter. 'Moving the Signposts: Changes in the Dedication of Suffolk Churches after the Reformation', in *East Anglian Studies*, ed. Longcroft, Adam and Joby, Richard (Norwich, 1995), pp. 201–05.

Okasha, Elisabeth. *Corpus of Early Christian Inscribed Stones of South-west Britain* (London and New York, 1993).

Olson, [B.] Lynette. *Early Monasteries in Cornwall* (Woodbridge, 1989).

Orme, Nicholas. 'The Dissolution of the Chantries in Devon, 1546–8', *Devonshire Association Transactions*, cxi (1979), pp. 75–123.

Orme, Nicholas. 'Two Saint-Bishops of Exeter: James Berkeley and Edmund Lacy', *Analecta Bollandiana*, civ (1986), pp. 403–18.

Orme, Nicholas. 'The Church in Crediton from St Boniface to the Reformation', in *The Greatest Englishman*, ed. Reuter, T.A. (Exeter, 1980), pp. 97–131.

Orme, Nicholas. 'Saint Michael and his Mount', *Journal of the Royal Institution of Cornwall*, new series, x part i (1986–7), pp. 32–43.

Orme, Nicholas. 'The Lost Parish of Dotton', *Devon & Cornwall Notes & Queries*, xxxvi (1987), pp. 1–5.

Orme, Nicholas. 'Indulgences in Exeter Diocese, 1100–1536', *Devonshire Association Transactions*, cxx (1988), pp. 15–32.

Orme, Nicholas. 'Saint Walter of Cowick', *Analecta Bollandiana*, cviii (1990), pp. 1–7.

Orme, Nicholas. (ed.) *Unity and Variety: a History of the Church in Devon and Cornwall* (Exeter, 1991).

Orme, Nicholas. 'The Life of St Breage: a Cornish Virgin Saint', *Analecta Bollandiana*, cx (1992), pp. 341–51.

Orme, Nicholas. 'Indulgences in Medieval Cornwall', *Journal of the Royal Institution of Cornwall*, new series ii, vol i part 2 (1992), pp. 149–70.

Orme, Nicholas. 'Church and Chapel in Medieval England', *Transactions of the Royal Historical Society*, 6th series, vi (1996) pp. 75–102.

Pearce, Susan M. 'The Dating of Some Celtic Dedications and Hagiographical Traditions in South-Western Britain', *Devonshire Association Transactions*, cv (1973), pp. 95–210.

Pearce, Susan M. *The Kingdom of Dumnonia* (Padstow, 1978).

Pearce, Susan M. (ed.) *The Early Church in Western Britain and Ireland*, (Oxford, 1982).

Pearce, Susan M. 'The Early Church in the Landscape: The Evidence from North Devon', *The Archaeological Journal*, cxlii (1985), pp. 255–75.

Ridyard, Susan J. *The Royal Saints of Anglo-Saxon England: a Study of West Saxon and East Anglian Cults* (Cambridge, 1988).

Rollason, David W. *Saints and Relics in Anglo-Saxon England* (Oxford, 1989).

Sharpe, R., and Thacker, A. (edd.) *Local Saints and Local Churches* (Oxford, 1996).

Shaw, Gareth, and Tipper, Allison. *British Directories: A Bibliography and Guide* (London and New York, 1988).

Sutcliffe, Sebastian. 'The Cult of St Sitha in England: an Introduction', *Nottingham Medieval Studies*, xxxvii (1993), pp. 83–9.

Taylor, T., Doble, G.H., Henderson, C.G., and Rogers, J.P. *Cornish Church Kalendar*, "Cornish Saints" Series, No. 31 (Long Compton, 1933).

Wade-Evans, A.W. 'Parochiale Wallicanum', *Y Cymmrodor*, xxii (1910), pp. 22–124.

Wade-Evans, A.W. *Vitae Sanctorum Britanniae et Genealogicae* (Cardiff, University of Wales, Board of Celtic Studies, History and Law Series, ix, 1944).

Wallace-Hadrill, J.M. *Bede's Ecclesiastical History of the English People: A Historical Commentary* (Oxford, 1988).

Whiting, R.J. *The Blind Devotion of the People: Popular Religion and the English Reformation* (Cambridge, 1989).

Wormald, F. 'The Calendar of the Augustinian Priory of Launceston in Cornwall', *The Journal of Theological Studies*, xxxix (1938), pp. 3–21.

INDEX TO THE GAZETTEER

This index is a cross-reference to all the cults of the Trinity and the saints which are listed in the gazetteer. It does not imply that all entries under the same heading are to the same person or are historically accurate — many are conjectures made since the eighteenth century.

The index contains every reference in the gazetteer to cults before 1600. After 1600, it includes those which have had some currency in practice or in directories, omitting most minor mistakes or conjectures which have never been influential.

References which relate only to the period after 1600 appear in italics. C: identifies places in Cornwall, and D: those in Devon. Cults of the Holy Cross, Holy Ghost, Holy Name and Holy Trinity are indexed under Cross, Ghost, Name and Trinity, but All Saints is listed under that heading.

Achevran C: St Keverne.
Adwen C: Advent.
Aethelthryth—*see* **Etheldreda**.
Agnes C: St Agnes, Scilly: St Agnes.
Alban *Beaworthy*.
Alexius Exeter St Alexius hospital.
All Saints C: *St Ewe*, Stoke Climsland. D: Alverdiscott, Bickleigh (Plymouth), Bishopsteignton, Blackborough, Bradford, *Broadwoodkelly*, Buckland *Tout Saints*, Cheriton Fitzpaine, Clovelly, *Combeinteignhead*, Cruwys Morchard, Culmstock, Dunterton, East Budleigh, Eggesford, Exeter All Hallows on the Walls, Exeter All Hallows Goldsmith Street.

D: *Fremington*, Hawkchurch, High Bray, Highweek, *Holbeton*, Holcombe Rogus, Honeychurch (?), *Huntsham*, *Kenton*, Langtree, Lapford, *Malborough*, Merton, *Monkokehampton*, Moreleigh, North Lew, North Molton, Okehampton parish church, Plymstock, Pyworthy, Rackenford, Rewe, *Ringmore*, Rose Ash, Southleigh, *South Milton*, *Thurlestone*, *Trusham*, *West Alvington*, Winkleigh, *Woolfardisworthy West*.
Alun (Allen) C: St Allen.
Alwys (Alweys) C: *Lansallos*.
Andrew C: St Buryan, Calstock, Launcells, Minster, St Pinnock, Stratton, Tywardreath Priory, Tywardreath parish church.

D: Alwington, Ashburton, *Aveton Gifford*, *Beaford*, Bere Ferrers, Berrynarbor, *Broadhembury*, Buckland Brewer, Buckland Monachorum, Chardstock, Clayhidon, *Clyst Hydon*, Colebrooke, Colyton, Coryton, Cowick Priory and early parish church, *Cullompton*, *East Allington*, Feniton, Halberton, Harberton, *Hittisleigh*, Ipplepen, Kenn, Kenton, *Knowstone*, Lifton, Littleham (Exmouth), *Moretonhampstead*,

Plymouth Sutton, *Rockbeare*, Sampford Courtenay, *South Huish*, South Tawton, *Stoke Damarel*, Stokeinteignhead, Sutcombe, Thorncombe, Whitchurch, Yarnscombe.

Anietus—*see* **Neot**

Anne C: *Advent, Whitstone*.

Anthony C: St Anthony in Meneage, St Anthony in Roseland, *Antony*, Bodmin St Anthony hospital.

Augustine D: Heanton Punchardon.

Austol C: St Austell.

Barnabas D: *Farringdon*.

Barri C: Fowey.

Bartholomew C: Lostwithiel, Warleggan. D: *Cadeleigh*, Coffinswell, *East Ogwell*, *Nymet Rowland*, *Nymet Tracey*, *Stoke Rivers*, Yealmpton.

Benedict D: Buckland Abbey, *Buckland Brewer*.

Blaise C: St Blazey. D: Haccombe.

Brandwellan D: Branscombe (?).

Brannoc D. Braunton.

Branwalader C: St Breward.

Breac (Breage) C: Breage.

Brendon (Brendan) *Brendon*.

Breward—*see* **Bruered**

Bridget C: Morvah. D: Bridestowe, *Bridgerule*, Virginstow.

Brioc (Breoc) C: St Breock, *Lezant*.

Bruered (Breward) C: St Breward.

Bryvyth (Brevita) C: Lanlivery.

Budoc C: Budock. D: St Budeaux.

Buryan C: St Buryan.

Calixtus D: West Down.

Carantoc C: Crantock.

Carroc C: St Carrock.

Catherine—*see* **Katherine**

Cecilia D: South Pool (?).

Cei—*see also* **Kea** D: Landkey.

Charles I, King C: *Falmouth*. D: *Plymouth Charles church*.

Christ D: *Churston Ferrers*, Crediton, Exeter St Martin.

Christina D: Christow.

Christopher D: *Aylesbeare*, Bradstone (?).

Ciarán of Saighir—*see also* **Kerrian, Keverne** C: St Keverne.

Ciricus—*see* **Cyricus**

Clair (Clarus) C: St Cleer.

Cleder C: St Clether.

Clement C: St Clement, Withiel. D: Kennerleigh, Powderham, Townstall.

Clether—*see* **Cleder**

Coan (Cohan) C: Merther.

Colan (Culan) C: Colan.

Columb C: St Columb Major, St Columb Minor.

Columba of Iona C: St Columb Major.

Conet C: *Lesnewth* (?).

Constantine C: Constantine. D: Milton Abbot.

Corentin C: Cury.

Cornelius C: Cornelly.
Creden—*see* **Sancreed**
Cride (Creed) C: Creed.
Cross, Holy C: Grade. D: Crediton, *Cruwys Morchard*, Exeter St Martin, *Highampton, Newton Ferrers, Tetcott.*
Crowan (Crewan) C: Crowan.
Cuby (Cybi) C: Cuby, Duloe.
Cury—*see* **Corentin**
Cuthbert C: Cubert. D: Exeter St Cuthbert, Widworthy.
Cyricus (Ciricus, Cyriac) C: St Carrock, Luxulyan, St Veep. D: Newton St Cyres, South Pool.

David C: Davidstow. D: *Ashprington*, Dotton, Exeter St David, *Thelbridge.*
Dedymin (Dedimus) C: St Martin in Meneage.
Delech (Dilecta, Dilic?) C: Landulph.
Denis (Disen) C: St Dennis, *North Tamerton, Otterham.* D: Bradninch.
Dilecta—*see* **Delech**
Disen—*see* **Denis**
Docco (Dochau) C: St Kew.
Dominic C: St Dominick.
Dunstan C: Lanreath, *Manaccan.*

Ebbe C: St Ewe.
Edmund C: Illogan. D: *Dolton*, Exeter St Edmund, Kingsbridge.
Edward D: Egg Buckland, Exeter St Mary Steps, Shaugh Prior, Spreyton (?).
Elenn C: St Stephen in Brannel.
Elid—*see* **Lyde**
Endelient C: St Endellion.
Enoder C: St Enoder.
Enodoc C: St Enodoc.
Entenin C: St Anthony in Meneage, St Anthony in Roseland.
Erch (Erth) C: St Erth.
Erme C: St Erme.
Ermund D: Stoke Fleming.
Erney—*see* **Terney**
Erth—*see* **Erch**
Ervan C: St Ervan.
Etheldreda (Aethelthryth) D: Canonsleigh Priory.
Euny C: *Crowan*, Lelant, Redruth.
Eustace (Eustachius) C: St Ewe. D: Tavistock parish church.
Eval (Uvel) C: St Eval, *Withiel.*
Ewa C: St Ewe.

Faith C: *Saltash.*
Felec C: Phillack.
Felicity (Felicitas) C: Phillack.
Felix C: Phillack, *Philleigh.*
Filii C: Philleigh.
Finbar C: Fowey.
Fioc C: Feock.
Francis D: Exeter Franciscan friary (?).

Gabriel: D: Clyst Gabriel hospital, Stoke Gabriel.

Gennys—*see* **Guinas**

George C: Bodmin St George hospital, Treneglos. D: Beaford, Clyst St George, Cockington, Dean Prior, Dittisham, Exeter St George, Frithelstock Priory (?), Georgham, George Nympton, Goodleigh (?), Harford, Manaton, Modbury, Monkleigh, Morebath, Seaton, Shillingford St George, *Thrushelton*, Witheridge.

German C: St Germans, Rame. D: Germansweek.

Germoc C: Germoe.

Gerent C: Gerrans.

Ghost, Holy D: Totnes Trinitarian hospital.

Giles D: *Buckerell*, Kilmington, *Little Torrington*, Milton Abbot, *Northleigh*, St Giles in the Wood, St Giles on the Heath, *Sidbury*, Sidmouth.

Gluviac C: St Gluvias.

Gonand (Gunand) C: Roche.

Goron—*see* **Guron**

Grace C: *Probus*.

Grade C: Grade.

Gregory C: Treneglos. D: Dawlish, East Ogwell, Frithelstock Priory, *Frithelstock parish church*, Goodleigh, *Harpford, Seaton, Venn Ottery*.

Gueriir C: St Neot.

Guiland (Guilant) C: St Juliot.

Guinas (Genesius) C: St Gennys.

Gulval—*see* **Gwelvel**

Guron (Goron) C: St Goran.

Guy D: *East Buckland*.

Gwelvel (Gulval) C: Gulval, *Laneast*.

Gwenek C: Lewannick.

Gwenep (Gwenap) C: Gwennap.

Gwinear C: Gwinear.

Gwithian C: Gwithian.

Helans C: St Stephen in Brannel.

Helen (Helena) C: *Helland*, Scilly: St Helen. D: Abbotsham, Lundy, *Parracombe*,

Helie C: *Egloshayle*.

Hermes C: St Erme, St Ervan.

Hieritha—*see* **Urith**

Hilary C: St Hilary.

Hugh (Hugo) C: Quethiock.

Humbert (Hunbeorht?) D: Stokenham.

Hyacinth C: Blisland.

Hydroc C: Lanhydrock.

Hyldren (Heldenus)—*see* **Ildiern**

Ia C: St Ives, *Lanivet*.

Ida (Ide) D: *Ide*.

Idi (Issey) C: St Issey, Mevagissey.

Ildiern (Heldenus, Hyldren) C: Lansallos.

Illogan C: Illogan.

Issey—*see* **Idi**

Ivo (Ives) C: St Ive.

James the Great C: Antony, Jacobstow, *Kilkhampton*, Tregony. D: *Abbots Bickington, Arlington, Ashreigney, Bondleigh, Chawleigh, Christow*, Exeter St James Priory, Exeter St James parish church, *Halwill, Iddesleigh*, Jacobstowe, *King's Nympton*, Kingston, Luffincott, *Northleigh, Parkham, Sheldon*, Slapton parish church, Swimbridge, *Talaton*, West Teignmouth.

James the Less C: *Kilkhampton*. D: *Bondleigh, East Putford, Huish, Iddesleigh, Kingston*.

John the Baptist C: *Antony*, Helston St John hospital, St John, Morwenstow, *Sennen, Temple*. D: *Ashton*, Aveton Gifford, Axminster, *Bishop's Tawton, Bishopsteignton, Bradworthy, Broadclyst*, Charles, Clayhanger, *Colaton Raleigh*, Cookbury, *Countisbury, Dowland, East Down*, Exeter St John Arches, Exeter St John hospital, Great Torrington hospital, Hatherleigh, *Hawkchurch, Holcombe Burnell*, Instow, *Kennerleigh, Lustleigh, Lynton*, Marldon, *Membury, Meshaw, Nether Exe*, North Bovey, *Plymtree*, Salcombe, *Sampford Peverell, Stowford, Warkleigh, Witheridge*, Withycombe Raleigh, Woodland, Yarcombe.

John the Evangelist C: *St John*. D: Canonsleigh Priory, *Countisbury*, Great Torrington hospital.

John of Instow D: Instow.

Jude D: *Hockworthy*.

Julian C: Maker.

Julitta (Juliot) C: St Carrock, St Juliot, Lanteglos by Camelford, Luxulyan, St Veep. D: *Newton St Cyres*.

Just C: St Just in Penwith, St Just in Roseland.

Katherine (Catherine) C: *Temple*. D: Exeter St Katherine almshouse, Polsloe Priory, Totnes Trinitarian hospital, *Whitestone*.

Kea—*see also* **Cei** C: St Kea.

Kenwyn C: Kenwyn.

Keri C: Egloskerry.

Kerrian—*see also* **Ciarán, Keverne** D: Exeter St Kerrian.

Keverne—*see also* **Ciarán, Kerrian** C: St Keverne.

Kewa C: St Kew.

Keyne C: St Keyne, St Martin by Looe.

Kieran—*see* **Ciarán**

Knett (Knet) C: *Lesnewth*.

Ladoc C: Ladock.

Lallu C: Menheniot.

Lanty C: *Landewednack, Lanteglos by Camelford, Lanteglos by Fowey*.

Laud C: Mabe.

Laurence C: Bodmin St Laurence hospital. D: Bigbury, Clyst St Lawrence, Crediton hospital, Exeter St Laurence, Membury, *Molland*, Sheepwash, *Southleigh*.

Leonard C: Duloe, Landulph, Launceston hospital. D: *Clawton*, Exeter St Leonard, Halwell, Newton Abbot, *Sheepstor*.

Levan—*see* **Salamun**

Ludwan C: Ludgvan.

Luke D: Newton Poppleford.

Lyde (Lydus) C: St Issey, Scilly: St Helen.

Mab C: Mabe.

Mabon (Mabyn) C: St Mabyn.

Maccabees, Seven D: Cookbury.

Macra C: *Maker*.

Madern (Madron) C: Madron.

Manacca C: Manaccan.

Manakneu (Manac) C: Lanreath, *Manaccan.*

Margaret C: Shipstors hospital. D: Honiton hospital, *Littleham (Exmouth), Northam,* Pilton hospital, Plympton hospital, Stoodleigh, Templeton, Topsham.

Marina C: St Merryn. D: Mariansleigh.

Mark D: Aylesbeare.

Martin C: Camborne, Lewannick, Liskeard, St Martin by Looe, St Martin in Meneage, Scilly: St Martin, Werrington.

D: Blaxton, *Broad Nymet, Chudleigh,* Exeter St Martin, Exminster, Ideford, *Martinhoe, Merton, Nymet Tracey,* Rockbeare, Sherford.

Mary Magdalene C: Helston St Mary Magdalene hospital, Lamford hospital, Launceston St Mary Magdalene, Liskeard hospital.

D: Barnstaple Priory, *Barnstaple hospital,* Chulmleigh, Exeter St Mary Magdalene hospital, *Huntshaw,* Monkton, Okehampton hospital, Plymouth hospital, Plympton hospital, Stoke Canon, Tavistock hospital, Teignmouth hospital, Totnes hospital.

Mary the Virgin C: Bodmin Priory, Braddock, Botus Fleming, Callington, East Looe, Glasney collegiate church, *Kilkhampton, Maker,* St Mary de Valle, Scilly: St Mary, Sheviock, Truro, Week St Mary.

D: *Abbotskerswell,* Ashbury, Atherington, Awliscombe, Axminster, *Aylesbeare,* Bampton, Barnstaple Priory, *Belstone,* Berry Pomeroy, *Bickington, Bickleigh (Plymouth),* Bickleigh (Tiverton), *Bicton,* Bideford, *Bishop's Nympton, Black Torrington,* Bondleigh, Branscombe (?), *Bratton Clovelly,* Brixham, *Brixton, Brushford,* Buckerell, Buckfast Abbey, Buckland Abbey, *Buckland Brewer, Buckland Filleigh, Burlescombe,* Burrington, *Calverleigh,* Canonsleigh Priory, *Charleton,* Cheldon, *Cheriton Bishop, Cheriton Fitzpaine,* Chivelstone, Chudleigh (?), Churchstanton, Churchstow, *Churston Ferrers,* Clovelly, Clyst Hydon, Clyst St Mary, Cockington, *Coldridge,* Colebrooke, Colyton, Combeinteignhead (?), *Combpyne,* Cornworthy Priory, Cotleigh, Creacombe, Crediton, Cullompton.

D: Dartington, Denbury, *Diptford,* Dotton, Down St Mary, Dunkeswell Abbey, *Dunsford,* East Worlington, Exbourne, Exeter castle chapel, Exeter Cathedral, Exeter Dominican friary (?), Exeter Franciscan friary (?), Exeter St Martin, Exeter St Mary Arches, Exeter St Mary Major, Exeter St Mary Minor, Exeter St Mary Steps, Exeter St Olave, Exeter St Roche hospital, Exmouth (?), Filleigh, Forde Abbey, Frithelstock Priory, *Frithelstock parish church,* Hartland Abbey, Hatherleigh, Hemyock, Hennock, High Bickington, Holcombe Rogus, Holne, Honeychurch, *Huntsham, Huxham,* Iddesleigh (?), *Ideford,* Ilfracombe (?), Kelly, Kentisbeare, Kerswell Priory, Kingskerswell, King's Nympton, *Kingsteignton.*

D: Landcross, *Lifton,* Little Torrington, Lundy, Luppitt, Lympstone, *Lynton,* Mariansleigh, Marsh Barton Priory, Marystow, Marytavy, Meshaw, Modbury, *Molland, Morchard Bishop,* Mortehoe, Newenham Abbey, Northam (?), *North Huish,* Nymet Tracey (?), Offwell (?), Ottery St Mary, Payhembury, Pilton priory and parish church, Plympton St Mary, *Plymstock,* Poltimore, Poughill, Rattery, *Rewe, Rockbeare,* St Marychurch, *Salcombe Regis, Sampford Spiney,* Silverton, Slapton collegiate church, South Brent, *South Molton, Stockleigh English, Stockleigh Pomeroy,* Stoke Rivers, Sydenham Damarel (?).

D: Tamerton Foliot, Tavistock Abbey, Tavistock hospital (?), Tedburn St Mary, Thelbridge, Thorncombe, *Throwleigh,* Totnes Priory and parish church, Uffculme, Upottery, Upton Hellions, *Upton Pyne, Walkhampton, Washfield, West Worlington, Whimple,* Willand, Wolborough, *Woodleigh, Woolfardisworthy East.*

Matherian (Mertherian) C: Minster, Tintagel.

Matthew D: *Butterleigh, Cheriton Fitzpaine, Coldridge,*
Maudith C: St Mawes.
Maugan C: Mawgan in Meneage, St Mawgan in Pydar.
Maunan C: Mawnan.
Maurice D: Plympton St Maurice.
Melaine C: St Mellion, Mullion.
Melor C: Linkinhorne, Mylor.
Menfre C: St Minver.
Merewenne (Merwenn) C: Marhamchurch.
Meriadoc (Meriasek) C: Camborne.
Merther C: Merther.
Mertherian—*see* **Matherian**
Meubred C: Cardinham.
Meva C: Mevagissey.
Mewan C: St Mewan.
Michael C: Helston, Lamanna, Landrake, Lawhitton, Lesnewth, Lezant, Maker, St Michael Caerhays, St Michael's Mount, St Michael Penkevil, Michaelstow, *Perranuthnoe*, Porthilly, *Rame*, Trewen.

   D: Alphington, Awliscombe, *Axmouth*, Bampton, *Beer, Blackawton*, Brentor, Bridgerule, *Bulkworthy, Cadbury*, Chagford, Cheriton Bishop, *Clyst Honiton*, Colaton Raleigh, Cornwood, *Cotleigh, Creacombe*, Doddiscombsleigh, Dunchideock, *East Anstey*, East Buckland, East Teignmouth, Farway, Gittisham, Great Torrington parish church, Heavitree, Honiton parish church, Horwood, Ilsington, *Kingsteignton*, Little Hempston, *Loddiswell, Loxbeare, Loxhore*, Marwood, Meeth, Musbury, Otterton, Pinhoe, Shebbear, Shute, Sidbury, Sowton, *Spreyton*, Stockland, Stokenham (?), *Trusham*, Wembworthy.
Minver—*see* **Menfre**
Moren C: Lamorran.
Morveth (Morwetha) C: Morvah.
Morwenna C: *Marhamchurch*, Morwenstow.
Mylor—*see* **Melor**

Name, Holy C: *Boyton.*
Nectan D: *Ashcombe*, Ashton (?), Hartland Abbey, Hartland parish church, Welcombe.
Nennyd (Nunit) C: Pelynt.
Neot C: *Menheniot*, St Neot, *Poundstock.*
Newlyn C: Newlyn East.
Nicholas C: St Buryan, Fowey, *St Mawgan in Pydar, Perranuthnoe*, Saltash, Scilly: Tresco, Tresmere, *West Looe*, Whitstone.

   D: Bickington, *Broadwoodwidger*, Combe Raleigh, *Dunkeswell parish church*, Exeter St Nicholas Priory, Holcombe Burnell, Shaldon, *Sidmouth*, Spreyton (?).
Nonn (Nun) C: Altarnun, *Pelynt*. D: *Bradstone.*
Nyvett C: *Lanivet.*

Odulph C: Pillaton.
Olaf (OLave) C: Poughill. D: Exeter St Olave.

Padern (Paternus) C: Madron, North Petherwin, South Petherwin, *Werrington.*
Pancras D: Countisbury, Exeter St Pancras, Pancrasweek, Rousdon, Widecombe in the Moor.
Patrick—*see* **Petroc**
Paul the Apostle (jt indicates jointly with Peter) C: *Ludgvan*, Paul, Sheviock (jt).

D: Barnstaple Priory (jt), Barnstaple parish church (jt), Bovey Tracey (jt), Bratton Fleming (jt), Broadhempston (jt), *Churchstanton*, Combe Martin (jt) (?), Ermington (jt), Exeter Cathedral (jt), Exeter St Paul, *Filleigh, Holsworthy* (jt), Morchard Bishop (jt), North Tawton (jt), Paignton (jt), Plympton Priory and parish church (jt), Staverton (jt), Teigngrace (jt), *Thornbury* (jt?), Tiverton (jt), Uplowman (jt), Uplyme (jt), *Zeal Monachorum* (jt).

Paul de Leon C: Paul. D: *Staverton*.

Paulinus C: Paul.

Perran—*see* **Piran**

Peter (jt indicates jointly with Paul) C: *Landrake, Mevagissey*, Sheviock (jt).

D: Affeton, Arlington, *Ashford*, Ashwater, Barnstaple Priory (jt), Barnstaple parish church (jt), Berrynarbor, Bishop's Tawton, *Bittadon*, Bovey Tracey (jt), Bradworthy, Brampford Speke, Bratton Fleming (jt), Broadhempston (jt), Buckland in the Moor, Buckland Tout Saints, Chawleigh, *Clayhanger*, Combe Martin (jt) (?), Cornworthy parish church, *Dalwood, Dowland*, Ermington (jt), Exeter Cathedral (jt), *Fremington, Gidleigh*, Halwill, Holsworthy (jt?), *Knowstone*, Lamerton, *Lew Trenchard*.

D: Malborough, *Meavy*, Monkokehampton, Morchard Bishop (jt), North Tawton (jt), Oakford, Paignton (jt), *Parracombe*, Peters Marland, Petertavy, Plympton Priory and parish church (jt), Revelstoke, *Roborough, Rose Ash, Salcombe Regis, Satterleigh, Shirwell*, Shobrooke, *Sidbury*, Staverton (jt), *Stoke Fleming*, Tawstock, Teigngrace (jt), Thornbury (jt?), Tiverton (jt), *Trentishoe, Twitchen, Ugborough*, Uplowman (jt), Uplyme (jt), *Washford Pyne*, West Buckland, *Westleigh*, Zeal Monachorum (jt?).

Petroc C: Bodmin Priory, Bodmin parish church, Egloshayle, *Egloskerry*, Little Petherick, Padstow, Trevalga.

D: Clannaborough, Cotleigh, Dartmouth St Petrox, Dunkeswell parish church (?), Exeter St Petroc, Farringdon, *Harford*, Harpford, Hollacombe, *Inwardleigh*, Lydford, Newton St Petrock, *Parracombe*, Petrockstow, South Brent, Tormohun, West Anstey, West Worlington.

Philip C: *Kilkhampton*. D: *East Putford, Huish, Iddesleigh*.

Pinnock—*see* **Pynnoc**

Piran C: St Keverne, Perranarworthal, Perranuthnoe, Perranzabuloe.

Pratt C: *Blisland*.

Probus C: Probus.

Protus C: Blisland.

Pynnoc C: St Pinnock.

Roche C: *Roche*. D: Exeter St Roche hospital.

Rumon C: Ruan Lanihorne, Ruan Major, Ruan Minor. D: Romansleigh, Tavistock Abbey.

Salamun (Selevan, Levan) C: St Levan.

Sampson (Samson) C: St Sampson (Golant), Scilly: St Samson, South Hill.

Sancreed C: Sancreed.

Sativola—*see* **Sidwell**

Saviour D: Dartmouth St Saviour, Exmouth, Kingsbridge (?), *Tormohun*, Torre Abbey.

Senan (Sennen) C: Sennen.

Senar (Sinar) C: Zennor.

Sennian (Sinian) C: Helland.

Sidwell C: Laneast. D: Exeter St Sidwell.

Silvanus C: St Levan.

Simon D: *Hockworthy*.

Sithney—*see* Sydhni
Spirit, Holy—*see* Ghost, Holy
Stephen C: Launceston Priory, Mawnan, St Stephen in Brannel, St Stephen by Launceston, St Stephen by Saltash.
 D: Buckfast Abbey, Exeter St Stephen, Huish, *West Putford.*
Stithian C: Stithians.
Sulyen C: Luxulyan.
Swithin C: *Launcells.* D: Littleham (Bideford), *Pyworthy,* Sandford, *Shobrooke,* Woodbury.
Sydhni C: Sithney.
Sylvester D: *Chivelstone.*
Symphorian C: Forrabury, Tintagel, Veryan.
Syth D: South Molton.

Tallan C: Talland.
Tean C: Scilly: Tean.
Terney (Torney) C: St Erney, North Hill.
Tetha C: St Teath.
Tewynnoc—*see* Winwaloe
Theobald D : Tavistock hospital.
Thomas the Apostle C: Launceston St Thomas. D: Cowick later parish church, Exeter St Olave, *Kentisbury, Mamhead, Oldridge.*
Thomas Becket (Thomas the Martyr) C: St Buryan, Glasney colegate church, Laneast, Launceston St Thomas, *St Merryn.*
 D: *Bovey Tracey, Bridford,* Cowick later parish church, Dodbrooke, Kingswear, *Lapford,* Loddiswell (?), *Mamhead* (?), *Newton Tracey, North Lew,* Plympton St Maurice, *Puddington, Sourton, Thorverton,*
Trinity, Holy C: *St Austell.* D: *Bicton,* Buckfastleigh, *Buckland Filleigh,* Burrington, *Challacombe,* Dartmouth St Saviour, *Drewsteignton,* Exeter castle chapel, Exeter Trinity, Exeter Wynard's almshouse, Exmouth, Great Torrington hospital, *Ilfracombe, Landcross, Littleham (Exmouth), Milton Damarel,* Newenham Abbey, Plymouth hospital, *Salcombe,* Tetcott, *Torbryan,* Weare Giffard, *Woolfardisworthy East, Woolfardisworthy West.*
Tudic C: St Tudy.

Unknown D: West Ogwell.
Uny — *see* Euny
Urith (Hieritha) D: Chittlehampton.
Ursula—*see* Virgins, Eleven Thousand.
Uvel—*see* Eval

Vepe C: St Veep.
Virgins, Eleven Thousand D: Exeter St Roche hospital.

Wendern (Wendron) C: Wendron.
Wenna C : Morval, St Wenn.
Werburg C: Warbstow. D: *Wembury.*
Winifred D: *Branscombe, Manaton.*
Winnoc (Wynnoc) C: *Lewannick,* St Winnow.
Winwaloe (Tewynnoc) C: Gunwalloe, Landewednack, Poundstock, Towednack, Tremaine, St Winnow. D: East Portlemouth.
Wulvella—*see* Gwelvel
Wyllow C: Lanteglos by Fowey.
Wynnoc—*see* Winnoc

GENERAL INDEX

Following practice throughout the book, places in Cornwall are indexed without reference to the word St